AGING
SOCIAL
POLICIES

Robbyn dedicates this book

to Jani, for her endless encouragement, love, and support

to Paola Guelpa, for her friendship, enthusiasm, and sense of adventure for our "projects," all of
which helped make this book a reality—grazie mille cara amica mia

to Dr. Patricia Keith, who was a valued mentor, colleague, and friend

to Alta Wacker, who faces aging with courage and humor

Karen dedicates this book

to Steve, for his continual love, support, and understanding of my needing time "to write"

to all the staff at the Center for Gerontology, who always do more than they are asked

to Robbyn, for having the vision and taking the lead in making this book a reality

We both dedicate this book

to the many older adults who agreed to be interviewed and/or photographed for this book,
who opened their homes and their hearts to us all in hopes that their stories would help us remember
the connection between the policies we create and the dignity they hope to have in later life

AGING

SOCIAL

POLICIES

An International Perspective

Robbyn R. Wacker
University of Northern Colorado

Karen A. Roberto
Virginia Polytechnic Institute and State University

Los Angeles | London | New Delhi
Singapore | Washington DC

For information:

SAGE Publications, Inc.
2455 Teller Road
Thousand Oaks, California 91320
E-mail: order@sagepub.com

SAGE Publications Ltd.
1 Oliver's Yard
55 City Road
London EC1Y 1SP
United Kingdom

SAGE Publications India Pvt. Ltd.
B 1/I 1 Mohan Cooperative Industrial Area
Mathura Road, New Delhi 110 044
India

SAGE Publications Asia-Pacific Pte. Ltd.
33 Pekin Street #02-01
Far East Square
Singapore 048763

Printed in the United States of America

Library of Congress Cataloging-in-Publication Data

Wacker, Robbyn R.
Aging social policies : an international perspective/Robbyn R. Wacker, Karen A Roberto.
     p. cm.
Includes bibliographical references and index.
ISBN 978-1-4129-3909-6 (pbk.)
     1. Population aging—Government policy. 2. Older people—Government policy. 3. Older people—Services for. 4. Older people—Social conditions. I. Roberto, Karen A. II. Title.

HQ1061.W26 2011
362.6—dc22   2010033451

This book is printed on acid-free paper.

10   11   12   13   14   10   9   8   7   6   5   4   3   2   1

Acquisitions Editor:	Kassie Graves
Editorial Assistant:	Courtney Munz
Production Editor:	Eric Garner
Copy Editor:	Megan Speer
Typesetter:	C&M Digitals (P) Ltd.
Proofreader:	Theresa Kay
Indexer:	Judy Hunt
Cover Designer:	Bryan Fishman
Permissions Editor:	Adele Hutchinson

Contents

Preface

Authors' Purpose

The genesis for this book came during a 2-week study-abroad experience for gerontology students that Robbyn led a few summers ago. During that experience, she was reflecting on the fact that after having taught aging social policies for many years, there were two pedagogical issues that were always particularly challenging. First, because of a dearth of in-depth information available on aging social policies in other countries, students rarely had an opportunity to compare, discuss, and analyze the different ways other countries approached and constructed their policies. Taking students on a study-abroad course and seeing how they responded so positively to learning about various countries' approaches to aging social policies was confirmation that we needed to replicate this learning experience as best we could in a textbook.

Second, teaching about aging social policies is naturally focused at the macro level of analyses and on the elements contained in such policies. Thus, it is easy to lose sight of the fact that the way in which governments choose to construct their aging social policies will have a direct effect on an older adult's quality of life. We thought that this link—the policy-person link—was an important element missing from textbooks on aging social policies, and we wanted to write a book that attempted to make the macro-micro connections apparent to the reader.

Using these two issues as our framework, the purpose of this book is to describe U.S. aging social policy alongside a select sampling of other countries' aging social policies and weave into our thinking interviews that we conducted with older adults from various countries around the globe to help give you some insight into their daily lives, thoughts, and concerns, which can be used as a reminder of how policies touch the day-to-day lives of older adults. While we were unable to include all the interviews we conducted, we have included photographs of many of the older adults we met or interviewed. We are very grateful to those who were kind enough to be interviewed.

The book is organized as follows. All chapters begin with pictures of older adults, many of whom we interviewed, and end with interviews we conducted with older adults from different countries. The first chapter introduces you to the demographics of the worldwide aging phenomenon, and to get you thinking about the policy-person link, we conclude with a case study of an older adult to which you can refer back as you learn about the specifics of other countries' social policies. You can use this case study to see the different effects these policies would have on one's life circumstances.

Chapter 2 provides a brief discussion of the elements of the policymaking process and a discussion about key U.S. and international aging social policy initiatives. Chapters 3 through 9 cover specific aging social policies and provide an in-depth review of U.S. policy, along with three to five other countries' equivalent social policies for comparison. We provide additional information or examples of programs influenced by policy in text boxes within many of the chapters and conclude each chapter with additional resources. We end the book with a summary of the challenges facing the future construction of aging social policy.

As we selected the countries to highlight within each chapter, we attempted to provide a rich array of the ways aging social policies are implemented in countries facing the challenges of an aging population. Although it was not possible to include a description of aging social policies from every country throughout the world, we hope that you will be inspired to investigate other countries on your own. Finally, public policy is dynamic and ever-changing; as we sent this book to press, President Obama signed into legislation the Patient Protection and Affordable Care Act (2010), which marks the first major change to U.S. health care legislation in more than 40 years, and the government in France announced its intention to increase the retirement age. Thus, we encourage you to keep an eye on the ongoing changes in the social policy arena. We hope you enjoy reading this textbook, and we welcome your comments and suggestions.

Robbyn R. Wacker
University of Northern Colorado
robbyn.wacker@unco.edu

Karen A. Roberto
Virginia Polytechnic Institute and State University
kroberto@vt.edu

Acknowledgments

We are so very grateful to a number of people who supported us in this endeavor and helped make this book a reality. We would like to thank the many people in countries around the globe who helped arrange, conduct, and interpret the interviews—Paola Guelpa, Paola Corazza, Enrica Interlandi, Chiara Rimoldi, Eric Rousson, Veronique Frison, Enrico Terzo, Dott. Adriano Guala, Alberto Mello Teggia, Dott. Enrico Negrone, Agueda and Miguel Mazarrasa, John Kinski, Liz Jeannet, Phil Ochiltree, Rebecca Rogers, Annemieke Lippes, Laurens v. Hulst, Jérôme Pellerin, Chrysostomos Giannoulakis, Anastasia Giannoulakis, Vickki Klingman, Frances Braafhart, Guei-ying Lin, and Aditi Divatia.

Thanks to Susan Collins, faculty member in the University of Northern Colorado's gerontology program, for sharing her insights and suggestions and to Sonja Rizzolo, who cheerfully lent her assistance in tracking down references. Jeanette VanGalder, Gloria Reynolds, Raul Cardenas, Thomas Smith, and Michelle Quinn—UNC colleagues—and Kisha Wacker Conroy all provided frequent support and encouragement from the beginning and at many points along the way.

We also appreciate the assistance of the staff and graduate students at the Virginia Tech Center for Gerontology for their help in locating information, developing the chapters, and reviewing drafts—Carlene Arthur, Katie Barrow, Ryan Cook, Lauren Ermann, Laura Eubanks Gambrel, Brandy Renee McCann, and Marya McPherson.

We are grateful to the reviewers who provided us with insightful and valuable suggestions on early drafts of the chapters:

Heying Jenny Zhan, *Georgia State University*

Stephen D. Gresham, *Brown University*

William H. Dailey, Jr., *California State University, Fresno*

Kathy Segris, *Ball State University*

James H. Swan, *University of North Texas*

Phyllis A. Greenberg, *St. Cloud State University*

Finally, we wish to acknowledge the staff at Sage and especially Kassie Graves, our editor, who managed to have the perfect combination of patience, insight, and encouragement and who contributed greatly to our thinking about the book's direction.

Robbyn R. Wacker
Karen A. Roberto

Part I

The Context of Aging Social Policy

Alta, age 88, United States

Arghaben, age 75, India

Aging Societies

The Setting for Aging Social Policy

> *The world stands on the threshold of a demographic revolution with few parallels in humanity's past. It's called global aging, and in the coming decades it will subject nations around the world to extraordinary economic, social, and political challenges.*
>
> —Center for Strategic and International Studies

> *I am a dressmaker, and I always worked at home. My husband who worked in a factory nearby died 6 years ago, and now I get his pension, [as] I haven't got my own pension. I have one son who lives in the flat above mine and one daughter who lives 2 km away. [My] small pension is not a lot, but I do not have great needs. The house is mine, I have no car, I do not buy clothes because I make my own; so I manage to get by. I do not think a lot about the future, perhaps during the night, but then I say to myself, "Let's live day by day," and I do just that. I hope to be healthy, and I hope not to be a burden to my son and daughter later on in life.*
>
> — Mrs. C., age 70, Piedmonte Region, Italy

Introduction

For the past 25 years, politicians, academics, and laypeople have been discussing the fact that the world's population—in the United States and elsewhere—is aging. The year 2000 marked the first time in human history that the number of older adults reached 600 million, and that number is expected to climb well into the middle of this century to a projected 2 billion (United Nations, 2007). Virtually all countries, with the exception of Africa, have experienced or are on the verge of experiencing a marked growth in their aging population. This population aging has caused a discussion across the globe about how social policy should respond to this demographic shift. Should retirement age increase? What can be done to protect the solvency of public pension systems and health care services? How should our communities respond with regard to providing social services, housing environments, and transportation? How will social policies support families in their role of primary caregiver? We are indeed living through a unique period in history and a time in which governments will be compelled to consider myriad aging social policy questions.

We use two approaches to introduce you to aging social policy. First, we have chosen to use an international comparison approach that will give us the opportunity to compare and contrast U.S. aging social policy with policies in other countries. Learning about U.S. aging policy can be enhanced by becoming aware of how other countries approach the same social policy issues. As Hill (2006) points out, social policy comparisons have a practical purpose—they show us that there are alternative ways of doing things, and we can learn from the experiences of other countries.

However, making international comparisons is a challenging undertaking for a number of reasons. Terminology and meanings vary by country (e.g., *home health, homemaker*) and many countries, such as Italy, have a decentralized approach to social policy implementation; so one must be cautious when making generalizations about an entire country. Perhaps the biggest challenge is the variability between countries in the amount of information and data readily available about a given social policy topic. Thus, the selection of countries to include in each chapter was somewhat restricted, because in some cases, particularly for non-European countries, there was not sufficient data available to make meaningful comparisons. In contrast, data on European countries are gathered and regularly reported by organizations such as the Organization for Economic Cooperation and Development and EuroStat. We did, however, attempt to include non-European countries when possible. In addition, and not surprisingly, some topics such as retirement income and family care offer quite an extensive amount of data and information from which different countries can draw. Information about other topics such as mental health is a bit more scant. Thus, you will notice that some chapters provide a more in-depth discussion than do others.

The daunting task of selecting only two to five non-U.S. countries for each chapter was guided by how well a country could help illustrate the different governmental approaches to the social policy issue being discussed. The countries selected will provide you with some insight into the different social policy choices that are made to address the same social issue, such as retirement income in later life. We hope that by the end of each chapter, you will be compelled to find out more about the social policy approaches of countries we discussed, as well as countries we did not discuss. It should also be noted here that our approach to select four or five different countries to compare differs from other notable texts that briefly discuss policy topics for 20 or more countries (e.g., Giarchi, 1996; Kosberg, 1994) or those that take an in-depth look at a handful of countries with regard to a particular topic, such as family care (e.g., Blackman, Brodhurst, & Convery, 2001).

Our second approach in writing this book was to draw attention to the link between policies and people. Social policy discourse and analyses occur at the macrolevel and can easily become separated from the impact that such policies have on the day-to-day lives and quality of life of older adults—in other words, what occurs at the microlevel. We refer to this as the *policy-person link*. The policy-person link is a reminder that the existence and characteristics of a policy will influence the conditions that older people experience—for example, the quality of their retirement experience; their access to medical care, transportation, and housing; and even facilitate their social interactions. Consider the following circumstances of a caregiver in the United States:

> My mother needs kidney dialysis three times a week for 3 hours a day. I work full-time, so I tried to arrange for specialized public transportation provided by the city to take her to and from the dialysis clinic. But they tell me they have limited service—so they can

drop her off, but they can't arrange to pick her up. I could arrange to use my vacation days and take off from work to take her myself, but I am not strong enough to transfer her in and out of my car. I asked the staff in the dialysis clinic to help me take her from the clinic to my car in the parking lot, but they tell me they are prohibited from leaving the clinic to help me. She also needs help with basic needs—meal preparation, bathing, and cleaning. But we can't afford the cost of home help. I need help, but I've run out of options.

It is possible that this caregiver's experience would be different if there were policies in place that made specialized transportation services more accessible, that provided assistance to help pay for a home help aid, or that provided paid leave from work to engage in caring activities. Being mindful of the policy-person link is one way to think about social policy outcomes and the role governments play in addressing the economic, health, and social needs of older adults. At the end of this chapter, we provide a case study of an older adult that you can use throughout this book to illustrate how aging policies in different countries influence the day-to-day lives of older adults.

Organization of Remaining Chapters

We begin each chapter by highlighting the policy-person link with two quotes—one from a politician or leader in the field of gerontology, public policy, or an organizational body involved in policymaking and one from an older adult whom we interviewed for this book.[1] We then provide, if available, macrolevel country data on the topic at hand to give you a sense of the scope of the issue on a global scale. This is followed by a separate discussion of each country we selected to include; by the end of the chapter, you will be able to compare and contrast the different policy approaches. We also embedded text boxes in each chapter to illustrate a connection between policy and people or policy and practice. At the end of each chapter, we provided more resources so that you can further explore the topic. We concluded with an interview of an older adult that will give you some insight into their daily lives and concerns and give you an opportunity to consider how their lives are influenced by the existence or absence of social policies.

Chapter 2 discusses the social policy process and the different factors that influence the creation and characteristics of social policies. We include a brief explanation of the federal legislative process in the United States and end that chapter with an overview of key international and U.S. aging policies. The next five chapters explore specific social policy themes of retirement income (Chapter 3), employment (Chapter 4), housing (Chapter 5), health care (Chapter 6), and mental health (Chapter 7). The next two chapters examine social policies that are more community-based. Chapter 8 examines community-based support policies, and Chapter 9 closes this section of chapters with a discussion about family care policy. Our last chapter (Chapter 10) summarizes the future challenges for aging social policy. We hope that this book expands your knowledge about aging social policy in the United States and elsewhere and increases your awareness that social policy decisions can make a marked difference in the quality of life of older adults.

We should also mention how we deal with different terminology and their spelling in this book. You will notice that in many chapters, we use the words *aging* and *ageing*

---

1. Please note that these interviews are not meant to be generalized to a country's elderly population as a whole; rather, they are used to illustrate the policy-person connection.

interchangeably, as the latter is the common spelling used outside the United States. The same is true for the words *caregiver* and *carer*, the latter word being most often used in European countries to identify a person in the family designated to provide care and support to an elderly family member. Because we feel that it is important to honor these and other linguistic distinctions throughout the book, you will see differing spelling and usage of these terms.

For the remainder of this chapter, we will discuss in more detail one reason why aging social policy has risen to the forefront of political discourse across the globe—the growing number of older adults. We will discuss what has contributed to this increase and provide an overview of population aging statistics worldwide.

Population Aging

When we use the term *population aging,* we are referring to the demographic characteristics of a country whereby its older adults—usually those over the age of 60 or 65—account for an increasing proportion of the total population. In this next section, we will discuss factors that are responsible for an increase in the aged population and the extent of population aging in the United States and other countries. We have provided definitions of the demographic terms we use in this chapter in Box 1.1.

BOX 1.1   Demographic Definitions

Total fertility rate: the average number of children a woman would bear over the course of her lifetime if current age-specific fertility rates remained constant throughout her childbearing years (normally between the ages of 15 and 49)

Life expectancy: the average number of additional years a person of that age could expect to live if current mortality levels observed for ages above that age were to continue for the rest of that person's life. So *life expectancy at birth* is the average number of years a newborn would live if current age-specific mortality rates were to continue, and *life expectancy at age 65* is the average number of years a person at age 65 would live if current age-specific mortality rates were to continue

Youth dependency ratio: the number of persons aged 0 to 14 years per one hundred persons aged 15 to 64

Old-age dependency ratio: the number of persons aged 65 years or older per one hundred persons aged 15 to 64

Total dependency ratio: the number of persons under age 15 plus persons aged 65 or older per one hundred persons aged 15 to 64; the sum of the youth dependency ratio and the old-age dependency ratio

Population ageing: the process whereby older individuals account for a proportionally larger share of the total population

Source: United Nations, (2007).

Fertility Rates and Life Expectancy

There are two primary reasons why the vast majority of countries in the world have experienced population aging. First is the decline in fertility rates, or the number of

Figure 1.1 Fertility Rates and Population Aging

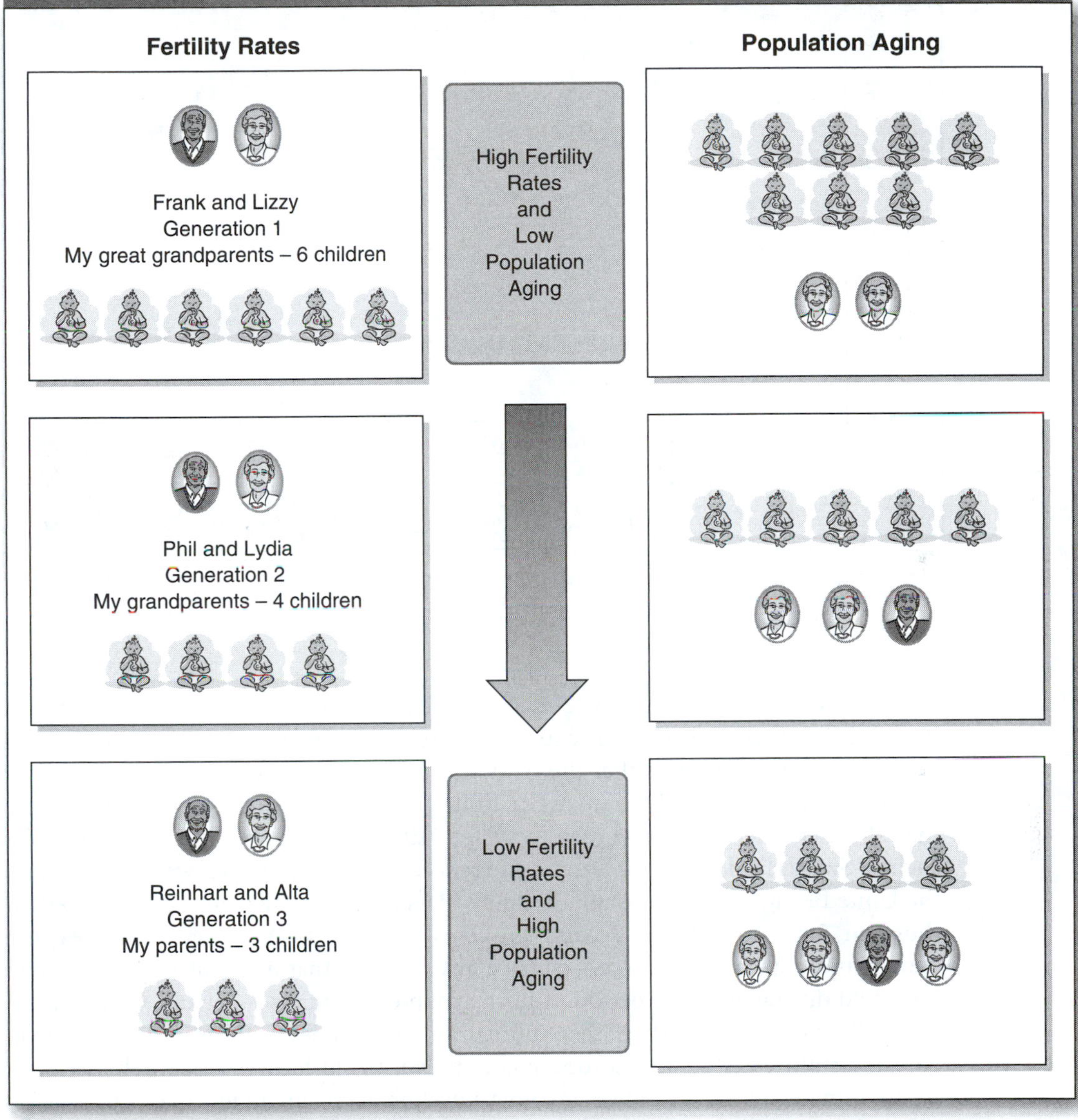

children being born. When fertility rates decline, the result is fewer younger people in the population relative to the number of older adults. When successive cohorts are having fewer children, the proportion of older adults to children expands (see Figure 1.1). As an example, consider Robbyn's great-grandparents, who had six children in the late 1880s and early 1900s. This is reflective of a time when families had high fertility rates, resulting in a higher number of children relative to older adults and resulting in low population aging. Her grandparents had four children, and her parents had half the number of children that her great-grandparents did—three. As the fertility rates decline with each successive generation, the result is high population aging. Figure 1.2 illustrates the numeric change in world fertility rates from 1950 to 2050, which fell from 5 children

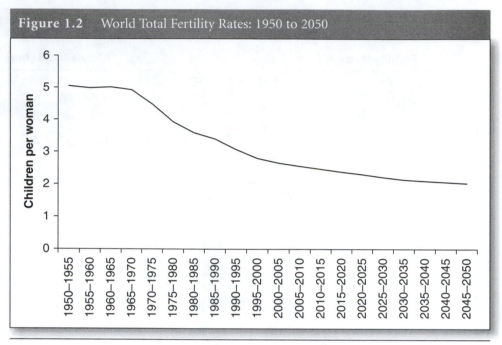

Figure 1.2   World Total Fertility Rates: 1950 to 2050

Source: United Nations (2008).

born to women in 1950 to 2.7 in 2005 to 2010 (United Nations, 2008). The world fertility rate is expected to drop further to 2.1 children per woman in 2045 to 2050.

It is important to note that the reduction in fertility rates also varies by country (see Figure 1.3). The fertility rate in the United States has declined from slightly more than three children born to women in 1950 to 1955 to two in 2005 to 2010. Countries such as Switzerland, Belgium, Denmark, France, Germany, Italy, Norway, Sweden, and the United Kingdom show a slight decline of less than one child from 1950 to 1955 to those in 2005 to 2010. A second group of countries—Australia, New Zealand, Netherlands, Spain, and Greece—all have fertility rates that have fallen by more than one child during that time period. A third group of countries—Canada, China, India, Japan, Brazil, and Chile—have seen more dramatic declines, with drops by more than half in fertility rates. All the European countries listed in Figure 1.3, as well as China, Japan, Canada, Australia, and Chile, show a decline in fertility to less than 2.0, which is below the population replacement rate of 2.1 children born per woman.

The second reason behind the increase in population aging is the increase in life expectancy. Life expectancy at birth, or the average number of years a newborn will live if current age-specific mortality rates continue, has steadily increased globally by 20 years, from 46.4 in 1950 to 1955 to 67.2 in 2005 to 2010 (see Figure 1.4 on page 10; United Nations, 2007).

The life expectancy worldwide is projected to increase another 8 years to 75.4 in 2045 to 2050. Just as in the case of fertility rates, the increase in life expectancy varies by country. Table 1.1 displays the life expectancy at birth of men and women by country

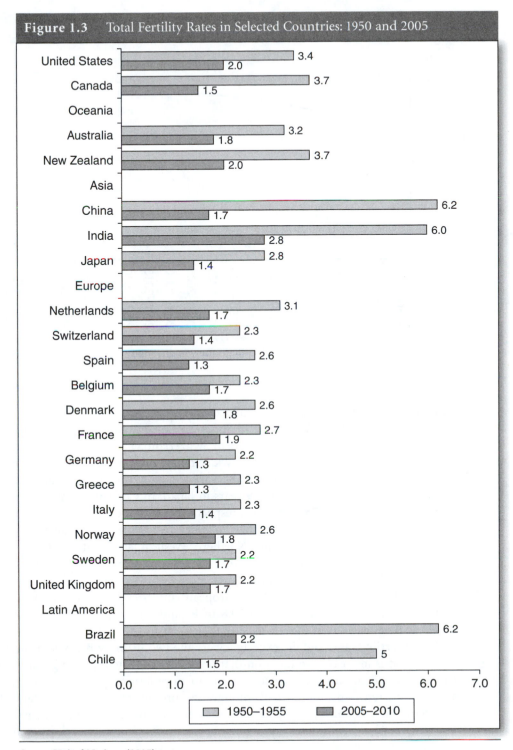

Figure 1.3   Total Fertility Rates in Selected Countries: 1950 and 2005

Country	1950–1955	2005–2010
United States	3.4	2.0
Canada	3.7	1.5
Oceania		
Australia	3.2	1.8
New Zealand	3.7	2.0
Asia		
China	6.2	1.7
India	6.0	2.8
Japan	2.8	1.4
Europe		
Netherlands	3.1	1.7
Switzerland	2.3	1.4
Spain	2.6	1.3
Belgium	2.3	1.7
Denmark	2.6	1.8
France	2.7	1.9
Germany	2.2	1.3
Greece	2.3	1.3
Italy	2.3	1.4
Norway	2.6	1.8
Sweden	2.2	1.7
United Kingdom	2.2	1.7
Latin America		
Brazil	6.2	2.2
Chile	5	1.5

Source: United Nations (2007).

Figure 1.4 World Life Expectancy at Birth: 1950 to 2050

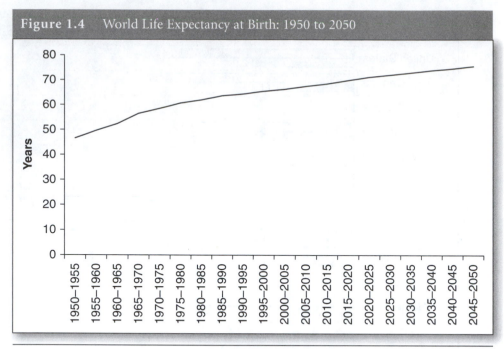

Source: United Nations (2008).

in different geographic regions. The life expectancy at birth for men in the United States, Canada, Northern, Western, and Southern Europe, and Oceania ranges from 75.6 years in the United States to 79 years in Switzerland. The life expectancy at birth pattern for men in Eastern Europe has a wider range, from 59 years in Russia to 73.4 in the Czech Republic. Asian countries also vary widely, as the life expectancy at birth for males is 63.2 years in India and 79 years in Japan. In Chile and Brazil, life expectancy at birth for men is 75.5 and 68.2, respectively. Without exception, women's life expectancy at birth is greater than men in every region and every country. Again, women in the United States, Canada, Northern, Western, and Southern Europe, and Oceania have life expectancies at birth that range from 80.6 in Denmark to 84.2 in Spain, which has the highest life expectancy at birth for women of all the countries listed in Table 1.1. Women in Eastern European countries have life expectancies at birth ranging from 72.6 in Russia to 79.8 in Poland. Life expectancies at birth for women in Asia range from 66.4 in India to 86.1 in Japan.

While fertility rates and life expectancy are the two primary reasons for population aging, it is important to mention that one additional factor, in-migration rates, also has the potential to influence the rate of population aging. This is because in-migration rates—the number of immigrants coming into a country—can offset low fertility rates, as immigrants tend to be younger and have more children (Gavrilov & Heuveline, 2003). Migration may have a more prominent role in influencing population

Table 1.1   Life Expectancy at Birth for Selected Countries by Region for Years 2005 to 2010

Country	Life Expectancy		Country	Life Expectancy	
	Male	Female		Male	Female
North America			**Western Europe**		
United States	75.6	80.8	Austria	76.9	82.6
Canada	78.3	82.9	Belgium	76.5	82.3
			France	77.1	84.1
Northern Europe			Germany	76.5	82.1
Denmark	76.0	80.6	Netherlands	77.5	81.9
Finland	76.1	82.4	Switzerland	79.0	84.2
Ireland	76.5	81.4			
Norway	77.8	82.5	**Southern Europe**		
Sweden	78.7	83.0	Greece	77.1	81.9
United Kingdom	77.2	81.6	Italy	77.5	83.5
			Spain	77.7	84.2
			Portugal	75.0	81.2
Asia					
China	71.3	74.8	**Eastern Europe**		
Japan	79.0	86.1	Bulgaria	69.5	76.7
South Korea	75.0	82.2	Hungary	69.2	77.4
Thailand	66.5	75.0	Poland	71.3	79.8
Vietnam	72.3	76.2	Russia	59.0	72.6
India	63.2	66.4	Czech Republic	73.4	79.5
Oceania			**Latin America**		
Australia	78.9	83.6	Chile	75.5	81.5
New Zealand	77.0	81.3	Brazil	68.2	75.7

Source: United Nations (2008).

aging in the future, particularly in low-fertility countries such as Italy, Canada, and the United States.

Scope and Speed of World Population Aging

Now that we have explained how and why population aging has occurred over the past half-century, let us briefly examine the scope and speed at which population aging has occurred. As shown in Figure 1.5, there were 205 million persons aged 60 and older in the world in 1950; by 2007, that number increased to 705 million, with 11 countries reporting more than 10 million people over the age of 60 (United Nations, 2007). By 2050, the number of elderly adults 60 and older is expected to rise to 2 billion, with 32 countries having 10 million or more elderly adults. The growth in the older adult population aged 80 and over shows a similar pattern. According to the United Nations (2007), there were 14 million older adults aged 80 and over in 1950, and by 2007, that number had increased to 94 million. By 2050, the number of oldest old is expected to have increased fourfold to 394 million (see Figure 1.6).

The increase worldwide in the number of older adults is also reflected in increases in individual country demographics. Figure 1.7 on page 14 shows a selected number of countries and their expected percentage increases in the elderly population. In the United States, the older adult population is expected to increase 102% from the year 2000 to 2030 (Kinsella & Velkoff, 2001). Canada and Australia are also expected to

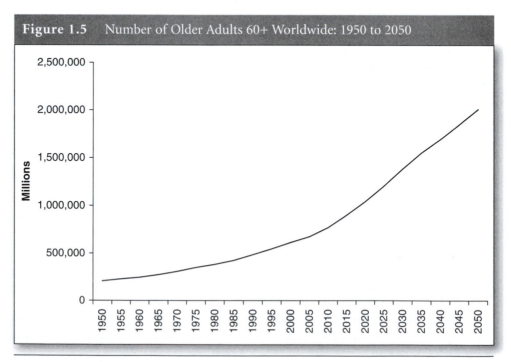

Figure 1.5   Number of Older Adults 60+ Worldwide: 1950 to 2050

Source: United Nations (2008).

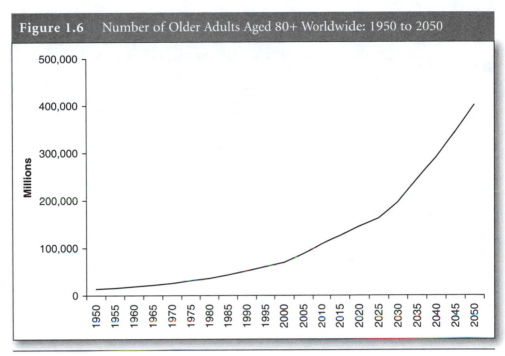

Figure 1.6 Number of Older Adults Aged 80+ Worldwide: 1950 to 2050

Source: United Nations (2008).

experience an increase in elderly by 126% and 108%, respectively. Interestingly, European countries are expected to experience a smaller percentage increase in their elderly population over the next 30 years. The percentage increase is expected to vary from 43% in Greece to 64% in Denmark. The less-developed countries of Thailand, Brazil, India, and China all have an expected increase of more than 150% over the next 30 years. So the percentage increase of older adults is expected to vary by country, as is the percentage of older adults over age 65 and 80 in any given region.

Figure 1.8 on page 15 illustrates the expected increase in the percentage of persons aged 65 and older by geographic region. In the United States, the percentage of persons aged 65 and older is expected to increase from 12.3% in 2005 to 20.2% in 2035. Europe is expected to see increases from 15.9% to 24.2%. However, the percentage of the population aged 65 and older is expected to double during the years 2005 to 2035 in Asia and Latin America.

The increase in the percentage of persons aged 80 and older in the world's regions is expected to increase markedly between the years 2005 and 2035 (see Figure 1.9 on page 16). In the United States in 2005, 3.5% of the population was adults aged 80 and older, and that percentage is expected to rise to 5.9% in 2035. Europe's and Canada's increase are expected to be greater, going from 3.5% to 6.9% and 7.4%, respectively. Asia's and Latin America's percentages are expected to increase by more than double from 1% to 2.7% and from 1.2% to 3.2%, respectively. Although Africa has a small percentage of older adults over age 80, the percentage is expected to double.

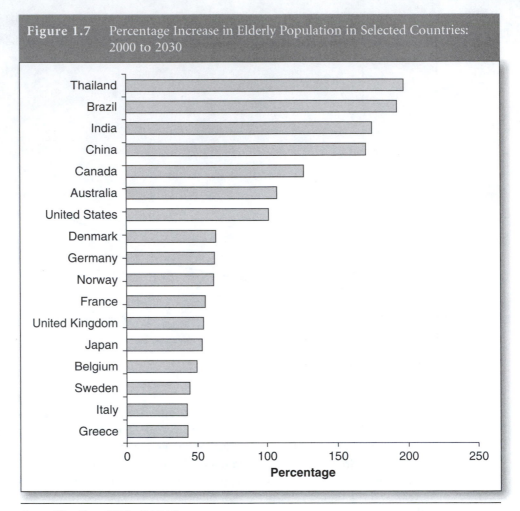

Figure 1.7 Percentage Increase in Elderly Population in Selected Countries: 2000 to 2030

Source: Kinsella and Velkoff (2001).

When examining characteristics of population, it is also constructive to consider the speed at which a country will experience population aging. Figure 1.10 on page 17 illustrates the number of years required or expected for the percentage of a country's population aged 65 and older to increase from 7% to 14%. For example, it is estimated that it will take a period of 69 years (1944–2013) for the United States to experience an increase from 7% to 14% (Kinsella & Velkoff, 2001). This slower rate of population aging is consistent in most other developed countries with the exception of Japan, which increased to 14% in only 26 years (1970–1996). The speed of population aging is much more rapid in developing countries. China is expected to reach 14% in 27 years (2000–2027)—something that took France 115 years to do (1865–1980).

The final demographic characteristic of population aging that we will discuss is dependency ratios. The total dependency ratio is the number of people under 15 years

Figure 1.8   Percentage Aged 65 and Over in Selected Regions: 2005, 2020, 2035

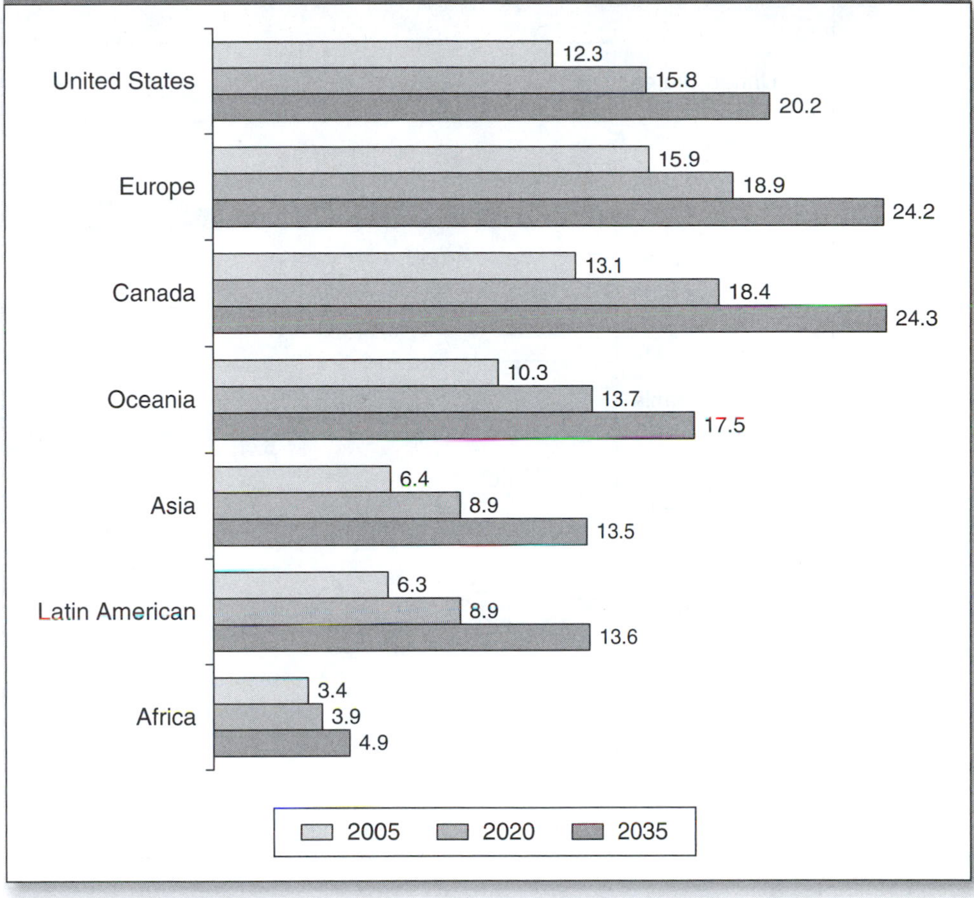

United States
- 12.3
- 15.8
- 20.2

Europe
- 15.9
- 18.9
- 24.2

Canada
- 13.1
- 18.4
- 24.3

Oceania
- 10.3
- 13.7
- 17.5

Asia
- 6.4
- 8.9
- 13.5

Latin American
- 6.3
- 8.9
- 13.6

Africa
- 3.4
- 3.9
- 4.9

☐ 2005   ☐ 2020   ☐ 2035

Source: United Nations (2008).

of age (i.e., youth dependency ratio) and the number of people aged 65 and older (i.e., old-age dependency ratio) to the number of people between the ages of 15 and 64. It is assumed that those under age 15 and over 65 are likely to be dependent on those assumed to be in the working ages of 15 to 64. It is important to discuss the total dependency ratio rather than present only the old-age dependency ratio, as this ratio provides a more complete picture of the potential social costs of caring for the young as well as elderly adults (Mullan, 2002). Figure 1.11 on page 18 shows the dependency ratio, which is composed of youth and old-age dependency ratios, for selected countries in the years 1950 and 2025. For example, the total dependency ratio in the United States was 54.5 in 1950 and is expected to increase slightly to 57.1. Although the total dependency ratio is expected to increase only a small amount, there should be a shift in the youth and old-age ratios. The youth ratio in 1950 in the United States was 41.7, and it is projected to drop to 29.3 by 2025. The old-age dependency ratio in the United States

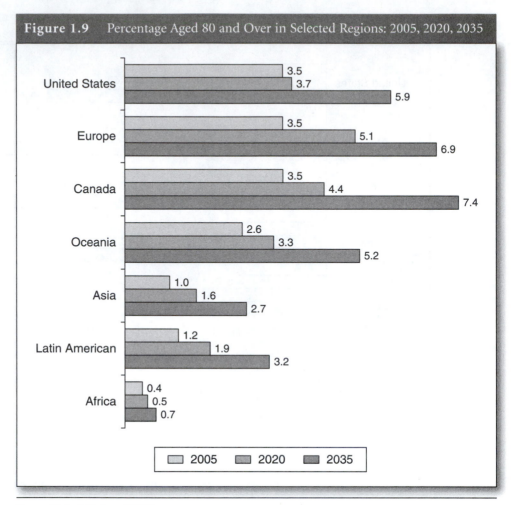

Figure 1.9 Percentage Aged 80 and Over in Selected Regions: 2005, 2020, 2035

Source: United Nations (2008).

is projected to increase from 12.8 in 1950 to 27.9 in 2025. Japan, Canada, and Australia/ New Zealand are projected to experience a modest increase in their total dependency ratios, whereas Switzerland, France, and Italy are expected to have a greater increase in their total dependency ratios. Interestingly, China and India are expected to experience a decline in the total dependency ratio from 1950 to 2025. All countries listed in Figure 1.11 show a decline in youth dependency ratios from 1950 to 2025 and an increase in old-age dependency ratios. The country with the highest expected rate of increase in the old-age ratio from 1950 to 2025 is Japan, with an increase from 8.3 to 49.7.

In summary, the demographic evidence shows declines in fertility rates and increases in life expectancy, which have contributed to the increase in worldwide population aging. In some European countries—notably, Italy, Greece, Germany, and Spain—the fertility rate will be slightly above one child per woman. Life expectancy gains will result in individuals living well into their seventh, eighth, and even ninth

Figure 1.10   Speed of Population Aging in Selected Countries
(Number of years required or expected for percentage of population aged 65+
to rise from 7% to 14%)

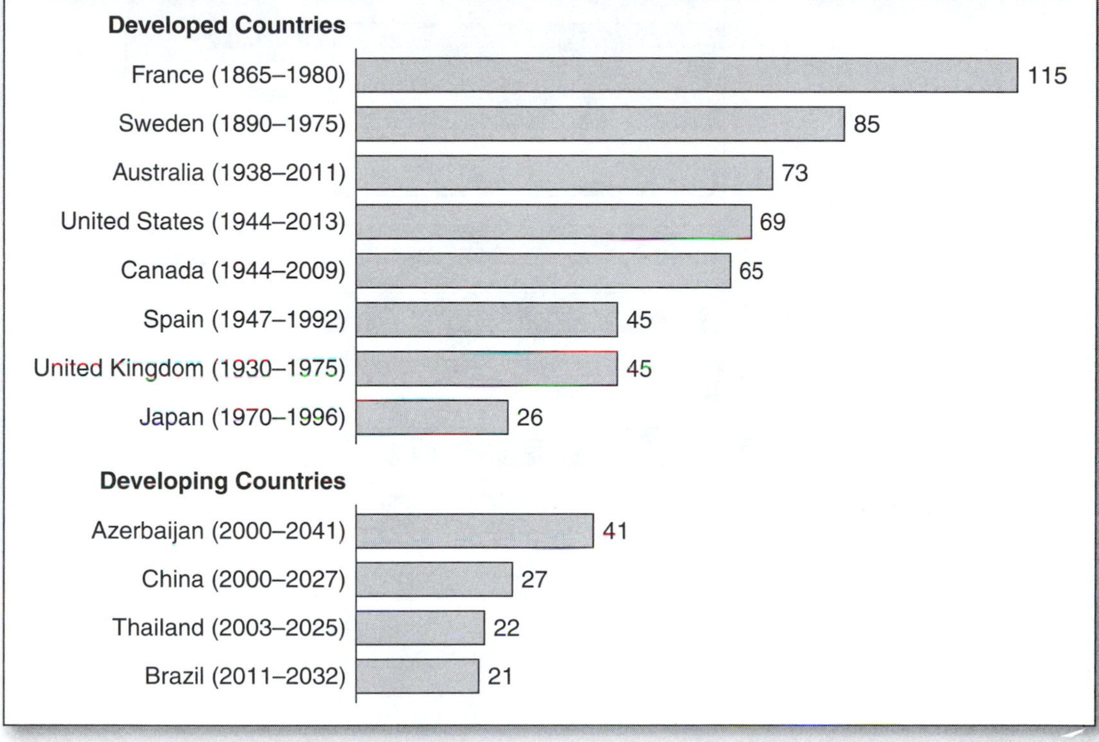

Developed Countries

France (1865–1980)	115
Sweden (1890–1975)	85
Australia (1938–2011)	73
United States (1944–2013)	69
Canada (1944–2009)	65
Spain (1947–1992)	45
United Kingdom (1930–1975)	45
Japan (1970–1996)	26

Developing Countries

Azerbaijan (2000–2041)	41
China (2000–2027)	27
Thailand (2003–2025)	22
Brazil (2011–2032)	21

Source: Kinsella and Velkoff (2001).

decades. For some countries, the pace at which they experience population aging will seem sudden—as is the case in China, which will experience an increase in its aged population of 165% over a 30-year period. For other countries, such as Sweden and the United States, ageing populations will continue a pattern of steady growth. The growth in the oldest-old—those over 80 years—will experience the fastest rate of increase. Although the old-age dependency ratio will increase in the coming decade, the overall dependency ratio will remain relatively stable over a 75-year period.

These are the statistics of population aging, but what are the consequences relative to aging policy? How these data are interpreted and how they should inform social policy has been generally divided into two different perspectives. The first perspective maintains that such a growth in the number of older adults will cause tremendous strain on all facets of society—economic, social, and health—and warns of an impending old-age "crisis" in which countries will become bankrupt caring for the aged. Peterson (1999) warns, "We face a threat more grave and certain than those posed by chemical weapons, nuclear proliferation, or ethnic strife: the "age wave" (p. 1). We started this chapter with a quote from a government official in China that appears to echo these concerns.

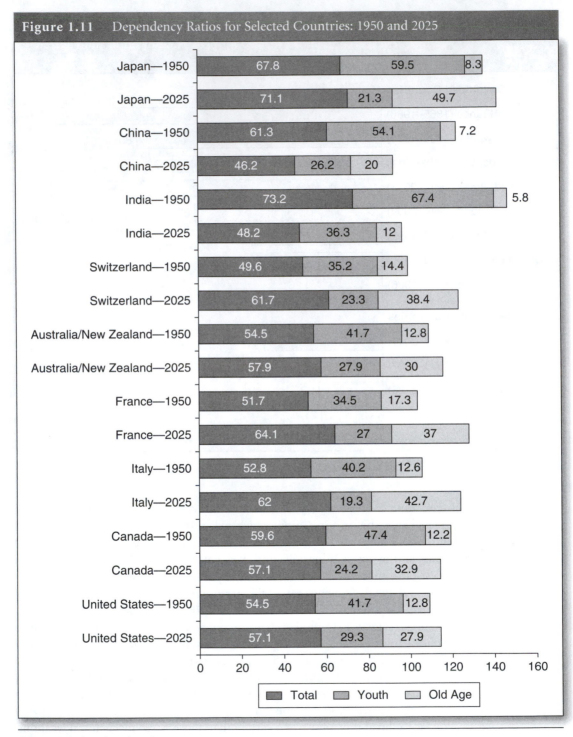

Figure 1.11   Dependency Ratios for Selected Countries: 1950 and 2025

Source: United Nations (2007).

The second perspective maintains that population aging has been happening since the 1900s and that societies have adapted. This perspective espouses that "demography is not destiny" (Friedland & Summer, 1999, 2005) and that policy choices, in conjunction with market forces and economic growth, can adequately address the needs of a growing older adult population (Friedland & Summer, 2005; Mullan, 2002). As you can imagine, how one approaches aging policy will be markedly different depending on which perspective of population aging one takes. We will revisit this topic again in Chapter 10 when we discuss the issues facing aging social policy.

There is little doubt that as baby boomers move into retirement age, they will once again change the demographic landscape—the same way they did as children and as adults moving through the life course. Of interest to our discussion in this book is how countries are responding to their population aging. As Hill (2006) aptly notes, "Ageing people have to come to terms with ageing, perhaps ageing nations have to do so as well" (p. 250).

Learning Activity: Policy-Person Link Case Study

We have created a case study based on the different circumstances of some older adults interviewed for this book. As you read through the chapters, use the case study of Luciana to examine how she would experience income, health, social, and economic support in each of the different countries we discuss.

CASE STUDY

Luciana is an 87-year-old widow of 20 years who lives alone in her single-family home and has a small dog named Zita. Both adult daughters, in their 50s, work full-time. One lives 30 minutes away, and the other lives in another region 5 hours away. Luciana worked for 30 years in full-time employment, and when she retired she was making $45,000 a year (€35,338). She has savings of $10,000 (€7,854.33).

Luciana has mild cognitive impairment, and although she is still very engaged and social, she is aware that her mental capacity is "slipping" and often cries about "what is happening to me." She is not able to drive, prepare meals, or manage her finances. She needs supervision to make sure she is dressed and has properly completed personal hygiene tasks both at night and in the morning. She also needs assistance in taking her medications. She ambulates with a cane and is able to ride specialized buses, with some assistance needed in getting on and off the bus.

Thus, Luciana needs the following support services:

- Assistance with shower, dressing, and personal care (e.g., hair, makeup, etc.) morning and evening, 7 days a week
- Meals morning and evening Monday through Friday and all meals on weekends

(Continued)

(Continued)

- Assistance with grocery shopping and laundry
- Help administering medications and paying her bills
- Help taking her dog for a walk
- Companionship in the evenings and on weekends
- Transportation to doctor visits and community events
- Yard care and snow removal in the winter and home repair when needed
- Mental health support

Select three or four different countries and identify the types of support to which Luciana would have access if she were living in that country. How much would she receive from her government pension? What support would she have paying for her doctor's visits and prescriptions? What types of assistance would be available for her daily living needs listed above? What alternative housing environments might she consider given her needs and income? How much would she have to pay for these services? As you will discover, her daily living circumstances will be very different depending on which country she happens to reside in.

For More Information

1. Population Pyramids: U.S. Census Bureau, International Database
   http://www.census.gov/ipc/www/idb/informationGateway.php

   Use this site to compare population pyramids for any country in the world.

2. United Nations: World Population Ageing: 1950 to 2050
   http://www.un.org/esa/population/publications/worldageing19502050/

   This report was prepared by the United Nation's Population Division as a contribution to the 2002 World Assembly on Ageing and its follow-up. The report provides a description of global trends in population ageing and includes a series of indicators of the ageing process by development regions, major areas, regions, and countries.

3. Center for Strategic and International Studies
   http://csis.org/program/global-aging-initiative

   The CSIS Global Aging Initiative explores the long-term economic, social, and geopolitical implications of demographic trends in the United States and around the world. Its website has a number of interesting publications on global aging, including aging issues in China and Latin America.

Mrs. V., age 71
Biella, Italy

I was born in Camburzano (a village nearby) in 1934. My mother was a weaver, and my father was a sewer. I have two brothers older than me and two sons but no grandsons because my sons want to keep me young so nobody will call me granny (haha)! Both I and my husband worked in a factory. I started to work when I was 10 years old.

A typical day for me is doing some work around the house. I go to see relatives or friends, I read and do some crosswords, I also do some embroidery and with my husband I play cards.

Together we go twice a week to the gym. I hardly see my sons. They are like white flies; from time to time, they come to visit us.

I haven't got any serious health problems, just some disorders due to old age.

I receive a pension, as I worked, but it is a very small one because for many years I stayed at home to look after my children. The amount I get, it is not adequate to my needs. I would need "Ciampi's" pension [ex Italian President] to sustain my needs or "Fazzio's" [ex director of the central Italian bank]. If my husband and I are sick, we go to the hospital or doctor through the national health system. If we want to choose the doctor or avoid the lines, we go privately and pay for the checkups. We get what the convent gives us [an old saying in Italy].

Teeth, eye checkups can be obtained through the national health system for free, but the lines are very long. Dental implants are half of the charge, so we have to pay for the rest. Hearing aid is free, but we hardly get the new inventions. Sometimes the models are 10 years, so a lot of people pay the difference to get the newer models. In Italy, we can buy private insurances but only up to the age of 70/75 years old. If you have an illness that you had in the past, the private insurance does not cover for any treatments for that particular illness.

If we were by ourselves unable to move with no family or any help and in need of food, there is the "Comunita' Montana" ["mountain community"; nongovernment run], which comes round to your house with warm meals every day. You pay a little amount towards it depending on your income. The maximum you pay is €7 per day. They come round once a day for 5 days a week. There is no help if you need transportation, but if you need someone to help you with cleaning the house there are people who come and charge €7 per hour, which is much less than the normal rate. Basically, unless you are really poor, you need to pay for all of these services. If you are really poor and have nothing, the local town hall will investigate your case, check your bank account, and then help you out.

How do I feel being an older person? Ah, it is the end of the world (hahahahaha). Well, there is something good. You can say what you want, but I don't like it because I feel I am at the end. When I was younger, I would not say everything about my life to my mother because I didn't want her to worry. Now my sons don't tell us all of their problems for the same reason, and I don't like that. For the future, I hope my husband and I can have some health and to be able to hold our hands and die together. Cats and dogs means more than elderly people sometimes. I think we tend to be neglected by society.

What advice would I give students about growing older? To do what you can but not to lose old values in life. Young people have too much today, and they do not know how to make sacrifices. We have gone to extremes, and their "getting older" will be harder than our getting old. I was born during the fascist time and saw the war, we worked hard, our generation made this country.

Catullo, age 90, Switzerland

Lucio & Domingo, ages 85 & 76, United States

2
Aging Social Policy

> *The moral test of government is how that government treats those who are in the dawn of life, the children; those who are in the twilight of life, the elderly; those who are in the shadows of life; the sick, the needy, and the handicapped.*
>
> —Last speech of Hubert H. Humphrey, November 1, 1977, Washington, D.C.

> *I receive the AVS (pension) as everyone. The age for retiring for women is 62, for men is 65. It is enough because we do not spend a lot of money.... If my pension was not enough for my needs or I had no family who could help, there are associations like Associazione ticinese terza età (Ticino Seniors Association) to help you, but it costs money unless you have nothing.... If someone is really, really poor, the government pays for everything.*
>
> —Mrs. G., age 78, Switzerland

We are all affected by the legislative decisions made by our local, state, and federal governments. Today, Robbyn's 88-year-old mother's bank account was credited with funds from her Social Security and state pension, and she took the senior care bus to go to her doctor's appointment and refill her prescriptions. When we got into our cars to go to work, we made sure our seatbelts were fastened and were mindful of the speed limit as we drove (at least, we tried to be mindful of that). Robbyn assisted students in getting financial aid to help pay their tuition; she has reviewed her office's operating budget in anticipation of next year's looming budget cuts in higher education from the state's budget. Her nieces and nephews attended their public elementary school and are preparing to take the state-sanctioned standardized test.

Each of these issues is in some way connected to a social policy—federal legislation that authorizes Social Security and pensions, Medicare, public transportation, and student financial aid and state legislation governing driving behaviors and funding decisions about higher education and K–12 education assessment. Indeed, many of the things you or your family does in a given day—from the seemingly minute (e.g., putting your seatbelt on) to the more noticeable (e.g., Medicare covering your grandparent's doctor visit)—are influenced by an existing social policy. For each of these and a myriad other actions—if you stop and think about them for a moment—you may be able to trace the policy that has been enacted to guide your behavior and help you or your family members gain access to social goods such as health care or a college education.

Why do some social issues become the focus of legislation and others do not? Why are some policies enacted the first time they are introduced and other policies take many decades to be enacted (e.g., health care reform) or never get passed at all (e.g., legalizing marijuana)? The purpose of this chapter is to help you understand the social policymaking process and the variables that influence both the form and content of social policy. In the last half of this chapter, we will review some key political milestones in U.S. and international aging social policy and close with an overview of the Older Americans Act legislation.

Social Policy Process

Before we discuss the steps in the policymaking process, let's first define what we mean by the terms *public policy*, *social policy*, and *aging social policy*. *Public policy* has been defined as "what governments do, why they do it, and what difference it makes" (Dye, 1976, p. 1). It is a collection of public interventions that have purposes and effects, including the distribution of life chances. The term *social policy* is often used when the policies being discussed are concerned with the social welfare needs of a society, such as education, health, poverty, housing, and the distribution of other social goods. Finally, *aging social policy* narrows the focus even further to those social policies that are directed toward older adults in particular.

When we use these terms throughout this book, we will be referring to policy either as a *product* (i.e., the actual legislation and programs and services it creates) or as a *process* (i.e., how social policy is created). Because social policy is a vast field of study that seeks to understand how societal problems are perceived to warrant a government response, how solutions to these problems are formed, and how policies are evaluated in order to understand the consequences of those solutions (Smith & Larimer, 2009), we can only hope to provide you with a brief overview of the key elements of the social policy process.

Figure 2.1 illustrates the six steps in the policymaking process: (1) a private problem emerges as a social problem, (2) the problem is defined, (3) the policy is designed, (4) the policy is adopted, (5) the policy is implemented, and (6) the policy is evaluated (Portney, 1986). Of course, policymaking in reality does not progress in the stepwise fashion that we have depicted here. Rather, the process of policymaking is very dynamic and iterative, moving back and forth between steps, but understanding each step will give you a good basic understanding of the policymaking process.

Problem Emerges

Social policies emerge because a private problem has been brought to the public's attention as a social problem or need. For example, legislation exists to assist family caregivers of older adults because the problems families were experiencing in the family unit in trying to adequately care for their older family members came to be identified as a public concern that required a public or governmental solution. Bradshaw (1972) identified four ways in which needs are identified and expressed, which helps them move from a private problem to a public problem. *Felt need* is what individuals perceive their need to be—such as feeling hungry. Needs cannot move into the public arena unless individuals are first aware of their own needs. An *expressed need* is a felt need turned into expressed demands, such as going to the local food bank for assistance. *Normative need* is defined by experts through the use of standards or data that can be quantified. For example, researchers conduct national studies on food insecurity among older adults, documenting the problem. Finally, *comparative need* is the perceived gap between what another group has relative to what one's own group has—for example, it is not the norm that all people in our society go hungry.

So the social policy process begins when private individual troubles or needs turn into public concerns because that need is expressed as a demand, when the need or

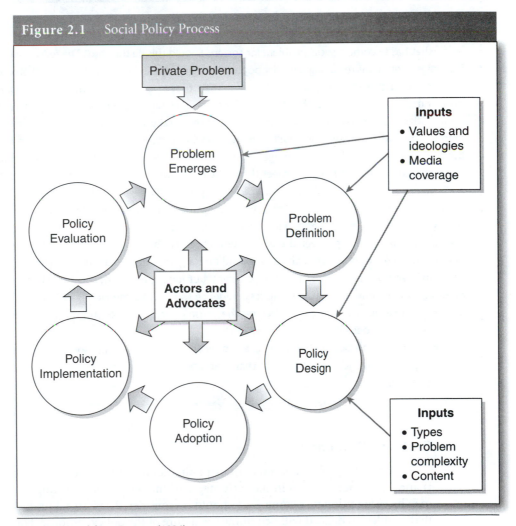

Figure 2.1   Social Policy Process

Source: Adapted from Portney (1986).

problem has been defined by experts (academics as well as advocacy groups; see Box 2.1), and when there is a relative judgment of need made against others in society. It is also important to note at this point that there is a difference between problems that can be classified as needs and those that are simply wants. We may *want* the newest technological gadget (and we do!), but not having such an item doesn't negatively impact our basic *needs* as human beings—such as not having food, shelter, or health care, which we might argue would be legitimate concerns of policy. To be sure, the advertisers for these gadgets will want us to confuse the two concepts so that we can convince ourselves that we have a need for whatever they're offering, but it is unlikely that this want for new technology will ever be defined as a public policy concern.

BOX 2.1 Is Population Aging a Social Problem?

We discuss in later chapters the issues older adults experience in later life that have become the topic of aging social policy. However, some authors often characterize the aged as a demographic subpopulation that has become a social problem for society. Should this be the case? The following are three examples of opinions regarding whether population aging should be defined as a social problem.

"We face a threat more grave and certain than those posed by chemical weapons, nuclear proliferation, or ethnic strife: the 'age wave.' As life expectancy grows and fertility rates decline, senior citizens will make up an ever-larger share of the total population. The effects of this demographic shift will be staggering. It will come with a whopping price tag, which will place a massive burden on an ever-smaller working-age population. . . . Unless the West recognizes the challenges to come and devises a strategy to meet them, the future will be gray and bleak." (Peterson, 1999)

"There is no ageing 'problem.' Greater longevity and falling early age mortality is a cause for celebration, not concern. Populations have been ageing and support ratios falling at pretty much the same rate for over 100 years, without generating the sort of financial and social crises being predicted today. . . . People over the designated retirement age do not become worthless dependents in need of support overnight and should no longer be treated as such. Ageing is not an illness. And with people living not just longer lives, but longer, healthier, and fitter lives, this myth of automatic dependence has less and less credence to it. . . . So the elderly neither represent an 'unsupportable burden' nor could they be the cause of weakened economic growth rates. The ageing 'problem' does not exist." (Mullan, 2002)

"Demography can be, and has been, used to reconstruct and redefine social problems in ways that fit a political agenda or, at the least, that calibrate with current and popular ideological positions." (Gee, 2002)

Problem Definition

As a private problem becomes more public, defining the exact nature of the problem is another important step in the early stages of the social policymaking process. There may be recognition that some issue should be considered as a social problem, but how that problem is defined will determine the nature of the policy response. For example, if we define the cause of caregiver stress as a lack of information about how to care for a person with Alzheimer's disease, then the policy design will seek to find ways to provide caregivers with the information they need to help them cope with caregiving challenges. Defining what causes a problem is a difficult and often controversial task that is the subject of great debate. It is difficult because the reasons why problems such as elder abuse and old age poverty exist are likely due to a complicated mix of societal and familial concerns. It is controversial because defining the nature of the problem is also influenced by a mix of values, ideologies, and the efforts of public policy organizations that work to shape the problem definition through the media.

Values and Ideologies

The process of identifying and defining problems that can eventually result in a social policy solution is debated within the context of personal and collective ideologies and values that direct one's opinion about whether such issues are a problem and whether government should respond with a solution. For example, consider the contrasting ideologies of individualism and collectivism (Gill & Ingman, 1994). Individualism espouses that individuals and families ought to find their own solutions to problems that they encounter with minimal involvement from the government. On the other hand, collectivism embraces a collective or state responsibility in helping people deal with problems that they encounter. So the ideological debate about caregiver stress is whether such a problem is a private matter to be solved by family members alone or whether families should be assisted in their role as caregiver by publically funded programs.

This level of governmental involvement is sometimes referred to as the level of social risk that a government wishes to undertake on behalf of its citizens (Watkins & Watkins, 1984). Social risk comes with simply being alive and existing within an economic structure. For example, you might contract a serious illness or you might be laid off from your job in bad economic times. To address the consequences of these social risks, the government response can range from taking on no risk (e.g., it is up to the individual to deal with the cost of health care or the loss of income) to taking on some or all of the risk (e.g., the government provides health care access or unemployment benefits).

To illustrate this notion of risk adoption further, we return to the issue of income adequacy in retirement. How should a government respond on behalf of individuals who may enter later life with no work history (e.g., a parent who chose to stay home to raise the children or a person with a disability that prevented him or her from working during his or her adult years) or those who have worked most of their lives in minimum-wage employment for an employer that did not offer a pension plan? Should there be a minimum level of income in retirement for all citizens, regardless of work history? The Social Security program is an example of the government taking on social risk on behalf of its citizens (see Box 2.2). In thinking about ideologies and values that inform the discussion regarding social problems and solutions—such as individualism and collectivism—other values such as social justice, fairness, and equity will most certainly come into play.

Public Policy Groups

Many public policy groups (we will identify those specifically concerned with aging policy later in the chapter) and think tanks involved in the social policy arena reflect

BOX 2.2 Social Security: An Example of Taking on Risk

We can never insure one-hundred percent of the population against one-hundred percent of the hazards and vicissitudes of life. But we have tried to frame a law which will give some measure of protection to the average citizen and to his family against the loss of a job and against poverty-ridden old age.

—Franklin D. Roosevelt, August 14, 1935

different ideological positions about the level of risk the government should take on to address social problems (i.e., none to a great deal). For example, the Cato Institute's (2010) mission is "to increase the understanding of public policies based on the principles of limited government, free markets, individual liberty, and peace." On the other hand, the Commonwealth Institute's (2010) vision statement says, "We believe in policies for the common good, which perform the basic functions of government of protecting and empowering individuals, enabling them to reach their highest potential, striving on an even playing field in a secure and environmentally sound world." These groups work through the media and other venues to promote their perspectives on defining social problems and the role of government in dealing with those problems.

Media Coverage

Whether a problem enters the public consciousness and how that problem is defined if it does are clearly influenced by media coverage in all its forms—TV, newspapers and magazines, blogs, YouTube, and other social media. The cover of *Life* magazine in August 1993 (see Box 2.3) is one example of the role printed media played in raising the public's consciousness about the challenges of family caregiving—a good example of a private problem moving to a public concern in the 1990s. The article chronicled a daughter's aging mother's physical decline and moves from independent living, to a separate mother-in-law apartment to moving in with the family and eventually a nursing home. With each move, the story described the daughter's challenges of caring for her mother's physical and social needs and the emotional, physical, and financial strain associated with caregiving. This article was among the first that made public, via the lay press, the notion of the "sandwich generation" and the fact that more people are living longer and "other solutions are desperately needed" (p. 36). Also during the early 1990s, there was extensive media coverage of the debate over whether the future of Social Security was a "problem" and the proposed solution to privatize the program (see Box 2.4). In 1995 alone, 25 stories appeared in five major news magazines, such as *Time* and *Newsweek* (Clawson, 2003). Jerit and Barabas (2006) found that Social Security was one of the most heavily covered topics in the national media (via the Associated Press) from March 1998 to May 1999, and much of the coverage conveyed misleading information about the program's financial future. The discussion that occurs in the public arena through various forms of media is an important factor in making an individual's problem a social problem deserving of a policy solution and in shaping the definition of that problem. As depicted in Figure 2.1, once a problem has been identified, the next step is to craft the policy solution or design.

BOX 2.3   Bringing Caregiving Into the Public Consciousness

Media exposure such as this edition of *Life* magazine from August 1993 (when print, television, and radio were the principle venues for social communication) is an example of bringing a private situation—caregiving—into the public spotlight and helping pave the way for public solutions.

Source: Cover: © Life Magazine; Photo: © Dana Fineman

BOX 2.4   The Public Debate to Define the Problem of Social Security

The public debate to shape or define a problem is an important step in the policymaking process. Take a look at these opposing opinions about defining the Social Security "problem."

"Social security, the most enduring and politically influential legacy of President Franklin D. Roosevelt's New Deal era of governance, is going through a crisis. Deficits are at hand and in prospect—small ones in the next few years, perhaps frighteningly large ones in the twenty-first century. Something must be done." (Cowan, 1978, p. 1)

"There is a long-run financing problem. But it's a problem of modest size. The Congressional Budget Office report finds that extending the life of the trust fund into the 22nd century, with no change in benefits, would require additional revenues equal to only 0.54 percent of G.D.P. That's less than 3 percent of federal spending—less than we're currently spending in Iraq." (Krugman, 2004)

"Social Security's actual problems are far less dramatic than its critics imply and thus require far less dramatic solutions than they have proposed." (Herd & Kingson, 2005, p. 200)

Policy Design

If policymakers agree that there is a social problem in need of a policy solution, then the next step in the policymaking process is the policy design or content. There are three different types of policies, and within those types, the policy design will be influenced by the problem's complexity and will include provisions that explain how the problem will be addressed, what benefit will be provided, and who will receive the benefit.

Types of Policies

Social policy design can be categorized into three types—distributive, regulatory, or redistributive (Lowi, 1964). *Distributive policy* refers to the granting of benefits to a small or well-defined interest group. Distributive policy is usually seen as eliciting consensus, and the typical result is legislation that provides something that is in the public interest and benefits a large number of people. These might be district-specific benefits advanced by members of Congress (often referred to as pork-barrel spending) or federal spending on infrastructure projects such as transportation (Birkland, 2001). *Regulatory policies* govern the conduct of business or professions or are designed to protect the public from negative effects of private activity, such as unsafe products or environmental pollution. *Redistributive policy* is the most controversial of the three categories because it involves manipulating the allocation of a valuable social good, such as wealth or personal and civil rights, among social classes. Under redistributive social policy, the transfer is from the well-off to the less-well-off, and such policies are difficult to pass because they require the less powerful to prevail over the more powerful groups in society (Birkland, 2001). For example, the Social Security program has an embedded redistributive element, as benefits are computed in a way that favors low-income elderly adults (Moon & Mulvey, 1996).

Problem Complexity

Problem complexity refers to how complicated the social problem under consideration is thought to be, and the degree of complexity will influence the policy's design (Ingraham, 1987). Legislation has been enacted over the past 50 years to address many social problems (e.g., poverty), but the fact that these problems still exist lends credence to the notion that the legislation to address these issues has perhaps not been very comprehensive in nature. In contrast, the problem of obtaining accessible parking for persons with disabilities is, relatively speaking, a simple one with a rather straightforward solution of providing handicap parking tags and spaces close to business entrances (however, that does not prevent nondisabled drivers from parking in those spots). Thus, the reasons why a social problem exists range on a continuum from simple to complex, and because of this complexity, some social policy solutions are incremental in design and may address only one or two elements of the problem. For example, providing an older adult living with little or no income a Supplemental Security Income benefit does not solve the socioeconomic factors that led them to poverty in later life but, rather, solves an immediate concern of providing some income on which to live.

A factor related to problem complexity is the consensus among key stakeholders regarding the degree of the problem (Ingraham, 1987). The more homogenous and like-minded the stakeholders are about the problem and its solution, the more likely that the policy design will be comprehensive in its approach to solving the problem. Conversely, if stakeholders are not aligned, the policy solution will be limited in scope and will not be seen as being very comprehensive.

Policy Content

When social policies are being formed, the content of the legislation will address three issues: what will be provided, to what extent it will be provided, and who will be eligible to receive benefits. What will be provided starts with determining the form of the benefit. The benefit can be a service—provided directly by the government or indirectly through a contract with a nonprofit or private sector entity (Birkland, 2001). An example of a service that is directly delivered by the government is the Eldercare Locator, an information and referral site that is a public service of the U.S. Administration on Aging. An example of a contract with nonprofits or private sector entities to provide services includes respite care services funded by the Older Americans Act but contracted with local home health agencies that deliver the services. The benefit may also be monetary in nature. An example of benefits in the form of monetary transfers includes Supplemental Security Income payments to low-income older adults. The extent of services or benefits defined in the legislation is symbolic of how much risk—as we discussed earlier—is taken on by a society via its government. For example, legislation to provide retirement income may be enacted, but the level of support for retirement income may be less generous if the benefit level is based on a poverty level definition linked to the monthly food cost for an individual. On the other hand, the benefit level can be more generous and based on median wage of the entire population.

Legislation that authorizes a service or program must also define who is eligible. Eligibility for services or benefits can be defined narrowly and targeted only at a specific subset of the older adult population or targeted more universally. If the eligibility for a benefit is very narrow in scope and limited only to the "truly needy" as a result of a breakdown in family support or the economy, then the implicit message here is that society wishes to accept taking on only a limited amount of risk. On the other hand, a universal approach is when the level of risk undertaken is greater and the benefit or support is spread across all citizens of a community. Using age as the basis for eligibility for programs authorized under the Older Americans Act is an example of a more universal approach to eligibility versus using a means test of income and assets such as those used to determine food stamp eligibility.

So far in this chapter, we have briefly discussed how legislative process begins with a problem that has risen to the level of public concern and some of the elements that must be considered in policy design. We turn now to policy adoption, or the process of how policies move from the design to adoption.

Policy Adoption: Process and Players

How does the bill become law? To aid in your understanding, we present Figure 2.2, "The Longest-Running Game in Town" (New York Times Company, 1985), which takes you through all the possible steps and missteps on the journey of a bill attempting to

Figure 2.2   How a Bill Becomes Law

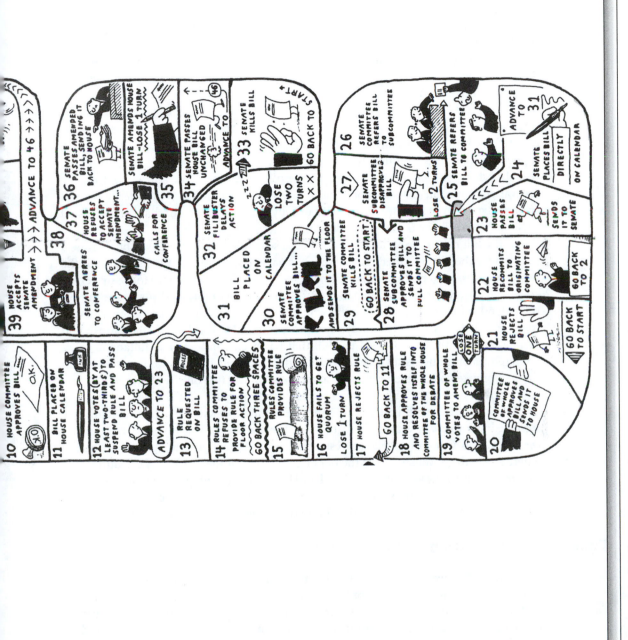

33

become law and shows why it is difficult to get bills passed into law. Proposed legislation can come from constituents, the president, lobbyists, or congressional members. Any senator or representative can introduce a bill by formally presenting it to the House or Senate clerk. Once the bill is introduced, it is given a number (H.R. __ for the House of Representatives or S. ___ for the Senate).

The rules of the House and Senate indicate which committee will consider the bill (Step 4 on our game board). Committees are where the legislative work happens, and each committee has subcommittees, procedural rules, and a chair. Chairs have a great deal of control over the schedule or if and when a bill will be considered. Hearings are often called to learn more about who is in favor of the legislation and its possible effect. Subcommittees usually rewrite the bill and vote on its approval, and if approved, it goes back to the committee. If the full committee approves the bill (Step 10 on the board), which also includes a report on the bill's estimated cost and impact on the federal government, it goes to be considered by the full House or Senate. If the full committee does not approve the bill, it is usually dead for the rest of that congressional session. Most bills die a silent death in committees.

If the bill makes it out of the committee, a schedule is set that allows the members to consider the bill and offer amendments. If passed by members, the bill heads to the other congressional body (i.e., House or Senate; Step 23). The other House or Senate committee may choose to either report on the bill favorably and place the bill on the calendar for consideration by the whole body or send it to a committee, where it may be killed or sent to the body for action (Steps 24–31). If both the House and Senate approve the bill (or a similar bill that has been considered simultaneously), a conference committee is set up to iron out differences between the two versions. When the conference committee reaches an agreement on the two bills, a conference report and final version of the bill are presented to both houses for a final vote.

If approved, the bill is sent to the president for consideration. The president may sign the bill into law or veto it. If two-thirds of the members of the house that originated the legislation vote to override a presidential veto, the bill goes to the second house, where a two-thirds vote will turn the bill into law without the president's signature. Bills that make it into law are given a Public Law (P.L.) number and published in the United States Code (U.S.C.). Funds must be appropriated in the budget process. You can follow a bill that has been introduced in the House or Senate by visiting www.thomas.gov.

Policy Implementation and Evaluation

As Figure 2.1 shows, the final steps in the policymaking process are policy implementation and evaluation. A review of the law and an implementation plan are conducted by the federal agency responsible for translating the law into action. Policy evaluation determines whether the legislation has resulted in some benefits or has achieved its stated goals. Policy evaluation is often conducted by external entities, including universities, think tanks, and advocacy groups, as well as the government's own investigative arm of Congress, the Government Accountability Office, which is charged with the auditing and evaluation of government programs. The House and Senate Committees also frequently hold hearings to gather feedback on the impact of legislation.

Actors and Advocates

As we briefly mentioned above, there are actors and advocates both within and outside government that seek to influence each step in the policymaking process (see Figure 2.1), and many are primarily concerned with aging social policy. Within government, the Senate Special Committee on Aging is a focal point in the Senate for discussion and debate on policy matters relating to older Americans. The Senate Special Committee on Aging was first established in 1961 as a temporary committee and was granted permanent status in 1977. The committee studies issues and conducts oversight of programs of concern to older adults. The House had a similar committee called the Select Committee on Aging, which began in 1975 with 35 members but was disbanded in 1992 (Wikipedia, 2010). The National Association of Area Agencies on Aging (N4A), which is the consortium of Area Agencies on Aging directors, advocates on behalf of its members for services and resources for older adults. Members of N4A (2010a) visit Capitol Hill annually to talk with congressional representatives regarding their concerns.

Advocacy groups outside government also play a critical role in the formation of aging policy. Perhaps the most recognized by the general public is the AARP. AARP was founded in 1958 and its Public Policy Institute, formed in 1985, is the division within the organization that informs and promotes the public debate on aging policy, particularly in the areas of economic security, health care, and quality of life (AARP, 2010).

Another notable nongovernmental organization is the National Council on Aging (NCOA), which is a prominent nonprofit advocacy group. According to the NCOA (2010a), members "work to improve public policies by being a national voice for older adults in greatest need and those who serve them, combining community service and advocacy, and empowering and engaging older adults." The Leadership Council of Aging Organizations (LCAO, 2010) is a consortium of 60 national aging advocacy organizations that advocates on behalf of older adults in the policymaking arena, serves as a source of information about issues affecting older persons, and initiates joint advocacy strategies among its members and other lesser known advocacy groups such as the Gray Panthers (www.graypanthers.org).

There are also issue-related advocacy groups such as the Alzheimer's Association (www.alz.org), the National Committee for the Prevention of Elder Abuse (www.preventelderabuse.org), and the Family Caregiver Alliance (www.caregiver.org). Advocacy groups also exist to promote the concerns of different subpopulations of older adults, such as the Older Women's League (www.owl-national.org), Asociacion Nacional pro Personas Mayores (National Association for Hispanic Elderly; www.anppm.org), the National Caucus and Center on Black Aged (www.ncba-aged.org), and Services and Advocacy for GLBT Elders (www.sageusa.org), to name a few.

Finally, older voters have been viewed by the media as a powerful voting block (Campbell, 2003). However, research shows that they are not monolithic in their voting behaviors, as older adults divide their votes along the same political, economic, and social lines as do voters in other age groups (Binstock, 2005). This is not to say that members of Congress have no reason to pay attention to older voters, because they do turn out to vote in high numbers—and, as we discussed in Chapter 1, the older adult population is growing exponentially.

We now turn to a discussion of key social policy milestones in U.S. and international aging policy and will conclude this chapter with a brief overview of one of the most influential pieces of aging social policy—the Older Americans Act.

The United States and International Aging Social Policy

Figure 2.3 provides a visual timeline of selected aging social policy milestones. The top timeline represents milestones in the Older Americans Act (OAA), and the bottom timeline represents milestones in other federal aging policy. International aging policy milestones appear below the U.S. timeline. We will start our discussion with U.S. federal and international aging policy milestones and conclude with a more in-depth discussion about the OAA.

Figure 2.3 Timeline of Older Americans Act Legislation and Other Key U.S. Federal and International Aging Policy

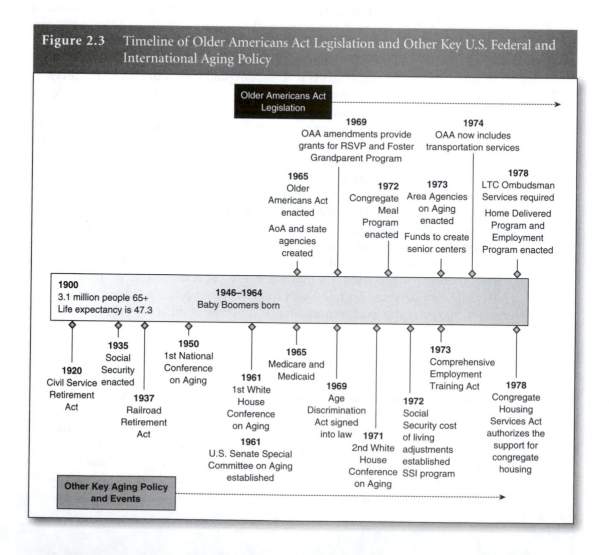

Figure 2.3 (Continued) Timeline of Older Americans Act Legislation and Other Key U.S. Federal and International Aging Policy

Older Americans Act Legislation

1981
OAA reauthorized; emphasis on community-based supportive services

1987
Disease Prevention and Health Promotion and Elder Abuse Prevention Activities enacted

Title III Priority Services defined as access, in-home, and legal services

1992
Reauthorization of OAA places increased focus on caregivers and protection of elder rights

2000
OAA amendments establish the Family Caregiver support program

2006
OAA amended to include home and community-based LTC activities and evidenced-based disease prevention and health promotion services enacted

2011
Congress will consider reauthorization and amendments to the OAA effective in FY 2012

2000
35 million people 65+
Life expectancy is 76.9

2011
First Boomer turns 65

1981
3rd White House Conference on Aging

1981
Medicaid HCBS waiver program

1987
Nursing Home Reform Act mandates access to ombudspersons

1990
Americans with Disabilities Act

Age Discrimination in Employment Act

1990
National Affordable Housing Act reauthorized HUD section 202 Elderly Housing Program

1995
4th White House Conference on Aging

2003
Medicare expanded to include private health plans; prescription drugs

2005
5th White House Conference on Aging

2006
Lifespan Respite Care

2010
Patient Protection and Affordable Care Act*

Other Aging Social Policy and Key Events

International Aging Policy and Events Timeline

1950
130 million people 65+ worldwide

2007
1.354 billion people 65+

1950
1st World Congress on Aging (113 participants from 14 countries)

1982
1st United Nation's World Assembly on Aging

1982
The *Vienna International Plan of Action on Ageing*

1990
UN declares October 1 as International Day of Older Persons

1991
UN adopts the Principles for Older Persons

1992
UN adopts the Proclamation on Ageing

1995
World Summit for Social Development

1999
Declared as International Year of Older Persons

2002
2nd World Assembly International Plan of Action

2009
19th World Congress on Aging (5,800 participants from 91 countries)

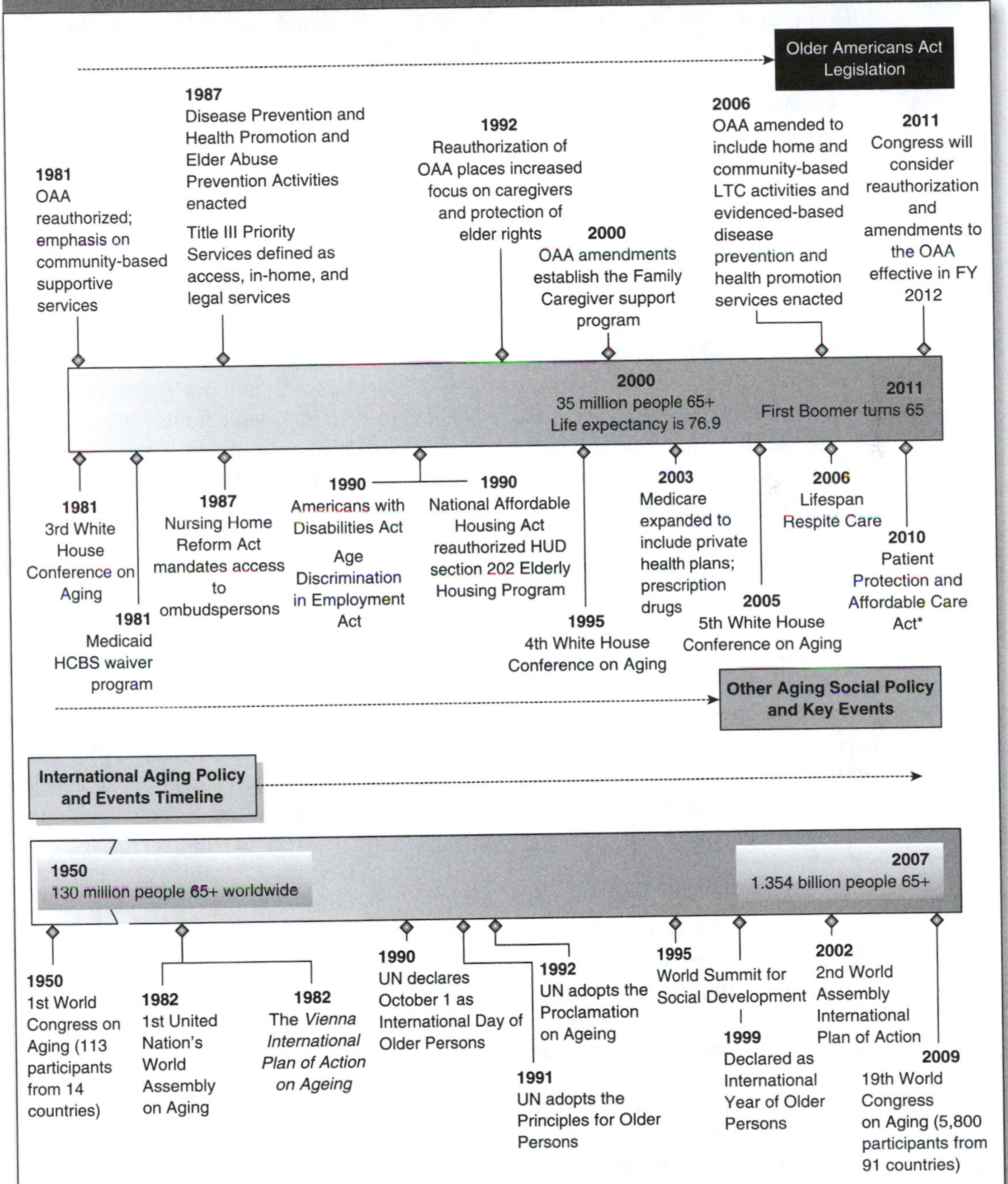

*As this book is going to press, President Obama has just signed the Patient Protection and Medical Care Act (2010), and it will be published shortly as Public Law (P.L.) 111–148.

Sources: AoA (2010b), O'Shaughnessy (2008), and United Nations (2009c).

Prior to 1950, aging social policy milestones were the enactments of income retirement programs in 1920, the passage of Social Security in 1935, and the Railroad Retirement Act in 1937.[1] The evolution of aging policy, beyond addressing retirement income to community-based legislation and social support for older adults, began to gain momentum politically in the 1950s and 1960s with the first national conference on aging; the creation of the Special Staff on Aging in the Department of Health, Education, and Welfare; the creation of the U.S. Senate Special Committee on Aging in 1961; and the first White House Conference on Aging (WHCOA) in 1961. It is believed that there were several outcomes of the 1961 conference, which included amendments to the Social Security Act providing additional support to beneficiaries, amendments to the Housing Act of 1961 and the Community Health Facilities Act of 1961 that made special provisions for older adults, and legislation in 1965 creating Medicare, Medicaid, and the OAA (WHCOA, 2010). During the 1970s, the second WHCOA was held (in 1971) and the Supplemental Security Income (SSI) program was enacted (in 1972), as were the automatic cost of living adjustments to Social Security. During the 1980s and 1990s, federal legislation was enacted to support the rights of older adults in nursing homes, of persons with disabilities, and of older workers. The fourth WHCOA was held in 1995.

As we move into the 21st century, aging policy has continued to focus on enhancing community-based care, health promotion activities, and changes to the Medicare program. In 2005, the fifth WHCOA was held, with the organizing theme of "The Booming Dynamics of Aging: From Awareness to Action." The fifth WHCOA was attended by 1,200 delegates selected by governors of all 50 states, Puerto Rico, the District of Columbia, and the territories; members of the 109th Congress; the National Congress of American Indians; and the Policy Committee. Fifty resolutions were passed on a variety of issues, including changes to the OAA, Medicare, and Medicaid, and changes to prepare the health care workforce to effectively assist older adults, to promote innovative noninstitutional models of long-term care, to improve mental health service for older adults, to strengthen Social Security, to provide incentives for older workers, to promote a national strategy for supporting informal caregivers, to develop incentives for businesses to retain older workers, and to provide older adults with protection from abuse and neglect, just to name a few of the resolutions (WHCOA, 2005).

On the international stage, the United Nations General Assembly (GA) has facilitated a number of key aging policy recommendations, which are also presented in Figure 2.3. The Vienna International Plan of Action on Ageing, endorsed by the GA in 1982, was the first international instrument designed to guide the formulation of policies and programs on aging worldwide and to strengthen the capacities of governments to deal effectively with population aging (United Nations, 1983). It included 62 recommendations for action in the following areas:

- Health and nutrition
- Protection of elderly consumers
- Housing and environment
- Family

---

1. History of aging policy is drawn primarily from the Administration on Aging (2010b).

- Social welfare
- Income security and employment
- Education

The GA designated October 1 as the International Day of Older Persons in 1990 and later, in 1991, adopted the United Nations Principles for Older Persons (see Box 2.5). In 1992, the GA adopted the Proclamation on Ageing. The Proclamation on Ageing urged partnerships among governments, nongovernmental organizations, academia, and the private sector to ensure that the entire population is engaged in preparing for the later stages of life and that needs of ageing populations are adequately addressed (United Nations, 1992).

BOX 2.5   United Nations Principles for Older Persons

Encourages governments to incorporate the following principles into their national programmes whenever possible:

Independence

1. Older persons should have access to adequate food, water, shelter, clothing, and health care through the provision of income, family and community support, and self-help.
2. Older persons should have the opportunity to work or to have access to other income-generating opportunities.
3. Older persons should be able to participate in determining when and at what pace withdrawal from the labour force takes place.
4. Older persons should have access to appropriate educational and training programmes.
5. Older persons should be able to live in environments that are safe and adaptable to personal preferences and changing capacities.
6. Older persons should be able to reside at home for as long as possible.

Participation

7. Older persons should remain integrated in society, participate actively in the formulation and implementation of policies that directly affect their well-being, and share their knowledge and skills with younger generations.
8. Older persons should be able to seek and develop opportunities for service to the community and to serve as volunteers in positions appropriate to their interests and capabilities.
9. Older persons should be able to form movements or associations of older persons.

Care

10. Older persons should benefit from family and community care and protection in accordance with each society's system of cultural values.
11. Older persons should have access to health care to help them to maintain or regain the optimum level of physical, mental, and emotional well-being and to prevent or delay the onset of illness.

(Continued)

(Continued)

12. Older persons should have access to social and legal services to enhance their autonomy, protection, and care.
13. Older persons should be able to utilize appropriate levels of institutional care providing protection, rehabilitation, and social and mental stimulation in a humane and secure environment.
14. Older persons should be able to enjoy human rights and fundamental freedoms when residing in any shelter, care, or treatment facility, including full respect for their dignity, beliefs, needs, and privacy and for the right to make decisions about their care and the quality of their lives.

Self-Fulfillment

15. Older persons should be able to pursue opportunities for the full development of their potential.
16. Older persons should have access to the educational, cultural, spiritual, and recreational resources of society.

Dignity

17. Older persons should be able to live in dignity and security and be free of exploitation and physical or mental abuse.
18. Older persons should be treated fairly regardless of age, gender, racial or ethnic background, disability, or other status and be valued independently of their economic contribution.

Source: United Nations (1991).

Another important international aging policy event was the World Summit for Social Development in Copenhagen in 1995 (United Nations, 1995). The more than 117 heads of state or governments in attendance reached a consensus on the need to put people at the center of the development of a "society for all," which included addressing the social, economic, community, and physical needs of older adults. The Second World Assembly on Ageing, held in Madrid in 2002, created the Madrid International Plan of Action on Ageing, which called for governmental action in three priority areas—developing older persons, advancing health and well-being into old age, and ensuring supportive and enabling environments (United Nations, 2002). Individual countries worldwide have responded to the Madrid Plan as well, and a sample of those plans is listed in Box 2.6.

BOX 2.6   International Ageing Policy Framework

The following are some examples of other countries' responses to enacting elements in the aging policy framework set forth in the Madrid International Plan of Action on Ageing.

1. African Union policy framework and plan of action on ageing
   www.helpage.org/Resources/Policyreports

Policy document that commits African Union member states to design, implement, monitor, and evaluate appropriate integrated national policies and programmes to meet the individual and collective needs of older people in Africa.

2. Ageing in the Arab Countries: Regional variations, policies, and programmes
    www.escwa.un.org/information/publications/edit/upload/sdd-07-tm2-e.pdf

Examines demographic trends in aging and its socioeconomic consequences.

3. Asia/Pacific: The Macao Outcome Document
    www.unescap.org/esid/psis/meetings/ageingmipaa2007/MacaoOutcomeDocument.pdf

This document is the culmination of the regional Asia/Pacific conference that took place in Macao in October 2007 to review progress to date on the implementation of the Madrid International Plan of Action on Ageing and make recommendations for the future.

4. China
    www.cncaprc.gov.cn/en/index.html

The National Working Commission on Ageing, established in 1999, is responsible for the development of strategies and major policies on ageing and coordinating and facilitating the relevant departments to implement the development plans on ageing. Policies and initiatives can be found on the Commission's website.

5. European Union
    http://eur-lex.europa.eu/LexUriServ/LexUriServ.do?uri=COM:2002:0143:FIN:EN:PDF

Communication from the Commission to the Council and the European Parliament of 18 March 2002, titled "Europe's Response to World Ageing: Promoting Economic and Social Progress in an Ageing World."

6. Central and Eastern Europe
    www.helpage.org/Resources/Policyreports

A *Generation in Transition: Older People's Situation and Civil Society's Response in East and Central Europe* draws on consultations with older people to provide principles and case studies for responding to their needs.

7. Brasilia Declaration
    www.un.org/esa/socdev/ageing/documents/regional_review/Declaracion_Brasilia.pdf

This declaration was the culmination of the Second Regional Intergovernmental Conference on Ageing in Latin America and the Caribbean to review progress on implementing the Madrid International Plan of Action on Ageing and make recommendations for the future.

Source: United Nations (2009b).

The Older Americans Act

The OAA is the only piece of legislation in the United States that provides a national statement about promoting the dignity and welfare of older individuals. President Lyndon B. Johnson signed the bill into law on July 14, 1965, and stated,

> The Older Americans Act clearly affirms our Nation's sense of responsibility toward the well-being of all of our older citizens. But even more, the results of this act will help us to expand our opportunities for enriching the lives of all of our citizens in this country, now and in the years to come. (Woolley & Peters, n.d.)

Older Americans Act Structure

The OAA creates the Aging Network structure, which consists of the Administration on Aging (AoA)—led by the assistant secretary for aging—and operates under the direction of the secretary of the Department of Health and Human Services. Under the administration's oversight, each state has an agency dedicated to creating statewide plans that are divided into planning and service areas. Within each planning and service area are Area Agencies on Aging (AAAs), whose directors develop local plans (O'Shaughnessy, 2008) and who are responsible for implementing programs authorized under the Act.

Specific Titles of the Older Americans Act

There are seven titles under the Act (see Table 2.1), and each is described below.

Table 2.1	Older Americans Act Titles at a Glance
Title I Objectives	*Declaration of Objectives/Definitions.* Provides 10 broad social objectives that provide the framework for the purpose of the Act. There are no funds associated with Title I.
Title II Aging Network Support	*Administration on Aging.* Establishes the Administration on Aging, the Aging Network, and the responsibilities of the assistant secretary for aging. It also authorizes the National Eldercare Locator and national resource centers.
Title III Community Programs	*Grants for State/Community Programs.* Authorizes community supportive services in five different Parts (A–E); accounts for the majority of the funding and programs delivered through the Act.
Title IV Research and Training	*Activities for Health/Independence/Longevity.* Funding in this title supports a small number of research projects, training to prepare individuals to work in the field of gerontology, and demonstration grants.

Table 2.1 (Continued) Older Americans Act Titles at a Glance	
Title V Employment	*Community Service Senior Opportunities Act.* The funding for Title V comes from the Department of Labor and is coordinated through the Aging Network.
Title VI Native Americans	*Grants for Native Americans.* These funds support Title III–type services for Native Americans, including Indian Tribal and Native Hawaiians.
Title VII Vulnerable Elders	*Vulnerable Elder Rights Protection.* Funding through this title supports the Long Term Care Ombudsman programs and elder abuse and prevention activities.

Source: Adapted from O'Shaughnessy (2008).

Title I: Declaration of Objectives/Definitions

Title I articulates the following 10 objectives that Congress declared the older population is entitled to. This title states that it is the job of federal, state, and local governments to ensure equal opportunity for older people by meeting these objectives:

(1) An adequate income in retirement in accordance with the American standard of living

(2) The best possible physical and mental health which science can make available and without regard to economic status

(3) Obtaining and maintaining suitable housing, independently selected, designed and located with reference to special needs and available at costs which older citizens can afford

(4) Full restorative services for those who require institutional care, and a comprehensive array of community-based, long-term care services adequate to appropriately sustain older people in their communities and in their homes, including support to family members and other persons providing voluntary care to older individuals needing long-term care services

(5) Opportunity for employment with no discriminatory personnel practices because of age

(6) Retirement in health, honor, dignity—after years of contribution to the economy

(7) Participating in and contributing to meaningful activity within the widest range of civic, cultural, educational and training, and recreational opportunities

(8) Efficient community services, including access to low-cost transportation, which provide a choice in supported living arrangements and social assistance in a coordinated manner and which are readily available when needed, with emphasis on maintaining a continuum of care for vulnerable older individuals

(9) Immediate benefit from proven research knowledge which can sustain and improve health and happiness

(10) Freedom, independence, and the free exercise of individual initiative in planning and managing their own lives, full participation in the planning and operation of community-based services and programs provided for their benefit, and protection against abuse, neglect, and exploitation (OAA, 1965)

Title II: Administration on Aging

Title II establishes the AoA and the position and responsibilities of the Assistant Secretary for Aging. The assistant secretary

- is an advocate for older adults within the federal government,
- collects and disseminates information about the aged and aging,
- administers the grants authorized in the Act,
- supports research in the field of aging,
- prepares and publishes educational materials dealing with the well-being of older adults,
- collects statistics about older adults and coordinates this effort with other federal offices,
- develops basic policies and sets priorities of the programs contained in the Act and coordinates with other federal programs, and
- develops a national plan for meeting the need for trained personnel in the field of aging.

Within the AoA are the offices for American Indian, Alaskan Native, and Native Hawaiian programs and the Long-Term Care Ombudsman programs.

Title III: Grants for State/Community Programs

Title III is the core of the Act, as it authorizes grants for a wide range of state and community programs. Part B includes supportive services and senior centers, Part C contains the nutrition services, Part D contains the disease prevention and health promotion services, and Part E addresses the National Family Caregiver Support Program. Details of the programs spawned under Title III are covered in later chapters.

Supportive services in Part B include a wide array of programs, and what is determined to be needed is identified in state and local AAA plans. Services under Part B may include transportation, information and assistance, home adaptations, personal care for assistance with activities of daily living, homemaker services, adult day services, legal assistance and counseling, physical activity and exercise, ombudsman programs, or elder abuse prevention programs.

The goal of the Nutrition Service programs under Part C is to reduce food insecurity and promote health, well-being, and socialization among older adults (AoA, 2010e). Programs funded include congregate meal programs delivered in senior centers, community centers, or churches and home-delivered meal programs—often referred to as Meals on Wheels programs.

Part D, disease prevention and health promotion funding, supports health education programs in areas such as diabetes and nutrition, as well as offering physical activity programs. Disease prevention and health promotion services and information are provided at multipurpose senior centers, at congregate meal sites, through home-delivered meals programs, or at other appropriate sites (OAA, 1965).

Part E contains the National Family Caregiver Support Program, which provides support to family caregivers who provide care for individuals with Alzheimer's disease and related disorders or to grandparents or older individuals who provide care for children with severe disabilities. Family caregiver services support elders and their family members by providing in-home assistance for daily living activities. Services include information and assistance to caregivers about available services and gaining access to those services;

individual counseling, support groups, and caregiver training; respite care to enable caregivers to be temporarily relieved from their caregiving responsibilities; and supplemental services, on a limited basis, to complement the care provided by caregivers (AoA, 2010f).

Title IV: Activities for Health/Independence/Longevity

The purpose of Title IV is to expand the nation's knowledge and understanding of the older population and the aging process; to design, test, and promote the use of innovative ideas and best practices in programs and services for older individuals; to help meet the needs for trained personnel in the field of aging; and to increase awareness of citizens of all ages of the need to assume personal responsibility for their own longevity (AoA, 2009d). Specific areas identified include career preparation, protecting older individuals from violence, health care service demonstrations projects in rural areas, computer training, innovations in transportation services, multigenerational and civic engagement, Native American programs, legal assistance, and ombudsman demonstration projects and community innovation projects to promote aging. It is the responsibility of the AoA to identify priority areas that will be addressed and funded. For example, in 2008, the priorities for grant-funded programs were as follows:

Priority 1: Empower older people and their families to make informed decisions about and be able to easily access existing health and long-term care options

Priority 2: Empower older people to stay active and healthy through evidence-based disease and disability prevention

Priority 3: Enable seniors who are at high risk of nursing home placement to remain in their homes and communities for as long as possible

Priority 4: Ensure the rights of older people and prevent their abuse, neglect, and exploitation

Priority 5: Promote effective and responsive management of AoA human capital resources and grant funds (AoA, 2008a)

Title V: Community Service Senior Opportunities Act

The Community Service Senior Opportunities Act supports programs that "foster individual economic self-sufficiency and promote useful opportunities in community service activities (which shall include community service employment) for unemployed low-income persons who are age 55 or older, particularly persons who have poor employment prospects" (OAA, 1965). The states and national organizations in turn recruit, train, and place older adults in community service jobs in locations such as hospitals and schools. The program is means tested, and those employed through the program receive an hourly wage.

Title VI: Grants for Native Americans

Title VI supports grants to Indian Tribal, Native Alaskan, and Native Hawaiian organizations to fund support and nutrition services that are comparable with those listed in Title III. Grants were awarded to 246 Indian Tribal and Native Hawaiian organizations in 2008 (AoA, 2008b).

Title VII: Vulnerable Elder Rights Protection

Title VII is the last of the titles in the OAA. Title VII provides funding for long-term care ombudsman programs, elder abuse and neglect prevention programs, and legal assistance development programs.

Eligibility for Older Americans Act Programs

The OAA was established for all older adults over the age of 60, and its programs are not means tested—which is prohibited under the Act. The Act does, however, mandate that the services provided be targeted to those having the greatest economic or social need and include those with low incomes, members of minority or ethnic groups, rural elders, those at risk of institutionalization, and those having limited English proficiency (OAA, 1965). Where feasible, participants are encouraged to make voluntary contributions, and states do have the option of implementing cost sharing for specific services, with contributions based on a sliding fee scale or cost of the program. The Act makes clear that no older adult can be denied services designed to have a cost-sharing component if that person is unable to contribute (OAA, 1965).

Funding for the Older Americans Act

Funding for the OAA has ebbed and flowed since it was enacted in 1965. Appropriated funding levels gradually increased from $6.5 million in 1966 to $18.8 million in 1970 (O'Shaughnessy, 2004). By 1990, the appropriated funding level for the OAA programs (including the Senior Community Service Employment Program funding through the Department of Labor) had reached $1.027 billion. During 2002 and 2007, funding increased slightly from $1.794 billion to $1.867 billion (NCOA, 2010c). In 2010, the appropriated funding was $2.341 billion (N4A, 2010b). As shown in Chart 2.1, the majority (58%) of the total OAA funding for FY 2010 is for Title III services. Two programs under Title III-Part C (Nutrition Services) and Part B (Supportive Services) receive 60% ($819 million) and 27% ($368 million), respectively, of the $1.368 billion earmarked for Title III services. Title V, the Senior Community Service Employment Program, which received funding from the Department of Labor of $825 million in FY 2010, represents a major portion of funding available for OAA programs. These federal funds flow from the AoA to the states according to a population-based formula, and the states then distribute OAA funds to local AAAs based on a state-determined formula.

Older Americans Act Legislative Milestones

Figure 2.3 provides an overview of the major amendments and milestones of the OAA since its inception in 1965. In 1970, a number of amendments were made, including the creation of the national nutrition program for the elderly in 1972 and the AAAs in 1973. Other amendments established the long-term care ombudsman program and a separate grant program for older Native Americans in 1978. The next decade, policies

Chart 2.1   Older Americans Act, FY 2010 Appropriations

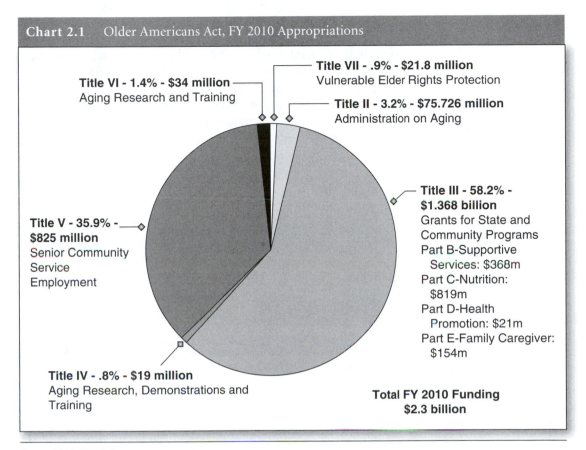

Title VII - .9% - $21.8 million
Vulnerable Elder Rights Protection

Title VI - 1.4% - $34 million
Aging Research and Training

Title II - 3.2% - $75.726 million
Administration on Aging

Title V - 35.9% -
$825 million
Senior Community
Service
Employment

Title III - 58.2% -
$1.368 billion
Grants for State and
Community Programs
Part B-Supportive
   Services: $368m
Part C-Nutrition:
   $819m
Part D-Health
   Promotion: $21m
Part E-Family Caregiver:
   $154m

Title IV - .8% - $19 million
Aging Research, Demonstrations and
Training

Total FY 2010 Funding
$2.3 billion

Source: N4A (2010b).

included the reauthorization of the Act in 1981, which included a new focus on supporting community-based programs and services. The amendments in 1987 reauthorized the Act for another 4 years and included programs to prevent elder abuse and neglect, health promotion and disease prevention programs, and a new provision that required AAAs to conduct outreach activities to identify and serve older Indians (Koff & Park, 1999). Three service areas, access services (e.g., transportation, information, and referral), in-home services (e.g., home health assistance, homemaker services), and legal services were defined as priority services and, as such, were to receive a set minimum amount of funding. Additional emphasis was put on serving older adults with the greatest economic and social needs, including low-income minorities (AoA, 2010b). The 1992 amendments created Title VII, authorizing programs that focus on protection of the rights of vulnerable older persons, and a long-term care ombudsman program. The reauthorized Act also placed an increased focus on caregivers and intergenerational programs, as well as calling for a White House Conference on Aging in 1995. In 2000 and 2006, amendments created the National Family Caregiver Support Program and an increased focus on home- and community-based services and health promotion (AoA, 2010b). The Act is due for reauthorization in 2011.

The degree to which the Act has been successful in achieving its objectives has been the source of much debate (see Estes, 1979, 1993). It is clear that the funding levels make achieving the Act's objectives impractical and limit the scope of the Act and the number of older adults that can be served. On the other hand, the planning, coordination, and advocacy activities conducted by entities located at various points within the Aging Network do serve to support the needs of older adults. The Act has been the driving force of a number of social policy directives in the arena of aging policy over the years, such as caregiver support, protection against abuse, and support for aging in place. As the baby boomers continue their slow march into later life, the Act will no doubt be tested as it tries to serve the needs of an increasing number of older adults.

We will return to discuss the challenges and future of the OAA, as well as future directions in U.S. and international aging policy, in Chapter 10.

For More Information

1. United Nations Programme on Ageing
   http://www.un.org/esa/socdev/ageing/

The UN Programme on Ageing is the division within the United Nations that facilitates and promotes policy development in support of older adults worldwide.

2. AGE Platform Europe
   http://www.age-platform.eu/en

AGE Platform Europe is a European network of around 150 organizations of and for people aged 50+, which aims to voice and promote the interests of the 150 million senior citizens in the European Union and raise awareness on the issues of concern.

3. Europa
   http://europa.eu/index_en.htm

Europa is the website of the European Union. Here, you can find an overview of European aging policies and statistics.

4. Administration on Aging
   http://www.aoa.gov

Best site for everything you wanted to know about the Older Americans Act and federal aging social policy.

5. United States Senate Special Committee on Aging
   http://aging.senate.gov/

The Special Committee on Aging website is a great resource for anyone needing information about what aging policies are getting congressional attention, as well as links to hearing reports and other legislative data.

Mr. S., age 63
Mumbai, India

I was born in 1942 at Umreth, a small town near Dakor, a well-known pilgrimage place in Gujarat state. My father was an advocate at Umreth. I have three brothers and two sisters.

I married in May 1974 and have two children, one boy and one girl. I see them every day because we all stay together.

My wife has remained a house maker throughout, barring a short span of 2 years during which she had a job in a school as a teacher. I served in one leading nationalized bank for 36 years.

I work in a tension-free job for about 4 to 5 hours a day, along with a hobby which I can pursue during my spare time.

I meet my friends almost daily during my morning walk. I meet my outstation friends once/twice a year, including our family members. I enjoy good health. I had to undergo a heart valve change surgery in December 1999, and I had a stroke in March 2005. I take medicines for smooth functioning of a heart valve, and I have to keep my blood pressure normal. To maintain my health, I take a morning walk for about 45 minutes daily, practice yoga beneficial to my health, and take medication as prescribed by doctors.

To stay active, I take my morning walk every day for about an hour, attend to family work relating to banks and other offices, and general reading during my spare time.

Do I receive a pension? The pension scheme was available in my organization as one of the options of terminal benefits. One pension was worked out as based on his/her length of service in the organization. I did not opt for pension, so I cannot comment on its adequacy for my needs.

Presently, there is a limited scope for work for [older] adults, since liberalization and globalization is taking shape in India. However, I had found some work, but it did not click owing to various reasons.

There is a very limited option for older adult housing in my locality. I am considering moving out of the house after my son marries, as the present area of my house is small. I may go in the vicinity of my native place, where I have some acquaintances.

Barring hospitalization charges, I have to bear regular medical expenses out of my own resources. Yes, ailments present at the time of taking the health coverage are not available for reimbursements. Except yearly premiums, other terms/conditions remain the same.

The daily activities like preparing meals, cleaning the house, etc. are not performed by me, except transportation and shopping, others are performed by my family members and/or maid-servant. The kind of meal programs that you have available for older adults in USA are not available in India. Maid servant charges are about Rs.600 per month for the present domestic chores in my house. Government has no role to play in assistance with transportation, shopping, preparing meals, health care in your home, and so on.

Growing old is one phase of life which is inevitable. Hence, positive attitude towards life is very necessary to enjoy the new phase of life, besides keeping a healthy life.

What I like about being my age is this phase of life (i.e., growing older) offers the opportunities to view and analyze the new trends coming up in life and also related to the past career and other areas of interest based on one's education/qualification, knowledge, and vast experience.

What I dislike about being my age is health problems coupled with limited income limits some activities to pursue. I look forward to a pleasure trip at the places of interest, good company of friends, and leading a healthy life.

What advice would I give students about growing older? Adopt a positive attitude and pragmatic view of life. Pursue hobby/other interesting activities which you wanted to pursue in life but could not do so for any reasons. Take interest in new invention/developments/happenings in area of personal interest/likings. Lead a healthy life and continued relationship with friends and relatives.

Part II

Aging Social Policy Comparisons

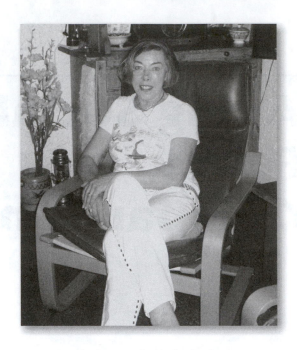

Janine, age 67, Netherlands

Walter and Frank, ages 79 and 82, United States

Retirement Income Policies

> *If you work hard your whole life, you ought to have every opportunity to retire with dignity and financial security. And as a nation, we ought to do all we can to ensure that folks have sensible, affordable options to save for retirement.*
>
> —President Barack Obama, September 5, 2009

> *My parents and I were singers when I was growing up. . . . I sang opera and performed in theaters in Paris, Rome, and Amsterdam until age 35. I returned to Amsterdam, where I worked in two different jobs until I retired at age 65. I received a pension called AOW from Holland, but it's a small amount because I didn't work in Holland my whole working career. But I get three other pensions, one from my husband's and two others from my work in addition to my AOW. . . . They are very adequate for me.*
>
> —Ms. G., age 67, Amsterdam

Retirement income programs serve a number of important purposes, including providing financial autonomy, protection from poverty in later life, some level of income predictability once workers leave the workforce—either through retirement or disability—and financial stability for surviving spouses, partners, and children. Although providing for later life income security seems like a fairly straightforward idea, the policy implementation is rather complex. For example, what percentage of one's preretirement income should be guaranteed via a pension plan? How much should workers and employers contribute? What eligibility requirements should be considered before one can begin receiving these benefits? How can the income security program's financial viability be maintained as the population ages and people spend more time in retirement? What is the appropriate mix between public- and private-sector retirement plans? As you can imagine, the answers, as reflected in retirement income policies, will be different in every country.

In this chapter, we will explore retirement income security policy by first discussing the workforce demographics that influence such policies and the framework used to categorize different retirement income policies. Next, we will compare four countries that illustrate different approaches to retirement income policies and programs.

Demographics Affecting Retirement Income Policy

Population aging, the increase in life expectancy, and the rate of labor force participation in later life are all factors that contribute to the context of deciding how to provide retirement income. As we discussed in Chapter 1, the population aging worldwide is increasing markedly, which means that more people will be retired from the workforce, and because of an increase in life expectancy, they will be drawing pensions for longer periods—possibly for 25 years or more for someone who retires at age 55 or 60.

Thus, because of the increase in the sheer number of older adults in or approaching retirement age, retirement income policy must also consider the interface between employment rates of older adults and the official age at which older workers can draw retirement benefits. Higher employment rates among older adults result in more workers contributing to the retirement income program and possibly fewer workers drawing retirement benefits. However, it is well-documented that labor force participation falls dramatically in most countries after age 65. The percentage of economically active persons between the ages of 50 and 54 and 65 and 69 for two time periods (1980–1981 and 2006–2007) in selected countries is shown in Tables 3.1 and 3.2.

Table 3.1 Percentage of Economically Active Population in Selected Countries at Age 50 to 54 for Years 1980 to 1981 and 2006 to 2007

| Country | 50 to 54 Years Old | | | | | |
| | 1980 to 1981 | | | 2006 to 2007 | | |
	Total	Men	Women	Total	Men	Women
Canada	71.5	90.9	52.1	83.6	87.9	79.4
Denmark	79.2	91.4	67.4	85.7	88.6	82.6
Finland	75.6	80.4	71.1	86.2	85.7	86.7
France	71.2	91.8	50.9	84.1	90.4	78.3
Germany	69.6	93.3	47.2	84.9	91.2	78.7
Italy	57.2	85.5	30.5	71.2	89.0	54.0
Japan	77.7	97.3	58.7	83.3	95.8	70.8
Netherlands	55.4	85.4	26.0	80.7	89.6	71.5
Norway	79.0	90.9	67.5	84.5	87.9	81.0
Spain	57.7	90.8	26.8	73.3	88.7	58.3
Sweden	83.7	89.8	77.8	88.0	90.1	85.8
Switzerland	71.1	96.9	46.9	87.6	94.3	80.5
United States	71.7	88.5	56.3	80.4	86.4	74.7

Source: LABORSTA Internet (2010).

Table 3.2   Percentage of Economically Active Population in Selected Countries at Age 65 to 69 for Years 1980 to 1981 and 2006 to 2007

| Country | 65 to 69 Years Old | | | | | |
| | 1980 to 1981 | | | 2006 to 2007 | | |
	Total	Men	Women	Total	Men	Women
Canada	17.1	26.1	9.3	*	*	*
Denmark	25.2	38.4	13.8	15.9	23.0	9.2
Finland	7.4	11.1	4.9	7.7	9.8	5.8
France	*	*	*	2.8	3.3	2.3
Germany	15.1	23.5	10.5	6.6	8.5	5.0
Italy	6.8	11.1	3.4	7.3	12	3.2
Japan	43.6	65.2	26.7	36.7	48.5	25.8
Netherlands	*	*	*	9.7	13.6	6.1
Norway	32.3	46.8	19.2	22.2	26.7	19.1
Spain	13.8	21.5	7.9	5.4	7.8	3.3
Sweden	10.0	14.4	6.1	15.0	19.1	11.1
Switzerland	16.7	25.5	9.5	17.0	22.5	12.7
United States	21.3	29.2	15.0	29.7	34.3	25.7

* Data were not available for these ages for these years.
Source: LABORSTA Internet (2010).

The Netherlands has the highest percentage change of employment among those aged 50 to 54 over those years—a 25.3% increase (see Table 3.1). Other countries with a significant change in employment rates for persons aged 50 to 54 are Switzerland (16.5%), Spain (15.6%), and Germany (15.3%). The United States experienced a modest 8.7% increase in labor force participation. Although the total employment rate for those aged 50 to 54 from 1980 to 2007 increased for every country listed in Table 3.1, this increase was largely due to the marked increase in the percentage of women actively employed in the labor force. Generally speaking, the percentage change for men over these years went up or down just a few percentage points. In contrast, women's employment rates increased markedly. For example, the employment rate for women in the Netherlands increased by 45.5% between 1980 and 2007. Other countries such as Switzerland (33.6%), Spain and Germany (31.5%), France (27.4%), and Canada (27.3%) have all experienced significant gains in employment rates for women between the ages of 50 and 54. In contrast, the employment rate for women in this age group in the United States increased by only 18.4%.

The rate of employment for those aged 65 to 69 over the time period between 1980 and 2007 shows a mixed pattern. The rate of total employment declined in five countries and increased in five countries listed in Table 3.2. For example, in the United States, the rate of employment for those aged 65 to 69 increased from 21.3% in 1980 to 29.7% in 2007. In contrast, Norway's employment rate dropped from its 1980 level of 32.3% to 22.2%

in 2007. The rate of employment by gender over the time period between 1980 and 2007 also shows some mixed trends. Only two countries, the United States and Sweden, saw an increase in employment for both men and women over this time period, whereas Germany, Japan, Norway, and Spain show a decrease in employment for both men and women; Denmark, Finland, and Switzerland show an increase for women only.

Finally, when we compare employment trends between individuals aged 50 to 54 and those aged 65 to 69, we see that the percentage of older adults actively employed drops dramatically for each of the countries listed in Tables 3.1 and 3.2. For example, in Sweden in 2006, the total percentage dropped from 88% for those aged 50 to 54 to 15% for those aged 65 to 69. Although the United States and Japan show a similar pattern of decline in employment rates between ages 50 to 54 and 65 to 69, the rate of employment is considerably higher in the 65 to 69 age groups for these two countries (29.7% and 36.7%, respectively).

Two other demographic characteristics related to pensions are the average retirement age and the average years in retirement. Table 3.3 shows that the average retirement age from the workforce ranges from a low of 58.8 years in France to a high of 63.7 years in Sweden. On average, women's retirement age for the countries listed in Table 3.3 is slightly lower than that of men.

Table 3.3 Average Exit Age From the Workforce and Projected Average Retirement Period in Selected Countries

Country	Average Exit Age From the Workforce in Selected Countries (2005)			Projected Average Retirement Period (2010)	
	Total	Men	Women	Men	Women
Netherlands	61.5	61.6	61.4	21.6	28.8
France	58.8	58.5	59.1	21.4	27.5
Italy	59.7	60.7	58.8	20.1	27.8
Belgium	60.6	61.6	59.6	23.1	30.9
Denmark	60.9	61.2	60.7	14.6	19.8
Germany	61.3	61.4	61.1	20.2	26.6
Switzerland	62.5	63.1	62.0	14.8	21.7
United Kingdom	62.6	63.4	61.9	18.9	25.0
Sweden	63.7	64.3	63.0	19.4	23.9
United States[*]	N/A	62	61.8	14.5	19.9

* Based on 2005 data, total data not available

Sources: Eurostat (2010) and Nyce and Schieber (2005).

As life expectancies increase and the age at retirement lowers, the amount of time spent in retirement increases. For men, the average number of years spent in retirement ranges from 14.5 years in the United States to 23.1 years in Belgium (see Table 3.3). In contrast, women will spend longer periods of time in retirement, ranging from 19.9 years in the United States to 30.9 in Belgium.

These three demographic characteristics—employment rates, average age of retirement, and time in retirement—influence the demand on pension resources, and the pension system characteristics influence individuals' retirement decisions. As policymakers work to keep pensions systems stable in the future, these three factors will be watched closely and will likely be the subject of retirement income policy initiatives.

Pension Characteristics

There are two basic pension characteristics that most people are concerned about—at what age they are eligible for their pension and how much they will be getting. Table 3.4 compares the ages for standard and early retirement benefits among selected countries. France has one of the lowest early retirement ages (56), as does Italy (57). Most countries listed in Table 3.4 have standard retirement ages of 65, although Sweden has the highest age at 67 years. The retirement age in the United States, which is linked to claiming full Social Security benefits, is currently 65 and will increase to 67 in 2027.

Table 3.4 Age of Entitlement to Early and Standard Pension Benefits in Selected Countries

Country	Age of Entitlement to Early Pension		Age of Entitlement to Standard Pension	
	Men	*Women*	*Men*	*Women*
Netherlands	None	None	65	65
France	56	56	60	60
Italy	57	57	65	60
Belgium	60	60	65	65
Denmark	None	None	65	65
Germany	63	63	65	65
Switzerland	63 to 64	62 to 63	65	64
United Kingdom	None	None	65	60
Sweden	None	None	61 to 67	61 to 67
United States*	62	62	65	65

* Will gradually increase the age of standard benefits to 67 in 2027
Source: European Commission (2007).

Pension Wage Replacement Rates

One way to determine the level of the "pension promise" a country makes to its citizens is to compare the level of retirees' income replacement rates once they leave the workforce. The pension replacement rate gives us some indication of how generous the policies are in ensuring adequate income in later life. There are two ways to examine how well a country's pension program provides income security in retirement—the net replacement rate and the relative pension level (Organisation for Economic Co-operation and Development [OECD], 2005c). The *net replacement rate* tells us to what extent pension systems attempt to maintain a certain standard of living in retirement by preserving a percentage of individual preretirement earnings. The net replacement rate is the percentage of preretirement income replaced by pension schemes (minus personal income taxes and social security contributions paid by workers and pensioners; OECD, 2005c).

Charts 3.1, 3.2, and 3.3 show net replacement rates by individual level of earnings as defined by low-wage earners, average-wage earners, and high-wage earners who earned half of the average, the average, and double the average country's earnings, respectively. For the average-wage earner (see Chart 3.1), Italy and the Netherlands exceed 75% net replacement rate, whereas the United Kingdom and the United States provide around 50% net replacement rate. France, Sweden, and Canada all provide a midlevel net replacement rate. For low-wage earners, all countries listed in Chart 3.2, with the exception of the United States, have a net replacement rate of more than 75%. The United States provides a replacement rate for low-wage earners at 61.4%. For those high-wage earners who have earnings double the average, Italy and the Netherlands have a replacement rate of more than 75%; Sweden and France have rates of more than 50%; and the United States, Canada, and the United Kingdom have rates lower than 40% (see Chart 3.3).

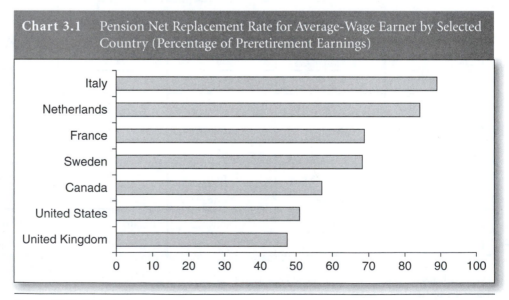

Chart 3.1 Pension Net Replacement Rate for Average-Wage Earner by Selected Country (Percentage of Preretirement Earnings)

Source: OECD (2005c).

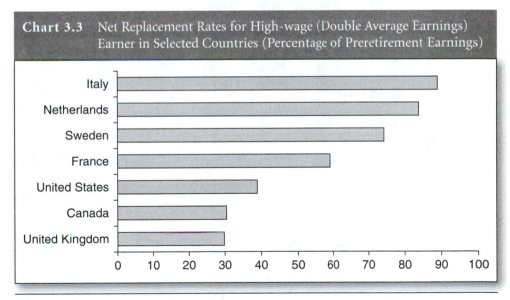

Chart 3.2   Net Pension Replacement Rate for Low-Wage (Half Average Earnings) Earner by Selected Country (Percentage of Preretirement Earnings)

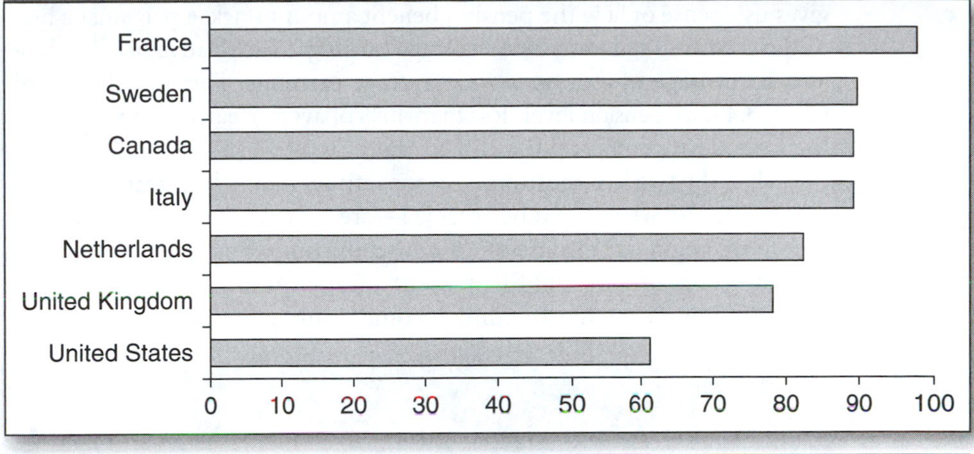

Source: OECD (2005c).

Chart 3.3   Net Replacement Rates for High-wage (Double Average Earnings) Earner in Selected Countries (Percentage of Preretirement Earnings)

Source: OECD (2005c).

For example, let's consider Sarah, who lives in the United States, and Paola, who lives in Italy. Sarah and Paola both have lifetime average salaries of $23,900 (we will use U.S. dollars for our calculations), and after taxes and social security contributions, their net salary is $19,120, which places them in the low-earner bracket. If Sarah's net replacement rate is 61.4%, then her benefit is $11,739 compared with Paola's replacement rate of 89.3%, which provides her with a benefit of $17,074.

Next, we can examine the *relative pension level,* which is the pension benefit level in relation to the average-wage earner in a given country. So a retiree may have a high net replacement rate of his or her own preretirement income, but the relative pension level gives us a sense of how the pension benefit amount stacks up against a broader measure of the country's economy-wide average earnings. The relative pension level is expressed as a percentage of economy-wide average earnings. Three of the countries listed in Chart 3.4 have pension levels less than 40% of average earnings in that country (Canada, the United Kingdom, and the United States, at 39.9%, 37.1%, and 36.5%, respectively).

Thus the two key pensionquestions retirees have—how much will their retirement income be and when can it be accessed—are answered very differently in each country. Before we begin our discussion of how countries set up their retirement income policies and programs, we will first present a framework that we will use to categorize the different approaches to providing income security.

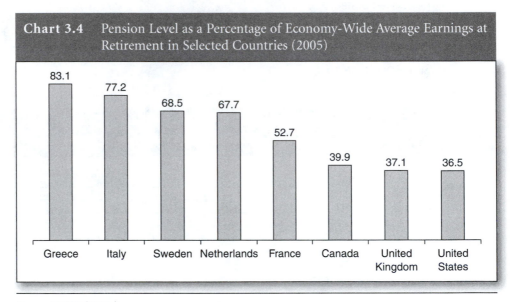

Chart 3.4 Pension Level as a Percentage of Economy-Wide Average Earnings at Retirement in Selected Countries (2005)

Source: OECD (2005c).

Overview of Retirement Income Program Framework

We have chosen to use the Organisation for Economic Co-operation and Development's (OECD) classifications of retirement income programs, which are based on two main objectives of retirement income programs—redistribution and savings (OECD, 2009b; see Chart 3.5). The objective of *redistributive programs* is to ensure that retirees receive some minimum standard of living. This is accomplished through a benefit formula that provides a higher replacement percentage to lower-income individuals compared with higher-income individuals (OECD, 2009b).

There are three types of redistributive programs—basic programs, resource-tested programs, and minimum pension programs. Basic programs provide a benefit that is the same to every retiree or is based on the years a retiree was employed (but not on

Chart 3.5   Framework for Types of Retirement Income Programs

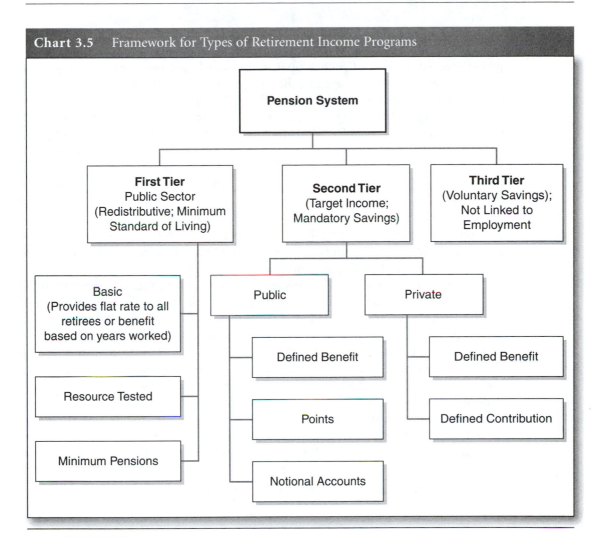

Source: OECD (2009b).

the amount of past earnings). Additional income in retirement does not change the benefit amount. Resource-tested programs assist poorer retirees at a greater rate than better-off retirees, and the value of the benefit is provided after other income and assets are considered in the benefit formula. Finally, a minimum pension program provides an additional amount to an earned pension benefit to bring workers with very low earnings to a minimum benefit level. Other nonpension income or assets are not considered when calculating this benefit.

The second-tier Mandatory Savings Pension programs are provided through the public and/or private occupational sectors and are based on employment history. These pension programs are designed to achieve some specified level of wage replacement in retirement and thus provide a targeted standard of living in retirement. These programs are set up as either defined-benefit or defined-contribution plans.

Defined-benefit (DB) plans pay pension benefits based on number of years contributed to the plan and level of earnings. These types of retirement plans provide a predetermined amount of money upon retirement based on average salary over a predefined number of years, age, and the number of years worked at the company. One type of plan, called a flat DB plan, pays a flat dollar amount for every year of service; a career-average DB plan may use a percentage of the career-average salary multiplied by the employee's number of years of employment. For example, under a flat DB plan, an employee receives 60% of his or her preretirement income based on completing 30 years of employment. Thus, if a worker's average preretirement income was $50,000, he or she would receive $30,000 a year pension benefit (60% x $50,000). These plans also contain annual cost of living increases.

Another pension type offered in the public sector is the points plan. The points plan provides retirement benefits based on the number of points earned for each year of employment. The total number of points is multiplied by a pension-point value to determine the actual benefit payment.

Defined-contribution (DC) plans are financed via contributions made to individual accounts that are invested in the financial markets, and the accumulation of this investment over time is paid out as pension benefits upon retirement. DC plans do not promise a specific benefit amount as do the DB plans discussed above, nor is there a redistributive element in the program as in the Tier 1 programs; rather, the amount of the contribution an individual and/or employer contributes to an individual's account in the plan is specified. For example, an employer might contribute 10% of an employee's annual salary on a yearly basis, which on an annual salary of $50,000 would be $5,000. The individual is responsible for selecting how these funds are invested. The amount available upon retirement is unknown, as the total amount will be based on how well the investment performs minus the fees charged against the account to manage it. Thus, in a DC plan, the *employee* bears the investment risk, whereas in a DB plan, the *employer* bears the investment risk (Purcell, 2008).

BOX 3.1 Policy to People Link: Defined Benefit Versus Defined Contribution: A Tale of One Family's Retirement Income Picture in the "Great Recession" of 2008

Different types of retirement programs have very different income payouts in retirement and are affected differently during difficult economic times. Florence, now age 75, worked for a local school district for 35 years and participated in a DB retirement plan offered by the state. Her pension pays out $3,400 per month. She also earned enough credits in Social Security to receive a monthly payment of $1,100 per month. In spite of the financial crisis that hit the market in 2008, she continues to receive her monthly income of $4,500. Although she will not receive a cost of living adjustment for her Social Security this year (2010), her benefit remains unchanged. The state pension program is looking for ways to deal with its short-term and long-term liabilities due to the economic downturn, but to date, Florence's benefits from her state pension and Social Security remain fixed and she is able to afford the cost of assisted living and her other expenses.

In contrast, her daughter Patty, age 52, has worked for a public university for 18 years and over that time participated in the university's DC plan. In December of 2007, the value of her DC portfolio totaled $423,894. The portfolio dropped in value by $90,231 and 1 year later totaled $333,663. Since she can most likely work for another 10 to 15 years, there may be time for this retirement portfolio to regain its value. If she had retired in December of 2007, her monthly retirement benefit would have dropped significantly—compared with Florence's retirement income, which did not change dramatically during this difficult economic time.

Notional accounts are similar to DC plans in that the pension benefit is based on contributions and the investment rate of return on those contributions is tracked in individual accounts. The accumulated amount earned over time is then paid out using a formula based on life expectancy data, and the rate of return on the contributions is set by the government through fixed rules for calculating benefits. Thus, fixing the rate of return acts as a buffer for the swings in investment returns in the financial markets (Settergren, 2001; World Bank, n.d.).

Finally, the third-tier voluntary savings programs provide additional funds in retirement that are not linked to an employment relationship. The plans are available via a pension fund broker or a financial institution acting as pension provider without any participation from employers. Individuals independently purchase and select how they wish to have such funds invested.

In the majority of countries, redistributive income security programs and DB programs are financed through what is called a pay-as-you-go (PAYGO) scheme (OECD, 2007). In a PAYGO-financed retirement program, premiums or taxes paid by current workers are used to pay current retirees and a reserve is established to help even out disparities between the revenue collected and the benefits paid, often due to demographic changes and employment patterns.

Now that we have covered some of the basics about pension benefits and program types, we will compare retirement income programs in four different countries—the United States, Canada, Sweden, and the Netherlands. We have selected these four countries because they illustrate four very different approaches to retirement income policies, as well as varying levels of net pension replacement and pension. Sweden and the Netherlands have more generous retirement income programs compared with Canada and the United States.

United States

The United States has a first-tier redistributive income benefit program, targeted to low-income individuals through the Supplemental Security Income program, and a second-tier mandatory savings program through Social Security. The United States also has voluntary private-sector retirement plan options. We start first with a review of the Social Security program.

Social Security

The Social Security program (SSP) was signed into law on August 14, 1935, as the Social Security Act, and according to Schulz (2005), the program was designed to

1. be compulsory and universal, in that high- and low-income workers alike were included;

2. be an earnings-related program and thus tied to employment;

3. have a weighted benefit formula that would favor low-income workers in order to achieve social adequacy for those at greatest risk of poverty;

4. be one of many sources of income in retirement; and

5. be a non-means-tested program, as all workers in various social classes earned their right to receive benefits.

Table 3.5 provides a summary of the amendments made to the SSP since it was enacted in 1935.[1] These amendments were designed to protect the integrity of the benefits and expand coverage. Coverage for SSP is now almost universal, as it is estimated that 88.6% of elderly couples and 91.2% of single elders receive income from Social Security (Employee Benefit Research Institute [EBRI], 2008).

Program Details

The SSP is a second-tier, public mandatory insurance program for U.S. citizens. It has broad, almost universal coverage, and payment is based on a defined-benefit approach. The SSP is financed by a PAYGO system, as described above.

Eligibility for Retirement Benefits

The SSP pays benefits to individuals who have reached retirement age as defined in the act and discussed below. In order to be eligible for SSP retirement benefits, an individual must have been working in covered employment, have earned enough "credits," and have reached the appropriate retirement age. Covered employment, which is participation in the SSP, includes virtually all employment, including those who are self-employed. A notable exception is federal or state employees who have the option to participate in their own retirement programs. Employees working in covered

1. The history section draws from Social Security Administration SSA Publication No. 21-059 ICN 440000 Unit of Issue—HD (one hundred), October 2007.

Table 3.5	Summary of the Legislative History of Social Security
Year	*Milestone*
1935	Social Security Act is passed.
1937	Employers and workers begin paying payroll taxes into the SSP, and workers begin acquiring benefit credits on January 1.
1939	Amendments to the law accelerate the start of benefit payments to 1940 and add two new categories of benefits—dependent benefits for the spouse and minor children of a retired worker and survivor benefits paid to the family in the event of the premature death of the worker. The first monthly benefit payment is $22.54 to Ida Fuller.
1950	One-time cost of living adjustment (COLA) is passed. Prior to 1950, the recipient's monthly benefit amount remained flat unless Congress passed legislation to increase benefit amounts. Ida Fuller received $22.54 per month until 1950, when Congress legislated the first general COLA benefit increase of 77%.
1956	The Social Security Act is amended again to provide cash benefits to disabled workers aged 50 to 65 and disabled adult children.
1956 1961	Amendments lower the eligibility age for women and men to age 62.
1972	The law is altered to provide for automatic annual COLAs based on the annual increase in the Consumer Price Index (CPI-W). Wage-indexing of the initial benefit amount upon retirement is introduced in order to ensure that benefits keep up with inflation.
1975	CPI-W increases go into effect.
1983	An amendment includes partial taxation of Social Security benefits, coverage of federal employees, raising the retirement age beginning in 2000, and increasing the reserves in the Social Security trust funds.
2000	Amendments eliminate the Retirement Earnings Test for beneficiaries at or above full retirement age, thus allowing older adults to continue working without having their benefits reduced.
2010	For the first time since the COLA law was enacted, Social Security beneficiaries do not receive an automatic adjustment to their benefits. This occurs because the CPI-W in the third quarter of 2009 fell below the third quarter of 2008 (Social Security Administration, 2010a).

Source: Social Security Administration SSA Publication No. 21-059, ICN 440000 Unit of Issue—HD (one hundred), October 2007.)

employment pay 6.2% of covered earnings, and employers pay 6.2% as well. Those who are self-employed are required to pay 12.4% of covered earnings. An employee's entire earnings amount is not subject to the 12.4%. In 2009, covered earnings were limited to $106,800 and any income above that was not subject to Social Security participation (Social Security Administration [SSA], 2009).

Next, the insured must have earned a total of 40 "credits." In 2009, 1 credit was earned for each $1,090 in earnings, and a maximum of 4 credits per year can be earned. Thus, a worker in covered employment who earns at least $4,360 a year can earn 4 credits a year and accumulate the 40 credits needed in 10 years. The amount of money needed to earn one credit increases every year.

Having met the eligibility criteria described above, beneficiaries can begin drawing early retirement benefits at age 62, but the benefits will be reduced by one-half of 1% for each month before full retirement age (SSA, 2009). Full retirement benefits in 2009 were payable at age 65 and 65 and 10 months for individuals born prior to 1937 and 1942, respectively. The full retirement age will increase gradually to age 67 by the year 2027, and payments will be deferrable up to age 70.

Benefit Amount

The benefit amount is calculated using the worker's covered lifetime earnings and is the basis for determining benefit amounts for the insured and the insured's family members as described in the next section. The pension benefit is calculated by adjusting or "indexing" monthly earnings against inflation since 1950 and then using the average monthly earnings during the highest 35 earning years (SSA, 2009). SSP does not make any exceptions for the years individuals are unemployed for reasons such as child rearing or pursuing an education. Earnings in years outside this period may be substituted, if higher. There is no minimum pension for insured persons reaching age 62 after 1981. The maximum monthly pension for workers retiring in 2009 at the full retirement age is $2,323; the average monthly benefit is $1,160.20 (SSA, 2010b). Social Security benefits are taxable if individual income is greater than $25,000—or $32,000 for a couple.

Individuals drawing benefits may continue to work without having their SSP benefits reduced if they wait to draw benefits after the full retirement age. If a person is working and elects to begin drawing benefits before the full retirement age, the monthly benefit amount will be reduced by $1 for every $2 in earnings above the annual limit, which was $14,160 in 2009 (SSA, 2009). If benefits are accessed in the year a worker reaches full retirement age, benefits will be reduced by $1 for every $3 in earnings above $37,680 in 2009.

Auxiliary Benefits: Dependents and Spouses

Family members of a retired worker may also qualify for benefits under the Dependence Allowance if they are not eligible for benefits under their own work history. Fifty percent of the insurance amount may be paid to a wife or a husband at the full retirement age (reduced from age 62 up to the full retirement age). An unmarried divorced spouse may also draw dependent benefits if the marriage lasted at least 10 years. Currently, unmarried partners are not eligible to receive benefits.

Auxiliary Benefits: Survivors

Social Security also provides benefits to survivors of deceased eligible workers who have met the same requirements for retirement benefits. Those groups eligible are surviving widows or widowers, a surviving divorced spouse (if the marriage lasted at least 10 years) aged 60 or older, surviving children younger than 18 or aged 18 to 19 and attending elementary or secondary school full-time (no limit if disabled before age 22), and surviving dependent parents aged 62 or older and at least 50% dependent on the deceased worker. Survivors receive from 75% to 100% of the worker's retirement benefit.

Disability Benefits

Social Security Disability benefits are payable to workers who meet both an earnings and disability requirement. Workers must have met two different earnings tests when they become disabled. A "recent work" and a "duration of work" test to determine if required length of employment was met under Social Security. Recent work is based on age and work history. The impairment must result in death or last for at least 12 months in a row. Disability must be due to a documented physical or mental impairment that causes the inability to work in one's previous occupation or in any other type of work that would be appropriate to one's age, education, and work experience.

Auxiliary Social Security Disability Benefits: Survivors

Survivors of a disabled beneficiary may qualify to receive benefits if they are disabled and meet the definition of disability or if they meet the nondisability requirements for a surviving spouse or a surviving divorced spouse described above.

Supplemental Security Income

In 1974, the Social Security Act added the Supplemental Security Income (SSI) program as Title XVI, which provided for the first time a national minimum income program for low-income individuals aged 65 and over, blind or disabled. The program is funded by general federal and state tax revenues. There are specific eligibility criteria for meeting the definition of blindness or disability. Once a person qualifies in one of these categories, eligibility is contingent on income, asset levels, and residency.

Eligibility and Benefits

Single individuals over age 65 are limited to a monthly income below $674, and couples are limited to below $1,011. Single individuals are limited to owning $2,000 worth of assets and couples to $3,000 worth, excluding personal belongings, a home, a car, funeral insurance, and life insurance (the last two assets up to $1,500 in value; SSA, 2009). Participants must be residents of one of the 50 states, the District of Columbia, or the Northern Mariana Islands and may not be absent from the country for a full calendar month or more than 30 consecutive days or apply for other benefits to which they may be entitled, such as Social Security. Single people over 65 can be eligible for up to $674 a month and a couple for $1,011 a month, depending on other sources of income, which can reduce the benefit amount. The average monthly benefit is $405.30 and benefit rates are equivalent to around 20% of the national average wage for individuals (OECD, 2007).

States can also choose to supplement the federally determined SSI benefit. 12 states pay only the federal minimum, 28 administer their own system, and twelve offer supplements that are operated by the SSA. The average additional payment in these 12 states is 13% for individuals and 18% for couples of the federal benefit amount (OECD, 2007).

Private Sector Plans

The American Express company established the first corporate pension plan in the United States in 1875 (Allen, Clark, & McDermed, 1993). Pensions were viewed as beneficial for employment reasons, as they offered retirement income benefits that provided for insurance against accidents, death, or disability as a reward for long-term employment and a payment when employment was terminated (Sass, 2003). Pension legislation was first enacted through the Revenue Act of 1921 (EBRI, 2009); by the mid-1940s, the number of private pensions rose to 400 and they were primarily offered in mature big businesses such as banking, railroad, and public utilities. By the 1960s, private-sector plans covered 40% of private-sector workers (Sass, 1997), and by 2007, 59.9% of full-time employees worked for firms that sponsored some type of retirement plan—down slightly from 62.8% in 1990 (Purcell, 2008).

Private employer retirement pension plans can be either DB, DC, or some combination of both. In order for the employer to receive the tax benefits of contributing to a retirement plan, the plan must comply with the rules contained in the Employee Retirement Income Security Act of 1974. As you recall, the DB plan provides employees a benefit amount at retirement based on a flat dollar amount, a career average of earnings, or average earnings at the end of a worker's career. In DC plans, employers and employees contribute a set amount of money into an account established for the employee. The final retirement income will be contingent on the account's investment gains and losses. There are different types of DC plans, including profit-sharing plans, stock-bonus plans, plans that set a standard contribution amount (money purchase plans), and a 401k plan that gives an employee the option of contributing a portion of pretaxed income to an investment account.

Eligibility for Private Sector Pensions

In order to be eligible for a private-sector pension, employers must choose to offer pension plans to their employees, as such plans are offered voluntarily. Next, the plan identifies which employees are eligible to participate. Finally, there are rules in pension plans that dictate when employees have ownership of the pension benefits.

Assuming that the employer decides to offer a pension plan, most plans require that an employee meet age and length of employment criteria in order to participate in the pension plan, but plans may not exclude workers under the age of 21 or require that employees be on the job for one year (EBRI, 2009). Employers may choose to cover all employees or to cover employees by job pay type (e.g., salary vs. hourly, full-time vs. part-time). All plans, however, must meet nondiscriminatory rules that ensure that plans do not discriminate in favor of higher-salaried workers (EBRI, 2009).

Employees gain legal rights to their accrued pension benefits—called *vesting*—when they meet the criteria contained in a formula that considers years of service and age. For DB plans, vesting rules generally fall under three different variations for the employee's accrued benefits: *general vesting* occurs after 5 years of participation in the plan, *cliff vesting* occurs prior to 5 years, and *gradual vesting* of 20% occurs after 3 years of service and 20% each year after that until 100% vesting has been reached (EBRI, 2009). For DC plans, employer contributions are required to vest more quickly, with either a 3-year cliff vesting or 2- to 6-year schedule. Immediate vesting occurs in both DB and DC plans for benefits attributable to employee contributions. Access to benefits occurs upon the retirement age set forth in the plan (usually 65) but also upon disability or death.

Benefits

Once vesting has occurred, pensioners can elect to receive the benefit in a lump sum or as an annuity, payable monthly over the lifetime of the employee. If an annuity option is selected, the employee may elect to provide his or her surviving spouse with a payment upon death that provides at least one-half of his or her monthly income to the surviving spouse over the spouse's lifetime. However, if this option is chosen, the employee's payable monthly benefit amount is reduced.

It is also important to note that some pension benefit amounts take the anticipated Social Security benefits into consideration when determining plan benefits. When this occurs, the actual benefit amount may be reduced by a dollar amount or a percentage of the person's annual Social Security payment. One type of integration plan offsets the pension by one-half of the Social Security benefit. For example, let's say that Jeanette's final salary was $50,000 at Tech Solutions. Her pension from Tech Solutions was a DB plan that took her final salary multiplied by the 30 years she was employed there and then multiplied by 1.5% (or 0.015), which totals $22,500. Jeanette also qualified for a Social Security benefit of $10,000. Under Tech Solutions' integrated pension plan, her pension can be reduced by $5,000, which is half of her Social Security benefit. Thus, Jeanette's total pension from Tech Solutions will be $17,500 ($22,500 minus $5,000), along with $10,000 from Social Security.

In conclusion, retirement income in the United States is addressed via three types of nonuniversal programs: Social Security, which is based on employment history; SSI, which is a means-tested program for very low-income elders; and private-sector retirement income programs offered through employers. Next, we will review the Canadian retirement income system.

Canada

Income security in Canada is addressed by four programs—Income Supplement Programs for very low-income individuals; the Old Age Security (OAS) Pension, which is a universal pension program for all Canadians; the Guaranteed Income Supplement (GIS), which supplements the OAS pension benefit; and the Canadian Pension Plan (CPP), which provides retirement, disability, and death benefits and private-sector retirement programs (Service Canada, 2009d). Thus, Canada has both first-tier redistributive programs and second-tier insurance income support programs. As with the United States, the first pension programs were established in the private sector in the late 1880s in the railways and banking sectors (Maser & Bégin, 2003). In 1927, Canada enacted a means-tested benefit program called the Old Age Pensions Act to persons 70 or over, regardless of their employment history. This program was later altered in 1952 into the Old Age Security Act, which provides a flat rate benefit to all persons 70 or over meeting residency requirements. The CPP was established in

January 1966 by the Canadian Parliament and is available in every province except Quebec, which offers the same program under its Quebec Pension Plan. Legislation supporting registered retirement savings plans in the private sector was added in 1957, and legislative changes in each of these programs have occurred over the years (Maser & Bégin, 2003). We will briefly review each program below.

Income Supplement Programs

Income Supplement Programs are the responsibility of provincial governments and are for very low-income individuals. The province of Ontario was the first to pass such legislation in 1974, and Alberta was the last province to enact an income supplement program in 1994 (Maser & Bégin, 2003). Because these programs are created and run by the provincial governments, eligibility criteria vary, but all programs are means tested. The maximum monthly benefits paid by the provincial government range from C$25 to C$200[2] (Government of New Brunswick, 2009; Maser & Bégin, 2003).

Old Age Security and Guaranteed Income Supplement

The universal basic pension program, OAS, provides benefits to residents regardless of income or employment history. Benefits are paid from the federal government's consolidated revenue fund, and no contributions are required (Maser & Bégin, 2003). Eligibility is based on residence (at least 10 years) in Canada to receive any benefit. Full pension benefits are provided at 40 years of residency, and benefits are reduced proportionately if one has lived in Canada for fewer than 40 years. Canadians can begin drawing OAS pension at age 65 irrespective of their employment status. The benefit amount is taxable, and the average monthly benefit in 2009 was C$489.53 (Service Canada, 2009e). The GIS provides a monthly nontaxable benefit to low-income OAS recipients aged 65 and older. The GIS is based on annual income or the combined annual income of the spouse or common-law partner. The average monthly GIS benefit for a single person is C$452.61 (Service Canada, 2009c, 2009e).

Auxiliary Benefits: Spousal Allowance

The Spousal Allowance is a monthly benefit for low-income seniors between the ages of 60 and 64 whose spouse or common-law partner is eligible for, or currently receiving, the OAS pension and the GIS. There is also an allowance for the unmarried surviving spouse or partner who has not entered into a new common-law relationship for more than 12 months and whose spouse or partner died on or after January 1, 1998 (Service Canada, 2010a).

Canadian Pension Plan

The CPP is a first-tier insurance program and is directed at the employed. It includes provisions for retirement, disability, and death benefits.

---

2. The current exchange rate between the U.S. dollar and the Canadian dollar is 0.99. Because these two currencies are so close in value, we will report only the Canadian value (C$).

Eligibility

Like the Social Security program in the United States, both workers and employers contribute to the CPP. Both contribute 4.95%, and self-employed workers contribute the full 9.9%. Every worker over 18 who earns more than C$3,500 per year pays into the CPP, and the maximum pensionable earnings were capped at C$44,900 in 2008. The minimum level is frozen by law, and the maximum level increases in January of each year (Capretta, 2007b; National Union of Public and General Employees [NUPGE], 2009).

According to Service Canada (2009a), early retirement benefits can be accessed between the ages of 60 and 64 if the beneficiary is not employed in the month prior to or during the pension start date or has earnings that are lower than C$884.58 in the month prior to or during the pension start date. As in the United States, pension benefits starting before age 65 are reduced. Starting at age 60, the monthly pension benefits reduce by 30%. There is no financial advantage to delaying pension benefits after the age of 70.

Benefits

Benefits under the CPP are based on the amount and length of time a worker has contributed to the plan (Service Canada, 2009a) and age of retirement. The CPP replaces 25% of workers' average lifetime earnings between a minimum and maximum threshold. Before the average lifetime earnings are calculated, 15% of low earning years—due to times when the worker may have been unemployed, enrolled in postsecondary education, and/or disabled—are dropped from the calculation (OECD, 2009b). In addition, the CPP includes a "child rearing" provision, which allows the years when workers stopped work or had lower earnings while they had a child under age 7 to be excluded from the calculation of pensionable earnings. There is no limit to the number of years that can be dropped for this purpose. The child-rearing dropout measure ensures that workers (primarily women) who leave the workforce to take care of children will not be penalized by having lower pensions when they retire (Torjman, 2002). In 2008, the maximum monthly pension benefit was C$884.58 and the average monthly pension was C$481.46 (Service Canada, 2009a). Benefits are adjusted for inflation. Working after beginning the CPP does not affect the monthly pension amount, and future earnings do not change the CPP benefit amount.

Auxiliary Benefits: Spouse/Partner Benefits

Under the CPP, benefits can be shared with a spouse or partner. A spouse is someone to whom one is legally married, and a "common-law partner" is someone of either sex with whom one has lived in a conjugal relationship for at least 1 year. Spouses or common-law partners who are both at least 60 years old and who receive CPP retirement pensions can share pension benefits, and each can receive an equal benefit amount. This works by adding together the pension earned by each worker during the time they lived together, and the pension is divided equally between spouses or common-law partners. For example, if one person's benefit amount is C$800 and the other is C$400, when added together and divided equally, each person's monthly benefit is C$600. Any pension benefit a worker earned outside the time he or she was married or lived with someone remains a separate benefit and is not combined. If only one spouse or partner is a beneficiary, that pension may be shared with the non-CPP-eligible spouse or partner (Service Canada, 2009a). The combined maximum OAS and CPP benefits replaced 39.9% of average earners' wages in retirement (OECD, 2007).

Auxiliary Benefits: Survivor Benefits

The CPP also pays survivor benefits to the spouse or common-law partner, as well as providing a death benefit payable to the estate of the deceased worker. Eligibility is based on the deceased spouse or partner's having contributed for one-third of the time between the ages of 18 and the death of the spouse or during a minimum of 10 calendar years (Service Canada, 2009b). If the surviving spouse or partner is not eligible for his or her own retirement or disability benefit and is over age 65, the benefit paid will be 60% of the deceased's retirement pension. If the surviving spouse or partner is under 65, the benefit will be a fixed amount plus 37.5% of the deceased's retirement pension. The maximum monthly benefits in 2008 for a survivor 65 and over and a survivor under age 65 were C$530.75 and C$493.28 per month, respectively (National Union of Public and General Employees, 2008). The surviving spouse or partner's maximum monthly benefit, when combined with their pension and survivor's pension, is C$884.58 (NUPGE, 2008). Survivors are entitled to receive these benefits even if they remarry; however, no beneficiary can receive more than the maximum benefit amount, regardless of the program from which they draw their benefit.

When a qualified beneficiary dies, the estate receives a lump-sum death benefit. The death benefit is calculated using the current deceased's retirement pension amount or the amount it would have been if he or she had been 65 when death occurred. The death benefit is equal to 6 months' worth of this calculated retirement benefit, up to C$2,500 (Service Canada, 2009b).

Second Tier: Public and Private Retirement Income Programs

The public- and private-sector tier retirement plans in Canada are composed of voluntary employer-based pension programs—the Registered Pension Plans (RPP) and the Registered Retirement Savings Plans (RRSP). The RPP programs exist in the public sector for employees in the federal, provincial, and municipal governments, the Royal Canadian Mounted Police, and the Canadian Forces. Private-sector programs are available via individual companies, unions, and other nongovernment entities. Legislation governing RPPs allows both the employee and employer to contribute funds up to a yearly maximum amount. Contributions into the plans are not taxed, but benefits paid out to the beneficiary are taxed. Now, let's turn to Sweden's pension programs.

Sweden

The Swedish pension system was first enacted in 1913 and by the 1960s had evolved into a universal program covering all Swedes (Palme & Svensson, 1997). Most recent reforms occurred in 1994 and were designed to

> provide an adequate earnings-related retirement benefit with universal coverage for all persons working and residing in Sweden, backed up by a safety net that guarantees an adequate standard of living for the elderly. (Palmer, 2000, p. 2)

The reforms included a change in the way its pension programs were funded in order to respond to the projected increase in the number of older adults and created a combined approach of a universal flat benefit with an earnings-related supplement. The discussion below relates to the new programs and applies to those born after 1938.

Sweden has two programs in the first tier—a minimum program called Maintenance Support (*Äldreförsörjningsstöd*) and a targeted retirement program called Guarantee Pension (*Garantipension*). These two programs work in tandem to provide universal coverage so that all Swedes have a basic standard of living in later life that is not contingent on employment history.

Maintenance Support Program

Eligibility for the Maintenance Support program is based on residency, income, and housing costs. For people aged 65 and older who reside in Sweden and intend to stay for at least 1 year, the benefit is prorated based on the number of years living in Sweden, and available if other pension benefits are insufficient. The benefit amount is means tested, and in 2008 benefits were provided to persons with income below SEK4,421 per month ($622.90) for an individual or SEK3,704 per month ($521.84) for married persons (Försäkringskassan, 2008a).

Guarantee Pension Program

The Guarantee Pension (GP) is referred to as a "top-up" pension that supplements the Maintenance Support benefit for individuals who have not earned an adequate pension amount as defined by the government each year. The GP program is also based on residency rather than employment history.

Eligibility and Benefit

To qualify for the program, beneficiaries must be aged 65 or older and have residency of at least 3 years in Sweden or in another European Union country (i.e., Norway, Iceland, Liechtenstein, or Switzerland). The GP is means tested, and eligibility is based on income from other pensions under the national pension system, but income from other work-related pensions (discussed below) is not included in the income calculation. Eligible persons must have incomes below SEK10,959 ($1,543.87) per month for a single person and SEK9,713 ($1,368.32) per month for a married person (includes a same-sex partner and cohabitating partners). A full pension benefit is given if an individual has lived in Sweden for 40 years; for each year of residence fewer than 40, the amount is reduced by one-fortieth. The total GP amount is SEK6,777 ($954.58) a month for a married person or SEK7,597 ($1,070.09) a month for a single person (Försäkringskassan, 2008b).

A GP survivor benefit is payable to individuals younger than 65 who were married to or who cohabitated (under certain conditions) with the deceased for at least 5 years. The full pension benefit is SEK7,046 ($992.52) a month if the deceased spouse resided in Sweden for 40 years and the surviving spouse does not receive an earnings-related pension (SSA, 2008b). The pension ends if the surviving spouse or partner remarries (or is cohabitating under certain conditions) or when the survivor reaches age 65 (Försäkringskassan, 2008b).

Income Pension

The Income Pension (*Inkomstpension*) is a second-tier mandatory pension based on employment history. The Income Pension is a notional defined contribution account for which the return contributions earn is set by the government through fixed rules for calculating benefits, which act to buffer swings in investment returns in the financial markets (Settergren, 2001; World Bank, n.d.).

Eligibility

Like the United States and Canada, eligibility is based on earnings from pensionable income and amounts from employment throughout one's life. There is no cap on the number of years for which one can earn pension credits. In 2008, income above SEK17,343 ($2,202.07) per year and up to SEK387,360 ($49,183.80) counted as credited income for pension entitlements (*Penionsrätterna*). Sweden also has a provision for individuals in nonemployment situations to earn pension entitlements. Pension entitlements are earned for one parent for a period of 4 years per child and one child per year; for students in postsecondary study; for persons serving in the national service armed forces; and for persons with a disability to prevent a reduction of a future pension benefit due to a loss of income during these life events (Försäkringskassan, 2008c). Benefits are based on fixed contributions paid over a lifetime of earnings.

Benefits

Benefits are based on the pension contribution of 18.5% of pensionable income from employee, employer, and self-employed—16% of which goes to the Income Pension and 2.5% to the Premium Pension program (discussed below). Pensions are payable at 61 years of age. Full and partial pension benefits are possible as well; however, the longer one waits to get benefits, the higher the benefit amount will be. Pensioners can also work while drawing a pension without such income reducing the pension benefit (Ministry of Health and Social Affairs/ Riksförsäkringsverket, 2003). The average monthly benefit is SEK10,489 ($1,505.53).

BOX 3.2   Policy to People Link: The Orange Envelope

Every year in February/March, the Swedish Social Insurance Agency and the Premium Pension Authority send the annual account statement—the Orange Envelope—to more than 6 million recipients. The Orange Envelope contains the latest data available and provides pension projections each year for every individual insured based on that individual's actual pension credit earned. The statement sent out each year in the Orange Envelope enables the insured to watch their own income pension and premium pension accounts grow from year to year. In Sweden, the Orange Envelope has become a familiar trademark, and today, its color symbolizes pensions as a universal concept rather than just the national public pension.

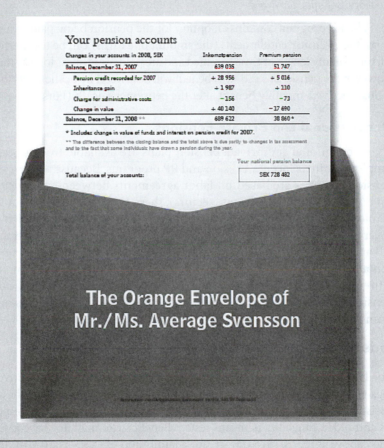

Source: Swedish Social Insurance Agency (2008).

Auxiliary Benefits: Survivors

Survivors are also entitled to receive benefits under the Income Program. Survivors' pension is 55% of the deceased's accrued pension paid to a spouse or partner of at least 5 years. The pension ends at remarriage or at age 65 (SSA, 2008b).

Premium Pension

The Premium Pension (PP) program is a defined contribution plan that takes 2.5% of the 18.5% contribution on earned income and invests it in individual accounts of the employee's choosing. Pensioners can choose from hundreds of different investment funds or default into a government-managed fund (Capretta, 2007a). As with all defined contribution plans, in the PP program there is no guarantee of the value of the pension. The pension amount will be based on how much money was paid into the PP account, the investment value, and when the funds are withdrawn. Benefits can be drawn as early as age 61, and one-fourth to full pension amounts are available.

Auxiliary Benefits: Survivors

The PP program contains an option for the pension being paid to a surviving spouse or partner. Pension entitlements (the amount one earns) can be transferred to a spouse or partner for any length of time specified and are paid monthly as long as the pensioner lives. However, the pensioner's monthly benefit will be lower if he or she elects to have a surviving spouse receive a monthly benefit after the pensioner's death (Försäkringskassan, 2008d).

Occupational and Private Pensions

Occupational and private pension plans are available to employees who wish to supplement their Income Pension and PP programs. Because most of the occupational pension schemes are based on labor agreements between employer and employees (in both the public and private sectors), these pensions cover about 90% of Swedish employees (Vidlund, 2009). These occupational pensions—of which the four largest cover 80% of white-collar and wage-earning employees—are usually a combination of DB and DC plans, although there has been an increase in the number of DC provisions contained in these plans (Invest in Sweden Agency, 2007). Plans contain provisions for retirement benefits, disability, and survivors. In addition, Swedes can buy a private pension policy through an insurance company, but only 7% of pension income comes from private pensions (Ministry of Health and Social Affairs, 2008).

Netherlands

The Netherlands has retirement income programs that are redistributive (first tier), savings via the private sector (second tier) and voluntary (third tier). The Work and Social Assistance Act (WWB) is a first-tier program that provides income support for persons 18 and older. Eligibility is means tested. Beneficiaries may not have assets (car and savings) above €10,910 ($16,031.41) for a family and €5,455 ($8,016.48) for an individual. One's home value may not be more than €46,100 ($67,746.93; Ministry of Social Affairs and Employment, 2009). The total household income is considered, and beneficiaries are expected to look for work (Ministry of Social Affairs and Employment, 2009).

Benefits

Assistance levels under the WWB for couples/cohabiting partners and single individuals between the ages of 21 and 65 is 100% and 70% of the net minimum wage, respectively—which in 2009 was €15,540.84 ($22,832.70) and €7,770.48 ($11,414.53) (Ministerie van Sociale Zaken en Werkgelegenheid, 2008). For persons aged 65 and older, the benefit amount is the net amount of the Old Age Pension benefit (discussed below). For married couples/cohabiting partners and individuals 65 and older, the social assistance levels are €16,416.12 ($24,112.53) and €11,935.68 ($17,531.68), respectively. Since municipalities are financially responsible for and administer the program, additional benefits may be added under special circumstances.

General Old Age Pension

The Old Age Pension (*Algemene Ouderdoms Wet;* AOW) is the compulsory public social security pension for all Dutch who reside or work in the Netherlands. The AOW provides all residents with a flat pension benefit, which, unlike Social Security in the U.S., is not connected to employment history. Thus, by default, those who have periods outside paid employment (e.g., caring for children, postsecondary education) are covered under the program. The AOW is financed through payroll taxes on a PAYGO basis. The contribution rate is currently set at 17.9% of earnings, up to a ceiling of 18.5%. Persons aged 65 and older are exempt from contributions (Capretta, 2007a).

Eligibility

All residents between the ages of 15 and 65, regardless of employment status, are considered to be participating in the AOW program. Every year a person lives in the Netherlands, he or she accrues 2% toward a full benefit at age 65. The only exception to this pathway to entitlement is when a person resides outside the Netherlands. There is no means test of eligibility, and other forms of income do not affect the AOW benefit.

Benefits

AOW benefits vary based on whether one is living with a spouse/partner (or another individual, as long as both individuals contribute toward household costs or take care of each other) or as a single individual. At age 65, the AOW pays a flat rate pension of at least 70% of the net minimum wage.

AOW pensions are tied to the nation's minimum wage as determined by law, which is about 55% of the average wage of Dutch employees. Single persons get a full-rate benefit equal to 70% of the minimum wage, while each member of a couple gets a benefit equal to 50% of the minimum wage (Ministerie van Sociale Zaken en Werkgelegenheid, 2008). Because benefits are based on the ratio of the minimum wage to the average wage, AOW benefits are effectively indexed to wage growth; so as the average wage increases, so do AOW benefits. Persons aged 65 and older who do not have retirement incomes of at least 70% of the minimum wage receive the WWB means-tested social assistance discussed above to "top up" or bring their incomes up to the minimum level.

Private Defined Benefit

The Netherlands does not have a second-tier public mandatory insurance program, but rather workers supplement their retirement benefits via private-sector DB programs. More than 90% of employees participate in an occupational pension plan. Plans usually promise a yearly replacement rate of approximately 2% of the final salary or average career salary; so 35 years of work would result in 70% of the final salary (Ministerie van Sociale Zaken en Werkgelegenheid, 2008). Since the occupational pensions are considered supplementary to the AOW, the AOW is used in the final occupation scheme; the combined pension amount reaches 70% of the net minimum wage.

As a rule, occupational pensions, together with the AOW, provide benefits equal to 70% of a full career worker's final salary, although replacement rates in some schemes are pegged to average career earnings. Occupational pensions are explicitly integrated with the public pension system through the "AOW franchise"—which, like similar arrangements in some U.S. DB schemes, allows private pension benefits to be offset by the amount of a retiree's public benefit.

Private-Sector Voluntary Savings

These are individual accounts that are taken out with an insurance provider and are not linked to employment history. Anyone can participate in these private pension schemes, which are either annuity or endowment insurance. Annuity pays the holder a fixed periodic benefit—contributions are tax deductible. Endowment pays a lump sum in connection with a person's life. Income from these private pension schemes may be used as a supplement to the AOW and/or with the occupational pension.

Summary

All four of the countries discussed in this chapter take a different approach to their retirement income policies and programs, and as a result, older adults in each country experience a different retirement income benefit amount. Table 3.6 summarizes the different key elements of the retirement income programs in each country. While all countries have Tier 1 programs, Canada and the Netherlands have a basic program that is based on residency and is not means tested. However, the average benefit amount differs significantly, as the Canadian benefit is less than one-third of the benefit amount provided in the Netherlands. Sweden's Maintenance Support (which is means tested) and the minimum pension—the Guaranteed Pension (based on residency and other nonpension income)—brings Swedish residents' retirement income up to an average minimum benefit amount of more than $1,076. The SSI program in the United States is a means-tested program for the very poor that provides benefits for those who aren't qualified to receive Social Security benefits, or it can "top up" very small Social Security benefits to the maximum SSI benefit amount if the resource limit has been met. The average monthly benefit under SSI is $405.30. The Netherlands' Tier 1 program provides a basic pension for all Dutch citizens that is more than three times the benefit level possible in the Tier 1 programs of Canada and the United States.

For Tier 2 programs, 65 is the age at which full benefits are available, and all countries except the Netherlands have an age at which partial benefits are available. With the exception of the United States, all other countries provide pension credits for periods of unemployment and include cohabitating partners in eligibility criteria.

Table 3.6 Comparison of Key Public Pension Characteristics in the United States, Canada, the Netherlands, and Sweden

Country	*Tier 1: Mandatory Adequacy, Retirement Income Programs*			*Tier 2: Retirement Income Programs, Savings Public Sector*				
	Coverage type Name of program	*Sets a minimum benefit amount Average Monthly Benefit*	*Age at full benefits Age at partial benefits*	*Pension credits for periods of unemployment (e.g., child rearing, going to school)*	*Includes cohabiting partners in worker benefits*	*Employment after drawing pension benefit does not reduce monthly benefit amount*	*Average monthly benefit*	*Net pension replacement rate for the average wage earner*
Canada	*Resource tested:* GIS *Basic program:* OAS	yes $433.51 (C$447.70) $474.15 (C$489.53)	65 60	X	X	X	$466.80 (C$501.32)	57.9%
Netherlands	*Resource tested:* WWB *Basic program:* AOW	yes $1,393.74 (€944.91) $1,439.27 (€975.78)	65 N/A	*	*	**	Offered via "social partners" in the occupational sector; a target income replacement rate of 70% is the norm	103.2%

(Continued)

Table 3.6 (Continued) Comparison of Key Public Pension Characteristics in the United States, Canada, the Netherlands, and Sweden

Country	Tier 1: Mandatory Adequacy, Retirement Income Programs			Tier 2: Retirement Income Programs, Savings Public Sector				
	Coverage type Name of program	*Sets a minimum benefit amount Average Monthly Benefit*	*Age at full benefits Age at partial benefits*	*Pension credits for periods of unemployment (e.g., child rearing, going to school)*	*Includes cohabitating partners in worker benefits*	*Employment after drawing pension benefit does not reduce monthly benefit amount*	*Average monthly benefit*	*Net pension replacement rate for the average wage earner*
Sweden	*Resource tested:* Maintenance Support *Minimum pension:* Guarantee Pension	yes $1,076.54 (SEK7,597)	65 61	X	X	X	$1,505.53 (SEK10,489)	64.1%
United States	*Resource tested* SSI	$405.30 (€299.14)	65 62			X (only after age 65)	$1,160.20	44.8%

* These situations are covered in the Tier 1 program.

** Most occupational plans allow for work while drawing a pension benefit. Benefit amounts were for 2009.

All countries allow continued employment after full retirement age, which does not reduce pension benefits. The net pension replacement rate in each country for the average earner ranges from a low of 44.8% in the United States to a high of 103.2% in the Netherlands (OECD, 2009b).

We began the chapter by posing some questions about how retirement income policy approaches the complexities of providing for income in later life. As you can see from our review of these four countries, the approach varies markedly. The question facing many government leaders is "How can income security programs maintain their financial viability as the population ages?" We will revisit this issue in more detail in Chapter 10.

For More Information

1. Center for Retirement Research, Boston College
   http://crr.bc.edu/

The Center for Retirement Research at Boston College provides decision makers in the public and private sectors with critical information to better understand the issues facing an aging population. The center's research program spans the four main areas that affect a household's retirement income: (1) Social Security, (2) employer-sponsored pension plans, (3) household saving, and (4) labor market trends among older workers.

2. Social Security Administration
   http://www.ssa.gov

Spend some time visiting the Social Security Administration's website. Everything you need to know about Social Security is there, from the history of the program to current benefit information and hundreds of research publications.

3. Employee Benefit Research Institute
   http://www.ebri.org/

The mission of the Employee Benefit Research Institute is to contribute to, encourage, and enhance the development of sound employee benefit programs and sound public policy through objective research and education.

4. Retirement Research Center, University of Michigan
   http://www.mrrc.isr.umich.edu/

The Retirement Research Center (RRC) promotes high-quality research on retirement and Social Security policy, communicates findings to the policy community and the public, enhances access to relevant research data, and helps train new scholars. The RRC serves the public and policy community as an authoritative source of information on a range of issues related to retirement income security.

5. European Commission
   http://ec.europa.eu/employment_social/spsi/pensions_en.htm

The European Commission on Social Protection offers a number of reports on pensions and pension reforms in the European Union countries. It's a good place to start if you are interested in learning more about other pension programs.

6. Organisation for Economic Co-operation and Development
   http://www.oecd.org

The Organisation for Economic Co-operation and Development (OECD) provides a setting where governments compare policy experiences, seek answers to common problems, identify good practice, and coordinate domestic and international policies. OECD is one of the world's largest publishers of reports and books in the fields of economics and public policy.

7. Pension Calculator: Country-by-Country Comparison
   http://www.oecd.org/document/12/0,3343,en_2649_34757_43024076_1_1_1_1,00
   .html

How much of your earnings will be replaced when you retire? What is the impact of taxes on your future income? Find out what future pension entitlements will be in your country. The OECD has a website that has incorporated all the rules and regulations of the pension systems into a simple pension calculator so that you can assess your future entitlement. For each country, you can choose the age at which you entered the labor market, the rate of return in place for funded, defined contribution pensions, if relevant, as well as your earnings level. Results can be calculated separately for men and women.

Mrs. G., age 82
Canton Ticino, Switzerland

My history is that I was born at Quartino, a village nearby, in 1928. I was the only child, which was very unusual in those days, and I felt special. But in reality, it was harder, especially at school. I had no brothers or sisters to help me, so at times I was a bit aggressive. My mother was a dressmaker. We lived with my grandparents. I went to school but only for few years like all of the other children. I would have liked to go longer, but when I told a school friend about it she was so surprised that she made me feel I was doing the wrong thing. So I started to work in a factory at 21 years of age. I got married and came over here to live; I am still here. I have a son who does not live very far and two daughters. I see them quite often, especially the daughter who lives here with us.

I get up not too early, I clean the house, I make lunch for myself, my husband, one of my daughters, and my niece, so we eat all together. In the afternoon, I do laundry, ironing; I never stand still. Maybe in the evening. I go to the swimming pool once a week, because it helps to ease muscular pain. I do not go out for walk because I have no time. I am always going up and down this house, including lots of stairs. In the evening, I watch TV, I read the newspaper. I never go to bed before 1 a.m. or 1:30 a.m.

My health could be better, but it could be worse. I cannot complain. I have the basic "cassa malati," which covers also for my swimming lesson, as I do it for health reasons. I just pay 10% towards it. For the doctor or medication, I pay 10% towards it. If I need to go to the dentist, the "cassa malati" covers only SRF500 per year. When I got my hearing aid, only SFR1,000 were covered; the rest, I had to pay it. It depends what kind of insurance you have; some cover more some less. If you need a visit to the eye doctor, it is covered. I just pay 10% and SFR300 towards new glasses.

I receive the AVS [Swiss pension] as everyone. The age for retiring for women is age 62; for men is age 65. It is enough because we do not spend a lot of money; we never go on holiday, not because we cannot afford it but because we like to stay at home. If my pension was not enough to meet my needs or I had no family who could help, there are associations like *Latte* to help you, but it cost money unless you have nothing. They check your income, but while alive, nobody can check your bank accounts. If someone is really, really poor, the government pays for everything.

How am I experiencing aging? This is a million Swiss Francs question. Aging is not that nice. Before 70 years old, I was okay, and then I started to think that I had only few years left to live. I guess what really scares me is thinking about illnesses. It is normal that years go by and that you get old, but you hear it all the time about people who don't understand anything anymore or live like vegetables, and you become a burden to your relatives. Obviously, you cannot think about it all the time, and you must take all of the good things that happen to you day after day.

What I like about my age? Perhaps the thought of not going to work every day, but besides that, nothing has really changed in my life. My husband and I have arguments all the time for silly things, who is coming to dinner or lunch, are there going to be too many people or too few, what are we going to eat, silly things really. We are very fortunate because we have a nice family and our arguments are never really serious. If we are in a bad mood, someone might come, like my granddaughter, and the mood must change, will change. We are fortunate because without our children, our life would be very sad and flat.

What I expect from the future? Health, for us, my family, and other people, too, win the lotto, but I never play so I will never win.

What advice would I give students about growing older? I don't know . . . look after their body and health . . . be affectionate with words and gestures with the people you really care for. I say this because I have never been affectionate, perhaps because my family understands I love them because of what I do for them, but it is true that I was never taught how to express freely my feelings.

Ruth, age 74, England

Mrs. X, age, mid-80's, China

4

Employment Policies

> *The bottom line is that population aging is both a challenge and an opportunity, . . . a tremendous opportunity for all of us to spend more rewarding years at work and in retirement. . . . Seizing this opportunity will require the cooperation of government, employers, trade unions, and civil society to adopt and implement a new agenda of age-friendly employment policies and practices.*
>
> —Organisation for Economic Co-operation and Development, 2006

> *I was forced to quit my job at age 52 and 1/2. I never found work after that. . . . I sent out thousands of letters. . . . I was told at age 53 I was too old, too expensive. I was willing to take positions I was overqualified for, . . . but no one answered me, . . . not even one interview during the 4 years I looked.*
>
> —Ms. L., age 65, Paris

With the aging of the population, many countries face a talent drain as their older workers retire or are removed from the workforce at a very young age, like Ms. L. (Charman, Feinsod, & Arthurs, 2007; Organisation for Economic Co-operation and Development [OECD], 2006). The workforce aged 15 to 49 in most developed economies is shrinking, and these employees do not have the long-term knowledge and experience that characterizes the over-50 workforce.

Countries such as Australia, Canada, the Netherlands, the United Kingdom, and the United States that have higher birth rates and supportive employment policies for older adults are better positioned to manage changes in the workforce than countries such as France and Germany, whose workforce and policies are in transition (Cook, 2006). Countries such as Italy and Japan are especially challenged because of their lower birth rates and few supportive age-related work policies. As we discussed in Chapter 3, the employment rates in most countries decline after the age of 50, but in some European countries, such as Belgium and France, labor force participation drops precipitously and few people are still working after age 65.

Table 4.1 shows labor force participation statistics for men and women aged 25 and older in a variety of countries throughout the world. The majority of European, North American, and Oceania

Table 4.1 Labor Force Participation Rates by Age and Sex for Selected Countries: Circa 2006

Country	Year	Male						Female					
		25 to 44 years	45 to 49 years	50 to 54 years	55 to 59 years	60 to 64 years	65 years and over	25 to 44 years	45 to 49 years	50 to 54 years	55 to 59 years	60 to 64 years	65 years and over
Western Europe													
Austria	2006	94.4	93.1	87.6	69.1	21.9	5.5	81.7	82.6	75.0	41.9	10.1	2.2
Belgium	2006	93.6	91.4	85.2	58.3	22.6	2.7	82.0	72.8	61.1	36.2	10.3	1.0
France	2005	94.6	94.1	90.3	62.5	15.4	1.6	80.8	83.2	77.3	53.4	13.4	0.8
Germany	2006	93.8	94.3	91.2	82.0	42.3	5.0	79.7	83.5	78.7	65.6	24.4	2.2
Greece	2006	95.4	95.6	89.4	74.0	45.2	7.4	74.2	64.0	51.3	33.5	21.8	2.1
Italy	2006	91.2	94.0	89.0	58.0	28.9	6.1	67.0	62.3	54.0	32.8	10.2	1.2
Eastern Europe													
Bulgaria	2006	86.7	84.1	79.2	66.1	38.6	4.6	79.2	82.8	76.5	53.4	11.7	1.5
Czech Republic	2006	95.8	94.6	90.6	83.1	36.1	6.6	77.3	91.8	88.2	51.2	13.1	2.5
Poland	2006	92.5	84.7	75.7	51.6	26.8	8.2	79.3	77.9	59.8	25.3	12.4	3.3
Northern America/ Oceania													
Australia	2006	89.9	89.2	86.1	75.7	56.4	12.1	73.0	78.3	73.4	57.9	33.5	4.3
Canada	2006	92.0	90.8	87.8	76.1	53.3	12.1	81.8	82.6	78.1	62.3	37.1	5.2
New Zealand	2006	91.1	92.6	91.6	87.2	73.1	16.8	74.3	81.9	80.0	71.7	50.0	8.0
United States	2006	91.9	89.8	86.1	77.7	58.6	20.3	75.2	77.2	74.7	66.7	47.0	11.7

Table 4.1 (Continued)   Labor Force Participation Rates by Age and Sex for Selected Countries: Circa 2006

Country	Year	Male						Female					
		25 to 44 years	45 to 49 years	50 to 54 years	55 to 59 years	60 to 64 years	65 years and over	25 to 44 years	45 to 49 years	50 to 54 years	55 to 59 years	60 to 64 years	65 years and over
Africa													
South Africa	2003	82.9	80.8	73.7	63.5	40.6	25.6	65.4	62.6	50.9	38.4	15.2	9.6
Uganda	2003	(NA)	97.1	94.6	93.9	91.4	72.9	(NA)	93.5	92.2	87.1	80.3	53.7
Asia													
Bangladesh	2003	99.2	99.5	99.2	97.3	87.8	66.1	27.3	22.6	19.9	17.1	13.4	8.7
Japan	2006	96.1	96.9	95.7	93.2	70.9	29.3	68.0	74.0	70.5	60.3	40.2	13.0
Pakistan	2006	97.3	97.6	95.8	90.7	77.5	49.3	23.1	26.5	22.5	22.8	19.1	11.5
Singapore	2006	97.1	96.5	93.3	81.9	62.5	22.0	74.5	66.2	59.5	44.6	26.2	8.3
South Korea	2006	90.5	93.1	89.7	79.9	68.5	42.0	61.4	64.4	58.5	49.7	43.8	22.7
Turkey	2006	93.2	82.0	65.4	51.3	39.8	22.0	30.8	24.8	21.8	18.5	14.5	6.6
Latin America													
Argentina	2006	95.1	95.3	92.6	87.3	76.8	28.3	68.3	67.2	62.1	55.6	38.7	10.7
Brazil	2004	94.7	92.1	85.8	77.6	64.9	35.1	71.6	65.4	57.3	45.5	30.9	14.1
Chile	2006	93.9	95.3	91.4	86.1	73.2	26.9	55.6	51.9	48.4	40.1	25.3	7.7
Guatemala	2004	94.7	91.4	93.8	92.5	92.2	66.7	52.0	53.2	44.6	39.7	30.3	23.7
Mexico	2006	96.0	95.4	92.5	88.2	74.0	45.8	52.6	50.4	44.0	35.3	28.5	14.7
Peru	2006	95.3	98.7	94.6	87.0	65.5	28.8	70.1	67.0	56.2	39.2	34.9	15.3
Uruguay	2006	99.7	97.9	96.4	91.2	68.8	19.7	75.4	75.9	69.4	58.7	39.0	8.4

(NA) Not available.
Source: Kinsella and He (2009).

countries have labor participation rates of less than 9% among older females aged 65 and over—with the exception of the United States, which has a female participation rate of 11.7%. Like their female counterparts, labor participation rates for older males living in European countries also are less than 9%. However, in North America and Oceania, a higher percentage of males than females are in the labor force (ranging from 12.1%–20.3% for males compared with 4.3%–11.7% for females). Many of the countries in Africa, Asia, and Latin America report higher labor participation rates, particularly among the male 65+ age group.

Each country has its own retirement and work policy culture that shapes how an aging workforce is handled and how an "older worker" is defined and treated. Across the globe, many countries have well-established *early* retirement cultures. As an example, India is a country where an estimated one-fifth of the current workforce—from shop-floor workers to top managers—are expected to leave the workforce by the year 2010 because they will have passed India's retirement age of 58 (Srinivasan, 2007).

Increasing life expectancy and low fertility rates in numerous countries also mean that there are fewer active workers to support retirees than in the past (see Figure 4.1). High levels of pension spending have driven many nations to reform their pension systems and encourage people to remain in the workforce longer. In the European Union, for example, increasing employment rates for all workers, in particular women and older people, is a key element in the strategy for making social security systems sustainable at the height of population aging (Hessel, 2009).

The worldwide economic crisis of recent years has further challenged labor markets and shaped the climate facing policymakers (United Nations, 2009c). There is a tension between the temporary boom of job openings when workers in economies with high unemployment rates retire and the added pressure placed on income security systems (e.g., pensions). In addition, gains in life expectancy after traditional retirement age have many older individuals reassessing the feasibility of their plans, considering the impact of retirement on access to health insurance, and often exploring options for remaining in the workforce. Along with personal and financial motivations for continued employment in later life, labor systems are encountering an increased desire among aging adults to work longer, particularly among those who are well-educated—those for whom more meaningful jobs may be available that can be performed well into older ages (Copeland, 2010). In this chapter, we will highlight policies influencing late-life labor participation and government-supported work training programs for older adults being implemented in the United States, Brazil, Japan, Finland, France, and Italy.

United States

In 2011, the first of the baby boomers will turn 65, the age at which generations preceding them—as well as their own cohort—expect to retire. The percentage of individuals in the labor force beyond the age of 65 drops significantly. In 2008, 73.1% of adults aged 55 to 59 were in the civilian labor force compared with 16.8% of persons aged 65 and older (Copeland, 2010; U.S. Department of Labor, 2010). In addition to age, labor force participation varies by sex and race/ethnicity. Approximately 22.0% of men and 13.0% of women aged 65 and older were in the civilian labor force in 2008.

| Figure 4.1 | Ratio of Retirement-Aged to Working Aged Population by Sex: 2005 and 2040 |

Males

Country	2005	2040
Australia	21	42
Denmark	23	44
Finland	31	58
France	37	62
Italy	36	76
Japan	19	40
Netherlands	29	59
Spain	31	72
Turkey	11	29
United States	18	34

(x-axis: 0, 10, 20, 30, 40, 50, 60, 70, 80)

Females

Country	2005	2040
Australia	31	60
Denmark	39	65
Finland	45	79
France	46	76
Italy	48	96
Japan	35	71
Netherlands	37	72
Spain	36	77
Turkey	14	36
United States	28	48

(x-axis: 0, 20, 40, 60, 80, 100, 120)

Legend: ☐ 2005 ☐ 2040

Notes: Ratios represent the number of people at or above the average effective retirement age per 100 people between age 20 and the average effective retirement age as calculated by OECD for 2005. Ratios for 2040 assume no change in the average age of retirement between 2005 and 2040.
Source: Kinsella and He (2009).

Older White Americans had the highest labor-force participation, followed by Asian Americans, Hispanic Americans, and Black Americans.

Many older Americans want to continue working beyond the traditional age of retirement or need to do so for financial reasons. But as noted in a report by the Taskforce on the Aging of the American Workforce (2008), older individuals often face challenges to full participation in the labor market, including a difficult job market for older workers with outdated skills, negative perceptions of older workers' abilities, health issues and disabilities, and the lack of flexible work arrangements to enable a greater work-life balance. Although the United States does not have an overarching policy regarding the employment of older workers, some initial retirement income policies created incentives for early retirement, whereas more recent government policies have encouraged older individuals to continue working.

Age Discrimination Policies

Challenges facing the aging of the American workforce came to light with the passage of the Age Discrimination Employment Act (ADEA) in 1967. The original legislation stipulated that employees 40 to 65 years old could not be discriminated against on the basis of age in any employment decision, including hiring, discharges, layoffs, promotions, wages, and health care coverage. The 1986 amendments to the ADEA prohibit most employers from setting a mandatory retirement age. The responsibility of enforcing the ADEA falls to the Equal Employment Opportunity Commission, but most states also have their own protections in place.

In 1990, Congress enacted the Older Workers Benefit Protection Act, which further clarified and reinforced that discrimination based on age in virtually all forms of employee benefits is unlawful. Specifically, the Act established regulations prohibiting age discrimination for most employee fringe benefits (Wiencek, 1991). It provides statutory recognition of early-retirement programs and enacted into law the "equal benefit" or "equal cost" principle, requiring employers to provide older workers with benefits at least equal to those provided for younger workers, unless the employers can prove that the cost of providing an equal benefit is greater for an older worker than for a younger worker.

Additional legislation to support and sustain the aging workforce passed in 2000. The Senior Citizens' Freedom to Work Act eliminated the earnings limitation for Social Security (see Chapter 3 for details about the Social Security program) for workers older than 65. The passing of this Act was heralded by some members of Congress as the "dawn of a new age for older Americans." This law allows those older adults already working to receive more wages without reduction of their Social Security earnings and is intended to encourage older adults to remain in or rejoin the labor force.

Employment and Training Programs

The federal government has also been instrumental in creating employment programs for older adults. Experience Works (2009; formerly known as Green Thumb) is the United States' oldest and largest operator of employment and training programs for older Americans. It was founded in 1965 by the National Farmers Union as part of President Johnson's War on Poverty. Through Experience Works, low-income individuals 55 years or older receive training experience at an approved government or private nonprofit agency, educational opportunities, counseling, and information to help them find and keep a job.

The Senior Community Service Employment Program (SCSEP) provides subsidized minimum-wage jobs in community service positions in public and nonprofit organizational settings for persons aged 55 and older whose family incomes are no more than 25% above the poverty level (U.S. Department of Labor, 2009a). This program began as a demonstration project funded by Congress in 1969. As a result of its success, regulatory financing was established in 1973. In 1978, the program became Title V of the Older Americans Act (see Chapter 7 for details about the Older Americans Act). SCSEP is managed by the Department of Labor.

Although not focused specifically on older adults, there are other government-funded programs available to assist citizens in retaining their place in the labor force. For example, the Trade Adjustment Assistance (TAA) program is a federal program established under the Trade Act of 1974. The TAA program provides aid to workers who lose their jobs or whose hours of work and wages are reduced as a result of increased imports. Administered by the Department of Labor in cooperation with the states, the TAA offers a variety of benefits and reemployment services to assist unemployed workers in preparing for and obtaining suitable employment. Support services for this program include training, job search and relocation allowances, income support, and other reemployment services (U.S. Department of Labor, 2009a).

The Workforce Investment Act of 1998 mandates integration of national and state job training programs. The Workforce Investment Act replaced the Job Training Partnership Act of 1982, which established federal assistance programs that provide job training to the economically disadvantaged and other individuals facing serious barriers to employment. Incorporating many of the functions and services delivered through the Job Training Partnership Act, the goal of the Workforce Investment Act is to find jobs and arrange for training for all workers who are laid off, including older workers and homemakers who were formerly dependents. Under this act, a locally driven "one-stop" service delivery system is mandated, integrating a broad array of employment and training programs.

Brazil

Among members of the OECD, Brazil claims an unusual combination of a relatively young population and relatively high expenditure on social security (Giambiagi & de Mello, 2006). Currently, there is no minimum retirement age for those working in the private sector in Brazil. The average retirement age in this sector is 53 years. Men and women in the civil service who were active as of 1998 can still retire at 53 and 48 years, respectively, while those who entered service later can retire at 60 and 55 years, with exceptions for even earlier retirement among some special groups (e.g., teachers). Because these policies support relatively early retirement, pension benefits are paid approximately 5 years longer to Brazilian citizens than to persons in many other systems. Thus, Brazil's government and economic system is ill-prepared to face the expected doubling of the share of population members 60 and older between 2005 and 2030 (Giambiagi & de Mello, 2006). Despite struggling with early retirement trends, Brazil's employment rate of individuals 65 and older—at 24.3%—is higher than that of the United States (Bureau of Labor Statistics and International Labor Office, 2009). Labor participation of those 55 to 64, however, is substantially higher at 56.8%.

Before the mid-1990s, labor market policies in Brazil were very sparse and rarely enforced. During the mid- and late 1990s, however, the government began to expand and diversify programs in response to strain from high unemployment and poverty across the nation (Berg, Ernst, & Auer, 2006). Beginning in 1994, the Brazilian government began pushing for a number of changes to improve its pension fund and retirement system. Most central to the executive branch was the issue of preventing individuals from retiring before age 60 (Marques & Batich, 2003). But despite numerous attempts to establish a consistent public and private sector minimum retirement age, the government was unable to pass any comprehensive legislation due to strong opposition from labor unions and others concerned with the prolonged employment of poor citizens who typically begin working when they are still in elementary school (Marques & Batich, 2003).

Age Discrimination Policies

Article 3, Section IV of Brazil's Federal Constitution of 1988 states that one of the fundamental objectives of the Republic of Brazil is "to promote the well-being of all people without prejudice based on origin, race, sex, color, age, or any other form of discrimination" (Inter-American Commission on Human Rights, 1997). Aside from the broad discrimination protections set forth in this constitution, however, aging adults in the workforce are not yet afforded many special policy safeguards. In the late 1980s and early 1990s, in fact, favoritism toward younger technically skilled and better-educated workers in the Brazilian marketplace became prevalent (Ius Laboris, 2009). Another aspect of age discrimination that also drew the attention of policymakers at this time was the existence of an age limit for employment in certain state positions, allowing the hiring of only workers 18 to 35 years old.

With increased awareness of age discrimination coming to light in the mid- to late 1990s, Brazil's government began to strive for some protections for older workers; however, many of these policies are still up for national debate. Rather than passing specific age discrimination policies, the government has passed laws offering financial incentives to companies that maintain a certain quota of workers 45 years and older (Ius Laboris, 2009). Plans for additional incentives for employers maintaining a significant contingent of workers over 45 are still pending official passage.

Employment and Training Programs

Government-subsidized employment programs did not exist in Brazil until 2003, when *Primeiro Emprego* (First Employment) was introduced. But this program specifically focuses on the generation of decent jobs for *younger* workers aged 16 to 24, excluding employees at the other end of the age spectrum from any assistance (Berg et al., 2006). There is no job-training program specifically targeting older adults in Brazil. Some aging workers might access services through the *Plano National de Qualificacao do Trabalhador* (PLANFOR; National Professional Training Program). This program was implemented in 1996 to improve the skills of the overall labor force (Berg et al., 2006). Training focuses on the unemployed, those at high risk of becoming unemployed, micro- and small producers, and self-employed workers. Although records have not captured how many older adults fall into these target categories in Brazil, it is likely that some struggling older workers have represented at least a small portion of the 11 million workers trained under PLANFOR between the years of 1996 and 2001 (Berg et al., 2006).

Japan

Japan has a higher labor force participation rate among older workers compared with most other industrialized nations. In 2006, 30.2% of persons aged 60 and older were employed, placing Japan third among OECD countries (International Labor Organization, 2008). Among males, 73.1% of those aged 60 to 64 and 50.1% of those aged 65 to 69 work. The percentages of older females who work in the same age groups are 43.5% and 28.2%, respectively (Yamada, 2009). Five factors help explain why Japanese older workers—men in particular—remain in the labor force as long as they do:

1. Economic necessity

2. Prevalence of self-employment

3. High cultural value placed on work

4. Good health and long life expectancy

5. The government's active role in facilitating the labor force participation of older workers (Williamson & Higo, 2009)

In 1971, the government enacted the Law Concerning Stabilization of Employment of Older Persons (Stabilization Law), which fosters policy measures designed to comprehensively extend working lives of older citizens for whom renewed labor force participation is necessary (Williamson & Higo, 2009). The 2006 revision of the Stabilization Law mandated that employers fully implement at least one of the following three measures by April 2013:

1. Fully abolish mandatory retirement rules in the workplace

2. Gradually increase the compulsory retirement age to at least age 65

3. Introduce employment policies designed to continually employ older workers until at least age 65 (Ministry of Health, Labor, and Welfare [MHLW], 2007)

Age Discrimination Policies

There are no age discrimination laws in Japan. The main policy endeavor to protect the employment of older workers is to raise the mandatory retirement age as outlined in the Stabilization Law (Higo & Yamada, 2009). Under the law's 2004 amended form, mandatory retirement age was raised from age 55 to age 60. The three measures mandated in the latest revision of the Stabilization Law (see above) also have supported prolonged employment. To comply with the Stabilization Law's mandate while simultaneously dealing with pressure to reduce costs, most firms in Japan have chosen the last option of introducing employment policies to continue employing workers aged 65 and older (Williamson & Higo, 2009). With this option, they are still allowed to enforce mandatory retirement but can rehire retired employees in temporary or part-time positions with reduced wages and responsibilities. Approximately 91.5% of Japanese corporations have mandatory retirement age rules, including 100% of corporations with more than 5,000 employees and 99.8% of those with between 1,000 and 4,999 employees (MHLW, 2007).

Employment and Training Programs

The government has taken two directions in its continual efforts to extend the working lives of older citizens. Since 1980, Silver Human Resource Centers (SHRCs) have operated nationwide, with each chapter fully subsidized by the national and municipal governments. The SHRCs provide persons aged 60 and older with opportunities for regular employment, as well as temporary, contract, part-time, or other forms of paid work (Williamson & Higo, 2009). In addition, with the 2002 amendments of the Stabilization Law, a program called Senior Work Programs has been organized by the Federation of SHRC chapters. Registered members receive free skills training, education, counseling services for job matching, and job interview preparation with the cooperation of a variety of business owners' associations and public employment security institutions.

The 2002 amendment of the Stabilization Law also introduced a subsidy program called Partial Subsidy to Promote Older Persons' Business and Self-Employment Opportunities, which provides financial support for older retirees seeking to start their own businesses. The program pays up to two-thirds of the entire cost for the first 6 months of the start-up process (MHLW, 2007). In collaboration with the private sector, this subsidy program offers free training, education, and consultation for participants.

The second effort to retain older employees in the labor force provides incentives for employers to continually employ them until at least age 65. In 1995, the government passed the Employment Continuation Benefit for the Aged as part of an employment insurance system to motivate employers to continually employ workers until at least age 65. The program allows employers to reduce the wage level of their older workers to as low as the maximum amount of the benefit, which, in theory, maintains the overall income from work of older workers (OECD, 2004b). Specifically, the program compensates workers aged 60 to 64 who experience a wage reduction of more than 25% after mandatory retirement. Older workers are eligible to receive this subsidy for up to 2 years. In FY 2007, the government spent about 267,000,000 JPY ($3,120,242) on this benefit program (Williamson & Higo, 2009). Critics of this incentive plan have noted that the benefit is not targeted at the most disadvantaged groups among older persons—such as the unskilled long-term unemployed—but, rather, supports older workers who have benefited the most from lifetime employment practices and seniority wages (OECD, 2004b).

France

In France, as in many European countries, older workers compose a small percentage of the labor force (International Labor Organization, 2008). Only 1.6% of men aged 65 and older and less than 1% of their female counterparts are gainfully employed. Although the official age of retirement in France is 60, labor force participation begins dropping by age 55. Approximately 90% of men aged 50 to 54 are employed compared with 62.5% of men aged 56 to 59. Similarly, 77.3% of women aged 50 to 54 and 53.4% aged 55 to 59 are employed. Retirement and unemployment policies that make early retirement attractive contribute to the lack of workforce participation among older people in France (OECD, 2005a). Although a number of French policy reforms in recent years have attempted to restrict this heavy access to early formal retirement, the phasing out of early retirement schemes has been offset by a rise in the number of unemployed older adults exempt from active job search (Zaidi, 2008). Disability benefits are another pathway through which adults circumvent new policies and adhere to the traditional culture of early retirement in France.

But France may be facing major reforms to its pension system in the coming years. Compared to other OECD countries, French social security benefits have historically been very generous (Zaidi, 2008). President Sarkozy and Prime Minister Fillon have committed to plans for "major" pension reform, the freezing of core public spending, and raising the retirement age within the year 2010 (Reuters, 2010). Government officials are in agreement that impending reforms are necessary before government debt levels become unsustainable. Workers and unions in the country have been highly resistant to any suggested changes in retirement policy in recent years and have already voiced strong opposition to the current planned reforms, setting the stage for major policy dispute during the remainder of 2010 (BBC News, 2010).

Age Discrimination Policies

Nondiscrimination is a central aspect of French labor laws and has been incorporated in several statutes of the labor code (Lokiec, 2008). As of 2001, age was added to the list of prohibited discriminations in Article L 122-45 of the labor code. Articles 122-14-2 and L 321-13 also directly address the issue of age discrimination by (a) negating any work contract that specifies age as a grounds for termination of employment and (b) requiring employers that dismiss an employee of age 50 or older who is eligible for unemployment benefits to pay a significant contribution (sometimes a year's wages) to the unemployment insurance administration (Lokiec, 2008; OECD, 2006). Because prosecution of labor law violations is often difficult, French labor policies even go so far as to include provisions for discrimination *prevention* by the National Commission for Collective Bargaining. According to Bloch (2006), however, antidiscrimination laws have been applied generously and consistently in French courts. In fact, "French courts tend to extend the application of labor laws against discrimination to every employment contract, even if the work is limited to a definite period of time or to training" (p. 724). The labor code has also been modified to place the burden of proof

---

BOX 4.1 Policy to People Link: ANACT's Management of the Ages: France

To address low-employment problems in France, the National Agency for Improvement of Working Conditions (ANACT in French) assumed "management of the ages" as a policy priority. This arm of ANACT focuses on the prevention of discrimination against older workers and encourages company leaders to fully capitalize on the knowledge and expertise of older employees—reframing the image of senior workers in France so that they are seen as an asset rather than a burden to employers.

(Continued)

(Continued)

A limited number of companies have fully embraced this initiative—each in its own way—and those that have report successes in dealing with an aging workforce. For example, Pierre Lionet of Lionet Décor, an interior decorating company in France—realizing that a quarter of his employees were over 50 and that he may soon see a talent drain in his business—chose to implement age management by placing an emphasis on revitalizing training arrangements and knowledge transmission. Lionet implemented a company-wide "age asset" program that consisted of a formalized tutoring system for exchanges between senior and younger workers. The company reported a resultant network of ongoing trusting relationships and satisfying educational exchanges between older "tutors" and their "students" in the business. For more information, go to http://hal .archives-ouvertes.fr/docs/00/26/48/01/PDF/Art-GENDRON-Cedefop-OW-HAL.pdf.

in discrimination cases on the employer (to prove lack of guilt) as opposed to placing that burden on the victim of age discrimination.

Employment and Training Programs

In addition to strong legal protections against age discrimination, France has implemented programs that attempt to combat the loss of older members of the workforce. The "inter-occupational fund" (OECD, 2006, p. 120) is a government program supported by employees and employers that focuses on promoting lifelong learning. The program takes a case management approach by auditing the skill levels of experienced, individual workers, providing "training passports" that act as resumes, and building "credits" that workers can use to apply for training (if they have been at the company for more than 1 year)—or if they lose their job, they can use the credits to subsidize the training costs to qualify for new employment. Additionally, ANACT (active from 2004–2008; OECD, 2006, p. 132) brought together policymakers, trade union officials, and employers to raise awareness and help employers facilitate older workers in the labor market. The focus of this program is the maintenance of good age-management practices in the workplace. According to the OECD (2006), regional arms of ANACT advise companies; innovate new ways to confront technological, organizational, and social change; and disseminate best practices regarding optimal administration of an aging workforce.

Finland

Approximately 14% of men and 10% of women beyond the official retirement age of 65 participate in the Finland labor force (International Labor Organization, 2008). Unlike some other European countries, persons in Finland are more likely to remain in the labor force throughout their 50s and mid-60s. Approximately 87.3% of men aged 50 to 54, 75.1% aged 56 to 59, and 42.7% aged 60 to 65 are employed. Likewise, 88.5% of women aged 50 to 54, 75.1% aged 55 to 59, and 40.1% aged 60 to 65 remain in the labor force.

Over the past decade, Finland, when compared with other OECD countries, has implemented one of the most comprehensive employment training and support networks to promote longer working lives for older adults (OECD, 2006, p. 131). After the serious economic recession of the 1990s, the Finnish National Program on Aging Workers (active from 1998–2002), the Workplace Development Program (begun in 1996), the VETO program (2003–2007), and other short-term initiatives have been implemented to extend success in the job market for aging Finnish citizens. These programs focus on occupational health and safety, continuous skills training, prolonged job satisfaction, and general health promotion. The policies supporting these national programs aim to change perceptions among employers in addition to increasing the employability of workers (OECD, 2004a); however, until unemployment and disability policies are reformed, many older workers and employers, similar to those in France, will use these generous benefits as gateways to early retirement.

Age Discrimination Policies

Age discrimination is covered under Finland's Nondiscrimination Act No. 21/2004. The Act addresses a wide range of discrimination issues in the workplace, community, and military settings, but Section 6 focuses exclusively on "prohibition of discrimination" in any of these settings. The national policy clearly states that "nobody may be discriminated against on the basis of age, . . . health, disability, or other personal characteristics" (Ministry of Labor, 2004, p. 2). The Act proceeds to specify that "a supplier of work or benefits . . . who has infringed the provisions of Section 6 or 8 based on age . . . shall pay the injured part compensation for the suffering caused by such discrimination" (p. 3). Compensation is limited, however, to no more than 15,000 euros.

Employment and Training Programs

One notable area in which Finland excels is adult and continuing education. Employment-related adult education is free, and enrichment adult education carries a fee that is either partly subsidized by the government or paid by individuals (Nyyssola & Hamalainen, 2001, p. 36; see also Turner, Toft, & Witte, 2008). However, the older adults who may most benefit from it—those with low levels of education—participate at lower rates than those with higher educational levels (Nyyssola & Hamalainen, 2001). Many older adult education participants are full-time workers but participate for personal rather than employment-related reasons (Nyyssola & Hamalainen, 2001).

Italy

Italy mirrors the European experience of low participation rates among older workers. In 2006, only 6.1% of men and 1.2% of women aged 65 and older were gainfully employed (International Labor Organization, 2008). Although the official age of retirement in Italy is 65 for men and 60 for women, overall labor force participation for individuals between the ages of 55 and 65 is under 30% (Contini & Leombruni, 2006). The low employment rate of older workers is partly explained by their low level of educational attainment compared with younger cohorts, which is compounded by limited training opportunities throughout their careers (Rymkevitch & Villosio, 2007). For individuals between the ages of 55 and 64, 67% with a high school diploma are still active in the labor force as compared with 44% of those who finished only grade school and 22% of those with only elementary schooling. This gap is even larger for women, as the employment rate of highly educated women between the ages of 50 and 64 is more than three times the rate of their less-educated female counterparts.

The decline in labor force participation patterns began when recession conditions stimulated the development of schemes to encourage older workers to retire early (Contini & Leombruni, 2006). For example, the Italian Social Security System, as well as large companies that had high numbers of older workers, offered financial incentives to those who agreed to retire early. Since the mid-1990s, the Italian pension system has been substantially reformed, and due to stricter age and contributions requirements, the general trend toward early retirement seems to have slowed.

Age Discrimination Policies

In November 2000, Italy established a general framework for antidiscrimination, which also prohibited age discrimination. The 2003 legislative decree, titled "Equal Treatment in Employment and Conditions," outlined provisions concerning the implementation of equal treatment of persons regardless of religion or belief, disability, age, or sexual orientation (Italian Republic, 2003). The principle of equal treatment with regard to employment and occupation applies to all persons in both the private and public sectors and includes access to employment, conditions of employment, career advancement and training, remuneration, and conditions of dismissal. However, employees of all ages are required to meet the demands of a particular job, and there may be differential employment based on legitimate goals of labor policy, labor market, and training. Beginning in December 2005 and continuing every 5 years thereafter, the Ministry of Labor and Social Policy submits a report to the Commission Chamber of Deputies and the Senate of the Republic regarding the application of this law.

According to Rymkevitch and Villosio (2007), age discrimination and the social inclusion of older people in Italy attracts little attention from employers and government. The main issue of concern in the Italian labor market has been how to promote the employment of younger people, even if this is to the detriment of older workers. Promotion of early retirement schemes has generally not been considered as discriminatory by trade unions, and in fact for many decades, based on a broad social consensus, these schemes have been used extensively in economic restructuring. However, empirical

BOX 4.2 Policy to People Link: The Biagi Law at the Local Level: Italy

One way in which the Italian government has attempted to curb its high unemployment rate among older adults is by expanding workplace flexibility. The 2003 Biagi law addresses this issue by changing the rigidity in the Italian labor market regarding employment options. In concert with the law's provisions against age discrimination in the workplace, it paves the way for companies to expand part-time, fixed-term, and temporary positions. Reforms are slowly reaching smaller communities, such as the Italian province of Bergamo, where local leaders signed an agreement in 2004 regarding the introduction of part-time work options and incentives to expand such employment at local companies. The agreement is intended to adapt the law to the unique local labor market, and province leaders plan to revisit the plan on a yearly basis in order to optimize its impact in the region. For more information, go to www.eurofound.europa.eu/eiro/2004/08/inbrief/it0408102n.htm.

studies show that forcing older workers into retirement in order to stimulate employment among the young does not work and may even be counterproductive (Pestieau, 2003).

There is limited and often contradictory data on the existence of age discrimination in Italy (Rymkevitch & Villosio, 2007). For example, a multicountry study of more than 70,000 workers found that almost one-third of the Italian workers who reported acts of discrimination encountered age bias. Reports of age discrimination were most common both among younger workers (under age 20) and older workers (aged 45–54) when applying for a job. Analyses of more than 5,000 position announcements published between 1993 and 2004 revealed that 42.4% included explicit age requirements, with most advertising for persons under the age of 44; only 13.1% sought a person over the age of 45. Others reporting discrimination against older workers suggest the problem also exists with regard to job training (Paulli & Tagliabue, 2002).

Employment and Training Programs

Employment and training programs in Italy targeting older workers are limited and often underutilized (Focarelli & Zanghieri, 2005). Even though about 50% of older workers are employed in firms that run training courses, less than 15% of them attend the courses. Moreover, only 7% of older workers with low qualifications receive training compared with 20% of those with higher qualifications. Until the passing of Act No. 236/1993, which explicitly stipulated and financially supported vocational training for workers between the ages of 45 and 64, older workers typically were excluded from such programs (Rymkevitch & Villosio, 2007). Apart from Act No. 236/1993, there is no national-level policy aimed at lifelong learning for a specific age group.

The few work incentive programs that exist in Italy generally aim to postpone retirement. Law 243/2004 supported the Superbonus program, which gave a tax incentive to workers who worked past retirement age (Focarelli & Zanghieri, 2005). From October 2004 through December 2007, those individuals who were eligible for retirement (i.e., those who were at least 57 years old and had made at least 35 years' worth of social security contributions) but decided to postpone retirement for at least 2 years and continue to work were granted a tax-free incentive equal to their contribution to social security. One critique of this plan was that only high-income workers really benefited and thus participated in the program (Boeri & Brugiavini, 2008). Confcommercio, an employers' organization representing small businesses in the service sector, reports that its affiliates wish to keep older workers in employment in order to enable them to transfer their skills to younger workers and supports the use of older workers as instructors for younger ones (Rymkevitch & Villosio, 2007). Other programs are regionally based, such as the L'Incontro Cooperative (Naegele & Walker, 2007), a nonprofit organization that recruits older maintenance workers from the region's local industries to work as instructors in protected job centers. The cooperative offers part-time and flex-time benefits to retired workers.

Summary

Labor policy leaders in both developed and developing countries are in agreement on one matter—it is paramount, in the face of rapid population aging, that workers remain in the workforce longer now than they have at any other time in history. Solutions to an aging workforce, however, are fraught with dilemmas based on individual national scenarios. At the crux of many policy debates is the struggle between protecting workers' rights and allowing companies to remain competitive in the global marketplace. Raising the age of retirement makes sense in many countries but generates questions such as how will this change affect workers in developing countries where individuals typically enter the workforce at a very young age? How will employers be able to absorb increases in retirement package and wage costs or accommodate the health needs of a substantially older workforce?

Governments are struggling to determine what constitutes a reasonable expectation of lifetime employment and what support employers can realistically provide for older workers while maintaining a viable business. Increasing flexibility regarding employment options or providing cash incentives to older workers and employers who extend workplace participation are strategies that have proven successful in many locations. But these approaches have a tendency to favor older workers who are already economically advantaged while having little impact on the lives of less-skilled employees. Depending on policy interpretation and implementation, workplace flexibility may even open loopholes for companies to manipulate options in order to avoid paying adequate benefits (e.g., use of part-time or temporary hires).

Another central dilemma with respect to employment policy across the globe is whether to develop laws and programs that focus specifically on older workers or to implement policies and practices that impact the entire workforce equally. Both training programs that target older adults and those that support lifelong learning have met with some initial success, but few countries have distributed training programs widely enough to gauge their potential for nationwide change in employment trends. Additionally, there is a question as to whether employee skill sets or employer attitudes are more responsible for the marginalization of older workers in the labor market. Governments must grapple with where to focus their attentions first—on changing ageist stereotypes that affect hiring practices or on supporting older worker development to optimize their late-life contributions to the workplace.

Longstanding cultural values and societal patterns may ultimately have the most powerful impact on late-life work and retirement choices. Countries with entrenched early retirement cultures and developing countries in which many employees operate outside the formal labor market cannot expect rapid change with even the most drastic shifts in employment policy. In these settings, policymakers must develop unique and creative strategies to gradually reframe the role of older individuals in the labor market and draw workers into the net of formal financial security schemes. One area that may be more clear-cut is that of antidiscrimination policy. Our review of labor practices suggests that the implementation and consistent enforcement of laws forbidding age discrimination are crucial steps to which every nation must commit in order to fully embrace older adults as highly valued members of the labor market.

For More Information

1. The Asia-Pacific Research and Innovation Centre
   http://www.watsonwyatt.com

This private-sector center serves as Watson Wyatt's Asia-Pacific focal point for human capital, benefits, investment, and financial services research. See the aging workforce report on Asia-Pacific elders at http://www.watsonwyatt.com/images/database_uploads/ageing_ap_06/AP_AgeingWorkforce2006.pdf.

2. AARP International
   http://www.aarpinternational.org/topics/topics_list.htm?topic=1974

AARP International provides resources on a number of topics related to aging, including economic and retirement security. Subtopics include research and news on age discrimination, the mature workforce, and pensions and can be searched by world region.

3. Asia Economic Institute
   http://www.asiaecon.org/

This is a web-based organization that conducts and disseminates research on Asian economies. The organization publishes some articles specifically on aging workers.

4. Centre for Senior Policy
   http://www.seniorpolitikk.no/informasjon/english

The Centre for Senior Policy is a Norwegian advocacy group that publishes reports and news briefs (with English translations) related to older workers. Its mission is to reduce rates of early retirement and raise awareness of the benefits of an older workforce.

5. Hofacker, D. (2010). *Older workers in a globalizing world: An international comparison of retirement and late-career patterns in western industrialized countries.* Cheltenham, UK: Edward Elgar.
   http://www.thefreelibrary.com/Older+workers+in+a+globalizing+world%3B+an+international+comparison+ of...-a0233056143

In this book, Hofacker develops and tests a life-course approach to understanding early retirement transitions in Europe and North America. He identifies economic globalization as the main contextual force that has contributed to the decline of older workers in the labor market but also considers impacts of national education and training systems and specific welfare and labor market characteristics that influence the continued participation or retirement of older workers in the labor market.

6. Senior Select Retain and Retrain: Ireland
   http://ec.europa.eu/employment_social/equal/data/document/age-ie-sen_en.pdf

In 2005, Ireland implemented Senior Select Retain and Retrain (SSRR), a nationwide effort to improve workforce participation among older workers. The purpose of the project was to engage in a participative action research process to explore the recruitment and retention of older people in employment with a view to inform relevant policy and practice. SSRR efforts have inspired regional programs such as "Choices at 50+," an initiative piloted in South County Dublin. This program offered a combination of workshops, one-on-one career coaching sessions, and in-house CV/interview help for local company employees over 50. Positive outcomes for program participants included skills acquisition and increased confidence.

Mr. M., age 62
Rethymnon, Crete, Greece

I was born in Rethymnon, Crete, in 1948. My father was a bus driver, and my mother did not work; she was taking care of the house and the children. I have three brothers, one younger and one older than me. I am married and have three girls. I see my children on a daily basis.

My wife is working in the public sector and simultaneously at a business that her father owned. I have been doing the same work for 30 years. I own a sales company for agricultural machines, such as tractors, etc.

A typical day . . . waking up at 7 a.m. and preparing the kids for school, since my wife usually leaves for the school that she teaches around 7:15 a.m. I drive the kids to school, and then I go straight to my business. I end my work around 2:30 p.m., and then I drive my kids to a private school for foreign languages, since we live in a suburb outside Rethymnon, which is 10 minutes from downtown. And then I am back to the house usually by 8 p.m.

I would say we visit or get together with family and friends quite often. During weekdays, whenever my kids do not attend the foreign language school in the evening, then I always take the opportunity to visit family and friends in Rethymnon. Sometimes I do that on Sundays as well.

My health is not really good. I had recently a heart attack, 15 months ago, and now I am still recovering from this very serious cardiac incident. I remain very active but with great difficulty indeed. But I have to continue working, since it is difficult to maintain a good living and take care of my life without working.

I do not receive a pension yet, since I am still working. I am thinking about retiring pretty soon. However, I am not quite sure whether the retirement plan will provide with enough financial support. I will be eligible for retirement after 35 years of documented work. Due to my cardiac incident, I have the right to retire earlier than I am supposed to. At this point, I have been working officially and being insured for 33 years. So I will receive 33/35 of what I am eligible for if I retire right now, which means not the full retirement money. Will the amount of money I receive from my retirement be enough to cover my personal and family needs? By any means, no. And I say that because my kids have a lot of expenses. However, I think that in conjunction with my wife's salary and some income that I have from apartments that I rent, the retirement money will be enough to maintain a living.

When in need of health care, there are specific doctors that are cooperating with my insurance company and that I always visit. In this case, my expenses are fully covered by the insurance. If I do want to visit doctors that are not in compliance with my insurance, then I have to personally cover the expenses. Due to the seriousness of my health condition, I do need to visit an external doctor four to five times per 6 months. In this case, it is quite expensive to cover all the expenses by myself. My insurance does not cover dental issues, but it covers everything else.

I know that in case an older adult cannot take care of his or her daily living needs, there is a service offered by the municipality of Rethymnon, and it's called "care in your house." But I do not believe that this service, which is free, provides enough to support everything that older adults in need must receive. In addition, when an older adult is hospitalized and there is nobody from his/her close family environment to take care of the adult, then the insurance may provide an exclusive nurse for only one night without any expenses. I know that especially an exclusive (personal) nurse beyond one night of service may cost a lot of money. I think it costs around $80 per night for a personal nurse, and the government will only support you when you are officially insured by a federal or private insurance company.

In Greece, the majority of older adults do have some type of insurance. For those that do not have insurance at all, then there are public nursing homes that would take care of those individuals.

I think the aging process is something natural. And when this process does not involve any serious health problems, then I believe that one can really enjoy the aging process, even being an older adult. But when one has health issues, then this process is really frustrating.

What I like about my current age is that I really enjoy when I get together with old friends, friends from high school, the army service, and college friends. I particularly enjoy when we all get together and recall beautiful moments that we shared in the past, since we usually avoid talking about negative experiences and memories!

I cannot really distinguish something that I really do not like about my current age. I think that it's a normal evolution, the fact that we are aging. I wish that I could reverse the process and become younger, but unfortunately I can't. I can only hope to be healthy from now on, and that my kids have a good life as well.

What message would I send to the readers of this book? Only one thing: that they should always be proactive in terms of their health. Namely, they should always take care of themselves and look after their health even from a young age. When one is healthy, then he/she can always overcome any kind of difficulty or obstacle.

Luciana and Primo, age 74 and 78, Switzerland

Helen, age 96, United States

5

Housing Policies

> With the number of Americans over the age of 65 expected to more than double from 40 million to 81 million by 2040, it is paramount that policymakers, program managers, and researchers work to maintain and create housing options and communities that meet the needs of older adults and facilitate aging in place.
>
> —AARP, *Strategies to Meet the Housing Needs of Older Adults*, n.d., p. 1

> There is a very limited option for older adults housing in my locality. I am considering to move out of the house after my son marries, as the present area of my house is small. I may go in the vicinity of my native place, where I have some acquaintance.
>
> —Mr. S., age 63, Mumbai, India

Comparisons of older people's living arrangements reveal substantial differences between developed and developing regions of the world (Kinsella & He, 2009). As shown in Table 5.1, older adults—and older women in particular—in developed countries often live alone, whereas living with family is more the norm in the developing world. That is not to say that multigenerational living arrangements do not occur elsewhere. Cultural norms of filial responsibility and the transfer of assets across generations, as well as availability of alternate living arrangements, influence where older adults live in their later years. In Spain, for example, about 66% of widowed older adults and 34% of married couples live with at least one child (Zunzunegui, Beland, & Otero, 2001). But in many countries, there has been a decline in multigenerational residence. Karagiannaki (2005) found that between 1974 and 1999, the proportion of unmarried older people in Greece living with a married child dropped from 23% to less than 9%, and the proportion of older couples residing with a married child declined from 14% to 5%. The decline of intergenerational co-residence has also occurred in Japan, where the extended family structure has historically been a prominent feature of society (Takagi, Silverstein, & Crimmins, 2007). Researchers speculate that factors contributing to a greater number of older adults living independently include an increase in

Table 5.1 Percentage Distribution of Population Aged 60 or Older by Household Composition and Sex: Average for Major Areas and the United States

Major Areas	Alone	Couple Only	Child/ Grandchild	Other Relative	Nonrelative
Male (M)					
Africa	6.1	10.6	75.6	6.3	1.4
Asia	2.8	14.9	78.1	2.9	1.3
Europe	14.7	54.6	24.5	3.8	2.5
Latin America and Caribbean	7.8	14.8	65.2	8.3	3.8
United States	14.9	60.1	16.8	4.3	3.9
Female (F)					
Africa	9.9	6.2	71.1	11.2	1.5
Asia	7.9	8.8	76.0	5.5	1.9
Europe	34.7	29.5	28.7	4.1	3.0
Latin America and Caribbean	8.7	10.6	65.6	11.2	4.0
United States	34.5	39.7	18.5	4.9	2.4
Sex differential (F-M)					
Africa	3.8	−4.4	−4.5	4.9	0.1
Asia	5.1	−6.1	−2.1	2.5	0.6
Europe	20.0	−25.1	4.2	0.4	0.5
Latin America and Caribbean	0.8	−4.3	0.3	2.9	0.2
United States	19.6	−20.4	1.7	0.6	−1.5

Source: United Nations (2005).

BOX 5.1 Policy to People Link: Supporting Elderly Population's Ability to Age in Place

Since 2000, Holland has seen the development of Green Day Care Farms that provide day care for older adults with dementia. More than 900 farms provide work such as gardening, meal preparation, and animal care for small groups of older people. Farms typically work with local health care agencies and are funded by the Dutch national insurance system (Bruin et al., 2009).

their personal resources and greater mobility and independence of their children (McGarry & Schoeni, 2000; Ruggles, 2007).

In general, housing policies supportive of older adults are prevalent only in countries with a strong individualistic or socially supported old-age system. For example, in countries with liberal economic policies, such as Switzerland and the United States, housing policies and the programs they support intersect with policies around aging or poverty. That is, the market economy determines housing for most people, but the government has developed policy to support populations with special needs. Even for countries such as Norway, with more universal government social welfare policies, the market approach is changing policy. In these countries, adequate housing for all has been a civil right throughout much of the 20th century. However, as these countries' economies become more market-based, there is a movement to allow the market to determine housing.

Older individuals are best able to remain in their homes and care for themselves when there is an appropriate "fit" between their level of competence (i.e., cognitive abilities, physical abilities) and the demands of their environment (Lawton, 1980; Lawton & Nahemow, 1973). Thus, the need for alternative living arrangements often is prompted by a need for greater physical, psychological, social, and financial security. Some countries have developed universal systems of residential or long-term care for their older populations that usually include assisted-living and nursing home facilities.

As shown in Figure 5.1, the highest use rates of long-term care facilities are in some of the world's demographically oldest countries (Kinsella & He, 2009). Policies directing the provision of long-term care typically are independent entities, except in

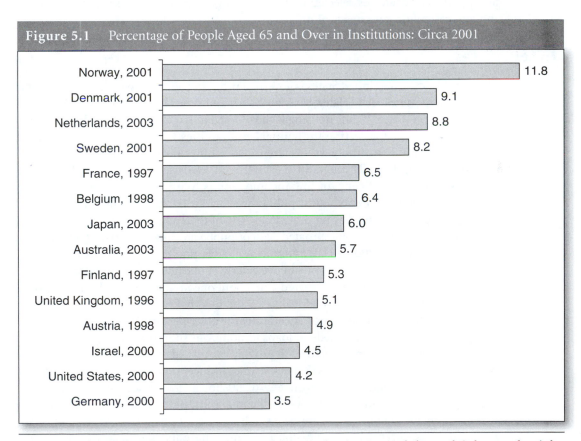

Figure 5.1   Percentage of People Aged 65 and Over in Institutions: Circa 2001

Country	Percentage
Norway, 2001	11.8
Denmark, 2001	9.1
Netherlands, 2003	8.8
Sweden, 2001	8.2
France, 1997	6.5
Belgium, 1998	6.4
Japan, 2003	6.0
Australia, 2003	5.7
Finland, 1997	5.3
United Kingdom, 1996	5.1
Austria, 1998	4.9
Israel, 2000	4.5
United States, 2000	4.2
Germany, 2000	3.5

Note: Netherlands and the Nordic countries include people in service housing; Japan includes people in long-stay hospitals.
Source: Cited in Kinsella and He (2009).

countries with an integrated social services system, such as Sweden and the United Kingdom. In countries with more extensive social welfare policies, older adults with increasing needs enter the social services system and are assessed by a social worker or case manager who takes their needs and wishes for housing, as well as health care and other services, into consideration (see Chapter 8). A number of countries have recognized that even when families provide much of the care and support for their older members, changing demographics and socioeconomic conditions influence the feasibility of multigenerational living arrangements. Consequently, many countries have adopted new policies aimed at alleviating current and anticipated housing needs for their older citizens (United Nations Department of Economic and Social Affairs, 2007).

Facilitating older adults' ability to *age in place* (i.e., remain in their homes as long as possible) is increasingly recognized in most countries as being important for the well-being of society's elders and for society as a whole. In the United States, for example, there is recognition that institutional care is much more expensive than home care services for the majority of older adults. Thus, housing policy and related programs are often related to a country's approach to long-term care. In this chapter, we will review the housing policies of the United States, Brazil, Japan, Norway, Switzerland, and Spain. The countries selected represent a range of policies that support the housing and residential care needs of older adults.

United States

Housing policy in the United States is governed primarily by the Department of Housing and Urban Development (Haley & Gray, 2008), and states have jurisdiction over how policy is implemented. Public housing is the oldest and largest federal housing program in the United States, assisting individuals and families with low incomes. In 1956, Congress for the first time gave preference to seniors in public housing (Milbank Memorial Fund, 2006). Throughout the 1960s and 1970s, a large number of developments were built specifically for low-income seniors. With very few exceptions, these were traditional apartments. Local public housing authorities usually operate these housing units, and renters pay no more than 30% of their adjusted monthly income for rent. Older renters occupy an estimated 31% of public housing units (U.S. Government Accountability Office, 2005). They typically are older, poorer, and perhaps frailer than most elderly households. Almost one in five elderly public housing households is headed by someone aged 85 or older, compared with about one in nine households nationwide.

The Section 202 Supportive Housing for the Elderly Program is the only federally funded housing program designed specifically for older persons (Haley & Gray, 2008). The program makes low-cost federal loans to nonprofit sponsors for new construction or rehabilitation of existing structures to provide subsidized rental housing for low- and moderate-income elders 62 years and older. Since its inception in 1959, the program has supported the creation of approximately 6,200 housing facilities for older persons, accounting for approximately 250,000 residential units. Beginning in 2002, appropriations have included funding to convert a small number of projects to licensed assisted-living facilities. Tenants living in Section 202 units have incomes below 50% of their area's median income (Bright, 2005). These housing complexes usually offer supportive services, such as transportation, housekeeping, and home-delivered meals.

The Section 8 Housing Choice Vouchers Program gives rental subsidies to landlords who agree to rent to low-income individuals and families. Public housing authorities can allocate up to 20% of their allotted funds to landlords who make their properties available to low-income residents or who agree to renovate their properties to meet Housing and Urban Development quality standards. Typically, the subsidy covers the difference between the tenants' contribution—an amount that totals 30% of their adjusted income—and fair market rents. Older adults are heads of households in 48% of project-based Section 8 housing (U.S. Government Accountability Office, 2005).

In contrast to the Section 8 project-based vouchers, most participants in the housing choice voucher program find their own housing, including single-family homes, townhouses, and apartments. They are free to choose any housing that meets the requirements of the program (e.g., rent that is not higher than the fair market value) and are not limited to units located in subsidized housing projects. Tenants are responsible for paying 30% of their income for rent. If the rent is higher than the fair market value, the renters are responsible for the difference. Older adults are heads of households in 16% of tenant-based Section 8 housing (U.S. Government Accountability Office, 2005).

Two government programs that help low-income older adults maintain their homes are the Department of Energy's Weatherization Assistance Program and the Low-Income Home Energy Assistance Program (LIHEAP). Under the Weatherization Assistance Program, low-income homeowners apply for funds to make energy-efficient changes to their homes, from installing new appliances and heating systems to adding weather-stripping or insulation. The federal government provides the funds, and governments manage them. Any household at or below 150% of the poverty level may be eligible for services. The program provides energy-efficiency services to approximately 100,000 homes every year and has weatherized more than 6.2 million families since its inception in 1976 (U.S. Department of Energy, 2010). In addition to reducing the utility costs for homeowners, the program helps improve health and safety by reducing carbon monoxide emissions and eliminating fire hazards, as well as creating jobs for those who provide the weatherizing services.

The U.S. Department of Health and Human Services began LIHEAP in 1981. LIHEAP provides heating and cooling assistance to low-income families, regardless of age, either directly through vendors or to landlords for home heating and cooling costs, energy crisis intervention, or low-cost weatherization. Particularly, households where at least one member receives Temporary Assistance for Needy Families, Supplemental Security Income, or Food Stamps qualify for LIHEAP. Applicants to LIHEAP services can apply for bill-paying assistance, energy crises assistance, or energy-related home repairs. Most LIHEAP funds are consumed during the winter months (U.S. Department of Health and Human Services, 2009). In 2003, about 36% of households receiving heating assistance and 47% of households receiving cooling assistance had at least one member 60 years of age or older (U.S. Department of Health and Human Services, 2006). There is wide variation in states' average household benefit levels for various types of fuel assistance.

Home repairs and maintenance are a considerable expense for many older adults, because they have likely lived in their homes for more than 3 decades. Besides needing specific repairs, many homes do not support frail older adults in conducting daily activities within the home. Older adults who are aging in place may need to modify their home's structure to accommodate their physical limitations. Modifications in lighting, accessibility, mobility, and bathing facilities can improve functioning and enhance safety (Wardrip, 2010). In response to the increasing demand for assistance with housing upkeep and repairs, a number of home repair programs have emerged across the United States. Home repair programs provide assistance with home maintenance or minor repairs. The funding for many of these programs comes from community development block grants or Title III monies from the Older Americans Act (see Chapter 8 for details). Programs vary with regard to the type of repairs they subsidize but typically include emergency repairs for plumbing, electricity, heat, and leaking roofs; minor repairs; exterior painting; and the removal of debris.

BOX 5.2   Policy to People Link: Housing Assistance

The U.S. Department of Agriculture's Rural Development initiative provides help for housing in several ways. Residents of rural areas who are over 62 years old can apply for funds to help with weatherization, home repairs, and rental assistance. It is not uncommon for local Rural Development offices to partner with other governmental agencies, nonprofits, and community groups to help individual older adults maintain independent living. For example, a widow from Utah who applied for a weatherization grant was put in touch with her local Rural Development office when an assessment showed that her home was beyond repair. The Rural Development office teamed up with three other government agencies and local businesses to build the woman a new home that she could afford on her fixed income. Find more Rural Development success stories at www.rurdev.usda.gov/rd/stories/index.htm.

Residential Care

Long-term care facilities are group-living arrangements that provide a wide range of restorative, rehabilitative, and medical services. The growth of the long-term care industry parallels the passage of federal income (see Chapter 3) and health care policy (see Chapter 6). Prior to the enactment of Social Security, Medicare, and Medicaid, many older adults had few options if they needed medical and personal care. In the early part of the century, almshouses or "poor farms" cared for many frail older adults, persons with mental illnesses, and those who were chronically ill. An estimated 60% to 90% of the persons living in almshouses were over the age of 65 (Fischer, 1978). Older adults who were financially well-off had the option of living in old-age homes run by ethnic or religious groups. German and Scandinavian immigrants built Lutheran Homes, and Jews and Methodists built their own facilities (Waldman, 1985). The 1950 amendments to the Social Security Act of 1935, allowing residents of institutions to receive benefits and health providers to directly receive payments for services, helped expand the creation of nursing homes. But the real impetus to the creation of the nursing home industry came with the enactment of Medicare and Medicaid. Both Medicare and Medicaid provide payments to nursing homes—Medicare for acute care and Medicaid for long-term care for those with low incomes. Since the enactment of Medicare and Medicaid, the percentage of adults aged 65 and older living in nursing homes increased from 2.5% in 1963 (Small, 1988) to 4.1% in 2008 (Administration on Aging, 2009e).

In 2004, there were about 16,100 nursing facilities in the country (Jones, Dwyer, Bercovitz, & Strahan, 2009). Nursing homes average around 108 beds, ranging from fewer than 50 to more than 200. Most nursing homes are certified by the Centers for Medicare and Medicaid Services and are eligible to receive reimbursement for their services to persons qualified for Medicaid and Medicare. Prior to federal legislation passed in 1987, nursing homes had two levels of care—skilled nursing and intermediate care—on which reimbursement was based. Skilled nursing facilities were designed to care for residents who needed care that was more medically oriented. Residents in intermediate-care facilities required custodial care. Because the two levels of classification did not accurately reflect the variations in the functional abilities of nursing home residents, the federal government replaced the dichotomous classification with one designation—the nursing facility. The Centers for Medicare and Medicaid Services designed a different classification system in 1998 called the Resource Utilization Groups: Version III. Instead of paying facilities retrospectively after services were delivered based on "reasonable costs," facilities are now paid prospectively based on a patient's care needs (e.g., rehabilitation, extensive services, special care, clinically complex care). This classification system (most recently updated in 2006) reflects the many types of older adults in need of nursing home care.

In the late 1970s, long-term care insurance became available to help cover the costs of long-term nursing home care. Such insurance policies are indemnity policies that pay a fixed amount for each day of care received once the individual reaches specified disability levels. Policies generally limit benefits to a maximum dollar amount or days of care, and some pay benefits for a limited number of years. In 2006, Congress passed legislation giving states the permission to coordinate the purchase and payment of long-term care insurance with Medicaid. The law permits Medicaid to cover long-term care needs beyond the terms of the policy, and policyholders are not required to "spend down" their assets to meet the Medicaid eligibility guidelines (Capretta, 2007b). Although long-term care insurance policy sales have steadily risen since being introduced into the market, older adults have been slow to purchase such policies because of the availability, the cost, the limited benefits, and a belief that Medicare or Medicaid will cover long-term care costs.

Insurance companies are increasingly allowing holders of long-term care policies to use their benefits for assisted living if the services are cost-effective. Although definitions of assisted living vary across states, the term is generally defined as a residential setting that provides or coordinates personal care services, 24-hour supervision, scheduled and unscheduled assistance, social activities, and some health-related services (Wright, 2004). These settings may include personal care boarding homes with additional services, residential care units owned by and adjacent to nursing homes, congregate housing settings that have added services, purpose-built assisted-living programs, or the middle level of continuing care retirement communities. Nationwide, there are about 39,500 assisted-living facilities accommodating more than a million residents (MetLife Mature Market Institute, 2009). Public payment for assisted living includes supplemental payments to the facility for housing for services for residents receiving Supplemental Security Income (see Chapter 3), reimbursement in Medicaid, Medicaid waiver, state long-term care programs, or some combination of these sources.

Brazil

Brazil is a country with many discrepancies in the distribution of income and wealth and acute problems of poverty. As such, there is great disparity among the lifestyles of its citizens, including housing options available to older adults. Only about 9% of Brazilians aged 60 and older live alone; 18% live independently with their spouse, while 61% live with adult children, grandchildren, or other relatives (United Nations, 2005). Co-residence often is beneficial for both generations. For many new families (i.e., young adult children) and working-class families, economic conditions make independent living difficult. In joint households, older adults can get the care and support they need while sharing both property and the benefits of their government old-age pension (e.g., purchasing food, clothes) with their family members (VanWey & Cebulko, 2007).

In describing housing policy in Brazil, da Piedade Morais and de Oliveira Cruz (2010) noted that until the 1930s, access to housing for middle- and low-income families was gained predominantly through the rental markets, which were privately supplied by the upper classes because there was no official housing financial system. This started to change when the principle of "self-owned housing" gained momentum. The 1942 Tenants Law provided incentives for the construction of housing to sell for owner occupation. The development of self-owned housing was closely related to the increasing construction of high-rise buildings in central areas, self-help construction in the periphery areas, and the emergence of slums and peripheral settlements in the main metropolitan areas of the country (cited in da Piedade Morais & de Oliveira Cruz, 2010). In 1964, the federal government created the Housing Financial System (SFH) and the National Housing Bank (BNH), under the military regime. BNH was the first effective initiative of the government to promote a national housing policy (cited in da Piedade Morais & de Oliveira Cruz, 2010). It also made the promotion of self-owned housing one of the main objectives of its national housing policy. The SFH/BNH System divided the housing market into three income segments: popular (up to three minimum wages), affordable (three to six minimum wages), and medium (above six minimum wages). Despite generating a real-estate boom, the BNH subsidized medium- to high-income households and was incapable of reaching the low-income population, therefore increasing slum formation and horizontal expansion toward the peripheral areas.

Although Brazil still lacks a comprehensive housing policy that would enhance housing conditions for all people throughout the country, much has improved in the housing sector since the end of the military government in 1986, including the development of a number of housing programs and supporting legislation (Valença & Bonates, 2010). Government leaders have sought to consolidate financial instruments in line with global markets and restructure the way private interests operate within the system. Such reforms and modernization have tended toward benefiting market solutions to housing policies (Valença & Bonates, 2010).

Following market-based economic policies means that class matters for older Brazilians' living arrangements. For example, independent living among older adults rose from about 27% in 1980 to 32% in 2000 (De Vos & Andrade, 2005). The largest increase by race showed that White Brazilians, who are also the wealthiest group of elders, accounted for the most change. There was little or no change among Brown or Black elders. Thus, increased financial resources may help facilitate independent living among some groups of elders (e.g., Whites) and multigenerational living among others (e.g., Browns and Blacks).

Residential Care

Brazil reflects the roots of colonialization, as it shares the common European system of charitable poor homes taking care of the poor and disabled (Garcez-Leme, Leme, & Espino, 2005). Nursing homes are rare in Brazil; most are privately run religious institutions and are primarily found in urban areas (Garcez-Leme et al., 2005). They typically serve the most frail and vulnerable elders and have a heterogeneous structure, with some providing medical care via a professional nursing staff and others providing social support.

Japan

Traditionally, pre– World War II, the eldest son in a Japanese family took care of his parents and inherited family property when the parents died. Government reforms after World War II deinstitutionalized this system, though many families continued to practice it (Izuhara, 2002, p. 69). Indeed, the 1950 National Assistance Act stated that public assistance should be considered as a supplement to family care (Izuhara, 2002). Thus, although the oldest son no longer had exclusive inheritance rights and care responsibilities, families were still expected to provide care for aging members. Older people can expect not only their spouses and children to provide care but also siblings and grandchildren (Izuhara, 2002). This state policy with explicitly stated expectations for familial care resulted in uneven public assistance, so Japan provides universal pensions and health insurance but very little if any other social services (Izuhara, 2002). Moreover, while it used to be typical for adult children and parents to co-reside throughout the parents' old age, older adults are increasingly living by themselves in couple or single households until they need care (25% in 1998; Izuhara, 2002; Takagi et al., 2007).

Although most older adults (85%) in Japan live in homes that they own, it is possible for two generations to purchase a home together with an extended mortgage period (Izuhara, 2002). Also, a new type of public housing, the three-generation home, features two living rooms (Izuhara, 2002). In 1984, Japan began giving a tax credit for intergenerational households and gave special "tax concessions" (p. 68) for building or remodeling because of intergenerational needs. The practice is changing somewhat, but the tradition of the family home makes it the least likely used asset to finance elder care (Izuhara, 2002).

As of 2001, in Japan, 58% of adults over 60 co-reside with their children (Takagi et al., 2007). Researchers examined determinants of three patterns of residency of older adults in relation to their adult children: non-co-residence, lifelong co-residence, and boomerang co-residence (parents moving in with children, or vice versa, after a period of non-co-residence); however, because their subsample was nonrepresentative and was generally healthier than the representative sample from which it had been taken, the experiences and prevalence of the non-co-resident (including those who were institutionalized) may have been underrepresented (Takagi et al., 2007). Those who were boomerang families (12.7%) tended to move in together again after a critical event, such as widowhood or acute illness, and were more likely to be found in regions with strong cultural norms of traditionalism. Surprisingly, those who were lifelong co-residents (44.7%) tended to be less traditional in their attitudes. The authors speculate that this may be because they had been living traditionally and the issue may be less salient than for those who may feel that they transgressed traditional norms and thus need to espouse them more strongly. Forty-two percent of the sample did not co-reside with children. Homeownership by older adults, availability of larger homes, and stronger local economies predicted co-residence among both co-residing groups, suggesting how structural factors and related policy influence family practices.

Residential Care

Municipalities cover 90% of the cost of long-term care insurance for everyone in Japan over the age of 40. Persons aged 65 and older needing care, or their providers, can apply for subsidies that support home-based or institutional care (OECD, 2005b). Individuals are assessed according to six levels of need, which determine the amount of funding. The majority of older adults who applied for long-term care provisions (over 73%) received home care services. One option that municipalities may incorporate as a feature of care is a cash allowance for family caregivers who do not use community long-term care services and provide higher levels of care (i.e., fourth level or above out of the six levels).

There is an increasing number of public and private large-scale nursing homes throughout Japan, as well as group homes and assisted-living complexes (Jenike, 2003). However, the availability of subsidized residential care facilities and services varies depending on the tax resources of an area and the foresight of local social welfare administrators. Typically, demand is higher than supply, particularly in high-density areas such as Tokyo. According to Jenike, in every district in Tokyo, the age of the caregiver, health status of the older care recipient as judged by the social welfare office, and household structure are taken into account in allocating these scarce resources. If an elder is accepted into the social welfare program, there are often 2- to 4-year waits for nursing homes within Tokyo wards and cities. In more sparsely populated rural areas, placements within federally subsidized nursing homes are more readily available.

Norway

Housing policy in Norway has changed since the 1980s from social-democratic to a "liberal welfare regime [featuring] market economics, low public expenditure, and subsidies for small, targeted groups" (Stamso, 2009, p. 194). Welfare states are supported by four pillars—health care, education, pensions, and housing—but housing is the most susceptible to the market because people buy and sell housing rather than the state providing it (Stamso, 2009). Prior to 1985, the Norwegian government actively sought to replace market conditions with state intervention (Stamso, 2009). Moves from an increasingly conservative government in 1984 and 1985 led to the deregulation of credit institutions and housing markets (Stamso, 2009). Unlike many other European countries, homeownership has historically been the norm, because Norway has been characteristically rural and without an aristocratic culture (Stamso, 2009). The Norwegian State Housing Bank began in 1946 and has financed up to three-fourths of housing construction. The Concession Act of 1974 has influenced the character of communities in Norway. For example, it established residency requirements so that homeowners in rural areas either must live in the home or rent the home. This was meant to stop people from purchasing a second home in the country and in effect creating urban bedroom communities.

Norway has the goal of homeownership for most people with three policy strategies: keep interest rates low and stable to promote a healthy housing market, ensure housing access for disadvantaged peoples, and encourage the development of environmentally sound and universally accessible housing and neighborhoods (Norwegian Ministry of Local Government and Regional Development, 2004). In anticipation of the aging population, the Norwegian State Housing Bank encourages universal design by adding these design criteria for loan applications. It also makes home modification loans to promote aging in place.

Residential Care

Norway follows the so-called Nordic model—as do Finland, Sweden, and Denmark—in which public services strongly promote aging in place and independence by providing in-home formal services when needed (Meeks, Nickols, & Sweaney, 1999). Moreover, Norway is known for its efficient and affordable public housing (Meeks et al., 1999). Family care is less prominent in Norway than in some other countries, but publicly supported programs such as adult day care and respite care help the many families that do provide informal care (Meeks et al., 1999). In Norway, there was a growth in assisted-living-type housing during the 1980s and 1990s (Meeks et al., 1999).

In Norway, approximately 50% of older people with dementia live in the community, mostly with family members (Norwegian Ministry of Health and Care Services [NMHCS], 2008). In 2007, the government declared that municipalities needed to prioritize day programs and home services to help independent living and provide respite to families involved in caregiving. Day programs may be offered at the homes of community-dwelling elders, at nursing homes, and at day care facilities. Moreover, there is increasing focus on making nursing homes and assisted-living facilities more amendable to the needs of those with dementia. The Norwegian State Housing Bank provides grants to such facilities to make living spaces smaller and more communal, with easy access to outdoor spaces (NMHCS, 2008). The primary aim is to change institutional housing to meet the needs of those with dementia, who compose around 80% of residents, as suggested by research findings. Some of these findings suggest that people with dementia have a higher quality of life when they do not change facilities, when they are in smaller spaces, and when they are served by professional staff members who understand dementia.

Though Norway has a reputation for its aging-related services, such as home care, the reality is that much of home care still depends on help from informal carers (Fjelltun, Henriksen, Norberg, Gilje, & Normann, 2009). Moreover, if an elder or his or her family decides to make the transition to a nursing facility, the elder must pay between 75% and 85% of his or her income for these institutional services. The transition process begins with a home nurse or family member requesting nursing home placement. Then, an assessment of the elder's care needs is made, and the result should be that the person gains admittance to a nursing facility. However, in most instances, older people are placed on a waiting list before entering the nursing home.

Switzerland

Most people (65%) in Switzerland live in rental housing dominated by the private market (Lawson, 2009; Van Wezemael & Gilroy, 2007). Although older persons in their 60s and 70s who wish to move into care homes can afford them, the oldest old (over 85) are at risk for poverty and often cannot afford the care they need (Van Wezemael & Gilroy, 2007). The three-pillar retirement system (state responsibility, individual responsibility, and employer responsibility) went into full effect in the 1980s and is based on a liberal market economy; however, the oldest old in Switzerland may be vulnerable, since they did not plan for the three-pillar organization of benefits that depends on employer contributions (Lawson, 2009; Van Wezemael & Gilroy, 2007). Medical and social services, collectively called "Spitex," are increasingly merging in Switzerland and are organized at canton (the regional) level and facilitate aging in place. Forty-four percent of Spitex customers are 80 years old or older (Van Wezemael & Gilroy, 2007). Services are a mix of public and private and are paid for by private insurance or out of pocket. Older adults occupy cooperative housing at a higher rate than other forms of housing because they typically facilitate aging in place, unlike tenants who live in flats that are ill-equipped for an aging population. Van Wezemael and Gilroy (2007) contend that landlords who are participating in the market economy do not see profitability in producing age-friendly flats, and therefore, there are few.

Public support for nonprofit housing has been intermittent in Switzerland, peaking at affecting 20% of households in 1992 to 1993 (Lawson, 2009). Cooperative began in the 19th century as a result of social housing policy arising from the labor movement response to deplorable living conditions during the Industrial Revolution. Instead of being managed by the state, however, most cooperative housing was run by particular labor enterprises (including public utilities) for their workers, such as the Swiss National Railway (Lawson, 2009). Cooperative policy attracts families and older people, and some places feature medical consultation rooms, day care facilities, fitness rooms, and studio space (Lawson, 2009).

Residential Care

Long-term care in Switzerland generally refers to home care. About 93% of home care organizations are nonprofit and private, which meets the conditions to receive government subsidies (OECD, 2005b). Historically, long-term care was a part of post-hospitalization and rehabilitation policy and has only recently emerged as an issue in its own right (OECD, 2005b). All citizens have health insurance, but the costs of long-term care are supplemented by public financing. Depending on municipality, sometimes clients receive tax breaks; other times, there are direct payments to the care provider or client. Private long-term care insurance is risk-based and therefore cost prohibitive, especially for aging women.

Spain

Housing policy in Spain is governed at the national level, the regional level (Autonomous Communities), the provincial level, and the municipal level (Gomez Jimenez & Koebel, 2007). Essentially, the national level provides money and general policy under the Spanish Housing Ministry, which was established in 2004, while the Autonomous Communities and their municipalities coordinate and implement policy on a local level. For example, all Spaniards have the right to "decent and adequate housing" (p. 27), though individuals cannot enforce this right; rather, it is a goal of the state. One plan that the Spanish government has to meet this goal is to subsidize homeownership rather than rental property. For example, the goal of the Spanish Housing Project (2005–2008) was to provide housing funding for disadvantaged groups, such as older people and those with disabilities; how it was implemented depended on the Autonomous Communities. Implementation included housing development for first-time buyers, renovating to facilitate accessibility, and redeveloping urban centers. But too often, services that affect housing, such as home help or other long-term care services, are not well-incorporated—or incorporated at all—into housing policy. Moreover, because the government is decentralized, the opportunities available from policy enactment in one region may be different from those in another region. Another type of policy that affects older persons is policy directed toward people with disabilities, which often makes explicit references to aging, such as the Spanish Disability Act and the National Plan for Accessibility (2004–2012). Such plans recognize that most people want to age in place or be cared for by family members and stress using funds to improve accessibility.

In the 1990s, 95% of older adults in Spain were community-dwelling, living in their own homes or in the homes of family (Rojo Perez, Fernandez-Mayoralas, Pozo Rivera, & Rojo Abuin, 2001). In 2001, 84% of all households were owned, with or without a mortgage (Population and Housing Census, 2001). Older women were more likely to live in their children's homes or alone, highlighting women's longer life expectancy; the age composition of homes where older men were present tended to be younger (Rojo Perez et al., 2001). In 1994, the Urban Letting Act affected the 13% of older adults in Madrid who rented homes (Rojo Perez et al., 2001). Until this Act, rents were fixed and contracts were automatically renewed and extended even to adult children; now, landlords can ask tenants to sign revised leases, which often ask for increased rent (Rojo Perez et al., 2001). Since this time, rentals have decreased by 3% from 1991 to 2001, though this follows a general pattern in Europe—and Spain in particular—of increasing homeownership (Population and Housing Census, 2001; see also Pareja Eastaway & San Martin Varo, 2002). Before the 1994 Act, there were similar measures in 1964 and 1985 (e.g., the Boyer Decree), but it wasn't until the 1990s that the deregulation of rental properties was clearly spelled out (Pareja Eastaway & San Martin Varo, 2002). However, rental contracts signed before 1964 still feature controlled rents and compulsory renewal for landlords, which means that older adults who have lived in the same rental home for decades may have very low rents based on their income (Pareja Eastaway & San Martin Varo, 2002). Gomez Jimenez and Koebel (2007) point out that these rental properties are notorious for their poor conditions and for the land the buildings rest on being far more valuable than the buildings themselves. Of the 14% of available rental property, only 8% was subsidized public housing (Pareja Eastaway & San Martin Varo, 2002).

Spain has a history of legislation that discourages rental development and encourages homeownership. The average number of bedrooms in family dwellings is five, with only about 12% of homes having three bedrooms or fewer (Population and Housing Census, 2001). There are three times as many women over 65 living alone than men over 65 living alone. Of the European Union countries, Spain and Portugal are the countries with the highest average number of persons per household; however, for those who are 90 years or older, 10% live in institutions, more than 25% live alone, about 44% live with someone of another generation, and 20% live with someone their own age (Population and Housing Census, 2001).

Residential Care

Although most elderly people in Spain live independently, those who are dependent typically live with a family caregiver; only 3% of elderly people rely on institutional or nursing home care (Rodríguez Cabrero, 2002). Older adults' reliance solely on family care is likely to decline with current demographic shifts. Specifically, Spain is experiencing

a. a decline in the number of women available to provide care at the same time as there is a growing number of elderly dependents,

b. a dramatic change in the traditional model of family because of growing rates of divorce, and

c. a change in the social role of women related to increased labor force participation that decreases their availability and the amount of time available to provide care (Rodríguez Cabrero, 2002).

The Spanish long-term care system is highly decentralized and can be characterized as a system of regional long-term care services (Costa-Font & Patxot, 2005). It is financed mainly through taxes and, to a lesser extent, copayments and charges (Comas-Herrera et al., 2006). In 2007, a marked change in Spain's long-term care policy began with the implementation of a national long-term care system. Changes will be implemented gradually, with full operation expected to be reached in 2015 (Costa-Font & Rovira-Forns, 2008). Previous to this system, long-term care was means tested and only the poorest people were able to get support for home services or institutional care. One of the chief characteristics of the "modern" Spanish state is its decentralized political structure (Costa-Font & Rovira-Forns, 2008, p. 22). There are 17 Autonomous Communities in Spain that will design their own specific policies to address perceived priorities while maintaining a basic long-term care system for the whole country.

Summary

Housing and long-term care policies are inextricably intertwined with overall governmental edicts and cultural values regarding who is ultimately responsible for the safety and care of older adults. Countries offer very different late-life housing options and support depending on whether tradition dictates that the national government, states/municipalities, or family members should shoulder primary responsibility for the long-term well-being of aging citizens. Political governmental leanings and societal belief systems also influence which older adults are deemed eligible for assistance in maintaining their homes, alternative housing, and long-term residential care. In some locations, a range of supports are available to all older adults, while other countries have policies and programs that target only the most vulnerable of aging citizens (i.e., those living in poverty, the oldest old, the sick and frail). What became apparent as we reviewed existing systems, however, is that most nations, regardless of ideological framework, are faced with the reality that their traditional systems of support are breaking down under the weight of population aging. Systems dependent on values of filial responsibility and care are seeing both demographic and cultural shifts that undermine the stability of family safety nets. Conversely, systems that rely heavily on public funding may potentially collapse under the financial burden of an expanded older population.

There is agreement across many nations on one particular issue of residential support and care in late life: It is crucial to find creative ways to support adults *aging in place* whenever possible. That is, for older adults, staying in their own homes and communities is the best option—economically, socially, physically, and emotionally. Even in countries with strong public systems of support, the large majority of late-life care is provided by informal family caregivers. Thus, the question remains—what's the best pathway for stabilizing lives of older adults in the community, and who is most responsible for ensuring the success of this process? The countries discussed in this chapter have developed a wide range of initiatives to support affordable housing and feasible in-home care in late life, including public and subsidized housing options, assisted-living options, and insurance schemes for long-term residential care. Although support programs differ considerably across countries, they all face two key challenges when trying to implement their unique systems of residential support—severe within-country discrepancies in regional programming and resources and generational decline in family support systems. Other factors that must be considered in any discussion of housing policies designed to support older adults include socioeconomic and class differences, rural/urban divisions, and the tensions between traditional and current societal values and norms.

For More Information

1. Assisted Living Federation of America (ALFA)
   http://www.alfa.org/alfa/Default.asp

   ALFA is the largest national association exclusively dedicated to professionally oper-ated assisted-living communities for seniors. It works to influence public policy by advo-cating for informed choice, quality care, and accessibility for all Americans.

2. Australian Housing Urban Research Institute (AHURI)
   http://www.ahuri.edu.au/

   This institute is dedicated to drawing together researchers, policymakers, the industry, and the community to achieve better housing market outcomes, to achieve an effective and efficient housing assistance program, and to build viable communities. One of its primary research themes examines how to integrate housing assistance with other care and support programs to improve overall outcomes for older adults.

3. Communities and Local Governments Ministers
   http://www.communities.gov.uk/corporate/

   This government entity in the United Kingdom works to create thriving, sustainable, vibrant communities that improve everyone's quality of life. Among its publications is Lifetime Homes, Lifetime Neighbourhoods: A National Strategy for Housing in an Ageing Society, available at http://www.communities.gov.uk/publications/housing/lifetimehome sneighbourhoods.

4. The European Center for Social Welfare Policy and Research
   http://www.euro.centre.org/broschuere_engl.pdf

   The European Centre provides expertise in the fields of welfare and social policy devel-opment, particularly in areas that require multi- or interdisciplinary approaches, inte-grated policies, and intersectoral action. Long-term care and personal social services is one of their primary research areas.

5. WHO Age-Friendly Environments Program
   http://www.who.int/ageing/age_friendly_cities/en/index.html

   The Age-Friendly Environments Program is an international effort by WHO to address the environmental and social factors that contribute to active and healthy ageing in societies.

Mrs. C., age 96
Greeley, Colorado, United States

I was born in Mystic, Iowa, in 1914. My grandfather was a Methodist minister. My dad served in WWI, and when he came home from the war, he worked in a coal mine office; he also had a small office where he edited a newspaper. He also worked in the oil business in Wyoming and worked in Utah as a deputy sheriff. My mother was a clerk and post mistress for the post office, did laundry and ironing for different companies. I had two brothers, one born in 1926 and one in 1920. I graduated from high school as a Salutatorian. I wanted to go to college, but I wasn't able to. But even though I didn't go to college, I feel like I got a lot out of life by just living it.

I've been married twice, once in Cleveland, Ohio, when I was 19. We kept it secret for a year because we didn't have the resources to set up a house, because this was during the Depression; so he lived at the YMCA, and I lived at the YWCA. We had a son, who is now 70 years old. I divorced in 1939. People didn't get divorces then, and so that was kind of a stigma. . . . I felt very bad about that. I met my second husband, who was a school teacher, and within 6 weeks after I married him, he was off to a WWII boot camp! That was a fast romance, but it lasted 53 years. I have a daughter from that marriage, who lives here in Greeley. I have grandchildren and great grandchildren. I see them all quite often.

My typical day? I live here in an independent living apartment, but they serve three meals a day. You don't have to be there for the meals, but it is an important part of the day for people who don't take part in activities. I participate in a drawing class, spelling bee practice and contests, exercise classes 5 days a week, and we have walks. I belong to PEO [a nationwide organization that promotes education], and we have meetings twice a month. I have been doing some dancing, too. For our talent contest, I learned how to do the River Dance. I won the talent contest! We have a nurse that comes and does pedicures and nurses that come and take our BP. We have a beauty shop and a bus that goes Monday through Thursdays that will take you to your doctors. On Thursdays, we go to Wal-Mart, and that is an expedition! They are always providing some kind of musical program. If people would just go to them, they would be busy every day. Some people come here and shut themselves up in their rooms, and that is too bad. I thrive on people and just have to be around people. I go to church every Sunday. My faith has been a help to me—a great source of strength to me. It has helped me through a lot of bad spots. The church has been a very important part of my life.

My daughter, who is a wonderful help, helps me if there is anything I need to do. I just moved here not too long ago, and it was very difficult. I lived in my house in Nebraska for 35 years. I really dug my heels in several times. . . . Finally, my children told me that "Mother, you have a decision to make because you can't move back into your house all by yourself." I knew they were right, but I didn't want to admit it. But I finally said okay, I will go, and I will be happy, but I don't want to go. It was like pulling a big tree out of the yard by its roots!

My health is pretty good. I have macular degeneration, and my hearing isn't great, but I have hearing aids that help. I have some aches and pains, but when I went to the doctor, he told me, "For 96 years, I think you are doing remarkably well!" I have rheumatism and congestive heart failure. I take five pills a day, and three are vitamins.

I do receive a Social Security check every month, which is based on one's working income. I get a small pension because my husband, who was a teacher, wasn't paid very well. I paid into Social Security when

I was working in Cleveland at a department store, and when I was in Wyoming, I worked at a feed mill in the office. My pension isn't adequate for my needs. It's $1,065 a month. Out of that, they take your insurance. What I am living on here is what we accumulated over a lifetime—my savings. I also have a small farm that my husband inherited from his grandfather in Kansas. I would say the income from that varies depending on the crop, and it is about $6,000 a year, but in some years it is nothing.

Medicare pays for my health care, and I have supplemental insurance that helps pay for the doctors. My supplemental insurance costs $207 per month. I am grateful for that because I can go to the doctor and I don't feel like I have to scrape to pay for it. None of my insurance covers my glasses, dental care, or my hearing aids. I pay for all of this by myself, and my insurance doesn't cover it. I have another insurance program, Well Care, and it costs me $30 a month, and that covers my prescription. It cuts the cost of each pill to $4 a month.

I have someone that works here that comes in and does light housekeeping for me. I do have a Long-Term Care insurance that I pay for every month, but it doesn't help with the costs of this place because it is independent living. I don't know if it would cover any costs if I needed additional nursing care while I was living here.

How do I feel about growing older? Well, I don't know. I got to 96 just day by day. . . . I don't know how I got here! I know I can't do the things I did when I was 16, but I do what I can. Some people say growing old is hell, but it really isn't. It is all in how you look at it. I just do it day by day. People are very nice to me, . . . my friends here, the people that work here. What I dislike about my age is that my eyes and ears are not like I would like for them to be. But there is nothing I can do about it. So I might as well accept it, as there are some things that are inevitable. So I try to work around them. I look forward to seeing my grandchildren and participating in their lives. I got to thinking about what I would like to leave for the kids, and I wrote a kind of legacy for each grandchild, which I hope they will appreciate when they get older. I had to do something. I am so privileged to know my grandchildren, because many people never get to know their grandchildren.

My advice about growing older is something I have been doing all my life—do exercise; keep those muscle and joints active, even if you are working. It is so important. I have always done that. At age 7 or 8, I found a magazine called *Physical Culture*—it was all poses, stretching. I have always done that. The body was made to move; you have to keep going. I was fortunate that I found that magazine. But all my life I have done that. Just keep active and keep your mind active.

Duilio, age 88, Italy

Mrs. U., age 82, Netherlands

6

Health Care Policies

> The fact that greater numbers of people are living longer is a huge achievement for our societies and our health systems. Life expectancy has risen much in the last fifty years, and will continue to do so also in the coming decades. However, demographic changes will also pose new challenges for our health and long-term care systems.
>
> —Council of the European Union (2003, p. 4)

> I pay a 105€ a month for health insurance. . . . It's for your doctor, the hospital, dentist, and medicines . . . . If I need medicines, I go the Apotheek (pharmacy). . . . I don't have to pay for anything. . . . Same with my hospitalizations. . . . But I do have to pay something if I go to the dentist. . . . They pay 75% for your dentist, 25% you have to pay for yourself. . . . I am very happy with my care.
>
> —Ms. K., age 69, Amsterdam

Policymakers and health service providers around the world are struggling to adapt to the current health care needs of older adults and, more importantly, to anticipate the changing health landscape based on dramatic projected shifts in the age distributions of their populations over the next 20 to 40 years. As we discussed in Chapter 1, life expectancy for the United States and most other developed countries now nears or exceeds 80 years (see Table 1.1 in Chapter 1). As the population ages and life expectancy increases, governments are concerned about two interrelated issues—providing the appropriate types of preventative and acute health care services and managing the access, and thus cost, of those services.

One way to track the amount a country spends on consuming health care services is to examine the relationship between the amount spent on all health care services and the Gross Domestic Product (GDP; a country's value of economic output). Figure 6.1 shows the total expenditure on health care as a percentage of the GDP of selected countries in 1990 and 2006.

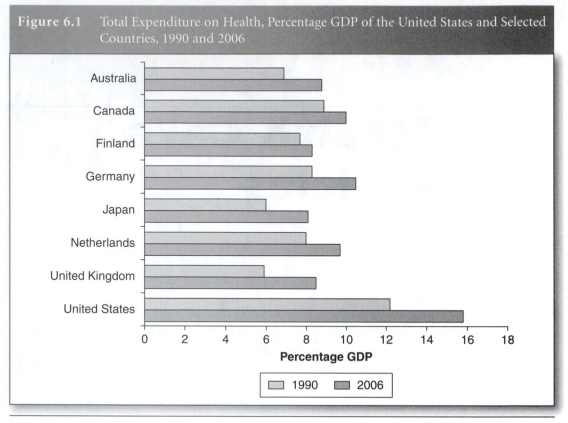

Figure 6.1 Total Expenditure on Health, Percentage GDP of the United States and Selected Countries, 1990 and 2006

Source: OECD (2009a).

In 1990, all countries—with the exception of the United States and Canada—were spending less than 9% of their GDP on health care; the United Kingdom was the lowest at 5.9% and the United States the highest at 12.2%. In 2006, all countries experienced an increase in the amount of GDP spent on health care compared with 1990. Among the countries listed in the figure, the percentage increase between 1990 and 2006 was greatest in the United States—a 3.6 percentage point increase to 15.8% of GDP spending on health care.

Another way to examine the amount of a country's health care cost is to identify the total amount spent per person, or per capita. As shown in Figure 6.2 on page 129, the per capita expenditure on health care services is close to $7,000 in the United States, which is double the per capita expenditure in six of the countries listed. Japan, Italy, and Finland have the lowest per capita expenditures on health care services, each spending less than $2,800 per person.

How much does population aging contribute to the overall cost of what countries spend on health care services? Indeed, population aging contributes somewhat to a country's overall health care costs because health expenditures by and for older age groups tend to be proportionally higher than their population share (Kinsella & He, 2009), and a large fraction of health care costs are incurred in the year or years just

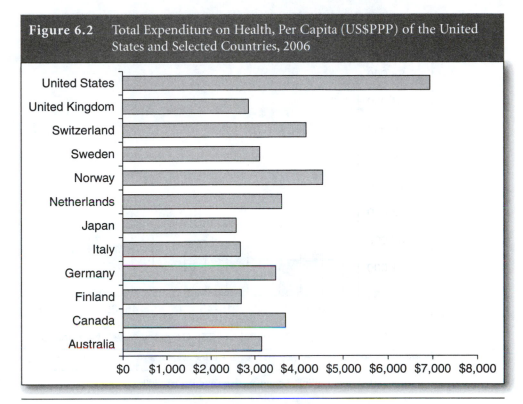

Figure 6.2   Total Expenditure on Health, Per Capita (US$PPP) of the United States and Selected Countries, 2006

Note: PPP stands for purchasing power parity, a criterion used as an appropriate exchange rate between currencies.

Source: OECD (2009a).

prior to death (R. D. Lee, 2007; Shugarman et al., 2004). As more people survive to increasingly older ages, higher health care costs are shifted from the younger to the oldest age groups (Kinsella & He, 2009). This cost can be examined as the cost of illness, which illustrates the economic burden of diseases and of course influences the overall cost of health care in a country (Heijink, Koopmanschap, & Polder, 2006). An example of the shift cost of illness across age groups in Australia, Germany, and the Netherlands is shown in Figure 6.3 on page 130, where in each country the cost of illness is greatest for those aged 65 to 85.

It should be noted, however, that researchers have identified other factors, in addition to population aging, that contribute to the rising cost of health care. The rises in per capita incomes (which enable people to consume more health care services), increases in health insurance coverage, new and expensive medical technologies, workforce demographics, and the way a country has organized its health care systems also affect the cost of health care (Lloyd-Sherlock, 2000; Reinhardt, 2003; Zweifel, Felder, & Werblow, 2004).

As health care service is an important social policy issue, countries have adopted an array of health care policies that guide the provision of preventative, routine health maintenance, long-term care, and palliative care needs of their elders now and in the

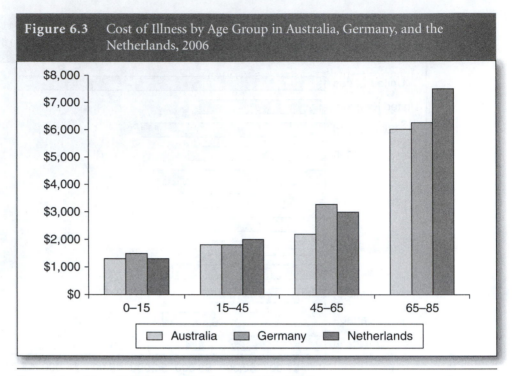

Figure 6.3 Cost of Illness by Age Group in Australia, Germany, and the Netherlands, 2006

Source: Adapted from Heijink, Koopmanschap, and Polder (2006).

future. In this chapter, we will examine how health care policies in the United States, Canada, Australia, China, Germany, and the Netherlands

a. structure health care for older adults,

b. incorporate consumer involvement in health care planning, and

c. confront issues of equity, regulation, and cost containment.

Because national health care policies and practices are inherently complex, we will necessarily focus on select aspects of each country's health care services to illustrate the most fundamental elements, strengths, and challenges present in different systems. We will address community-based care and family care in the context of broad policy trends, as these topics are explored more thoroughly in Chapters 8 and 9, respectively. While reviewing each country's policy foundation, system structure, and available care services, take time to reflect on how these different health care frameworks might shape the day-to-day lives of aging adults in each country.

United States

The United States is the only major industrialized nation in the world where health care policy has not emerged from a principle of universal care (Chappell, 1997). Rather, it uses a market approach to health care provision wherein competition between various private health care providers and insurers is intended to keep health care costs under control and therefore, theoretically, keep health care affordable for most citizens. More than 70% of adults purchase health insurance from private companies to cover their basic health care costs (Organisation for Economic Co-operation and Development [OECD], 2004d). As we were writing this chapter, President Barack Obama directed Congress to develop legislation that will result in a major overhaul of the nation's health care system, which will certainly affect health services for older adults. Visit the United States government websites provided at the end of this chapter for updates as this process evolves and health service changes unfold.

Acute Health Care

Current acute care services for older adults are covered, at least in part, through the federal Medicare program (Klees, Wolfe, & Curtis, 2009). President Harry S. Truman first introduced the idea of national health care for all people in 1945. After 20 years of political debates, a narrower plan focusing just on older adults and the poor was enacted in 1965 as part of President Lyndon B. Johnson's "Great Society" legislation. Medicare Part A provides persons aged 65 and older with hospital insurance, covering most costs associated with inpatient hospitalization and some post-hospitalization care. Almost all beneficiaries also purchase Medicare Part B, known as Supplemental Medical Insurance, which covers a percentage of the costs of physician care, outpatient care, and other medical services. Medicare is financed solely through mandatory Social Security contributions of employees to the federal government; thus, persons eligible for Social Security are automatically eligible for Medicare. Administered by the Centers for Medicaid and Medicare Services (CMS), under the direction of the U.S. Department of Health and Human Services, more than 45 million people are enrolled in one or both of parts of Medicare in 2009 (Klees et al., 2009).

Two optional components have been added to the Medicare program since it was first enacted. The Balanced Budget Act of 1997 established Medicare Part C, which gave beneficiaries the option of receiving their Medicare benefits through private health plans, mainly health maintenance organization (HMOs). Known as "Medicare+Choice," Balanced Budget Act legislation authorized Medicare to contract with local preferred provider organizations (PPOs), private fee-for-service plans, and medical savings account plans (Kaiser Family Foundation [KFF], 2009). The Medicare Modernization Act of 2003 renamed the program "Medicare Advantage" and authorized two additional plan types (regional PPOs and special needs plans) and boosted federal payments to plans to encourage plan participation. Consumer protections focusing on market practices were added in 2008 with the passage of the Medicare Improvements for Patients and Providers Act. Thus, over time, Medicare payment policy for these plans has shifted from one that produces savings to one that focuses more on expanding access to private plans under Medicare. In 2009, 23% of Medicare beneficiaries were enrolled in a private Medicare Advantage plan (KFF, 2009).

The passing of the Medicare Modernization Act in 2003 brought about the most significant legislative change to Medicare since its inception. In addition to adding more care plan options, it also established a voluntary outpatient prescription drug benefit to help reduce out-of-pocket drug spending for people on Medicare. Known as Part D, this option went into effect in 2006. It provides all elderly and disabled beneficiaries access to drug benefits through private plans approved by the federal government. Part D plans vary in benefit design, cost-sharing amounts, utilization management tools (e.g., prior authorization, quantity limits, and step therapy), and covered drugs (KFF, 2009). Although enrollment in Medicare drug plans is voluntary for most Medicare beneficiaries—unless they have drug coverage from another source (e.g., an employer plan) that is at least as good as standard Part D coverage—they face a penalty equal to 1% of the national average monthly premium for each month that they delay enrollment. In February 2010, 27.6 million beneficiaries were enrolled in Medicare Part D plans (KFF, 2010).

Long-Term Health Care

The Medicaid program, also enacted in 1965, is a federal-state, means-tested social assistance program funded through general taxation. It was designed to provide three types of medical assistance for low-income families and individuals:

1. Health insurance

2. Long-term care

3. Supplemental coverage for low-income Medicare beneficiaries for services not covered by Medicare and Medicare premiums, deductibles, and cost sharing.

Although states develop their own eligibility standards; determine the type, amount, and scope of benefits and the rate of payment for services; and administer their own program, they must provide the following basic medical services to Medicaid beneficiaries (KFF, 2009):

a. Inpatient and outpatient hospital services

b. Physician services and medical and surgical services of a dentist

c. Nursing facility services

d. Rural health clinic services

e. Home health care for persons eligible for skilled nursing services

f. Laboratory and X-ray services

g. Nurse practitioner services

Although not designed specifically for older adults, in 2005 older adults represented 10% of persons enrolled in Medicaid and accounted for 25% of Medicaid spending, most of which was used to cover costs of long-term care (KFF, 2009). Because Medicare does not cover either long-term care in institutions or home care services other than nursing care for people with acute conditions, older adults must pay for the full cost of institutional or in-home care. While they do have the option of acquiring private long-term care insurance to help provide for their care needs, the cost of private health insurance remains prohibitive for the majority of older adults (Kaiser Commission on Medicaid and the Uninsured [KCMU], 2006). Often, older adults requiring prolonged health care services start out with the resources to cover the cost of their care; however, most eventually "spend down" their assets and become eligible for Medicaid.

As a result of the growth in the cost of health care for older adults under Medicaid, managed care has emerged as a way to control health care costs. Another way legislators have acted to control Medicaid spending on long-term care costs is by allowing all states to enact legislation that links the purchase of long-term care insurance with Medicaid. In February 2006, Congress passed legislation that permits Medicaid to cover long-term care needs beyond the terms of the policy, with policyholders not required to spend down their assets to meet the Medicaid eligibility guidelines (Capretta, 2007b).

In 1981, Congress passed legislation creating Medicaid waiver programs, which enable states to provide a broad array of home- and community-based services (HCBS; e.g., personal care, respite, adult day health services, and personal emergency response systems). The intent of the waiver programs is to allow individuals to remain living in their own homes while receiving needed care and support, which is not only a priority for the majority of older adults but also a cost-effective alternative to nursing home care. While the majority of Medicaid long-term care dollars still go toward institutional care, about 41% of Medicaid spending is for HCBS (Burwell, Sredl, & Eiken, 2007). In 2006, the annual average spending for aged or disabled HCBS beneficiaries was $8,954 and $9,644 per participant, respectively (KFF, 2009), compared with $26,617 for beneficiaries in nursing facilities (Klees et al., 2009).

Fifty percent of waiver participants receive services through waivers targeting the aged or disabled (KFF, 2009). Forty-eight states and the District of Columbia offer services through (a) the optional 1915c HCBS waivers, (b) the mandatory home health benefit, and (c) the optional state plan personal care services benefit. Under the waiver programs, states may provide a combination of both traditional medical services (e.g., dental services, skilled nursing services) and nonmedical services (e.g., respite, case management, environment modifications). States also use a broad range of cost-containment strategies (e.g., restrictive financial eligibility standards, restrictive financial eligibility criteria, strict functional eligibility criteria) to meet federal waiver cost neutrality requirements and to limit waiver spending so that costs do not exceed state budget allocations (KCMU, 2009).

Over the past 3 decades, policymakers have responded to consumer preferences for alternatives to institutional care by expanding Medicaid HCBS programs. Most recently, as part of the Deficit Reduction Act of 2005, Congress "created new incentives and opportunities for states to refocus their Medicaid long-term services delivery systems away from nursing homes and toward a greater community orientation" (Crowley, 2006). For example, the Act provides options for states to apply for competitive awards for increased community services through the Money Follows the Person Program, aimed at helping Medicaid enrollees transition from long-term care institutions to the community (CMS, 2010b). It also created a new option for states to expand HCBS to low-income older adults and offers a "cash and counseling" option wherein states can allow for personal direction of self-assistance services without a waiver (Cash and Counseling, 2007). The details of these provisions are complex, but on the whole, they underline a shift toward increased attention to community-based care options as states deal with an increasing older population, health care center capacity limits, and the exorbitant costs of caring for persons within long-term care facilities.

Palliative Care

The Tax Equity and Fiscal Responsibility Act enacted in 1982 created the Medicare hospice program. Hospice service (i.e., physician services; nursing care; medical social services; home health aides; counseling; short-term inpatient care; physical, speech, and occupational therapy; homemaker services; and medical supplies, appliances, and equipment) are provided to terminally ill persons with life expectancies of 6 months or less who elect to forgo the standard Medicare benefits for treatment of their illness and to receive only palliative care (Klees et al., 2009). Such care includes pain relief, supportive medical and social services, physical therapy, nursing services, and symptom management. Originally, reimbursement for coverage was limited to 210 days. The passing of the 1990 Omnibus Budget Reconciliation Act removed this limitation. Medicare now provides for unlimited days of coverage for hospice care when provided by a Medicare-certified hospice program for as long as the doctor certifies that there is a need.

Although Medicare is the most common source of funding for hospice services, Medicaid provides hospice coverage in 48 states plus the District of Columbia. Medicaid hospice expenditures totaled $1.129 million in 2004 (Hospice Association of America, 2009). Hospices also receive reimbursement from private health insurance, HMOs, PPOs, and private-pay organizations—and to a lesser extent, from local (e.g., United Way), state, and federal sources (National Hospice and Palliative Care Organization, 2009).

Canada

Canada's health care system, called Medicare, is a government-funded universal system of medical insurance for every citizen, built on a culture of social solidarity. This system of social insurance covers the cost of basic preventative and acute medical care for Canadians of all ages. Although the funding base for this system involves a large federal contribution, the individual provinces actually have primary responsibility for managing health care under the Canadian Constitution (Steinbrook, 2006a). Because of this structure, rates of spending, available services, and degree of dependence on federal funds vary considerably from one province to another. Like the United States, Canada has a steep age-benefit profile (Kotlikoff & Hagist, 2005). In other words, the government spends a great deal more on health care for its older citizens than for younger members of the population.

Acute Health Care

Federal policy clearly states that no citizen can be denied physician and hospital services based on inability to pay. Even specialist and surgical care is equally accessible to all Canadian citizens. Demand for specialist services, however, has overburdened the universal system in some provinces, creating long waitlists for certain medical treatments and procedures (e.g., orthopedic surgeries, ophthalmological procedures). Though a wide range of services are available free of cost to all older adults, there has been critique that the system sometimes fails "to meet some patients' needs in a timely fashion" (Steinbrook, 2006a).

In an attempt to curtail waitlists for needed medical procedures, several provinces are experimenting with a shift in policy that allows for some combination of public and private care. Ongoing debate in Canada is fierce, however, over what positive or negative effects even a small infusion of private care options will have on the universal public system. A 2005 Supreme Court decision allowing patients to bypass some waitlists through private means if waits are "excessive" has opened the door for a widening role of the private sector, though it is still unclear what long-term impact this new flexibility will have on provincial health care management, national health policy, or overall patient care. Currently, private care accounts for only 1% of core health services in Canada (Steinbrook, 2006a).

Universal health care services acquired through Canada's mandatory state health insurance are financed through general taxation. Funding is provided jointly by the federal and state governments, with the federal government providing approximately one-third of each province's health care funding. The rest of health care expenditures are supported primarily by provincial personal and corporate taxes (Steinbrook, 2006a; Tanner, 2008a). With the aging of its population, Canada has decentralized control over the distribution of this funding, allowing each province to make changes aimed at reducing health care spending. To qualify for funding through the federal block grants, however, provinces must meet very specific criteria with respect to defined universality, comprehensiveness, portability, accessibility, and public administration (Tanner, 2008a). Current responsibility for ensuring standards of care in Canada are "widely distributed among professional and regulatory bodies" in different regions (OECD, 2005b). The most prominent national regulatory agency is the Canadian Council on Health Services Accreditation. On a voluntary basis, this organization assesses the quality of primary health care providers, hospitals, rehabilitation institutes, and long-term care facilities.

Canada is much further along than most other countries in developing a national health information infrastructure policy. In April 2001, the prime minister established the Commission on the Future of Health Care in Canada to study and make recommendations regarding the future of health care. The resulting report, known as the Romanow Report, contained 47 recommendations for a reform and renewal of the health care system. Five of the first 12 recommendations focused on building Canada's health information technology infrastructure. Implementing electronic personal health records (ePHRs; comprehensive records to which patients can have regular access) was viewed as one of the keys to modernizing Canada's health system and improving access and outcomes for all Canadians (Romanow, 2002). In support of this recommendation, the Personal Information Protection and Electronic Documents Act, passed in 2000, was extended in 2002 to the health sector to protect the confidentiality of ePHRs (Office of the Privacy Commissioner of Canada, 2006). ePHR is still in its early stages of development; as of early 2009, only about 17% of the process had been completed. However, each of the provinces has an established timetable and road map for full ePHR implementation by 2016.

Long-Term Health Care

Although part of the Canada Health Act, the government does not play as prominent a role in funding long-term residential- and community-based care for older adults as it does for acute medical costs. Both in-home and institutional long-term care programs are means tested—that is, they provide services free of charge or on a sliding scale to those who qualify for in-kind benefits. Eligibility for long-term care, similar to other components of Canada's health care system, varies considerably among provinces (OECD, 2005b).

Because health care spending in most provinces is growing at an unsustainable rate, Canada is looking to improve the efficiency with which it manages the health of older adults before demographic shifts overburden the Canadian tax base—hence, there is a push for integration of services (MacAdam, 2008). A 2002 Collaborative Strategy for Home and Community Care has increased policy emphasis in Canada on integrating care for older adults, particularly those with chronic conditions and disabilities. This policy is aimed at improving access to and quality and sustainability of medical services as the population ages.

A System of Integrated Care for Older Persons (SIPA in French) has also been piloted in some Canadian provinces, specifically with the goal of reducing the use and costs of institutional services (e.g., hospitals, nursing homes; MacAdam, 2008). The idea behind SIPA is that communities provide a full range of integrated services to meet the complex long-term care needs of frail older adults—health and social services, community services, hospital care, and institutional care. In collaboration with primary care physicians, a multidisciplinary team is responsible for assessing needs and organizing and delivering most of the health and social services in the community. The initial SIPA pilot projects have shown promise for substituting community-based for institutional services at no extra cost to the system and with increased client satisfaction (MacAdam, 2008).

Palliative Care

In 1974, about 7 years after the introduction of Canada's public health insurance, hospitals began operating palliative care wards (Canadian Hospice Palliative Care Association [CHPCA], 2009). Hospice palliative care grew quickly and became widely accepted as a societal movement reforming health to balance *high-tech* acute care with *high-touch* palliative care. Since becoming an option within the Canadian health care system, hospice care has expanded from hospital units to the home and long-term care facilities.

In 2000, the Senate Standing Committee on Social Affairs, Science, and Technology released a report on the growing need for a national strategy to address Canadians' palliative care issues. As a result, in 2001, Health Canada created the Secretariat on Palliative and End-of-Life Care (now known as the Palliative and End-of-Life Care Unit) to manage issues related to end-of-life care and advocate for the needs of dying Canadians to other government agencies (CHPCA, 2009). In 2004, as part of "A 10-year Plan to Strengthen Health Care," provincial and territorial government officials agreed to fund social services related to palliative home care, including nursing and case-management staff, medications, and other personal care needs (Romanow, 2002).

Palliative care is paid for in different ways across Canada. Only a small number of provinces have designated hospice palliative care as a core service under their provincial health plans. In the remaining provinces, hospice palliative care may be included in provincial home care budgets or other health service budgets, leaving the funding vulnerable to budget reductions (CHPCA, 2007; Health Canada, 2009). Funding for palliative care services comes from private donations from individuals, social agencies, service clubs, local cancer societies, and other similar organizations.

BOX 6.1   Policy to People Link: Access to Health Care

One way to reduce health care costs is to provide access to preventative health care services. Canadians have access to Telehealth Ontario, which is a confidential, free service offered by the Ontario Ministry of Health and Long-Term Care. Ontario residents call the toll-free number and are able to speak with a registered nurse and get health-related advice. Nurses can help clients develop self-care regimens for managing chronic conditions, give advice about when to seek medical treatment, or address lifestyle and wellness issues. The nurse operators can also direct clients to appropriate community services. The service is available 24 hours a day, 7 days a week. For more information on this service, go to www.health.gov.on.ca/en/public/programs/telehealth/.

In the Netherlands, more than 90% of citizens have access to after-hours medical clinics. The purpose of these clinics is to reduce emergency-room visits for nonemergency medical care. For example, the New West Clinic in Amsterdam opens at 6 p.m. Clients call the clinic seeking advice about their medical problems. Sometimes, they are advised to seek immediate care, but usually the staff determines whether the patients need to come in or require a home visit. Typically, older people with serious health problems receive home visits from a team of providers, which may include a general practitioner, nurse, and paramedic. For more information on these clinics, go to www.npr.org/templates/story/story.php?storyId=92606938 and www.commonwealthfund.org/usr_doc/Grol_qualityNetherlands_910.pdf.

Australia

The Australian system of health care is mixed and complex, with responsibilities divided between federal and state governments and involvement of both public and private (profit and nonprofit) sectors (Duckett, 2004; OECD, 2005b). The aim of Australia's national health care system is to give universal access to health care while allowing choices for individuals through a substantial private-sector involvement in delivery and financing (Commonwealth Fund, 2009). Although there are some significant discrepancies between access to health care by indigenous groups in Australia and the general population, as well as some challenges with regard to health care access for residents of remote rural areas, it appears that the large majority of Australians are able to access and afford regular preventative and acute medical care without major logistical or financial obstacles.

Acute Health Care

The government Medicare program, funded with general tax revenue, provides universal coverage for a large portion of the costs of medical and hospital visits for all Australian citizens. A benefits schedule guides the amount of benefit received for various services, procedures, or treatments. The gap between this scheduled fee and what physicians actually charge is covered by patients out-of-pocket (Commonwealth Fund, 2009). Public hospitals are owned and managed by the state and house about 70% of the country's hospital beds. Charitable nonprofit hospitals are also available, and the number of private for-profit hospitals has expanded in recent years (Duckett, 2004). The Australian central government also supports a Pharmaceutical Benefits Scheme that offers subsidies for the cost of medication. It covers almost all prescriptions, with a few exceptions. Cost sharing for prescriptions is lower for pensioners and Australians below a certain income threshold, but all citizens receive some assistance with prescription fees (Duckett, 2004). The federal government will additionally provide a subsidy of 30% for purchase of private health insurance, and leaders actively promote citizen purchase of private coverage to assist with any uncovered services or gaps between the Medicaid system and physician charges.

The responsibility for funding and provision of health services is distributed between the Commonwealth and the eight state and territory governments (Commonwealth Fund, 2009). The commonwealth government has primary responsibility for policy-making, broad public health initiatives and protections, and as funder/insurer of medical, pharmaceutical, and aged-care services. Central government also plays an important role in regulating and subsidizing private health insurance and contributing funds that support state/territory provision of services. State and territory governments, on the other hand, have much heavier involvement in service delivery. These governments own and operate public hospitals and directly deliver a full range of mental, dental, and promotional health services, as well as managing community and school health programs (Commonwealth Fund, 2009).

The federal and state governments provide support for the country's Medicare system through general tax revenues, and both tiers of government also help provide the majority of the funding for institutional and community-based long-term care. Overall, the government pays about 70% of health care costs (with 47% coming from the federal level and 23% from state governments). The remainder of health care costs is covered either by private insurance (8.6%) or private pay. Costs related to prescriptions and long-term care are scaled based on pensioner status and/or ability to pay, so some individuals are required to contribute more toward overall health costs than others. Since Australia embraces the philosophy that no patient should be refused, services are based on inability to pay and all older adults have access to the full range of medical and long-term care service options (OECD, 2005b).

Long-Term Health Care

With passage of the Aged Care Act in 1997, Australia placed a major policy emphasis on care for older adults. It developed a multifaceted, integrated "aged care system" that includes Residential and Aged Care services, Home and Community Care (HACC), Community Aged Care packages, and Extended Aged Care at Home packages. The Australian government also provides funding for expert Aged Care Assessment Teams, which provide eligibility assessment for institutional and or home care services based on the medical, physical, social, and psychological needs of older adults. In addition, they also provide recommendations and guidance regarding residential choices and navigation of the long-term care system (OECD, 2005b). Older adults are required to receive an Aged Care Assessment before receiving any Australian government subsidy for either institutional or community care. Once assessed, they may be eligible to participate in one or more of these programs and required to pay a portion of fees based on a government-subsidized sliding scale.

The Residential and Aged Care services provide accommodation and support with either "low" or "high-level" care for any older Australians who can no longer live at home (Australian Institute of Health and Welfare [AIHW], 2006). Aged care homes are legally permitted to charge several kinds of fees; however, the government calculates and regulates all care fees. Some fees are standard, while others are based on the person's income. Under the Aged Care Act of 1997, aged care homes are required to care for a certain minimum number of people who need help to pay for their aged care accommodation—known as concessional or assisted residents. For this, they receive extra government subsidies. Residences must be accredited under the Accreditation Standards for Residential Aged Care in order to receive subsidies from the Australian government. The standards cover such things as management, care, lifestyle, quality, and safety issues.

Most HCBS are offered through the HACC packages to enhance the independence of all adults with "moderate, severe, or profound" disabilities and prevent premature admissions to institutional settings (AIHW, 2006). It is a cost-shared program between the Commonwealth and state and territory governments. Some programs charge a small income-based fee for services; the amount and type of fees vary between states and territories. HACC programs offer a variety of services tailored to the unique needs of each adult, including home nursing services, meal delivery, housekeeping and home maintenance services, transportation and shopping assistance, allied medical care, home- or center-based respite care, and general support for effective coordination of services (AIHW, 2006). The National Guidelines for HACC Service Standards provide agencies with a nationally consistent approach to the standard, quality, and delivery of all HACC-funded services.

Community Aged Care packages, on the other hand, are offered to older Australians who desire to remain at home but have more complex care needs that would actually allow them to qualify for low-level residential care. Participants are offered a more intense level of service coordination and supervision from a central package provider (AIHW, 2006). The Extended Aged Care at Home services are similarly coordinated but are offered only to those who qualify for "high-level" care and wish to remain at home, and they include nursing input (OECD, 2005b). All community care service providers, including Community Aged Care and Extended Aged Care at Home, have to meet consistent Australian government standards in the quality and delivery of services.

Australia's spectrum of health care services also includes a range of formalized governmental supports for informal caregivers. These services include three different options for informal carers who wish to stay at home and provide care for family members or friends. Carer Payment is an income support payment for people who are unable, or minimally able, to participate in the workforce due to caregiving responsibilities. Carer Allowance is an income supplement for those who work but also commit a great deal of time to the care of an individual (adult or child) with a disability or severe medical condition. The National Respite for Carers Programme provides funding for short-term or emergency respite in the community (OECD, 2005b).

Palliative Care

As in other countries, a focus on and government support for palliative care has evolved over time (see Allen, Chapman, O'Connor, & Francis, 2008). In 1987, the Victorian Parliamentary Committee published "Options for Dying with Dignity," which focused on patients' right to oppose extraordinary and heroic attempts to keep them alive. This was followed by the passing of the Medical Treatment Act of 1988, giving persons the right to refuse treatment, a move that was replicated in many other Australian states over the next few years (Ramadge, 2000).

In 1989, the Australian government announced the Medicare Incentive Package, which funded homecare palliative care programs. This action was later augmented with further funding from the Australian government through the Palliative Care Program of 1993. This program provides support for palliative care in four broad areas (Commonwealth of Australia, 2009):

1. Support for patients, families, and carers in the community

2. Increased access to palliative care medicines in the community

3. Education, training, and support for the workforce

4. Research and quality improvement for palliative care services

The first guidelines for the delivery of palliative care services—Standards for Hospice and Palliative Care Provision—were developed in 1994 by the National Palliative Care Association and the Australian Council on Health Care Standards (Ramadge, 2000). These guidelines focused primarily on end-stage cancer care. Recognizing that people with a chronic or life-limiting illness besides cancer would benefit from the delivery of palliative care, the Australian government commissioned "Guidelines for a Palliative Approach in Residential Aged Care" (Allen et al., 2008; Australian Government National Health and Medical Council, 2006).

In October 2000 the Australian Health Ministers' Advisory Council endorsed the National Palliative Care Strategy, a policy document that the Australian government and state and territory governments used to guide palliative care policy development and service delivery across Australia (Commonwealth of Australia, 2009). Although palliative care programs are governed under the auspice of each state and territory, as part of the 2003 to 2008 Australian Health Care Agreements, the Australian government committed more than $200 million to national activities to support improvements in the standard of palliative care offered in the community. For example, with support from the Australian Health Care Agreements, states and territories work collaboratively to develop and assess common performance indicators, including access to and quality of palliative care services.

Responsibility for the funding of palliative care services in Australia varies depending on the type of service and the setting in which it is provided (Gordon, Eagar, Currow, & Green, 2009). Funding for out-of-hospital medical and pharmaceutical services is covered under the national Medicare system; thus, these services are accessed in a mostly consistent manner across the country. There is no national model for the funding for inpatient hospital services or community-based palliative care services. Funding for these services is the responsibility of the individual states and territories.

China

The Chinese health care system, along with other aspects of the national Chinese infrastructure, is struggling with the transition from a planned economy to a market economy (Zhang & Chen, 2006). Health services that used to be free for all citizens now require copayments from employed workers who are fortunate enough to have insurance and require full coverage of costs out-of-pocket from the majority of rural, poor, and an increasing number of working Chinese who do not have health coverage. Although the government is attempting to better serve the needs of vulnerable groups, such as older adults and disabled individuals, with community health care programs, there is an overall problem across the country with a high level of unmet needs and general underutilization of health services (Zhang & Chen, 2006).

Acute Health Care

China has never had a universal welfare system for all its citizens, but historically, it has entitled workers in urban areas to free health care for life and 50% coverage of health care costs for their dependents. Though health reforms in the 1980s meant to reduce the financial burden of the state, there has been a dramatic shift away from this nearly universal health care for urban employees and their extended families (Sun, 2004). Medical coverage is instead now shouldered by local government, employers, and individuals. Increasingly, as some employers are unable to provide coverage that is not mandated by government, access to health care that was once nearly universal has become based largely on the patient's ability to pay (Sun, 2004). There is also a Rural Cooperative Medical Scheme in China meant to provide those in rural communities with some access to health insurance. In reality, however, the majority of rural farmers and their families are not members of these cooperatives and end up paying all medical expenses out of pocket (Zhang & Chen, 2006).

In recent years, the Chinese government has openly recognized the weaknesses in its health support system and has made some progress toward increased insurance coverage through a new Urban Employee Basic Medical Insurance System and reestablishment of the Rural Cooperative Medical Scheme. By 2005, these efforts had made some strides toward improved health insurance rates, but both programs have significant drawbacks that have limited their overall impact (Hew, 2006). In response to economic recession and the extreme rural-urban health gap, the Chinese government is planning a major restructuring of its health care system to move toward improved care and more universal health coverage. Aware of the heavy burden health care costs in the current system place on Chinese families, particularly those in rural areas, the government has introduced a plan to revamp its health care system over the next 3 years (Lawrence & Liu, 2009; Wang, 2009). In what Wang describes as China's "stab at universal health care," the country plans to spend 850 billion yuan ($125 billion) to boost health insurance coverage to 90% of the population by 2011. An annual health subsidy and a system to more widely distribute vital drugs and vaccines to Chinese citizens are both part of this new health care plan (Lawrence & Liu, 2009; Wang, 2009).

Although China has begun to tackle some of the problems with its health care system infrastructure, Chinese citizens are still by and large shouldering the majority of health care costs directly. In 2003, almost 45% of China's urban population and 79% of rural citizens were without any type of health insurance coverage and therefore paying out-of-pocket for any medical care (Hew, 2006). Health care expenditures have been increasing steadily, while at the same time, the government percentage of the GDP spent on health care has been decreasing. The typical hospital in China receives less than 10% of its income from the government, spurring a trend in excessive prescription of expensive drugs and overutilization of costly medical tests so that hospitals can charge citizens enough in medical fees to sustain operation (Hew, 2006; Sun, 2004).

Currently, there is an absence of integrated policies to guide care at all of China's hospitals. There are also no accepted uniform national guidelines regarding minimum requirements for education and training of health care professionals (Hew, 2006). Because of the weaknesses in quality controls, the quality of patient care, quality of health care personnel, and monitoring of health care are highly variable and often weak across Chinese medical facilities. Rural areas in particular suffer from an extremely low quality of health care workers. A 2001 study of rural provinces found that 70% of village doctors had no more than a high school education and had received an average of only 20 months of medical training (Hew, 2006).

Long-Term Health Care

Long-term care for older adults is traditionally provided at home in China by adult children, with daughters-in-law providing the majority of care. This arrangement will become increasingly less feasible in coming decades when parents of the first generation of the one-child policy start reaching old age and retiring (Zavoretti, 2006). Referred to as the "4-2-1 problem," only-children will face the need to care for two sets of parents and several grandparents.

To meet long-term health care needs, China currently has two coexisting systems that provide institutional care for aging adults. These include the social welfare system, which operates welfare institutes, homes for the aged, and veteran care facilities, and the medical care system, which manages geriatric hospitals, nursing facilities, rehabilitation wards, and mental health hospitals for elders suffering from dementia (Wu, Mao, & Xu, 2008). The welfare institutions, elderly apartments, and homes for the aged are run by departments of civil affairs at national and regional levels. These facilities are operated by government organizations, nongovernment organizations, or private investors.

Most nursing homes in China are funded by public resources. In 2001, the Chinese Ministry of Civil Affairs initiated the Xing Guang Project (Wu, Mao, & Zhong, 2009), which asked that departments of civil affairs at the central and local government levels fund building township residential care facilities for elders in rural areas. The Ministry allocated 20% of social welfare lottery funds for this project. In 2006, the Ministry initiated the Xia Guang Project that again asked departments of civil affairs to allocate some proportion of the welfare lottery funds for building infrastructure specifically to support *wubao* elders (poor older persons guaranteed by the government to have the provision of the five basic needs of food, clothing, accommodation, health care, and burial service; Wu et al., 2009).

In rural areas, where the range of care options is more developed than in urban areas, poor and childless elders, as well as those not having any close relative with which to live, are likely to become nursing home residents. Policy documents, including the "Opinions on Accelerating Socialized Welfare Services" and "Opinions on Development of Social Services for the Aged," help speed the development of institutional care for elders in rural areas (Chu & Chi, 2008). If older residents require any hospitalization outside the institutions, insurance covers only 40% of these expenses, while the remaining 60% of medical costs is shared between the resident and the institution (Wu et al., 2008). Some facilities also receive land from the government to help cover daily expenses. They require staff members and elderly residents without major functional impairments to raise pigs and plant vegetables to help support themselves. Because most residents of long-term care facilities are not functionally disabled, the large majority of residents assist with the work in the field. Institutions that cannot fall back on this government provision of land for support admit elders who can afford to pay admissions fees and other expenses. In the past decade, privately run long-term care facilities have begun to emerge in some rural areas. These facilities rely almost solely on admissions fees from residents and usually do not accept wubao elders (Wu et al., 2008).

With the growing of China's aging population, the financial implications of building and operating the majority of nursing homes by government sponsorship has shifted some of the policy emphasis toward community and home care. For example, between 2001 and 2004, the Chinese government built 32,000 Star Light Centers for Seniors, which provide services such as emergency aid, day care, health care services, and recreational activities to more than 30 million elders (Chu & Chi, 2008).

Palliative Care

Palliative care was introduced into China in the early 1990s as care for a person approaching death (Kerr, 1993). Such care is localized and not widespread (Goh, 2008). Services are available primarily in hospitals located in major cities, including Tianjin, Beijing, Shanghai, Chengdu, and Guangzhou. Even where it is available, relatively few people in China seek this type of care. Experts suggest that because the pursuit of longevity is inherent in Chinese culture, people are ashamed to mention death, let alone go to a place to await death (China Daily, 2006).

Germany

The two predominant frameworks for supporting health care in the European Union are tax-financed National Health Service systems and Social Insurance collected in insurance funds that operate independently from the central government. Germany falls into this latter category, with a system built on compulsory social insurance. Citizens of all income levels and ages are able to participate in this social insurance scheme. Germany does provide an option, however, for citizens above a certain income threshold to opt out of social insurance if they prefer to purchase private coverage. Private health insurance can either substitute for or be supplementary to the statutory health insurance program in Germany (Lundy & Finder, 2009). Many Germans rely on private providers for their primary coverage or supplement with private plans (OECD, 2004c). Almost 90% of the total German population was covered by the public system in 2006, while 26% of Germans had private insurance (i.e., primary and supplemental) coverage (Lundy & Finder, 2009). As of January 1, 2009, and for the first time in German social history, all residents are obliged to have health insurance (Bundesministerium für Gesundheit, 2009).

Acute Health Care

The health care system in Germany is based on the key principles of social solidarity, decentralization, and self-regulation (OECD, 2004c). Central government provides only the legislative framework in which health services are delivered, while management of the various insurance funds and service providers falls under the jurisdiction of individual states (*Länder*). This "state centrism" or state "semi-sovereignty" has a long historical tradition in Germany (Altenstetter & Busse, 2005). One unique aspect of the German system is a strict separation of purchasers (the insurance funds are termed *sickness funds*) and the providers of health care services. Health care fees are then subject to intense negotiation between these two sectors of the health care system.

The basic benefits package for social insurance includes coverage of preventative, screening, diagnostic, treatment, and rehabilitation services, as well as some transportation for medical care (Jakubowski & Busse, 1998). Health insurance premiums are collected separately and managed by sickness funds within different German states. These funds are maintained by contributions from all German citizens participating in the public insurance scheme. In 2003, members of the German parliament agreed to raise copayments for general physician visits, copayments for hospital stays, and patient-shared costs for prescription drugs (Burgermeister, 2003). A controversial deal on health care reform that took place between 2004 and 2007 requires patients to pay much more for treatment than they have in the past. In 2006, about 77% of German health care funding was derived from compulsory and voluntary contributions to social health insurance, 10% was covered by private insurance or other private funds, and the remaining 13% of health care costs were covered by out-of-pocket payments from patients (Lundy & Finder, 2009).

The financing of the statutory health insurance system changed in January 2009 as part of the 2007 Health Care Reform (formally titled the Act to Strengthen Competition in the Statutory Health Insurance System; Bundesministerium für Gesundheit, 2009). All contributors now pay the same contribution rate, and an increasing amount of money from taxes will flow into the sickness fund. It is from the fund that the health insurance funds will receive the resources they need to ensure their members' care.

Long-Term Health Care

In 1995, Germany added an additional pillar to its health care system—long-term care insurance (Federal Ministry of Health, 2009). All insured persons are legally entitled to assistance if and when needed. Their financial situation has no effect on their long-term care entitlement. Rather, benefits are granted on the basis of the assessed level of care needed (i.e., considerable, severe, extreme). Regardless of the level of care received, prevention and rehabilitation (i.e., measures to overcome, reduce, or prevent an increase in the need for long-term care) are high-priority services, and home care is given priority over institutional care.

All citizens must have long-term care insurance that matches their health insurance. If a person, regardless of age, has social health insurance, long-term care insurance is automatic. Persons with private health insurance are also required to purchase long-term care insurance. Benefits provided under private long-term care insurance must be equivalent to those provided by statutory long-term care insurance. Private insurance companies are also required to offer reasonable terms and rates for older members. In this rather complex system, both social and private long-term care insurance is governed by the same regulation, wherein insurance beneficiaries must be assessed and qualify for long-term care services based on three different levels (considerable, severe, extreme) of care need (OECD, 2005b). The number of available spaces in institutional settings such as nursing homes has increased considerably since the adoption of the insurance scheme, meaning that the nation is able to handle current capacity for institutional care without waitlists. The number of home care providers in Germany since 1995 has also more than doubled and has been assessed as a sufficient infrastructure to support the current care needs of older adults (OECD, 2005b). Thus, long-term care insurance has made a marked contribution to the stabilization and expansion of professional services in home and inpatient care (Federal Ministry of Health, 2009).

Social assistance contributes to the funding of both institutional and in-home care when persons do not have a high enough income to cover out-of-pocket costs. The fixed rate of contribution for long-term care insurance is already not keeping pace with the care demands of Germany's aging population, and the picture is likely to get only bleaker as the oldest old—those most dependent on long-term care services—become a much larger proportion of the population seeking health care services in coming years (OECD, 2005b).

Germany's quality assurance program places the majority of responsibility on providers and sickness funds with a 2001 Long-Term Care Quality Assurance Law that states long-term care providers are responsible for producing quality outcomes and for establishing internal quality assurance mechanisms. The sickness funds are made responsible for ensuring equal access of all beneficiaries to quality care. Oversight and regulation are loosely monitored by individual states and broadly guided by the Federal Ministry of Health as the key health policy watchdog on the national level. The Advisory Council for Concerted Action in Health Care also plays an advisory role in many nationwide medical matters (Jakubowski & Busse, 1998). The ongoing price negotiations between health care providers and purchasers are also used as a regulatory mechanism for keeping health care pricing at a reasonable level.

Palliative Care

Unlike other Western countries, Germany does not have a strong practice of specialized hospice care (Schneider, Lueckmann, Behmann, & Bisson, 2009). The German hospice movement emerged in the 1980s but was not well-integrated into the public health care structure. In 1994, the German Association for Palliative Medicine was founded, which gave professional health caregivers a voice in the delivery of palliative care. However, as recently as 2005, the Enquete Commission on Ethics and Legislation in Modern Medicine noted that the quality and availability of palliative care in Germany was unsatisfactory. Specifically, the committee called for more services, education, financial support, and research (Schneider, Buser, & Amelung, 2006). In response to these recommendations, as part of the 2007 German Health Care reform, lawmakers gave citizens the right to receive "specialist outpatient palliative care." However, the reform did not strengthen nonspecialist services typically provided by local general practitioners (Schneider et al., 2009).

BOX 6.2   Policy to People Link: Out-of-Pocket Medical Costs

One aspect of health care financing policy is the determination of the level of out-of-pocket payments that individuals must pay when they consume health care services. As we mentioned at the beginning of the chapter, Ms. K., a retiree living in Amsterdam, pays 105€ ($140) out of pocket each month, which covers all her costs for basic health care services and prescription drugs in the Dutch health care system. The table below shows the variation in the out-of-pocket medical costs borne by adults with any chronic condition in five of the countries we reviewed in this chapter. As you can see, the direct out-of-pocket cost to older adults with chronic conditions is much lower in other countries compared with the United States.

Out-of-Pocket Medical Costs in the Past Year, Adults With Any Chronic Condition (2008)		
Country	*Less Than U.S. $500*	*More Than U.S. $1,000*
Australia	43%	25%
Canada	57%	20%
Germany	57%	13%
Netherlands	72%	8%
United States	31%	41%

Sources: Adapted from Commonwealth Fund (2008) and Schoen, Osborn, How, Doty, and Peugh (2009).

The Netherlands

The Netherlands defies the more predominant European trend of universally funding health care through general taxation. Instead, this country mixes a compulsory insurance fund scheme with private voluntary insurance (Jakubowski & Busse, 1998). Its system of insurance for health and long-term care is composed of three different pillars (OECD, 2005b):

1. Government health insurance, which is mandatory up to a certain income level

2. Private health insurance for those above the income threshold

3. A comprehensive public scheme for the total population to cover "catastrophic" or "exceptional" risks and expenditures that are regarded as "noninsurable"

This last pillar of the health system also covers acute care needs stemming from chronic conditions and a broad range of long-term care services across a range of care settings.

Acute Health Care

The history of health care in the Netherlands reflects the changing relationship between the government and voluntary organizations. Originating largely in private or charitable initiatives, almost all Dutch hospitals are still private and are all nonprofit organizations. Despite the predominance of private ownership, the government heavily regulates the Dutch health care system.

Health policies in the Netherlands are shaped by the interaction between the government and organized groups (Exter, Hermans, Dosljak, & Busse, 2004). Examples of the primary organizations are the Health Council (*Gezondheidsraad*), which is the statutory body that advises the government on the scientific state of the art in medicine, health care, public health, and environmental protection; the Council for Public Health and Health Care (*Raad voor de Volksgezondheid en Zorg*), which is an independent governmental body that advises on health care and welfare policy issues; and the Health Care Inspectorate (*Inspectie voor de Gezondheidszorg*), which supervises the quality and accessibility of health care.

Medical care in the Netherlands is largely funded by a system of public and private insurance schemes. As described in the "Health Care Systems in Transition" report (Exter et al., 2004), the Netherlands health care insurance system is divided into three compartments. The first compartment, covered under the Exceptional Medical Expenses Act (*Algemene Wet Bijzondere Ziektekosten*), covers the exceptional medical expenses associated with long-term care or high-cost treatment, where the expense is such that it cannot be borne by individuals or adequately covered by private insurance. With a few exceptions, everyone living in the Netherlands (irrespective of nationality) and subject to Dutch income tax is covered by the Act. The second compartment of the insurance program covers normal, necessary medical care and is largely covered by the Sickness Fund Act (*Ziekenfondswet*), private medical insurance (e.g., Health Insurance Access Act), or a health insurance scheme for public servants. All persons meeting income restrictions and receiving social security benefits are insured up to the age of 65 years under the Sickness Fund Act. As of January 1998, people 65 years and older who were insured under the Act before they turned 65 continued to be insured in this way after they reached the age of 65. Their income is no longer a significant factor. This is known as the "stay where you are" principle. The main motive for this legislated protection was that older adults were spending an unjustifiably large share of their income on premiums. Individuals with private insurance who turn 65 can opt to join a sickness fund, provided their income does not exceed a certain ceiling. The third compartment of the insurance program covers the supplementary forms of care regarded as being less necessary (e.g., dental, vision, alternative medicines). The costs here are largely covered by private medical insurance. Complementary sources of health care financing include taxes, out-of-pocket payments, and voluntary supplementary health insurance.

Long-Term Health Care

The Netherlands boasts an extremely comprehensive, diversified system of specialized long-term care, both in-home and in institutional settings. A wide range of acute and long-term care delivery pathways for aging residents were integrated at the District Health Board level by the Health of Older People Strategy of 2002 (OECD, 2005b). These programs are supported by insurance contributions from all; they are available to persons of all ages but require copayments based on personal income.

As previously noted, medical expenses associated with long-term care not covered by private insurance are covered under the Exceptional Medical Expenses Act (Exter et al., 2004). With a few exceptions, everyone living in the Netherlands and all nonresidents employed in the Netherlands and subject to Dutch income tax are covered by the Act. In the early 1990s, as part of ongoing health reforms, some entitlements shifted from the sickness fund and from private health insurance to the Exceptional Medical Expenses Act. However, this policy was reversed in 1996, and nursing homes and homes for the aged are once again included in the Exceptional Medical Expenses Act benefits package.

Compared with other European countries, the Netherlands has almost the highest rate of residential care for older adults (Exter et al., 2004). A range of specialized institutional settings are available for older adults with varying degrees of dependency or specific health care needs (e.g., dementia, sensory impairment, or psychiatric care needs). While the majority of older adults needing institutional care live in nursing homes or similar institutions, some also receive care in residential settings designed for persons with disabilities or in sheltered housing that provides psychiatric and psychosocial care for persons with mental health problems.

Nearly 58% of older recipients of long-term care live in their homes or in another community-based setting. Home care services in the Netherlands range from meals-on-wheels and home-making supports to adult day care and respite care to more intensive home nursing care (OECD, 2005b). Recently, the country has seen a trend toward increased prevalence and volume of in-home care with a simultaneous decline in nursing home use (Statistics Netherlands, 2008). The emphasis on further development of in-home care and universal availability of long-term care options is very interesting given the country's general rejection of the notion of extended family care responsibilities, which often occurs alongside use of formal services.

Given the wide range of service providers who contribute to the long-term care terrain in the Netherlands, this country takes a "self-regulatory" approach to service oversight. All member organizations of the major care service association in the Netherlands have to comply with a generic, formal system of internal quality management. Compliance with these guidelines is checked by an independent agency before service providers can be approved for certification (OECD, 2005b).

Palliative Care

In the Netherlands, palliative care is part of regular health care. As described in a policy report prepared by the Netherlands Institute for Health Services Research (Francke, 2003), the Dutch government began to develop a policy on palliative care as hospice units and care homes began palliative care work in 1996. The Minister of Health, Welfare, and Sport initiated a stimulation program based on the expectation that the need for palliative care would increase further in the coming decades and to support initiatives in the sector. The initiative encompassed three specific separate programs that informed policy decisions. The Health Research and Development Council/Medical Sciences Program was charged with the encouragement of research and innovative projects. Its work resulted in a better understanding of the nature and scale of palliative care. The Centers for the Development of Palliative Care were created to promote and guide the development of palliative care by six university centers. In addition to initiating numerous research projects, the Centers for the Development of Palliative Care introduced projects relating to consultation and training in the palliative care field. The Hospice Care Integration Project Group investigated ways to stimulate the integration of professionally staffed hospices, volunteer-run hospices, and hospice units into regular health care. This group made a major contribution to cooperation, coordination, and network creation between providers of palliative care.

Hospice care in the Netherlands is typically provided by general practitioners, nurses, and home care workers. General practitioners can be reimbursed for their care through both compulsory public and private health insurance plans. Services that a general practitioner provides include pain management and psychoemotional support to patients and their families. Likewise, workers in home care agencies are reimbursed through public and private insurance companies.

Summary

To address the growing health care needs and costs of their aging populations, countries have structured their health care systems in diverse and complex ways. They have negotiated various levels of universal versus market-driven care, public versus private funding and insurance schemes, for-profit versus nonprofit health provision, and mandatory versus voluntary citizen participation. They, as well as most other countries, are being pulled by considerations of balance between fiscal security and fair distribution of services. Market-driven structure, for instance, often leaves serious gaps, providing excellent care for some elders and neglecting the care of others entirely. Universal systems, on the other hand, may be stretched so thin by population aging that while everyone has equal access to medical care, very few receive optimal or timely services. Similarly, private funding and insurance schemes may disproportionately benefit the wealthy, and publicly funded schemes, while serving a broader array of individuals, may struggle to stay solvent. At the center of the struggle to find balance is this question: What level of responsibility do governments have for the health care of their older citizens? Every system has a different answer, and no system is ideal in every aspect. A review of the various health care models, however, suggests that those countries that embrace a diverse range of approaches—creatively combining market/universal systems, public/private funding schemes, for-profit/nonprofit care, and compulsory/optional participation in components of the system—tend to be the most stable and comprehensive.

Countries have implemented a range of strategies for regulation of health care systems at national, state/territorial, and local levels. Some rely on government entities, while others use independent regulatory agencies. Some countries have national standards, while others determine standards at the local level. Different cultures emphasize strict external oversight by government or independent regulatory agencies, while other health care cultures rely heavily on internal self-regulation by care providers. Most systems find it necessary to widely distribute responsibility for medical system management and service delivery, thus creating challenges regarding consistent regulation and equitable distribution of health services in different parts of the world.

Among the countries discussed in this chapter, Australia and the Netherlands demonstrate the greatest balance between public and private provision of health care between national, state, and individual costs. Their comprehensive systems of health care for older adults might serve as models for countries with more rigid or narrow approaches to health care delivery that have caused financial struggles or unequal distribution of services. The integrated policy tactics employed by these two nations have, for the most part, ensured older adults equal access to a full range of services from preventative to palliative care and created a smooth continuum of late-life care in both community and institutional settings. However, countries with substantial proportions of minority elders, such as Australia and the United States, face additional obstacles to providing comprehensive late-life care. Even the most successful health care systems rarely address the unique health needs of minorities. This holds true across the lifespan and across national borders.

For More Information

1. AARP Public Policy Institute (Health Research)
   http://www.aarp.org/research/ppi/health-care/

   The Public Policy Institute of the AARP conducts research and reports on a number of issues related to the aging population, including health, in the United States and around the globe.

2. Centers for Disease Control and Prevention (CDC)
   http://www.cdc.gov/aging/

   The CDC is an arm of the U.S. Department of Health and Human Services and provides information on a variety of health-related issues affecting older adults.

3. Global Action on Aging
   http://www.globalaging.org/

Global Action on Aging is a nonprofit organization that advises the United Nations on global aging issues.

4. International Association for Hospice and Palliative Care
   http://www.hospicecare.com

The vision of this organization is to help increase and optimize the availability of and access to hospice and palliative care for patients and their families throughout the world.

5. Health Care Reform
   http://www.healthreform.gov/

Just as this book is going to press, President Obama has just signed the Patient Protection and Affordable Care Act (2010), and it will be published shortly as Public Law 111-148.

6. Kaiser Family Foundation
   http://www.kff.org/healthreform/upload/8061.pdf

The Foundation provides an excellent summary of the new U.S. health care law.

7. Health Policy Monitor
   http://www.hpm.org

Health Policy Monitor is a German organization that brings together researchers and health policy analysts to examine health policies and best practices from countries around the world in order to advocate for reform to Germany's health care system.

8. The Henry J. Kaiser Family Foundation
   http://www.kff.org/

This nonprofit, private organization produces research reports on health policy in the United States and around the world. It also develops public health information campaigns, particularly targeted at HIV/AIDS awareness and prevention.

9. World Health Organization (WHO)
   http://www.who.int/en/

WHO is responsible for providing leadership on global health matters, shaping the health research agenda, setting norms and standards, articulating evidence-based policy options, providing technical support to countries, and monitoring and assessing health trends.

Mrs. G., age 67
Amsterdam, Netherlands

I was born in 1939. I was married before in Italy. I met my husband in Rome, but he died. That is why I still visit Rome, as I still have family in Rome. So my second marriage was in 1982 to a Dutch man. I am living here with him, in a very nice house. It is a very nice place here. I have four cats.

I was a classical ballerina in Italy when I was a child, and later I was dancing and in the opera here in Amsterdam. My whole family was in the opera; my mother was a costume designer, my father was in the orchestra, and I, too. Before I was in the opera here in Amsterdam, I was in Paris for 1 year and I was in Rome for 18 years. I worked with the [Italian] television (RAI) in Rome, and I did big shows in the theater and in television. I worked with Modugno [a famous Italian singer] and knew him very well. It was very exciting life. When I was 14 and working with the opera, I went to Germany, Spain, France, I saw the world; I was in America, New York. I don't travel anymore, only to Rome. *Basta* . . . means enough! Finished! So when I was 35 years old, I went back to Amsterdam. . . . You are finished as a ballerina at age 35.

When I finished being a ballerina, I went back to Holland where I worked in Amsterdam for a few years in marketing. Then I said at 60 years, I am finished with my work. I don't work anymore. I worked too hard already.

My typical day? I go to visit friends, I go shopping, . . . I read books, books, books. I am always reading. . . . I am crazy for needlework.

I have my pension from Holland. . . . I got it when I was 65. I get AOV [Dutch government pension], a little amount, but not like my neighbor, because I didn't work all those years in Holland, because I was living in Italy. I also get a pension from the work I did at the theater in Italy. I get a pension from when I was working for the shop here in Amsterdam also, because you paid for it out of your paycheck a little every month. So I have three pensions. I feel that my pensions are adequate, and I have my husband also. But you have to pay taxes on your pension income.

The health system has recently changed. Now everyone pays and contributes something to the health care every month. My husband and I each pay €105 a month. Some people pay a different amount based on the amount of coverage and what you use, . . . like doctor, medicines. So for me, I have to go for the medicines, for the blood [work], and get tests, and the government pays for everything. I have a card. . . . When they see the card, I don't have to pay for anything. If I need medicines, I go to the Pharmacia, they see the card, and I don't have to pay. When I go to Italy, if I need medicines, they see the card, and I don't pay while I am in Italy; it's international. So I pay the monthly amount (105€), and my medicines are covered. For the dentist, I have to pay a little—25%; for the hospital, I don't pay. The hospital is very nice. . . . It is close; I can walk. . . . It doesn't take long to get in to see the doctor. Eye glasses are not paid for, so you have to pay for yourself. I could pay extra for private insurance or more coverage if I wanted a private room if I was in the hospital.

For other things like transportation, if I need to get around I can take a taxi, and I pay and then get reimbursed for my cost, and it is free. There is a little autobus that you can use. . . . You call them, and they will take you for €1.50; you can also use the tram if you are 65 or older you pay less, half of it, which is good because taxis are very expensive. It is very easy to get around Amsterdam.

Every month, they have something you can do for free or reduced cost. . . . This month, you can go to the zoo, . . . another month to the movie or theater for half of the cost or trip on the boat and different things. . . . They send you the information. Every month there is something, and sometimes you don't pay or sometimes you pay a little something. But this benefit is only available in Amsterdam, not the other cities.

There are clubs for older adults if you want to go, you can also eat there, take a meal there if you want to, every day if you want to. . . . There is lunch or a dinner. At the end of the street, there is an apartment for old ones, there is a doctor available, you can cook for yourself, or if you don't want or you are sick, they will cook for you. The government does not sponsor this; these are private, but most people who are old want to stay in their home, like me. I have lived here since 1998.

If you need help in your home, you can ask to have someone come in to help. My neighbor has a girl that comes in to clean the house two times a week because she is not doing well, but there is a wait for that service.

The things in Holland are very good. We always say, "That is not good, that is not good," but also, for the health, it is good and also for the old people, it is good.

I don't think about growing older—no, no, no. I have always been that way. I think every age has something nice about it. But I had a friend who was 40, and she had a difficult time, a ballerina friend who killed herself because she retired from the ballet and she didn't think she had anything to look forward to. This is sad.

Sixty-seven is a good age for me. . . . I hope I get to 80, 90, in good health. There is nothing I dislike about my age. You see some people who are very young, but they are so old. Their mind is old. . . . The sun may be shining, . . . but they complain, "It's too hot, it's too cold, it's raining," always very negative.

In Holland . . . and in Italy, too, in general younger people are separated from older people, . . . but not all, but generally, yes. But I think it is in you. . . . I say to people, my name is _____, not signora! I think it is in yourself. . . . It is coming from your outside, if you are more outgoing. Some people think that they are old at 50. . . . It is all in your mind. In Holland, they say that if you are old, you just sit and watch through the windows to watch the flowers. I think many older adults in Holland do this.

The advice would I give to students about growing older is that you have to be upbeat. The world is not nice, but you have to make something. After the rain, is coming sunshine always.

Shirley and Herma, Ages 75 and 84, United States

Clint, Age 80, United States

7
Mental Health Policies

> As people live longer and populations get older, the number of people with mental disorders is likely to increase over the next few decades. This burden creates an enormous cost in terms of suffering, disability, and economic loss, and trends indicate that it will only increase in the future.... To improve the mental health of populations, it is essential that governments formulate and invest in a coherent and comprehensive strategy.
>
> —World Health Organization, 2001, p. 8

> If I am well ... I do not think about it [growing older]. I really don't care, but sometimes, I realize that I haven't got the energy I had, I see my life behind me and that there isn't too much to look forward to. I feel very gloomy at times, and I wish I could start my life all over again. Often I live off old memories, but sometimes I have no memory at all. ... I keep my feelings inside, which is not so good. ... This is why when I get in the car at times I scream for a while.
>
> —Mrs. A., age 76, Piemonte region, Italy

The World Health Organization (WHO) defines mental health as a state of well-being in which the individual realizes his or her own potential, can cope with the normal stresses of life, can work productively and fruitfully, and is able to make a contribution (WHO, 2009). The majority of people aged 65 years and older cope constructively with the changes associated with aging and maintain mental health. However, some older adults like Marisa experience poor mental health, often caused by depression or anxiety—or other conditions such as substance abuse and dementia that are not part of normal aging and that cause great personal suffering, social exclusion, disability, and poor quality of life. Take dementia as an example. There are an estimated 30 million people with dementia in the world (Alzheimer's Disease International, 2008). Based on available epidemiological data, the number of older adults affected will likely increase to more than 100 million by 2050. Although there is a trend for a lower prevalence of dementia in

155

developing compared with developed countries (see Table 7.1), Alzheimer's Disease International predicts that as patterns of morbidity and mortality converge with those of developed countries, so will dementia prevalence.

Table 7.1 Estimates for the Prevalence of Dementia (%), by Selected WHO Region and Age Group

WHO Region	Description	Age Group					
		60–64	65–69	70–74	75–79	80–84	85+
EU	West Europe	0.9	1.5	3.6	6.0	12.2	24.8
EU	East Europe	0.9	1.3	3.2	5.8	12.2	24.7
AM	North America	0.8	1.7	3.3	6.5	12.8	30.1
AM	South America	0.8	1.7	3.4	7.6	14.8	33.2
EM	Middle East	0.9	1.8	3.5	6.6	13.6	25.5
EM	North Africa, Middle East	1.2	1.9	3.9	6.6	13.9	23.5
WP	Japan, Australia, New Zealand	0.6	1.4	2.6	4.7	10.4	22.1
WP	China and neighbors	0.6	1.7	3.7	7.0	14.4	26.2
SEA	Indonesia, Sri Lanka, Thailand	1.0	1.7	3.4	5.7	10.8	17.6
SEA	India and neighbors	0.4	0.9	1.8	3.7	7.2	14.4

EU- Europe; AM- Americas; EM- Eastern Mediterranean; WP- Western Pacific; SE- South-East Asia

Source: Adapted from Alzheimer's Disease International (2008).

There is a universal ambivalence that appears to influence the development of policy, allocation of resources, and the establishment of services for the management of mental health problems in late life. Individual and societal barriers, including (1) a tendency of older adults to emphasize physical symptoms over emotional concerns; (2) a reluctance to disclose psychological problems due to stigma associated with mental health diagnoses; (3) a lack of provider training to identify manifestations of mental health disorders in late life; (4) stereotypes about "normal aging" held by both older adults and health and service providers that cause individuals to downplay the seriousness of cognitive, psychological, and behavioral symptoms; and (5) restrictive financial and regulatory structures, exacerbate the underuse of mental health services among older adults (Mauch, Kautz, & Smith, 2008).

Throughout the world, about 78% of countries accounting for 69% of the population have instituted mental health policies (WHO, 2005a). Although many countries report the existence of programs to address the mental health needs of their citizens, information on the specific type and quality of the programs, particularly for older adults, often is limited or unavailable. As shown in Figure 7.1, the presence of mental health programs for older adults varies considerably and is closely associated with the wealth and development of the area; the existence of programs ranges, with 15.6% of countries in the

Figure 7.1   Distribution of Mental Health Programs for Older Adults in Comparison With the Percentage of Elderly Population in Each WHO Region and the World

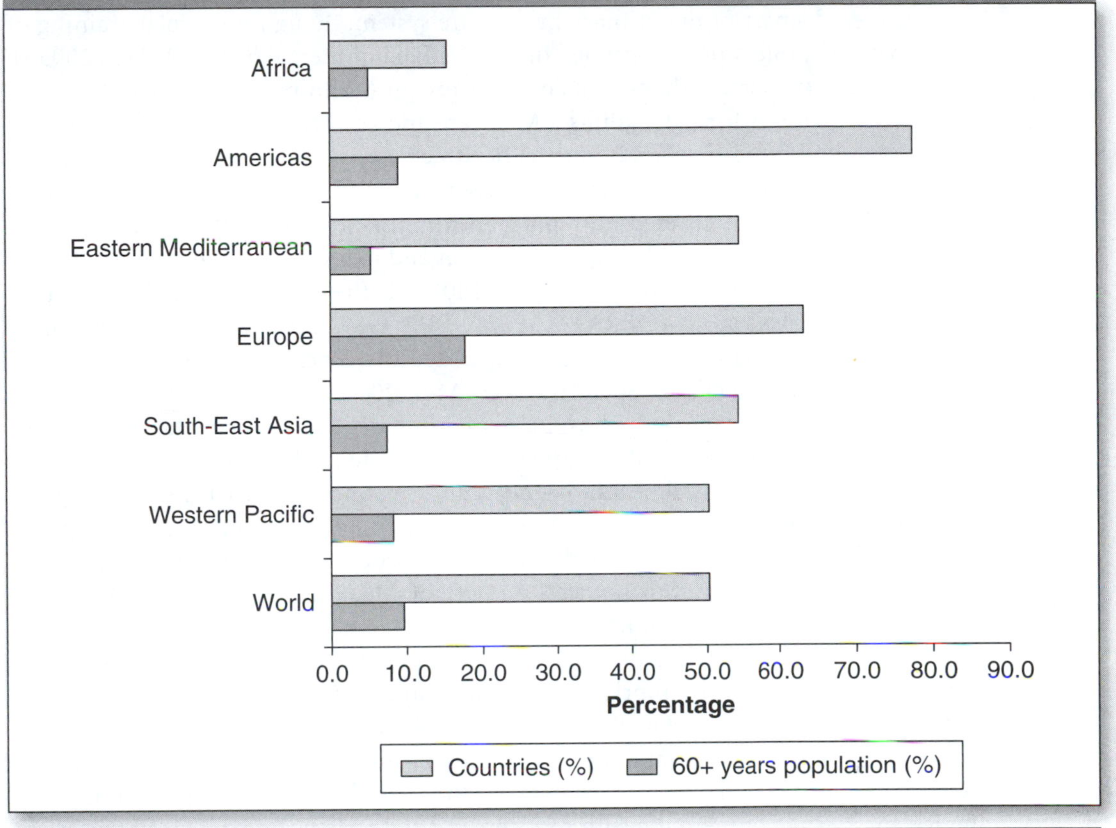

Source: WHO (2005a).

African region and 50.0% of countries in the Western Pacific Region offering programs and 77.4% of countries in the Americas making programs available (WHO, 2005a).

The countries discussed in this chapter take different approaches to supporting mental health services and represent different phases of mental health policy revision to accommodate their aging populations. We encourage readers to pay close attention to policy, regulatory, financial, and personal issues that can promote or interfere with effective provision of mental health services for older populations. As you read the unique profiles of the United States, Canada, Australia, Sweden, the United Kingdom, and Spain, note how decisions at different policy levels can begin to eliminate barriers so that older adults are able to access mental health services as easily as they access other health services.

United States

In the United States, less than 3% of older adults report seeing a mental health professional for treatment, a rate lower than that of any other adult age group (Bartels et al., 2004). Perhaps this is because the United States has no comprehensive national policy specific to mental health (WHO, 2005d). Rather, mental health treatment for all citizens is framed by general health policy, as it intersects with a multitude of different legislative decisions, national organizations, state programs, and private initiatives. Mental health is considered a part of the primary health care system, though no regular training of primary care professionals is carried out in the field of mental health (WHO, 2005d).

When first enacted, the two major government health policy initiatives that provide health services for older adults—Medicare and Medicaid (see Chapter 6)—made little reference to the specifics of mental health care provision. Over time, coverage of mental health services through these programs has gradually expanded. For example, until 1987, Medicare covered an annual maximum of only $250 of a beneficiary's expenses for outpatient psychological treatment and follow-up diagnostic services. The annual payment cap was increased to $1,100 with the enactment of the Omnibus Budget Reconciliation Act (OBRA) of 1987. OBRA 1989 removed the annual payment limit for mental health treatment and expanded the coverage for services provided by psychologists and clinical social workers. As of 2009, coverage under Medicare for mental health services includes hospital-based inpatient care for mental health treatment (Part A), physician and therapist services while in the hospital (Part B), outpatient services for mental health diagnosis and treatment (Part B), and prescription psychotropic drugs (Parts C and D; Medicare Benefit Policy Manual, 2009).

Individuals who qualify for Medicaid in conjunction with Medicare may be eligible for additional mental health services. As part of Medicaid reform, the OBRA 1987 requires that all prospective nursing home applicants who have a primary or secondary diagnosis of a major mental disorder undergo a preadmission screening to determine whether their cases are appropriate for nursing home admission and whether they need active treatment for mental illness. The mental disorders covered by OBRA 1987 include schizophrenia, paranoid disorders, major affective disorders, schizo-affective disorders, and atypical psychoses. States have the flexibility, however, to determine coverage for a range of mental health services, and state Medicaid benefits packages can differ considerably within federal guidelines. For instance, only 19 states cover psychologist services through Medicaid, and only 5 states provide Medicaid payment for medical social work services (Center for Medicare Advocacy, Inc., 2009).

Although the range of services has grown, a lack of parity continues between Medicare and Medicaid benefits for physical health compared with mental health diagnoses. For example, Medicare has an 80% reimbursement rate for general medical services versus 50% reimbursement for outpatient mental health services, there is no Medicare coverage of prescription drugs for mental health treatment unless the older adult has been hospitalized, Medicare lifetime limit on inpatient mental health service coverage is 190 days compared with no limit for coverage of general health inpatient care, and both Medicare and Medicaid place special conditions on reimbursement for mental health services (e.g., required designation of disorders as severe and disabling, limits and caps on number of mental health visits allowed) (Center for Medicare Advocacy, Inc., 2009; Sivis, McCrae, & Demir, 2005). Advances in Medicare payment parity for mental health services were made with the passage of the Medicare Improvements for Patients and Providers Act of 2008 (National Committee to Preserve Social Security and Medicare, 2008). Beginning in 2010, there is a reduction in the cost-sharing related to the treatment of outpatient psychiatric services. By 2014, beneficiaries will pay the standard 20% coinsurance rate for Part B services.

In 1996, Congress passed the Mental Health Parity Act (MHPA) in an attempt to give mental health benefits equal footing with other aspects of health support for individuals with private insurance. Under the MHPA, group health plans, insurance companies, and health maintenance organizations offering mental health benefits may not set annual or lifetime dollar limits on mental health benefits that are lower than any such dollar limits for medical and surgical benefits. A plan that does not impose such limitations on medical and surgical benefits may not impose such a dollar limit on mental health benefits. The MHPA provisions, however, do not apply to benefits for substance abuse or chemical dependency (U.S. Department of Labor, 2008).

Mental Health Policy and Older Adults

Although a sweeping policy initiative to improve mental health services for aging adults has not yet succeeded, some smaller-scale legislative and regulatory decisions have been made that have the potential to improve late-life access to mental health services (e.g., psychotherapy), both in the community and institutional settings. These steps include Medicare reimbursement for psychological services provided to dementia patients (enacted in 2001), expansion of the Medicare Health and Behavior Assessment and Intervention codes to cover a broader scope of services provided by psychologists (enacted in 2002), and establishment of a nationwide Graduate Psychology Education program to support universities and colleges that train psychologists to work with underserved populations, including older adults (enacted in 2002; Karlin & Duffy, 2004). Funds from the Older Americans Act (see Chapter 8 for details) also may be used to support mental health services for older adults. For example, Title III-F (added to the Older Americans Act in 1992) provides a small amount of funds for disease prevention and health promotion services, which can include screening for the prevention of depression, coordination of community mental health services, provision of educational activities, and referral to psychiatric and psychological services.

Continuing efforts influence policy that would increase support for late-life mental health services. In 2005, an expert panel of 24 mental health care consumers, providers, researchers, and governmental health officials were assembled to identify barriers faced by older adults attempting to access mental health services (Mauch et al., 2008). In their report, they specified a number of financial barriers, including

1. state Medicaid limitations on payments for same-day billing for a physical health and mental health service or visit;

2. lack of reimbursement for collaborative care and case management related to mental health services;

3. absence of reimbursement for services provided by nonphysicians, alternative practitioners, or contract practitioners/providers;

4. Medicaid disallowance of reimbursement when primary care physicians submit bills listing only a mental health diagnosis and corresponding treatment;

5. low reimbursement rates in both rural and urban settings; and

6. lack of reimbursement incentives for screening and providing preventative mental health services in preventative care settings (Mauch et al., 2008; Psychiatric Services Online, 2008).

Hence, the financial safety net for mental health care has many gaps through which older adults in need of mental health services can easily slip.

Similar to financing structures, approaches to regulation have the simultaneous potential to improve or hinder mental health services to older adults. The regulatory system for mental health services, like mental health policy and financing, is complicated by federal, state, and local community layers. The Centers for Medicare and Medicaid Services is the regulatory body responsible for managing the Medicare and Medicaid programs. It administers the Medicare program through contracts with private insurance companies around the country, known as Medicare carriers or intermediaries. These companies are then responsible for processing Medicare outpatient mental health claims.

Although the Centers for Medicare and Medicaid Services has 10 regional offices to oversee these carriers, the intermediaries and their medical directors determine local medical review policies for their service regions, which guide decisions about what constitutes "medically necessary" treatment worthy of reimbursement (Karlin & Duffy, 2004). Because of this decentralized system, local medical review policies vary considerably; some are overly restrictive or interpreted too narrowly, preventing proper reimbursement for mental health services. Mental health professionals in one region may be denied coverage for a service that is readily reimbursed in another part of the country. As mentioned previously, state governments have the power to determine the range of mental health Medicaid benefits they offer within established government guidelines, and many states have recently restricted Medicaid payments for psychological services in response to a strained economy. In addition, federal quality indicators used to assess nursing home care can also undermine the use of psychological services with residents, because only medicinal therapies are counted as valid antidepressant therapies in this system. Thus, diffuse and varied regulatory structures create inconsistencies and challenges that significantly impact older adults' access to mental health services.

A number of broader national directives and legislative efforts have drawn attention to and influenced the direction of mental health services available to older adults. The Americans with Disabilities Act of 1990 (ADA, 1991) and the Supreme Court's *Olmstead v. L. C.* decision (Cornell University Law School Legal Information Institute, 1999) were also pivotal moments regarding U.S. policy and legal foundations for those suffering from psychiatric disabilities. The Americans with Disabilities Act protects individuals with mental health disabilities from discrimination, and the later Supreme Court ruling confirmed their right to reside in community settings (President's New Freedom Commission on Mental Health [PNFCMH], 2003). While not establishing any comprehensive policy regarding mental health treatment, these events stimulated a shift in governmental climate, increased attention to the barriers encountered by those suffering from mental disabilities, and emphasized the importance of expanding nationwide community-based mental health care options. In the same vein, *Mental Health: A Report of the Surgeon General* (Surgeon General U.S. Public Health Service, 1999) helped raise national awareness, identifying mental health as a fundamental aspect of overall health and emphasizing the importance of confronting service barriers in this sector.

In 2002, President George W. Bush convened the New Freedom Commission on Mental Health. This group was charged with studying the nation's mental health delivery system and making recommendations for enhanced services that would allow those suffering from mental illness or emotional disturbance to "live, work, learn, and participate fully in their communities" (PNFCMH, 2003). Although the Commission's final report failed to address the unique needs of older adults, it did identify inadequacies of the mental health care delivery system at the federal level—a segue that many service providers hope will provide a "policy window" for change that can eventually impact services for older adults in positive ways (Karlin & Duffy, 2004). Of the six primary recommendations put forth by the Commission to improve mental health services for all citizens, implementation of at least four of these recommendations could profoundly reduce service barriers, increase the scope of services, and enhance the quality of mental health support available to older adults (PNFCMH, 2003):

1. Educating all U.S. citizens more fully about the relationship between physical and mental health

2. Making mental health care more consumer- and family-driven

3. Eliminating disparities in mental health care

4. Making early mental health screening, assessment, and referral common practice in preventative care settings

Canada

Approximately 20% of older Canadians currently suffer from mental illness (Canadian Mental Health Commission, 2006). The Canadian Mental Health Association (CMHA, 2009a) suggests that the rate of mental illness occurrence is similar among older and younger age groups but notes that adults in late life also have to contend with age-related psychiatric disorders such as dementia and delirium. Including these disorders and substance abuse in the estimates, prevalence of mental health problems among older adults may be as high as 30% (Elderly Mental Health Care Working Group [EMHCWG], 2002).

For the most part, the Canadian health system fails to recognize the unique and diverse mental health needs of older adults. The Canadian Mental Health Commission (2006) identifies several significant challenges facing Canada's mental health system in light of its aging population:

1. Inadequate availability of age-specific treatment and support services

2. Limited access to mental health services

3. Inefficiency and unnecessary disruption of appropriate care when transitioning from community-based to institutional-based mental health care

4. The tendency to place older adults with mental illness in acute or long-term care facilities rather than actively pursuing effective community-based treatment with the goal of recovery and sustained community living

Similar to the climate in the United States, a major issue in Canada is the societal tendency to stigmatize and apply fatalism to the normal aging process. Professionals, family members, and older adults themselves tend to dismiss real symptoms of distress in late life as attributable to "just getting old" (cited in Canadian Mental Health Commission, 2006).

Support for mental health services is part of Canada's overall health care system. Known as Medicare, it is a universal system of mandatory medical insurance for every citizen, built on a culture of social solidarity (see Chapter 6). This system of social insurance covers the cost of basic preventative and acute medical care for Canadians of all ages, including mental health treatment. The funding base for this system involves a significant (about one-third) federal contribution; the rest of health care expenditures are supported primarily by provincial personal and corporate taxes (Steinbrook, 2006a; Tanner, 2008b). Individual provinces have primary responsibility for managing health care under the Canadian Constitution; thus, mental health services vary considerably across provinces.

For older adults, primary care is the "backbone" of the mental health care system and the focal point of entry into the continuum of available care (EMHCWG, 2002). The gateway to this three-tiered system for older adults seeking mental health support is through general practitioners and other health care providers screening for home nursing admission or home care. Primary care physicians frequently report difficulties accessing mental health care for their older patients, a problem that profoundly disrupts how this three-tiered system is supposed to function. Thus, even those in need of specialty support often do not make it out of the primary level (Canadian Alliance on Mental Illness and Mental Health [CAMIMH], 2006). Secondary systems include specialized preventative, diagnostic, and therapeutic care from professionals who have specific training in geriatric mental health, psychiatry, or geriatric psychiatry. Only about 10% to 15% of older adults with mental illness require this level of care, but they often are turned away because of limited resources (EMHCWG, 2002). Tertiary care, the last level of Canada's three-tiered system, involves highly specialized services that come with professional or technical skills, equipment, or facilities—such as inpatient services, university research clinics, and rural/remote community outreach. These most complicated cases amount to about 1% of the total older adult population, or about 10% of seniors receiving secondary services.

Older adults needing residential long-term care often are removed from the flow of this care continuum. Most long-term care homes are not designed with mental health needs in mind, and most placements are based primarily on physical mobility issues (Zahradnik, 2007). Insufficient staff training in mental health continues to be an issue in long-term care facilities, and even physicians in these settings receive only minimal dementia and Alzheimer's education, rather than more comprehensive training regarding the broader spectrum of mental health issues that affect older adults (Zahradnik, 2007).

Funding levels for mental health programs in Canada are inadequate to meet societal demand—as evidenced by uneven and fragmented services—with mental health supports lacking in many jurisdictions (CAMIMH, 2006). The deficit in mental health services is so extreme that waitlists for mental health services are seldom maintained because the gap between need and supply is simply too large (CAMIMH, 2006). The absence of community supports such as low-cost transitional housing and adequate income support are also identified as gaps that impede recovery from mental health problems facing older adults and other Canadian citizens.

To help inform policymakers, CAMIMH produced *Framework for Action on Mental Illness and Mental Health* in 2006. Advocates hope the production of this framework and the consensus reached in 2005 among government leaders and territorial/ provincial ministers of health to create a Canadian Mental Health Commission (CMHA, 2009b) indicate momentum toward creation of a National Action Plan on Mental Health. The Commission is currently working on five key initiatives:

1. A countrywide mental health strategy toward recovery and well-being

2. An antistigma initiative

3. Homelessness research demonstration projects

4. A knowledge exchange center

5. A Partners for Mental Health Program to recruit members for participation in advocacy and change

Mental Health Policy and Older Adults

Formed in 2002, the Canadian Coalition for Seniors' Mental Health (CCSMH) advocates for explicit policy improvements for mental health services for older adults, particularly those living in long-term care facilities. They have made strides toward improving the research network for late-life mental health issues, disseminating best practice guidelines for older adult mental health services, and implementing pilot projects across Canada to test these guidelines (CCSMH, 2008). For example, in 2004, CCSMH formed a national Research and Knowledge Exchange Network on seniors' mental health. In 2005, through funding awarded by the Public Health Agency of Canada, CCSMH facilitated the development of Canada's first evidence-based recommendations for best practice guidelines in areas of seniors' mental health (CCSMH, 2008). Since 2007, CCSMH has been testing these recommendations through seven pilot projects across the country. The recommended guidelines are tailored for system responses to four specific mental health issues that disproportionately or significantly impact seniors:

1. Assessment and treatment of delirium

2. Assessment and treatment of depression

3. Assessment and treatment of mental health issues in long-term care

4. Assessment of suicide risk and prevention of suicide

The Public Health Agency of Canada has continued its support of CCSMH efforts, providing renewed funding in 2008 for expanded application of these guidelines in a variety of health and aging services settings across Canada.

Another Canadian national advocacy and research group, the Seniors Psychosocial Interest Group, is also spearheading countrywide policy change for late-life mental health care. This group was kindled by collaborative work between the British

Columbia Psychogeriatric Association and the Population Health Fund of Canada's Public Health Agency. Their original 2005 to 2008 project, titled "Best Practice in Seniors' Mental Health Program and Policy Design," helped integrate the Senior Mental Health Policy Lens—an instrument designed to promote social and health service environments that optimize older adult mental health (MacCourt, 2004)— into program and policy developments across the country and evaluate its effectiveness in improving mental health outcomes for seniors (Seniors Psychosocial Interest Group, 2004).

The Standing Senate Committee on Social Affairs, Science, and Technology also addresses the unique mental health needs of seniors in one chapter of its final policy report on mental health, mental illness, and addiction services (Canadian Mental Health Commission, 2006). Broadly, the committee members identify

1. a lack of specialized treatment programs or support services for older Canadians,

2. a lack of research knowledge and exchange in this area, and

3. societal ageism underlying a tendency to "warehouse" seniors in inappropriate facilities rather than striving for effective treatment and recovery (Canadian Mental Health Commission, 2006).

The report provides specific policy recommendations to begin addressing these system inadequacies, including (1) creation of a Knowledge Exchange Center as part of the Canadian Mental Health Commission that focuses on, as one of its primary goals, the sharing of information among gerontology researchers themselves, providers of specialist care to seniors, and mental health and addiction care providers for improved tailoring of mental health services to the unique and diverse needs of seniors; (2) provision of mental health support services to seniors in their own homes or homes of family caregivers at an equivalent level to those supports available for physical ailments; (3) efforts to shift older mental health patients from acute care to long-term care facilities or other appropriate housing and, accordingly, trained staff members of long-term care facilities to provide clinically appropriate mental health services onsite (Canadian Mental Health Commission, 2006).

Further insights for policy reform may soon be drawn from the final anticipated report from the Victorian Order of Nurses from Canada 3-year national research project, titled "Reach Up, Reach Out: Best Practices in Mental Health Practices for Culturally Diverse Seniors." This project wrapped up in 2008 and aimed at increasing the capacity of Canadian community organizations to effectively respond to the mental health needs of culturally diverse seniors, with a plan to provide additional best practice guidelines and measurement tools for work with culturally diverse older adults. The Center for Addiction and Mental Health (2005) has released a guide for workers and volunteers who encounter older adults who face substance abuse, mental health, or gambling challenges. Although national agencies and advocacy groups have set the stage for comprehensive mental health reform in Canada, the question remains whether government leaders and policymakers will weave these various efforts and insights into a connected national effort.

Australia

Mental health statistics characterizing older Australians do not differ much from older adults in other countries; about 14.5% of older Australians report mental health problems. The 2007 National Survey of Mental Health and Wellbeing found that one in five (20% or 3.2 million) Australian adults experience mental illness in any year (Australian Bureau of Statistics, 2007). Across all age groups, including older adults, the most common mental health concerns were anxiety disorders, affective disorders, and substance abuse. The majority of these individuals (approximately 2.1 million) were not using mental health services at the time of the survey but perceived the need for counseling, information, and social interventions.

Traditionally, psychiatric hospitals and institutions provided the majority of mental health care for persons in need of services and care. In 1992, policy was passed that changed Australia's approach of mental health care from an institutional to a community-oriented service. All Australian governments adopted a National Mental Health Policy (Australian Health Ministers, 2000), which is implemented and reaffirmed through a series of 5-year national mental health plans. Known as the National Mental Health Strategy, these plans have established a framework for the protection of rights and civil liberties of people with mental disorders and advanced the position that mental health should be part of the mainstream health system, including primary care. Specifically, the Australian and state and territory governments committed to decrease the size and number of stand-alone psychiatric hospitals, replacing them with acute beds in general hospitals and a range of community-based services, including residential accommodation.

BOX 7.1 Policy to People Link: Aged Persons Mental Health Services, Australia

In Victoria, Australia, Aged Persons Mental Health Services (APMHS) are available to individuals over 65 with longstanding mental illness or who have developed serious mental health complications in late life. Support is also available to those with severe behavioral or emotional disturbances stemming from cognitive disorders such as dementia. Through Victoria's regional arm, multidisciplinary mental health teams provide community-based assessment, treatment, rehabilitation, and case management. Services in Victoria also include specialist APMHS nursing homes and hospitals that serve long-term care patients who have persistent cognitive, behavioral, or emotional disturbances that cannot be managed in mainstream aged care facilities. Finally, acute inpatient treatment for severe short-term episodes of mental illness is provided in aged care facilities or general hospitals. For more information, go to www.health.vic.gov.au/mentalhealth/services/aged/index.htm.

The change in the mix of mental health services has been substantial. In 1993, only 29% of state mental health resources were directed toward community-based care; 73% of psychiatric beds were located in stand-alone hospitals, and these consumed half of the total spending by the states and territories on mental health care. By 2002, this had changed to 51% of state mental health resources for community-based care and 39% of psychiatric beds in stand-alone hospitals consuming 29% of state mental health resources (Whiteford & Buckingham, 2005). The need to improve the quality, as well as expand the quantity, of mental health services was one of the goals of the Mental Health Strategy. Service standards, one part of a quality and safety framework, are used by health service accreditation agencies. By June 2003, almost 90% of all public mental health services had begun the process of having their services reviewed in terms of the standards, and almost half had completed a review against these standards (Whiteford & Buckingham, 2005).

In 2008, the National Advisory Council on Mental Health was established to provide a formal mechanism for the Australian government to gain independent advice from a wide range of experts to inform national mental health reform (Australian Government, 2008). This 10-member, appointed panel provides independent and confidential advice to the minister for health and ageing on mental health issues, including (1) advice on strategies and broad directions in mental health policy; (2) implementation of mental health programs currently funded by the Australian, state, and territory governments; (3) guidelines on how to improve coordination and integration of existing mental health programs; and (4) advice on how to focus mental health programs for people with particular needs, including older people.

Mental Health Policy and Older Adults

The National Strategy for an Ageing Australia was launched in 2002 in response to the recognition that there will be an unprecedented aging of the Australian population during the first half of the 21st century. Two guiding principles of the strategy are particularly relevant for aged mental health services: (1) All Australians, regardless of age, should have access to care services that are appropriate to their diverse needs to enable them to optimize their quality of life over their entire lifespan; and (2) a strong evidence base should inform the policy responses to population aging (Hassett, Fortune, & Smith, 2007). Although access to specialized mental health care for older Australians has improved greatly in recent years, there is still inequitable access across urban and rural geographic areas.

Unlike most other countries, Australia has integrated its health and mental health services in an attempt to provide a seamless system of care for older adults. General practitioner physicians provide primary care for mental health, and community psychogeriatric nurses, psychologists, and geriatric psychiatrists provide advice and support as required. The key to the model is supported, collaborative, and shared care between primary care, community care, and specialist services, which include community-aged care, geriatric medicine, and old age psychiatry (WHO, 2005a). Despite the existence of a high level of coordination between mental health specialists and general practitioners in Australia, as well as a variety of community care packages available, the country still suffers from underusage of specialty mental health services by older adults (Trollor, Anderson, Sachdev, Brodaty, & Andrews, 2007).

In 2005, Australian Health Ministers jointly agreed to the development of a National Framework for Action on Dementia 2006 to 2010 (Australian Health Ministers'

Conference, 2006), making dementia care a national health priority (Ageing Research Online, 2006). Developed within the context of other national initiatives in health, community, and aged care, the framework is a national policy and implementation plan for a coordinated national approach to improve the quality of life of people living with dementia, their carers, and their families. Each state and territory contributed to the development of the framework by preparing its own dementia plan to provide direction for dementia services specific to the needs of older adults and their families living in a target area (e.g., Queensland's Directions for Aged Care 2004–2011, Tasmania's Dementia Care Plan 2000 and Beyond). The government committed $320.6 million over 5 years to support activities that improve service delivery, assessment, treatment, and management to enhance quality of life for people with dementia, their carers, and their families (Ageing Research Online, 2006). The framework is intended to inform policy and service developments, leading to more consistent, cost-effective approaches to dementia research, assessment, treatment, and care to minimize duplication of effort and funding (Australian Health Ministers' Conference, 2006).

Sweden

Mental health conditions affect about 10% of adults aged 65 and older in Sweden. The most common condition is depression (affecting 10% of the aged population), while 6% suffer from anxiety or some kind of psychotic condition (Berleen, 2004). Similar to the trends in other countries, older Swedes underutilize specialty mental health services and there are marked differences between service regions (municipalities) with respect to available mental health resources, methods of care, and service utilization (Silfverhielm & Kamis-Gould, 2000).

Sweden does not have a national mental health policy discrete from the country's overall health policy (WHO, 2005c). The opening paragraph of the Swedish Health and Medical Service Care Act of 1982, however, makes explicit the community's responsibility to provide high-quality mental health care, on par with primary care and in cooperation with the patients and their families (Silfverhielm & Kamis-Gould, 2000, p. 294). In other words, in agreement with the welfare state approach of Sweden's overall health system, mental health services are guaranteed by law as a fundamental right of all citizens, including vulnerable groups such as older adults.

Mental health services are governed by the Social Services Act (originally passed in 1982 and amended in 1995). According to this Act, citizens, including those with mental health diagnoses, have the right to receive public service and help at all stages of life (Socialstyrelsen, 2008, p. 4). Spurred by parliamentary critique of inadequate social services for persons with mental illness, the most recent amendment to this Act, the Mental Health Care Reform of 1995, specifies that municipalities have the same responsibility to care for persons with mental disabilities as those with physical disabilities (Silfverhielm & Kamis-Gould, 2000; WHO, 2005c). Despite lacking a distinct mental health policy, Sweden does make specific budget allocations for mental health and spends about 11% of the total health budget on mental health treatment (WHO, 2005c). Swedish mental health services are largely financed through a tax-based national health insurance. To limit costs for the individual there is a high-cost ceiling, which means that after persons reach the maximum costs for medical consultations in the 12 months following the date of the first consultation, services are free of charge (Swedish Institute, 2007a).

There are also different layers of regulatory guidance, under the broader umbrella of Swedish Health and Welfare Services, provided to the mental health sector. The National Board of Health and Welfare is the Swedish government agency that shoulders responsibility for supervision, evaluation and monitoring of social services, health and mental health care, dental care, environmental health, and control of communicable diseases (Silfverhielm & Kamis-Gould, 2000). One of this agency's primary responsibilities is to encourage county councils and municipalities to follow the guidelines set out in the national Health and Social Care Acts. Although this board has no power to impose sanctions on communities in Sweden that do not comply with recommended care guidelines, thus far, county councils have embraced these guidelines with respect to mental health provision (Silfverhielm & Kamis-Gould, 2000).

Like many other European countries that have shifted from institutional to community-based care, Sweden has moved toward a very decentralized system to manage mental health care in local areas. This shift to a community focus has been quite dramatic, with an almost 85% reduction in inpatient mental health beds over a 25-year period and a simultaneous increase in community-based services (WHO, 2005c). The responsibility for mental health services is divided between 23 elected county councils, charged with the provision of health and medical services, and 228 elected municipalities that are responsible for social and generic services (Silfverhielm & Kamis-Gould, 2000).

Mental Health Policy and Older Adults

Similar to the mental health regulatory system, the responsibility for the welfare of older adults in Sweden is explicitly divided between three government levels, creating overlap in the systemic oversight of mental health and age-related services (Socialstyrelsen, 2008). At a national level, the Parliament and government have set out policy aims and directives by means of legislation and economic steering measures. At a regional level, the county councils or regions are responsible for the provision of health and medical care for older adults. At a local level, the municipalities are legally obligated to meet the social service and housing needs of older adults. There is concern that older adults suffering from mental health problems are often overlooked or given improper treatment because of practices at point-of-entry (i.e., assessment) for aging services (Socialstyrelsen, 2008). When older adults seek help from social services, assessment of need for services is primarily based on a person's physical capabilities; mental health issues are seldom considered.

In 2003, the National Board of Health and Welfare was instructed to develop guidelines for health and social care of people with a dementia disorder (Swedish Association of Local Authorities and Regions, 2007). The national guidelines are based on a complete assessment of the best available expertise on the effects, cost-effectiveness, ethics, and intention of legislation of various dementia care measures. In 2006, the government mandated the National Board of Health and Welfare to develop a national center for excellence in the health and social care of the elderly, including issues regarding family members and dementia. The Swedish Dementia Centre opened in January 2008, along with a National Centre for Excellence: Family Carers; both centers are financed by the Swedish government.

An area of mental health intervention where Sweden's system has performed most favorably is suicide prevention. Between 300 and 400 people over age 65 commit suicide each year, which is about one-fourth of all suicides in the country (Swedish Association of Local Authorities and Regions, 2007). Since the establishment of the National Council of Suicide Prevention in 1993, there has been a nearly 50% reduction in suicides among men 65 years and older (Berleen, 2004). The frequency of suicide among men over 75 years, however, is still double that of Swedish men in general and four times that of women in the same age group.

Fredrik Reinfeldt, Swedish president of the European Union, identified "healthy and dignified aging" and "prevention of alcohol-related harm" as two of his priority issues for 2009. He has placed emphasis on the need for improved coordination and cooperation between institutions focused on health and social issues and the effects of harmful alcohol consumption on healthy and dignified aging (Ministry of Health and Social Affairs, 2009).

United Kingdom

Three million older people in the United Kingdom experience symptoms of mental health problems that significantly impact quality of life, and this number is set to grow by a third over the next 15 years (M. Lee, 2007). The Department of Health characterizes mental health problems in older adults across the region as common, estimating a prevalence of diagnosable mental health issues among individuals aged 65 and older to be approximately 40% among those who visit general practitioners offices, 50% of general hospital patients, and 60% of residents in long-term care facilities (Philp & Appleby, 2005). The Care Services Improvement Partnership (Care Services Improvement Partnership [CSIP], West Midlands, 2006) reported that depression is present in about 12% to 15% of older adults and dementia affects approximately 5% of the older population. People between the ages of 55 and 74 have the highest rates of alcohol-related deaths of any age group, and older men and women have some of the highest suicide rates of all ages in the United Kingdom (Age Concern, 2007).

With the exception of Scotland, countries in the United Kingdom are guided by a unified National Mental Health Policy established in 1998, a National Mental Health Program formulated in 1999, and a National Substance Abuse Policy passed in 2000 (WHO, 2005d). This unified policy includes the components of mental health advocacy, promotion, prevention, treatment, and rehabilitation, with a focus on primary care and access to services, effective services for people with severe mental illness, services for care providers, and action to reduce suicide.

The United Kingdom's budget allocations for mental health account for about 10% of the region's total health budget. These funds come primarily from national taxes, private insurance, social insurance, and out-of-pocket expenditures. The United Kingdom National Health Services support about 85% of the expenses for separate country systems of health and social care, with remaining costs shouldered by local authorities. The contributions vary between countries, with Scotland and Northern Ireland investing more heavily than either England or Wales (WHO, 2005d).

Mental health is considered a responsibility of the primary health care system in the United Kingdom, and treatment for severe mental health issues is available from general practitioners who receive regular training in the field of mental health (WHO, 2005d). There are also separate, specialized programs and services available for older adults across the United Kingdom. Systems are organized slightly differently across countries, with England and Wales receiving health care from the National Health Services but providing social services through local authorities. Scotland maintains a similar structure but within a different legal system, and Northern Ireland merges the health and social services sectors (WHO, 2005d).

There is mental health–related legislation specific to England and Wales. The 1983 Mental Health Act addresses the assessment, treatment, and rights of people with a mental health condition (Department of Health, 2009). Originally, this Act focused solely on mental health treatment in hospital settings, but revisions to the Act have been introduced that would enable compulsory treatment to take place in the community. The Mental Capacity Act of 2005 enshrined in statute current best practice and common law principles concerning people who lack mental capacity and those who make decisions on their behalf (Department of Health, 2007). Specifically, it provides a statutory framework to empower and protect people who may lack capacity to make certain decisions, including people with dementia and those with mental health problems. England also has a National Suicide Prevention Strategy that is aimed at reducing the death rate from suicide by at least 20% as of 2010 (CSIP, West Midlands, 2006). This policy, however, does not specifically address the issue of suicide among older adults, "who are extremely successful at killing themselves," with one completed suicide for every four attempts (CSIP, West Midlands, 2006).

A cornerstone of United Kingdom mental health policy, originally conceived in 1991, is the Care Program Approach. According to this directive, Mental Health Service Units must collaborate with the social services sector in development and execution of intermediate (institutional transition to community) and other community-based psychiatric services for U.K. citizens of all generations (WHO, 2003). Unfortunately, some of these collaborations exclude adults 60+ because of a policy bias that places emphasis on services provided to adults of working age (CSIP, 2005; Minshull, 2007). The Care Program Approach is a crucial component of the government's mental health programming that could, if implemented without such age biases, be pivotal to successful provision of services to older adults.

Mental Health Policy and Older Adults

The exclusion of mental health in policies for older people and the exclusion of older people in some policies for mental health have created gaps in services and provisions for older adults (Age Concern, 2007). The National Service Framework for Older People was launched in 2001 to root out "age discrimination in all aspects of health care financing, planning, and service delivery" (Alliance for Health and the Future, 2005) and to set standards to ensure that high-quality services are available to all older citizens (Department of Health, 2001). This framework requires that every health district in the United Kingdom have a fully resourced specialist service for late-life mental health by 2011 (CSIP, 2005; Minshull, 2007).

Even with the existence of the National Framework for Older People, concern has been expressed by many government and nongovernment constituents that mental health in late life is a much-neglected area (Age Concern, 2007). Currently, a widespread antistigma movement is underway with respect to mental illness in the United Kingdom, but the messages of this movement have not successfully breached age issues and the full spectrum of services to older adults. Perhaps stemming from the fact that mental health policy and services were originally formulated with a focus on improving circumstances for adults of working age, significant age inequities persist. Adults over 65 are often transferred to unfamiliar service settings or excluded altogether from psychological services (CSIP, 2005; Minshull, 2007).

As a result of these concerns, the Inquiry Into Mental Health and Well-Being in Later Life was launched in 2003. Its purpose is to investigate the neglect of older people's mental health in policy, practice, and research. While resulting publications have made concrete recommendations for improvements to all levels of the mental health service system for older adults (i.e., government, local authorities, health departments, education departments, public bodies, businesses, and nongovernment organizations), most of these recommendations have yet to result in specific policies or practices (Age Concern, 2007).

There is some movement in the United Kingdom toward improved multidisciplinary coordination of late-life mental health services. Stemming from the recent nationwide attention on older adult mental health, the Department of Health established a program board for older adult mental services that includes policymakers, the Care Services Improvement Partnership, the Health Care Commission, and the Commission for Social Care Inspection. The intention of this effort is to ensure that mental health and age-inclusivity are seen as cross-cutting themes across policy development (Philp & Appleby, 2005).

BOX 7.2   Policy to People Link: National Dementia Strategy Demonstrator Site Program, England

England's 2009 National Dementia Strategy (highlighted earlier in this chapter) received £150 million ($231 million) in support over its first 2 years. As part of this extensive plan, the Department of Health is allowing local authorities and their health partners to apply for funding to become demonstrator sites for implementation of innovative approaches to achieve two main objectives of the National Strategy—enabling easy access to care, support, and advice following dementia diagnosis and developing structured peer support and learning networks. The demonstrator site program is designed to provide robust evidence of the effectiveness or ineffectiveness of pilot initiatives so that the government reproduces only the most successful models as National Dementia Strategy programming expands. For more information, go to www.dh.gov.uk/en/SocialCare/Deliveringadultsocialcare/Olderpeople/NationalDementiaStrategy/index.htm and www.dh.gov.uk/prod_consum_dh/groups/dh_digitalassets/documents/digitalasset/dh_099134.pdf.

Spain

Findings from a national study indicate that approximately one in five adults in Spain experience mental health problems sometime in their lifetime (European Policy Information Research for Mental Disorders Consortium, 2008). As in other adult populations, the most common mental disorders among Spanish adults include depression (10.6%), a specific phobia (4.8%), alcohol abuse (3.6%), and dysthymia (3.6%). A recent study focusing on the prevalence of psychiatric symptoms and mental disorders among 293 older adults in primary care settings in the province of Huesca found that almost 50% of the elderly patients presented some type of psychiatric symptom on initial assessment, although only 29% of the study population had a previous psychiatric diagnosis (Olivera et al., 2008). Extrapolating from this one province, findings suggest the need to address psychiatric issues among community-dwelling elders.

Although Spain has a national mental health policy, mental health issues are not addressed by a single comprehensive plan at the national level but, rather, in an extremely decentralized system in which each of the 17 Autonomous Communities (i.e., independently governed regions that make up the country) in Spain are required to have a published mental health policy framed within the community health plan (Salvador-Carulla et al., 2006; WHO, 2001, 2005c). Each community's plan includes the elements of advocacy, promotion, prevention, treatment, and rehabilitation, but the organization and funding of resources for mental health vary considerably between these service areas.

At the national level, pivotal policy and legislative actions have guided mental health practices for citizens of all ages. These include the recommendations of the Commission for Psychiatric Reform of 1985 and the General Health Law of 1986. The Commission for Psychiatric Reform stimulated the movement from institutional psychiatric hospitals in Spain to more varied levels of community-based care, including community mental health units (WHO 2001, 2005c). The General Health Law, which guarantees the right to health care, includes a chapter on mental health, bringing "the care of psychiatric disorders to a level of equality with other diseases" (WHO, 2001, p. 82).

The universal right to health care is part of Spanish law, with a health system entirely financed by general taxes and inclusive of a wide range of services requiring no payment from patients (WHO, 2001). Psychiatric care is considered part of the national health care budget; thus, mental health services are financed most prevalently through taxes, followed by patient/family out-of-pocket expenditure, and least often, private insurances (WHO, 2001, 2005c). In addition, because mental illness is recognized as a cause of disability in the country, some individuals with mental health problems qualify to receive a disability allowance from Spain's social security system.

In 2002, health resources management was transferred from a national to a community level. This transfer of authority began in 1977, when increasing costs, poor conditions of national mental hospitals, and professional awareness of the benefits of community care sparked the initial establishment of Autonomous Communities and the trend toward transferring health care into decentralized units (WHO, 2005c). Regional Health Ministries of Autonomous Communities are now responsible for implementation and regulation of mental health services. Regional mental health policies are based on a model of community care, and each region uses different terms for naming their mental health resources (Navarete & Palanca, 2005). The public health system in each region is the main provider of mental health services. Because mental health care is considered part of the overall health care system, treatment often occurs at the primary care level, even though primary care professionals typically do not have specific training in mental health (WHO, 2005c). There is no centralized system for national oversight of the mental health services provided in the different regions.

Mental Health Policy and Older Adults

In most areas of Spain, there are no specialized mental health services for older adults. However, in some regions, reflective of the variance that exists between different community systems, there are services targeting the needs of aging adults. For example, the Madrid Mental Health Plan provides special programming designated for "vulnerable client groups" and includes older adults as one of these target populations (Navarete & Palanca, 2005). The Madrid plan outlines specific policies to improve service delivery and quality of care, involve service users and families in care planning, and provide adequate long-term residential facilities and respite services—all policy aims that have the potential to heavily impact services to older adults. This region's system includes not only outpatient care at community mental health centers but also home help coordinated with input from primary care and social services.

Although some of the individual provinces in Spain have identified relatively high prevalence of mental health problems (e.g., anxiety, depression, psychosis) and cognitive impairments (e.g., dementia) among older adults, national rates have yet to be established (Olivera et al., 2008). Thus, the true demand for age-specific mental health services in Spain is unknown. Based on existing research and projected population changes, however, it appears that general practitioners need improved training in psychogeriatric issues and assessment to address the spectrum of mental health concerns facing Spain's aging population.

BOX 7.3 Policy to People Link: Madrid Takes the Lead in Mental Health Needs in Spain

Madrid has taken important steps to improve supports for older adults with mental health needs. In this region of the country, mental health outreach by multidisciplinary teams, home treatment and psychosocial services, and additional specialty services for vulnerable client groups such as older adults are available in all 36 city districts. Madrid also offers a "carer subsidy" for individuals providing in-home support to older family members, including those with dementia. The Ministry of Health and Social Policy of Spain has also initiated attention to priority areas for older adults within the European Pact for Mental Health and Well-Being through a planned Presidency Conference on Mental Health of Older People in Madrid. For more information, go to www.eurofound.europa.eu/events/2010/confmadrid0410/index.htm.

Summary

The international frameworks described in this chapter present a range of systems, policies, legislation, and efforts designed to confront the immense challenges of providing effective mental health supports to an aging population. Though countries vary considerably in their approaches to mental health care provision, they share many of the same experiences when it comes to addressing the unique needs of older adults. Collectively, they face an array of insidious obstacles that are not easily overcome. Whether mental health policies are piecemeal or part of comprehensive national initiatives or specifically target older adults or envelop their needs in more general policy language, the issues of ageism, stigma attached to mental illness, deficiencies in specialty services for older adults, and overall underutilization of mental health services in late life persist across countries and systems. Admirable strides have been made for more equitable distribution of mental health care in many regions, but policymakers have a long way to go before they can answer the question of how governments can most successfully confront the entrenched societal resistance and fill the gaps in service that currently impede the provision of adequate mental health supports for elders in almost every location around the globe.

For More Information

1. Jane-Llopis, E., & Gabilondo, A. (Eds.). (2008). *Mental health in older people: Consensus paper.* Luxemburg: European Communities.
   http://ec.europa.eu/health/ph_determinants/life_style/mental/docs/consensus_older_en.pdf

This paper highlights figures and trends, discusses key aspects of mental health in late life, and identifies examples of evidence-based actions.

2. The Mental Health Foundation (United Kingdom)
   http://www.mentalhealth.org.uk/our-work/older-people/

This nonprofit group provides links and services specifically for older adults. Topics include community initiatives related to coping with life transitions, home improvements, dementia, and palliative care.

3. National Institute of Mental Health (United States)
   http://www.nimh.nih.gov/index.shtml

This is one of the 27 institutes and centers that make up the National Institutes of Health under the U.S. Department of Health and Human Services. The National Institute of Mental Health website provides information about specific mental health conditions and ongoing research.

4. National Institute of Mental Health and Neuro Sciences (NIMHANS, India)
   http://www.nimhans.kar.nic.in/

NIMHANS is a leading mental health center in India that specializes in clinical work, research, and education. It includes several clinics, including the Geriatric Clinic, which specializes in psychiatric disorders for persons over 60.

5. Oxley, H. (2009). *Policies for healthy aging: An overview* (OECD Health Working Paper 42). Paris: OECD.
   http://dx.doi.org/10.1787/226757488706

This paper covers policies related to healthy aging, including mental health, in several OECD countries.

6. Pan American Health Organization (Latin America)
   http://www.paho.org/English/DD/PIN/mentalhealth_index.htm

This site gives an overview of initiatives and developments in regards to mental health services in Latin America and the Caribbean.

7. World Federation for Mental Health (WFMH)
   http://www.wfmh.org/

WFMH is an international body of mental health workers, consumers, and policy-makers. It offers reports on a variety of mental health topics from an intercultural perspective.

Mrs. W., age 89
Colorado Springs, Colorado, United States

I was born in Loveland, Colorado, on December, let me think, the 23rd I believe, 1921. Yes, that is correct, 1921. I was the first born in my family. My father worked at the Great Western Sugar Factory, and he was a farmer and also worked in the beet fields. My mother worked at different jobs over her life—in a laundry, a bakery, and cleaned a business. Both my parents were Germans who came over from Russia in the 1900s. I am the oldest of four children. We were very poor and lived on the farm. My mother made all of our clothes out of flour sacks. She was very good at making things.

I married in 1945. My husband worked during the war at Camp Hale in Colorado, in a meatpacking plant and later worked for a local freight delivery company until he retired. I didn't finish high school, as my family needed me to work, so I worked as a nanny for a family until I got married. After I married, I worked cleaning houses, in a department store, as a secretary at the freight company my husband worked at. Then I worked at the local school district for—I think it was 35 years—as a parent coordinator, a teacher's aide, and in the human resources office. I got up every morning at 4 a.m. so I could be to work at 5 a.m. to call substitute teachers to come in and cover when a teacher was absent. I have three children—two girls and one boy. My son passed away unexpectedly a few years ago, maybe it has been 10 years. My one daughter lives here in the same town I do. I appreciate what my daughter does for me, her kindness. My other daughter lives in Southern Colorado. She is raising her grandkids. She does a good job with them.

A typical day for me is that I get up and get ready. I have some help when I shower. Then I go down to breakfast. I participate in all the activities they have here at the place I live. We have field trips that we go on quite often, lots of different ones. We play different games, Bingo, Wii—but I just watch that; I really can't do that one. She [the activity director] always takes us on field trips, shopping—but I don't go often because I like to go shopping with my daughter—bus rides, crafts, and Bingo and toning exercise. I just like to stay busy. I do these puzzles—I look for words, I want to keep my mind active. Here is the schedule. Now what is today? [April 28th]. Okay, here you can see what's going on tomorrow. Here, see, they have "happy hour" on Friday, too. I go to another part of the building for therapy on my knees. They have someone come by and give us pedicures, and they do our nails. We have a beauty shop here, too.

Yes, I do get a pension. I get Social Security for when I was working at the department store and the trucking company. I also get a pension from when I was working at the school district—PERA. The total has always been okay until recently. I have to pay rent here for this apartment, and it covers all of my utilities, heat, cable, and three meals a day and for the aides to help me make sure I get my medicines. My medicines cost me something, but I don't know how much—my daughter takes care of my bills. Medicare doesn't pay for any of my costs to live here, though, I know that. So my daughter helps me by making up the difference. But being here is hard for me. Oh, everybody here is so kind and nice, very helpful, very polite. They have so many things we can do. But I have a house that I lived in for 50 years in another town, and I don't know why I can't be there. But my daughters tell me I am not safe living there by myself, and I can't afford to have the people come in and help me. I had a wonderful lady—let's see, what was her name? Edie, yes, it was Edie—who came in to help me in the morning and in evening every day. But I got real sick over Christmas last year and was in the hospital with pneumonia. And

I ended up in this apartment. My whole life just went to pieces. All of my stuff is scattered all over, . . . some here, some at my house in the attic. I don't know where my things are. I can't really remember how all that happened. I miss my friends and seeing the people I used to work with at the school district. Sometimes, I just sit here and cry. I hate to be a crybaby, but I get so lonesome. I miss all the fun I had with my family. We used to be so close, but everyone lives somewhere else. You know, I just sit here watching TV. I try to read when I can, but I can't drive my car anymore. So I can't go out like I used to, you know, go out and about when you want to. So I just sit here stuck. I can't have company come visit. . . . This place is too small; where would they stay? I think it is so hard on me because I have never been alone. I lived with my parents, and then I was married for 53 years. Now I am alone. It doesn't matter where I go, where I put my head, I will be by myself.

My health is okay, I guess. Pretty good really. I have terrible arthritis in my knees—bone on bone, the doctor tells me. I don't have the brightest mind in the world, but I am glad for what I have.

How I feel about getting older? Well, to tell you the truth, I am glad I am still here and I am thankful I am well enough to get up and get out of bed every day. I have had things to do, like learning how to paint, learn crocheting, and other odds-and-ends that I didn't have time to do before. What do I like about being my age? Well, I don't know that I can say what I like about it, but I have seen and did a lot of things. I don't have to worry about going to work, but my joy was all the years I worked at the school district. I am not able to do some of the things I would like to do. You have to be careful that you don't fall down, that you worry about your health, and that you have to exercise to keep yourself going. They don't like for you to drive anymore; they feel like you are not capable, and that is a little bit annoying. I do lots of reading so you can keep up with what is going on in the world, so you can act intelligent. You don't want to sit and do nothing; you need to be able to know a little bit of what is going on in the world.

I look forward to being alive a good number more years. I want to see my great-grandchildren grow up. I want to see them go to school, to be healthy, enjoy life, and take trips.

My advice to younger people about growing older is to get an education, stay with education, and keep your vision broadened in different things; the world has lots of different things that you may need to come into contact with, that you may need to know about. That doesn't mean that everyone needs to go out and be a lawyer. . . . Even the person that learns to be a mechanic is important, too. Each one needs to find out what they want to do and be proud of what you can do and do it well.

Yvonne and Peter, Ages 78 and 79, England

Mary and Ted, Ages 76 and 82, England

Community Support Policies

Over the past decade, we intensified our efforts to build a "society for all ages" and to promote international commitment to the United Nations Principles for Older Persons. The Principles are founded on the need to build an inclusive society that emphasizes participation, self-fulfillment, independence, care, and dignity for all. To transform them into deeds, we have campaigned for policies that will enable older persons to live in an environment that enhances their capabilities, fosters their independence, and provides them with adequate support and care as they age.

—United Nations Secretary-General Ban Ki-moon (September 28, 2009)

[I was] married for 51 years, but at the age of 78 [my husband] died. We had no children, but I was happy because he was a very good man and we had a good life; we always got along well. He got diabetes. He was really sick, and he died. E' la vita (it's life!). After his death, I was all by myself—a bit isolated in that house in the countryside with nothing else to see than the sky and some trees. So I moved to a small town, and there I felt happier. In 1999, part of my body became paralyzed. I thought to myself, "What do I do? I have no children. I have no one!"

—Mrs. M., age 80, Province Rovigo, Italy

ommunity-based programs and services can help older adults like Mrs. M. stay connected and engaged in a community that promotes social and physical well-being. Community-based programs and services can be organized into those that provide elders with access to other services, such as transportation and information and referral/assistance; those that address social and physical well-being with services such as in-home services, legal assistance, nutrition, mental health counseling, and health information; and those that promote social engagement such as recreation and leisure activities, lifelong learning, and volunteering and civic engagement. Having access to programs and services can make all the difference in the day-to-day experiences that contribute to overall quality of life in later life. According to Kosberg (1994), community-based services and programs provide the support older adults need to remain independent, engaged, and protected so they can develop full capabilities in their personal, social, and community relationships, as well as maintain a desirable quality of independent living (p. xix). Imagine how different Alta's quality of life would be if that bus didn't come to her house each day and there was no senior center to attend.

Policy and Community-Based Services

Community services can certainly include a wide array of social, cultural, educational, health-related, housing, and transportation programs. So the starting point for community service policy begins with deciding which services should be in place for general population use and which services need to be adjusted or altered dramatically so that individuals whose physical or social life circumstances (i.e., targeted populations) prohibit them from accessing services made available to the general population are included.

Figure 8.1 provides a visual representation of how policy might address both general and targeted population community needs. The outer edge of the circle represents community programs available to the general population. The center of the wheel represents those programs and services that are in essence new programs to address the needs of a target population that is unable to access general programs. The connection between the general and targeted programs represent a continuum of services that are a variation, to a lesser or greater degree, of general population programs made more accessible to target populations. For example, a community provides all citizens with the opportunity to use its public transportation services; however, a policy may be enacted that facilitates access to the general public transportation systems among older adults by providing them reduced fares or altered routes during off-peak hours. However, a new transportation program may need to be created, such as a door-to-door transport service, because there are older adults or persons with disabilities who aren't able to use the general population transportation system, regardless of the variations made to the program. The question for social policymakers is "Where along this continuum of general population and targeted population community services should policy be enacted?" If there is such a determination, how are such services or programs financed and delivered? What is the mix between the public-government sector, the voluntary nonprofit sector, and the for-profit sector in providing for such services?

International Overview

Identifying indicators on a macrolevel that give us a picture of the depth and breadth of a country's community-based services is difficult at best. Not only are such expenditures, when quantified, spread across numerous government agencies, but included in the data are expenditures for a vast array of programs for all ages and all social programs such as employment programs, health programs, education, and so on. However, the Organisation for Economic Co-operation and Development (OECD) has compiled social expenditure data across 30 countries that excludes expenditures on health services—data that can at least give us an inkling as to the degree to which a country's policy supports social programs. The OECD public social expenditure data comprise cash benefits, direct "in-kind" provision of goods and services, and tax

Figure 8.1 Social Policy Continuum of Community Programs for General and Targeted Populations

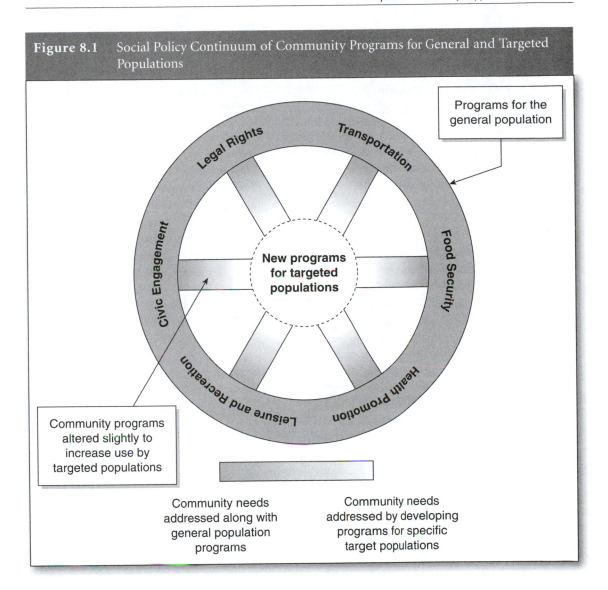

breaks with social purposes (OECD, 2009c). To be included, benefits have to address one or more social goals and may be targeted at low-income households, the elderly, disabled, sick, unemployed, or young persons. Thus, even though the OECD data capture a very broad look at how much countries spend on social programs, we know that programs that serve older adults are included within this data and it does give us some insight into the resources directed to social care by each country. Figure 8.2 shows that there is a wide difference among countries when it comes to social expenditure. Sweden has the highest percentage (7.8%) of their net national income directed toward social services and Mexico the lowest (0.1%). The United States is in the lower third of the countries with 0.8%. Many of the Scandinavian countries, such as Finland and Denmark, are in the top third; two of the Asian countries included in the analysis, Korea and Japan, are in the bottom third.

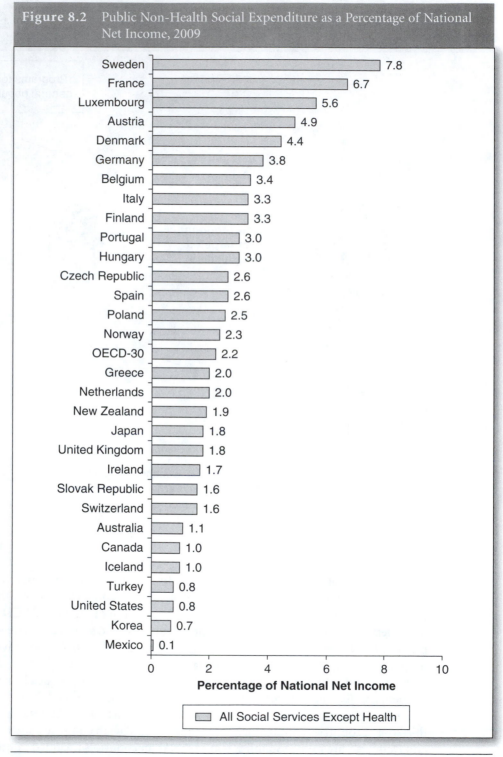

Figure 8.2 Public Non-Health Social Expenditure as a Percentage of National Net Income, 2009

The percentages that countries spend on social care programs will certainly be impacted due to the increase in the number of older adults worldwide over the next 20 years. As a result, there has been a growing interest in how the community-based support needs of older adults will be met in the coming years and which of these needs should be addressed through legislative action. The discussion about what community needs should be addressed legislatively has already begun on the international stage. The United Nation's Madrid Second World Assembly on Ageing in 2002, attended by more than 150 countries and international organizations, adopted the Madrid International Plan of Action on Ageing, which contains resolutions designed to encourage governments to address, among other concerns, the active participation of older adults in social, economic, cultural, sporting, recreational, and volunteer activities that contribute to the growth and maintenance of personal well-being.

The World Health Organization (2007) is also promoting the Age Friendly Communities initiative to help local city governments create "an inclusive and accessible urban environment that promotes active ageing." This initiative includes recommendations for adapting city structures and services that enable people to age actively. Structures and services identified as elements of age-friendly communities that need to be examined include transportation, outdoor spaces, housing, social inclusion, civic participation, communication and information, and community support services.

The purpose of this chapter is to examine the different ways in which social policies promote independence, well-being, and social engagement of community-dwelling older adults. Because there is such a wide array of community programs, we have elected to narrow our discussion to three countries and six important areas of community-based social policy—food and nutrition, recreation and leisure, transportation, legal assistance, information and referral/assistance, and civic engagement. We discuss in detail the United States, England, and Sweden, as these three countries represent three distinct ways in which national governments actively promote community programs and the varying amounts of government expenditure on social programs. We excluded from our discussion in this chapter community-based home health services, as these services are discussed in more detail in Chapter 9. We begin our discussion by reviewing the policies and programs in the United States.

United States

Social policy creating community-based services such as nutrition programs, transportation, community involvement, and legal assistance exists in a number of different legislative acts and is implemented through a number of different federal government agencies. These will be discussed in more detail when we review the policies below; however, it is important to again briefly mention that in the United States, the Older Americans Act (OAA; discussed in Chapter 2) is the one piece of legislation that serves to centralize the delivery of a number of community-based services for older adults.

The OAA, passed in 1965, is the landmark legislation that funds a wide array of community-based services for older persons. The Act created a structure and a system for advocating, coordinating, and delivering a broad range of community programs and services and spawned the "Aging Network," composed of federal, state, and local governments as well as myriad nonprofit organizations. Over the years, the OAA created a number of community-based programs, including a national nutrition pro-gram, programs to prevent elder abuse and neglect, programs for health promotion, long-term care ombudsman, and programs that support caregivers. Titles III through VII operationalized the health and community-based programs and services that we will discuss in more detail below. In most communities, the Area Agencies on Aging (AAAs) do not directly deliver services but, rather, contract with local agencies through a competitive grant process to implement the services outlined in the Act and identified in the state or local AAA plan. We will discuss the role of the OAA in providing com-munity-based services when we review the community-based services presented below.

Food and Nutrition Programs

The federal government first provided access to food via coupons to those "on relief" starting in 1939 via the Food Stamp program (U.S. Department of Agriculture [USDA], 2009c). The program was short-lived and ended in 1943, as it was determined that the conditions that brought the program into existence—widespread unemploy-ment and food surpluses—had ended (USDA, 2009c). It was not until 1964 that Congress passed the Food Stamp Act of 1964, which established a permanent program under the guidance of the USDA in partnership with the states, with whom it shares 50% of the state's costs to administer the program. The program's stated goals at its inception were to strengthen the agricultural economy and provide improved levels of nutrition among low-income households, and it was operational nationwide in 1974.

The Food Stamp Act has undergone numerous legislative changes that addressed program regulations, including eligibility guidelines and program administration. The most recent legislation, now called the Food and Nutrition Act of 2008, changed some aspects of the program—including changing the name of the federal program to the Supplemental Nutrition Assistance Program (SNAP), but states have the option to not change the name of the program. SNAP is based on a rather complicated set of financial eligibility guidelines and on whether a household contains an elderly adult or a person with a disability. One part of the financial eligibility guidelines covers the amount of a household's cash or savings. This amount cannot exceed $3,000 (it excludes home value, Supplemental Security Income Benefits, and retirement plan accounts such as a 401k) and one car per adult member in the household, whose fair market value can-not be more than $4,650—although some vehicles are excluded in the resource determi-nation if they are used for purposes identified in the guidelines (USDA, 2009c).

The second part to determining financial eligibility is assessing the household's gross or net income. If the household contains at least one adult over age 60, income eligibility is based on net monthly household income, which is 100% of the poverty level. Deductions include 20% of earned income, a standard deduction of $141 for a household of two, medical expenses over $35 paid out of pocket, and shelter costs that are more than half the household income after the other deductions. For a household of two older adults, the net monthly income cannot be over $1,167. If the household contains someone over age 60 who meets a permanent disability standard and cannot buy/prepare food separately because of his or her disability, the guidelines consider this individual to be his or her own food stamp household, and others living in the household must meet gross versus net monthly income standards. In 2009, the maximum benefit for a household of two eligible older adults was $367 per month. The program is administered through local departments of social services. Individuals apply for benefits in local offices and, if eligible, receive a debit card to purchase food. As of September 2009, there were 16.8 million households participating in the SNAP program—an increase of 19.9% over September 2008. The average benefit amount for all recipients was $275.53; the average monthly benefit for elders living alone was $76, and it was $172 for elders not living alone (USDA, 2010).

The federal government enacted the Agriculture and Consumer Protection Act of 1973, which funds the Commodity Supplemental Food Program that provides expectant and new mothers, infants and children, and older adults aged 60 and over with USDA commodity foods. The USDA purchases food and makes it available to participating states and Indian Tribal Organizations for distribution via public and nonprofit entities, along with the funds to support the administration of the program. Currently, 32 states (AK, AZ, CA, CO, IL, IA, IN, KS, KY, LA, MI, MN, MS, MO, MT, NE, NV, NH, NM, NY, NC, ND, OH, OR, PA, SC, SD, TN, TX, VT, WA, and WI) and the District of Columbia participate in the program (USDA, 2009a). Local agencies determine eligibility of the applicants, which for older adults is income at or below 130% of the federal poverty guidelines, which for a one- and two-person elderly household was $14,079 and $18,941 annually, respectively. In 2008, an estimated 444,000 elderly adults participated in the program (USDA, 2009a).

Another federal food distribution program is the Emergency Food Assistance Program, first authorized as the Emergency Food Assistance Act of 1983 (USDA, 2009b). The program provides low-income individuals, including older adults, with emergency food via nonprofit food banks or directly to those who qualify. The USDA buys surplus food and distributes the food to states based on the number of unemployed and the number of persons with incomes below the poverty level. The federal government provides the funds for operating programs, and states set eligibility guidelines and distribute the food to local charitable organizations such as food banks and food pantries, which distribute food directly to qualified individuals. For example, Feeding America (formerly known as America's Second Harvest) secures and distributes more than 2.5 billion pounds of food and grocery products annually and is the primary recipient of government commodities via the Emergency Food Assistance Program (Feeding America, 2010). The food is also distributed to congregate meal sites that provide meals to those in need.

Under the OAA, Nutrition Services (Title III-C) provides funds to establish and operate nutrition programs for both congregate and home-delivered nutrition services and the Nutrition Services Incentive Program, which is a food supplement program. Title III-C is the major source of funding for nutrition programs targeted at older adults and has the stated purpose of reducing hunger and food insecurity and promoting health and social well-being among older adults.

Formula grants to fund the Title III-C programs are given to the states and territories based on their share of older adults over age 60. The state or local AAAs in turn contract with local providers to implement the programs. All meal programs under Title III-C benefit from the expertise of nutrition science experts and dieticians to ensure that the meals are nutritionally sound.

Funding for the Nutrition Services under Title III-C in 2008 was $604.5 million, an amount that represented 54% of the 2008 Administration on Aging (AoA) budget (Napili, 2008). Although the programs do not charge for the meals, participants are asked to make the suggested donation of the cost of the meals, which nationally ranges between $2 and $4. In addition to participant contributions, other federal, state, and local funds and private donations help support these programs, as Title III-C funds cover less than half the cost to deliver congregate meal programs and less than 25% of the cost of home-delivered meal programs (AoA, 2009b).

The Congregate Nutrition Services section of the Act authorizes the delivery of meals, nutrition assessment, and education and counseling in a congregate setting such as a senior center. The Act requires that for five or more days a week (except in a rural area where such frequency is not feasible and a lesser frequency is approved by the state agency), the grantee provides at least one hot or other appropriate meal. The meals are to be offered in congregate settings, including adult day care facilities and multigenerational meal sites (OAA, 2006 as amended). In addition to the meals, programs also provide nutrition education, nutrition counseling, and other nutrition services, as appropriate.

Congregate meal programs are available to anyone over the age of 60 and to certain categories of individuals (e.g., spouses or persons with disabilities) under age 60. The majority of congregate programs offer a noontime meal, although there are some sites that offer breakfast as well. In 2008, the Congregate Nutrition program funding allocation was $410 million. In 2007, congregate nutrition meal programs served more than 94 million meals to more than 1.6 million older adults (AoA, 2009c).

BOX 8.1 Policy to People Link: Congregate Nutrition Services, Mackay, Idaho

The reach of the OAA congregate meal program extends to every state and territory and plays an important role in the nutritional well-being of rural and urban communities across the country.

Mackay is a small town of a little more than 500 people in rural, east-central Idaho, 100 miles northwest of Idaho Falls. According to Census data, almost a quarter of the population is 65 and over, and 19.8% of those over 65 are living below the poverty line. The town has one small grocery store (with four aisles) and two—sometimes three—local restaurants.

The congregate meal program is offered at noon on Mondays and Fridays in the two-room Mackay Senior Citizen Community Center. According to one 93-year-old participant, "I come for the company and associations with people. The meals I get at the center are the only hot meals I get all week."

The Home Delivered Nutrition Services Act provides funding for nutritional assessments, counseling, and the delivery of meals to homebound older adults. The Act stipulates that on five or more days a week (except in a rural area where such frequency is not feasible and a lesser frequency is approved by the state agency), at least one meal per day—which may consist of hot, cold, frozen, dried, canned, fresh, or supplemental foods and any additional meals that the recipient of a grant or contract under this subpart elects to provide—must be home-delivered. As with the Congregate Nutrition Program, formula grants are given to the states and territories based on the number of older adults over the age of 60 residing in the state or territory. In 2008, the Home Delivered Nutrition

Program's funding allocation under the Act was $193.8 million, and the program served more than 140.9 million meals to more than 900,000 persons (AoA, 2009c).

The Nutrition Services Incentive Program provides additional funding to states, territories, and eligible tribal organizations that is used exclusively to purchase food to supplement local food programs. States may choose to receive the grant as cash, commodities, or a combination of cash and commodities. The funding for the program in 2008 was $153.4 million (AoA, 2009c).

Recreation and Leisure

In the United States, senior centers have historically been the focal point of recreation and leisure programs for older adults. Although the first senior center opened in New York City in 1943, the passage of the OAA launched the modern era of senior centers (Leanse, Tiven, & Robb, 1977). In 1973, Congress enacted Title V of the OAA to provide financial support for the renovation or acquisition of "multipurpose senior centers" that provided a broad range of health, social, and educational services and were designated as "community focal points" to coordinate and integrate community services for older adults. Amendments to the Act in 1978 placed support for senior centers under Title III, and local AAAs were instructed to use senior centers, when feasible, as the central point for delivery of OAA services, thus promoting the rapid expansion of senior centers across the country. Although not all community focal points supported by OAA funds are senior centers, of the 9,240 focal points identified in 2008, 6,935 were senior centers (AoA, 2009h). There are now an estimated 15,000 senior centers, whose characteristics range from small nutrition sites that offer only occasional programming— such as the one in Mackay, Idaho—to large multipurpose senior centers with a broad array of social, cultural, health, leisure, and recreational programs (Dal Santo, 2009). The most common services provided at multipurpose senior centers are

- health and wellness programs and information,
- cultural events,
- arts and crafts,
- recreational and fitness programs,
- intergenerational programs,
- employment assistance,
- educational programs,
- information and referral,
- financial and legal assistance,
- leisure travel and local outings,
- meal and nutrition programs and education,
- transportation services,
- volunteer opportunities, and
- social networking opportunities (Dal Santo, 2009).

It is estimated that senior centers serve 10 million older adults each year (National Institute of Senior Centers, 2005). Senior center funding comes from multiple sources. In addition to OAA funds, senior centers receive funding from local and state governments, nonprofit agencies, grants, businesses, and membership fees.

Transportation

Transportation is a critical component in assisting older adults to access health care services, stay connected with friends and family, participate in civic events, and maintain an independent lifestyle.

Transportation policy for older adults tends to be organized in two categories: (1) essential or life-sustaining trips, which include trips for medical purposes, employment, shopping, banking, and other necessary trips; and (2) quality-of-life trips that include visiting friends and family and attending civic and cultural events, religious services, and volunteer activities (U.S. Government Accountability Office, 2004). Perhaps in part because of these varied purposes for transportation, transportation policy is fragmented and involves a number of different federal entities.

There are five different federal agencies involved in providing transportation services both to the general population and to older adults. Figure 8.3 shows the five different federal agencies, their departments, and the programs within those departments that provide transportation funding and services. The shaded boxes indicate which transportation programs are targeted toward older adults, and the nonshaded programs indicate that older adults are included in populations that can be served under those programs, such as the transportation services for veterans. Funding supports a variety of different types of transportation, including fixed-route, where vehicles operate along predetermined routes on a fixed schedule; rail transit systems, which include subways, elevated trains, or streetcar vehicles; flex-routes, which may include prearranged services in addition to the fixed routes in place; demand-responsive systems, which require advanced scheduling; and paratransit systems, which are for individuals whose disabilities prevent them from using regular fixed-route transportation systems (United We Ride, 2007).

As you can see in Figure 8.3, the Department of Transportation and the DHHS are two federal agencies that provide the majority of funding and programs for transportation services directed toward older adults. Recent legislation that created community transportation programs has been the Transportation Equity Act for the 21st Century, enacted June 9, 1998, and the Safe, Accountable, Flexible, Efficient Transportation Equity Act: A Legacy for Users (SAFETEA-LU), enacted August 10, 2005. Under the SAFETEA-LU legislation, the U.S. Department of Transportation (2010) is authorized to fund the following programs:

Formula Program for Elderly Persons and Persons with Disabilities (Section 5310): These funds are allocated by formula to the states for capital costs of providing services to elderly persons and persons with disabilities. States suballocate funds to private nonprofit organizations and to public agencies to provide coordinated service. States receive their allocation on the basis of the number of elderly and persons with disabilities.

Capital Investment Grants "New Starts" (Section 5309): These provide funds for new fixed transit systems or extensions to existing systems such as light rail, rapid rail (heavy rail), commuter rail, monorail, or a busway/high occupancy vehicle facility.

Urbanized Area Formula Grants: These provide public transportation capital investments.

Non-Urbanized Areas Formula Grants (Section 5311): These provide capital and operating assistance for rural and small urban public transportation systems and provide formula capital and operating grants to states for services in other-than-urbanized areas.

Figure 8.3	Overview of Federal Programs Supporting Transportation

Dept of Health and Human Services

Admin for Children and Families	Community Block Grants	Social Services Block Grants
Admin on Aging OAA	Grants for Supportive Services- OAA Titles III-B Grants for American Indian, Alaskan Native, Native Hawaiian Elders – Title VI	
Centers for Medicare and Medicaid	Medicaid Medical Services	
Health Resources and Services Admin	Rural Health Care Services Outreach	

Dept of Transportation

Federal Transit Administration SAFETEA-LU	Formula Program for Elderly Persons and Persons with Disabilities (Section 5310)
	Capital Investment Grants (Section 5309)
	Urbanized Area Formula Grants (Section 5307)
	Nonurbanized Area Formula Program (Section 5311)
	Job Access and Reverse Commute (Section 5316)
	New Freedom Program (Section 5317)

Department of Veterans Affairs

Veterans Health Administration	Beneficiary Travel Benefit

Dept of Education

Office of Special Education and Rehab Services	Independent Living Services for Older Individuals Who Are Blind

Department of Labor

Employment and Training Administration	Senior Community Service Employment Programs

Job Access and Reverse Commute (Section 5316): This provides funding for local programs that offer job access and reverse-commute services to provide transportation for low-income individuals who may live in the city core and work in suburban locations.

New Freedom Program (Section 5317): This provides funding to encourage services and facility improvements to address the transportation needs of persons with disabilities that go beyond those required by the Americans with Disabilities Act. Formula grants are given for associated capital and operating costs. Funds are allocated to states through a formula based on their population of persons with disabilities.

Transportation services are also funded under Title III-B of the OAA, which funds services designed to enable older adults to remain in their own homes and age in place in the community. Assisted transportation services are funded under Title III-B and vary in their type and scope, as each community determines how best to meet the transportation needs of its elders. Funds can support door-to-door transportation for medical appointments, transportation to senior centers or adult day programs, door-through-door services (which help seniors get in and out of their houses in order to access the door-to-door transportation), volunteer driver programs, and transportation voucher programs. In 2008, OAA funds for transportation totaled $219.5 million and provided more than 28 million rides to older adults to doctor's offices, grocery stores, pharmacies, senior centers, meal sites, and other necessary daily activities (AoA, 2008c; Napili, 2008). The majority of older adults who use OAA transportation services are over the age of 75 and live alone (AoA, 2006).

The Department of Veterans' Affairs, Department of Education, and Department of Labor also are authorized to provide transportation services to individuals who have qualified for their respective programs. For example, the Senior Community Service Employment Program under the Department of Labor is a community service and work-based training program for older workers, and transportation is a supportive service that can be provided to assist participants who live in remote places (U.S. Department of Labor, 2004). The Veterans' Administration has the authority to provide eligible beneficiaries a special mode of transportation (when medically justified) and in certain circumstances, such as a taxi or hired car. The Independent Living Services for Older Individuals Who Are Blind supports individuals aged 55 or older whose recent visual impairment makes competitive employment extremely difficult to obtain but for whom independent living goals are feasible. Services offered to eligible participants include transportation services.

Legal Assistance

Equal access to justice is a fundamental tenet in our system of government and law, a key component of which is to provide legal assistance programs to persons who are unable to afford legal representation for both criminal and civil matters. For our discussion, we will focus only on policies that support legal assistance for civil matters.

Older adults, and particularly low-income older adults, have been identified as a population in need of legal services. They and their families often need assistance with navigating the complex and sometimes inconsistent requirements of different benefit programs (remember the eligibility rules for food stamps described earlier in the chapter?), health care, income retirement benefits, assisted living and long-term care living environments, and issues surrounding cognitive capacity. There are two primary sources of federal legislation that provide low-income older adults access to legal advice and representation, the Legal Services Corporation Act (1974) and Title III of the OAA.

The Legal Services Corporation, a nonprofit organization, was established by Congress in 1974 under the Legal Services Corporation Act (1974). The mission of the LSC is to promote equal access to justice and civil legal assistance to low-income Americans, defined as those living at or below 125% of the federal poverty guideline. The LSC redistributes funds from the federal government to 137 local independent legal aid programs across the country (LSC, 2010). In 2008, LSC received federal funding of $350.4 million. Local legal aid offices provide no-cost legal representation to eligible clients, including older adults, in matters of family law, housing, consumer issues, and income maintenance.

Under the OAA, Title III-B mandates that legal services for limited types of civil legal problems will be provided in some measure in every state. States are to provide, under the direction of a state legal assistance developer, the coordination of the delivery of programs, technical assistance, and training for local providers. The qualified providers with whom local AAAs contract are to serve older adults with the greatest economic or social needs and are to give priority to legal issues related to income, health care, long-term care, nutrition, housing, utilities, protective services, defense of guardianship, abuse, neglect, and age discrimination (OAA, 2006). Programs must also work to involve the local private bar association in providing pro bono efforts to help supplement OAA-funded efforts. In 2007, $25.2 million was used to provide 943 million hours of legal assistance (AoA, 2009f, 2009g).

In addition, Title IV authorizes funding of demonstration and support projects for delivering legal assistance and creating a national legal support system. This system aids state and area agencies on aging in providing, developing, or supporting legal assistance for older individuals, including (a) case consultations; (b) training; (c) provision of substantive legal advice and assistance; and (d) assistance in the design, implementation, and administration of legal assistance delivery systems to local providers of legal assistance for older individuals (OAA, 2006). Currently, the National Legal Resource Center funds demonstration projects designed to expand or improve the delivery of legal assistance and elder rights protections to older persons with social or economic needs. Five programs receive funding to provide national-level support. The National Senior Citizens Law Center provides case consultation for professionals and advocates in the field of law and aging. The National Consumer Law Center provides training for professionals and advocates from aging and legal services networks. The Center for Social Gerontology provides technical assistance in the development of efficient and effective legal and aging service delivery systems. The Center for Elder Rights Advocacy provides technical assistance to a network of legal helpline professionals. The American Bar Association Commission on Law on Aging provides professionals and advocates in aging and legal services networks with information and resources on legal and elder rights issues impacting older adults. Funding for these programs in 2009 totaled $736,302 (AoA, 2010d).

Information and Referral/Assistance

Providing information about all available federal and state programs has been formalized through two governmental initiatives—GovBenefits.gov and, specifically for older adults and their families, the OAA's National Eldercare Locator. GovBenefits .gov, launched in 2002, is a partnership between 16 federal agencies and all 50 states and is the official benefits website of the federal government. Visitors to the site can find information and eligibility prescreening question for more than 1,000 benefit programs (GovBenefits.gov, 2010).

The National Eldercare Locator is a nationwide information service that links individuals looking for assistance with state and local area agencies on aging and community-based organizations. The locator is authorized and funded under the OAA. The Eldercare Locator, which is a 24/7/365 service, receives more than 135,000 calls every year and 250,000 visits to the website (www.eldercare.gov). The Eldercare Locator provides general and topic-specific information about financial assistance, health care and health insurance and services, caregiver support programs, transportation, legal services, and housing. The Eldercare Locator is administered in partnership with the National Association of Area Agencies on Aging and the National Association of State Units on Aging (National Association of Area Agencies on Aging, 2009). In 2008, funding for the Eldercare Locator program totaled $1.1 million (Napili, 2008).

The AoA also provided funding to create the National Center on Benefits Outreach and Enrollment (National Council on Aging, 2010b), which has funded a web-based decision support tool and 10 benefit enrollment centers located in various states to help older adults determine their eligibility for federal and state benefit programs. Finally, Title III-B funds are also used to establish information and assistance efforts through local AAAs.

Civic Engagement

Within the last decade and more recently since 2008, there has been a renewed interest in promoting civic engagement across all age groups. According to the American Society on Aging, late-life civic engagement "encompasses actions wherein older adults participate in activities of personal and public concern that are *both* individually life enriching and socially beneficial to the community" (American Society on Aging, 2010). Volunteerism, a key component of civic engagement, has played an important role in the delivery of OAA programs since its inception. However, with the recent renewed interest in civic engagement nationally, 2006 revisions to the OAA now specifically articulate strategies to engage volunteers, called the Multigenerational and Civic Engagement Initiative. Amendments included providing guidelines for the use of volunteers in all OAA programs, providing grants for multigenerational and civic engagement programs that involve older adults, and calling for collaboration between the AoA and the Corporation for National and Community Service (AoA, 2010a). The goal of the Multigenerational and Civic Engagement Initiative is for older adults to make important contributions to their communities through (1) demonstration and research projects for multigenerational and civic engagement activities, (2) a comprehensive national strategy for using older adults to address community needs, and (3) intergenerational programs that connect older volunteers with families that have special needs. The National Council on Aging received funding under the initiative for a 3-year project designed to provide technical support to local programs to assist them in the development of civic engagement programs.

The National and Community Service Act of 1990 and its most recent reauthorization, called the Edward M. Kennedy Serve America Act (2009), created the Corporation for National and Community Service, a federal agency created in 1993 to administer three nationwide volunteer programs—AmeriCorp, Learn and Serve America, and Senior Corps. The Senior Corps programs include the Foster Grandparents Program, which connects volunteers age 60 or older with children and young people with exceptional needs for 15 to 40 hours per week in a variety of settings, including schools, hospitals, drug treatment centers, and child care centers. Volunteers who meet income eligibility requirements receive a modest monetary stipend of $2.65 per hour. The Retired and Senior Volunteer Program provides older adults with a variety of service opportunities in their local communities, and volunteers choose how many hours per week they wish to volunteer. Volunteers are eligible to receive reimbursement for mileage and insurance coverage while volunteering. The Senior Companion Program connects trained volunteers age 60 and over with homebound and other adults who have difficulty with tasks of day-to-day living (Corporation for National and Community Service, 2004). Senior Companion volunteers provide between 15 to 40 hours of service per week, and those who meet income eligibility guidelines receive a modest monetary stipend of $2.65 per hour. Funding in 2009 for all the Senior Corps programs was $213 million (Corporation for National and Community Service, 2009). We now turn our discussion to England's approach to community resources for older adults.

England

Community-based social programs in England cover a wide range of activities, and the push for these programs originates at the national level from legislation as well as from position papers, called white or green papers, that outline in more detail the specific goals of providing community-based programs. Once legislative direction or position papers have been articulated, it is the responsibility of the local government counsels to ensure that services are being delivered. Services are in turn provided either by local government counsels or agencies in the charitable nonprofit and private sectors.

The National Assistance Act of 1948 and its reauthorized versions are the foundational piece of legislation that authorizes local authorities in municipalities to make residential and social care arrangements designed to promote the welfare of persons with physical limitations. More recently, a key government position paper called "Opportunity Age" (Department for Work and Pensions, 2005), led by the Department of Work and Pensions and the Minister of State for Pensions and the Ageing Society, presented a strategic focus to achieve a vision of society that "aims to end the perception of older people as dependent; ensure that longer life is healthy and fulfilling; and that older people are full participants in society." Three key areas targeted for change were (1) work and income to achieve higher employment rates and greater flexibility for over-50s in continuing careers, managing any health conditions, and combining work with family and other commitments; (2) active ageing to enable older people to play a full and active role in society; and (3) services that, when utilized, allow older adults to keep their independence and control. Outcomes of the "Opportunity Age" initiative for active ageing created additional programs in the areas of transportation, learning, leisure, and volunteering, which will be discussed below. The follow-up to "Opportunity Age" was the publication of the government's strategic vision, titled "Building a Society for All Ages," in July 2009. Building on the themes set forth in the 2005 document, additional programs in the areas of leisure and sport, learning, transportation, volunteering, and access to services were developed. Funds for these programs are given to local authorities, who contract with charitable/nonprofit or private-sector agencies to provide services. We begin our review of community programs in England with a discussion of nutrition programs.

Food and Nutrition Programs

Various types of home and community-based meal programs for older adults exist in England and are funded by the national government. Unlike the United States, the United Kingdom does not have a stand-alone food stamp program for low-income individuals; rather, the various monthly cash benefit amounts provided to low-income individuals is thought to cover the cost of food. The National Health Service and Community Care Act of 1990 (U.K. Acts of Parliament, 1990) places a duty on local councils to assess anyone who might need help with activities of daily living, and home-delivered meals can be included in the plan created to address care needs. Home-delivered meals—referred to as the Community Meals Service—are arranged and/or provided by the local social services departments for older adults who have been assessed by the local adult social care department to be unable to prepare a daily hot meal and are disabled, sick, or frail and, depending on local council policy, meet income guidelines. Those who do not qualify under the Community Care Act may participate in the program for a cost of approximately £3.12 ($4.75) per meal (Bath & North East Somerset Council, 2009). The availability of the meals varies, but most provide at least daily service Monday through Friday, and frozen meals are available for later consumption over the weekend.

Community-based nutrition programs are provided by charity organizations and funded through national and local governments. Charitable organizations such as Age Concern Resource Centres and WRVS provide nutrition support services such as shopping assistance or noontime meals. Various local nonprofit organizations such as local Age Concern Resource Centres provide shopping assistance. The staff in these local centers works with local supermarkets to have food delivered to elders. There is no Age Concern fee for this service, although the supermarket will charge for delivery. Noontime meals—often called Lunch Clubs—are also available for a small fee (£2.90 or $4.40; Age Concern, 2010b).

Recreation and Leisure/Sport

While programs to engage older adults in leisure and recreation (referred to as sport in England and elsewhere in Europe) have been in existence for quite some time. The white papers mentioned earlier—"Opportunity Age" (Department for Work and

Pensions, 2005) and "Building a Society for All Ages"—were the most recent national catalysts for creating new leisure, recreation, and lifelong-learning programs for older adults in England. In general, older adults have opportunities to participate in leisure activities through local Age Concern Resource Centres and other community associations. For example, Age Concern has used National Lottery grant funds to create and implement local chapters of "Fit as a Fiddle" programs, which include gardening, walking, yoga, swimming, and tai chi for those over age 50 (Age Concern, 2010a). Age Concern also recruits and trains volunteers who are 50 years or older to become senior health mentors who volunteer in the Ageing Well and Fit as a Fiddle programs. These volunteers then make contact with isolated people and community groups, providing vital links to health services and opportunities in local communities, and offering advice on a range of issues, including diet/nutrition, physical activity, and falls prevention. Other local community centers also provide a venue for leisure and recreation programs. For example, the Queen's Crescent Community Association and the Highgate Newtown Community Centre offer a variety of social and educational programs for individuals of all ages and programs targeted to older adults, including Older Peoples Luncheon Club, movies, exercise programs, bingo sessions, travel excursions, intergenerational workshops, an English language class, and computer classes (Highgate Newtown Community Centre, 2010; Queen's Crescent Community Association, 2010). The activities are provided free or for a small fee (£2 or $3).

Two programs initiated by the government via the 2005 Opportunity Age strategic plan were the TV license fee waiver for older adults over age 74 (the fee generally had to be paid to watch or record TV broadcasts to support the BBC's domestic broadcasting services). This waiver of the £148 ($224) fee was based on the notion that many adults 75 and older rely on TV for information and entertainment and providing access would keep older adults informed and engaged in their community (Department for Work and Pensions, 2009). The second program, the free swimming initiative run through local councils, provides free swimming to individuals aged 60 and over.

"Building a Society for All Ages" (Department for Work and Pensions, 2009) launched a number of different initiatives designed to increase participation in a variety of community activities. For example, the Active at 60 Programme is designed to increase active participation by older adults in cultural, educational, and social events and provide information about how to access these opportunities. Local authorities and charitable organizations collaborate to implement the program. In another strategy designed to make participation in community programs and services easy, local authorities are piloting the use of smart cards that provide all-in-one access to a range of local activities (e.g., sport clubs, bus travel, museums, libraries, business discounts). Other initiatives in "Building a Society for All Ages" included commissioning 46 national governing bodies of sport to create a community sport system that includes plans to encourage individuals over 50 to participate, piloting a program called Digital Mentors to improve digital literacy levels of older adults and providing £20 million ($30.2 million) for a learning transformation fund and in cooperation with the National Institute of Adult Continuing Education and the Third Age Trust to test new ideas for increasing access to informal learning opportunities.

BOX 8.2   Policy to People Link: Digital Smart Card

One of the goals of the "Building a Society for All Ages" white paper was to increase community involvement among older adults. In order to promote easy access to a variety of programs—for both government programs and private business—the Digital Smart Card was launched.

In Bracknell Forest, people over 60 can use their digital smart cards to access the library, free bus services, and sports clubs and get discounts from more than 100 local businesses. An added benefit is that people do not need to travel into town to register for free bus travel, as was the case before. Instead, it is possible to register for any service that is available on the card at any location that uses smart cards. This is a benefit for people with mobility problems, since it reduces the need for long journeys.

Derbyshire has a similar program, which includes discounts at more than 1,400 local businesses that have signed up to use the card. In addition, the library service is included on the cards automatically, and 20,000 people have registered for the library as a result. The card, combined with a communication strategy, including a magazine and regular road shows, has helped improve participation levels in local services. Derbyshire is looking for opportunities to expand the cards to include, for example, cycle hire or DVD rentals, as well as government entitlements.

Transportation

The Transport Act (U.K. Acts of Parliament, 2000) introduced a statutory requirement for local transportation authorities to produce a Local Transport Plan every 5 years and includes an obligation for local transportation authorities to address the transportation needs of older adults and persons with mobility difficulties. The revisions to the Act in 2008 broaden the scope of local transport legislation to bring it in line with the Disability Discrimination Act of 1995 and revisions of 2005. The Act ensures that the needs of older adults and those with disabilities are considered in the development of local plans and also enables the Secretary of State for Transport to make regulations that would facilitate the accessibility of taxis, public service vehicles, and rail vehicles for disabled people.

The Concessionary Bus Travel Act of 2007 enacted free off-peak concessionary local bus travel throughout England beginning April 2008. The concession guarantees free local bus travel for those people over 60 and eligible persons with a disability from 9:30 a.m. until 11 p.m. on weekdays and all day weekends and bank holidays (U.K. Acts of Parliament, 2007a). Local authorities may offer discretionary concessions beyond the statutory minimum based on local needs and circumstances, but such additional services must be funded from a local authority's own resources (Department for Transport, 2009). Examples of the types of discretionary concession that some local authorities offer include companion passes for those who are unable to travel alone, free travel on other modes of transport where buses are limited or scarce, and extension of the time restriction to allow travel in peak periods (Age Concern, 2009).

Other programs launched from the Transport Act include subsidies for taxi sharing and taxibuses that in turn allow older and disabled passengers to pay a smaller fare (rather than the exclusive fare normally associated with taxi travel) and institute a taxi-sharing program that allows passengers to prebook a cab and coordinate trips with a reduced fare for each passenger, who would pay his or her own fare for the trip. The Taxicard program is a door-to-door transport service in London for individuals with verifiable serious mobility impairments who aren't able to access other public transportation. Riders pay a flat fare based on the length of the trip, and fares range from £1.50 ($2.25) to £11.50 ($17.85). This program is financed by the London boroughs and administered by the London Councils Transport and Environment Committee. Dial-a-Ride is a free door-to-door local service for disabled people who aren't able to access buses or London's metro, called the Tube.

BOX 8.3 Policy to People Link: The Transport Act, Taxicard, and London's Capital Call Program

London's Capital Call program is a complementary service to the Taxicard program, and is for individuals who live in London boroughs where there is a shortage of London taxis—currently in the boroughs of Bexley, Ealing, Enfield, Haringey, Hillingdon, Hounslow, Kingston, Lambeth, Lewisham, Merton, and Southwark. The program provides subsidized door-to-door transport for people with mobility issues by using private-hire vehicles called minicabs. Riders call the Capital Call operator, who in turn contacts and books a participating minicab company.

Qualified individuals are given an annual personal travel budget of £200 ($302) to spend on Capital Call trips. Riders are required to pay an out-of-pocket cost of £1.50 ($2.25) for a trip that would normally cost £11.80 ($17.85) or less (about a 2-mile trip). The rider's contribution increases as the distance and value of the trip goes up. Once the £200 budget is used, a new allotment is provided each April.

Shopmobility is another mobility program offered throughout England that lends manual wheelchairs, powered wheelchairs, and powered scooters to members of the public with limited mobility (National Federation of Shopmobility, 2010). The equipment is loaned for any length of time with the goal of aiding access to shopping and leisure facilities within the town or shopping center. The program is available in various cities across England, and in some cities, programs operate with funds from local councils or charge a small fee for the use of the equipment. The Disabled Persons Transport Advisory Committee, a national advisory council, is encouraging local councils to support Shopmobility as a way to meet the requirements to address transport needs of persons with disabilities. The Forum of Mobility Centres, another charitable organization funded by the Department of Transport, offers a range of services, including a driving ability assessment, tuition for driving classes, and information on matters concerning independent mobility (primarily related to car and adapted vehicle use as a driver or passenger). Some centers also offer advice on the selection and use of wheelchairs and scooters and car adaptations.

Disability living allowance, an income benefit for adults with disabilities, includes a mobility component, which helps in covering the costs of transportation. The disability allowance is slightly higher if there is a demonstrated need for transportation services.

Legal Assistance

Legal assistance is funded by the national government and administered by the Legal Services Commission, which is authorized to provide civil legal aid under the Legal Services Act (U.K. Acts of Parliament, 2007b) with oversight by the Ministry of Justice. Legal advice is provided free of charge through the commission's Community Legal Advice program (Legal Services Commission, 2007a). Legal aid assistance beyond advice for individuals over age 60 for civil matters is available for those who meet income and asset eligibility guidelines through the Community Legal Service program. Individuals may be asked to pay some of the costs of their case either out of pocket or, depending on the outcome of the case, have the cost deducted from the judgment amount. Other organizations, such as the Citizens Advice Bureaux, receive funding from local authorities to offer legal advice for a nominal fee that covers incidental administrative costs (Legal Services Commission, 2007b).

Information and Referral/Assistance

Improving access to information and community services has received a lot of attention at the national level, and a number of initiatives have been launched in this regard. The LinkAge Plus program, under the direction of the Department of Work and Pensions, is designed to simplify and coordinate information about national and local governments and the third-sector services in the areas of housing, transportation, health and social care, and work and volunteer opportunities. The basic premise is that there is "no wrong door" through which people enter to find information and access services. This is primarily an intergovernmental initiative that is attempting to approach needs of individuals from a whole systems perspective that puts older people at the center of service delivery and joins the needed services across a number of areas (e.g., health care, housing, and employment).

The "Building a Society for All Ages" white paper (Department for Work and Pensions, 2009) proposed a strategy that would create one-stop information sites staffed by highly skilled, knowledgeable people who could assist individuals in locating the appropriate service or obtaining advice. FirstStop (www.firststopcareadvice.org .uk/) is a free information service about care, housing, employment, volunteering, and informal adult learning and is a joint project between the government and charitable and private-sector organizations (Department for Communities and Local Government, 2010). Funding comes from the Department for Communities and Local Government and a grant from the Big Lottery funds.

Another information site called Carers Direct, funded by the National Health Service (2010), provides a telephone helpline and a webpage for caregivers. The Carers Direct site provides information, advice, and support for carers with a comprehensive online resource about topics such as guidance on the different stages of caring, information for claiming benefits, contact information for local authorities and support groups, news articles, and case studies with videos.

Civic Engagement

The WRVS charitable organization is one of the primary organizations that utilizes volunteers to offer services to help and support older people to live well, maintain their independence, and play a part in their local communities. The typical WRVS volunteers are older, retired, or working part-time and from a mix of social backgrounds, and the beneficiaries of volunteer services are older adults. In 2008 to 2009, WRVS volunteers supported programs such as the Good Neighbours service (provides company or help with a range of tasks) to more than 4,500 older adults, the Meals on Wheels service to 24,538 older adults, assistance in emergency situations to 6,000 older adults, and shopping assistance or transportation assistance to 7,000 older adults (WRVS, 2010).

The Generations Together Programme launched by "Building a Society for All Ages" in April 2009 is designed to promote positive intergenerational interaction and address local community needs (Department of Health, 2010). Twelve local projects totaling £5.5 million ($8.3 million) have been funded by a wide coalition of national and local governments, including the Department for Children, Schools, and Families, the Office of the Third Sector in the Cabinet Office, the Department of Health and the Department for Work and Pensions, and the Department for Communities and Local Government. The specific goals of the Generations Together program are to (1) generate wider interest in and thinking about intergenerational work, (2) increase the number of volunteers working on intergenerational activity by 20,000 by the end of the program, and (3) provide evidence about the effectiveness of intergenerational initiatives. We now turn our discussion to Sweden's approach to community-based programs.

Sweden

The legislative framework for the existence of community services for older adults in Sweden is found in the Social Services Act of 1982 (Ministry of Health and Social Affairs, 2007). Under the Act, the objectives of social services are to promote people's economic and social security, equality of living conditions, and active participation in the life of the community. It is the responsibility of municipalities, under the guidance of the Social Welfare Committees, to provide services to those who are unable to provide for their needs or to obtain assistance in any other way. Committees are designed to ensure that older people are able to live independently in safe conditions and have an active and meaningful existence in the community with others and to support help at home and other readily available services. Committees are to work with the county council and other community agencies and organizations to develop municipal plans and provide needed services. Given that municipalities have been given wide latitude for identifying and providing community-based services and that there are 294 different municipalities, the scope and availability of community-based services vary across Sweden. We chose to use Stockholm for our discussion to illustrate a Swedish approach to community services.

Food and Nutrition Programs

Almost all municipalities in Sweden offer home-delivered meals to those who are no longer able to cook for themselves, grocery delivery, and communal meals at day centers. The cost varies based on the income of the older adult, but in Stockholm, for example, the distribution of a daily lunch box and home care for up to 2 hours per month has a maximum cost of SEK389 ($53.31) a month (Stockholm Government, 2010a). Nearly all local authorities offer meals on wheels (*Matdistribution*) to the elderly and disabled. In total, 57,300 people in Sweden received meals on wheels in 2006, an increase of about 5,000 recipients from 2004 (Swedish Association of Local Authorities and Regions, 2007).

BOX 8.4 Policy to People Link: Stockholm's Community Preventative Outreach Program

One of the policy goals for elder care in Sweden is that "elderly people shall grow old in safe conditions and retain their independence" (City of Stockholm, n.d., p. 6).

The city of Stockholm's care plan for the elderly includes actions that are designed to help older Swedes stay in their homes as long as possible. One such service is the preventative house call for older adults aged 75 or older. Trained city workers offer to meet with the elders in their own homes to provide information about the city's eldercare programs.

Another service is called the Janitor Service (*Vaktmästarservice*). This program provides help with simple daily tasks such as changing light bulbs or curtains, moving furniture, carrying heavy boxes up and down from the attic or basement, and so on, which might be difficult and place elders at risk of injury. The Janitor Service is offered free of charge, and the limit is 6 hours per year, per household.

For more information, go to www.stockholm.se/FamiljOmsorg/Aldreomsorg/.

Recreation and Leisure

There are a number of recreational, leisure, and educational venues available to older adults in Sweden. Lifelong learning opportunities, often referred to as adult education (*folkbildning*), are funded by grants from the national government and operated by municipalities and local nonprofit agencies (Folkbildningsrådet, n.d.). These learning opportunities are open to individuals of all ages and provided through folk high schools (*folkhögskolor*) and study associations (*studieförbund*). Some charge a course fee for participation. In addition to adult education offerings through folk high schools, the Study Vuxenskolan (*Studieförbundet Vuxenskolan*) offers a wide range of workshops, courses, and cultural events. One of the most notable is Study Circles. Study Circles is a method of learning via a small group of people (normally between 7–12 participants) who meet over a specified time frame to carry out planned study of a particular topic. In Stockholm alone, there are around 50,000 Study Circles available on almost any topic (Vårdguiden Stockholm, 2010). The Study Vuxenskolan also organizes more than 30,000 cultural events that include lectures, concerts, and other cultural events.

SeniorNet Sweden (2010) is a nonprofit, nonpolitical organization, started in 1997 with government funding to address the "digital divide" among older adults. The website is the virtual meeting point for all members with news from SeniorNet central as well as from all the local clubs about their programs and activities.

Transportation

In 1979, Sweden passed legislation mandating that public transport be adapted to the needs of persons with disabilities over a 10-year period. This legislation led to the development over the next 30 years of accessible urban and intercity transport services. More recently, the Swedish approach to transportation has been based on the notion that "no community can be fully served with a single transportation mode," and the framework under which transportation is provided has been called the Community-Responsive Public Transportation design (Stähl, 1999). Under Swedish law, each municipality is responsible for providing various types of transportation service and for the quality of those services.

The community responsive design in Sweden includes mainstream public transport services that operate on *fixed routes* and utilize low-floor buses that can accommodate riders who have some mobility challenges and *service routes* that use accessible low-floor midi- or minibuses on planned or regular routes close to housing for elderly and disabled people who are unable to navigate regular public transportation and travel to health facilities, shopping centers, and other common destinations. For those who are unable to use regular public transportation without assistance because of a disability, the mobility service (*Färdtjänst*) provides access to both ordinary public and specialized transport services. Riders in Stockholm who have medically documented disabilities travel free or at a low cost (SEK70 [$9.80] per 30 kilometers [18.6 miles]); however, there is a cap, and travelers pay no more than SEK420 ($58.80) per month (Vårdguiden Stockholm, 2010). Travelers also begin with a certain number of trips annually (190) and may request more if needed. As long as traveling companions have been preauthorized, they may travel at no cost. Journeys can be taken using special vehicles or taxis.

Legal Assistance

The Legal Aid Act (*Rättshjälpslagen;* cited in van Zeeland & Barendrecht, 2003) provides legal advice and assistance to individuals who are unable to privately secure legal support. Under the Act, Swedes in need of legal advice are obliged to access legal aid by utilizing the coverage provided by their private legal insurance policies. Legal insurance coverage is automatically included in their home insurance policies, and it is estimated that 97% of the Swedish population have such a policy (van Zeeland & Barendrecht, 2003). However, under the Legal Aid Act, every Swede has access to up to 2 hours of legal advice for SEK1,162 ($162), or less if the individual has limited financial resources (annual income of less than SEK75,000 [$10,500]; Legal Aid Authority, 2007).

If legal representation is not available through the legal insurance policy, legal aid is provided by the government through the National Courts Administration to those with a disposable annual gross income of less than SEK260,000 ($36,401; Legal Aid Authority, 2007).

Information and Referral/Assistance

Municipalities offer a service called *Äldre Direkt* (Mature Direct) that creates contact centers to provide information and assistance about programs and services for older adults (Stockholm Government, 2010b). The Stockholm Äldre Direkt website or staff provides information about home care services, the housing adaptation program, lifeline alarm systems, housing options, handyman-type services, community activities, and transportation (Stockholm Government, 2010b). In addition, the city has an Elder Ombudsman (*Äldreombudsman*) who provides advice, support, and guidance on matters relating to older adults.

Civic Engagement

The central government has adopted a policy that "people should have the best possible opportunities to organise themselves and take part in nongovernmental organisations (NGOs) and popular movements of various kinds" (Ministry of Integration and Gender Equality, 2008, p. 1). Moreover, the Ministry of Integration and Gender Equality is responsible for encouraging and supporting organizations and associations by providing a favorable climate for these organizations to operate and pursue their activities. Although recent data indicate that 90% of Swedes belong to an NGO and more than 50% of the population between the ages of 16 and 85 engage in some form of voluntary work (Ministry of Integration and Gender Equality, 2008), there is currently no national policy or initiative specifically designed to promote civic engagement among older adults.

Summary

All three of the countries we reviewed have stated goals of enhancing the quality of community life for older adults. The policy approach to accomplish this goal, however, differs across the three countries. The United States has a number of key legislations (e.g., the OAA) that are somewhat prescriptive in the type of programs they will fund, and local AAAs are given latitude in defining program specifics as well as determining the entity that will be responsible for delivery of programs. Community resources in the United States are also spread out among a number of different entities, but the OAA does serve to centralize some of the community services for older adults. In England, community programs are developed through national legislation that sets policy direction and goals for particular community programs that are then operationalized and funded by various units within the national government through strategic white papers. In contrast, Sweden is the most decentralized, as the national government sets a broad agenda through legislative acts and the municipalities are given the funding and authority to implement the agenda.

For More Information

1. Administration on Aging
   www.aoa.gov

The AoA administers the OAA and is your resource for information about the Act and its reauthorization status, new policy initiatives, and other information on older adult policy and programs.

2. Age Concern and Help the Aged (AgeUK)
   http://www.helptheaged.org.uk/en-gb

Age Concern and Help the Aged are two charitable organizations that have merged to create a new charity called AgeUK. In addition to its U.K. focus, Help the Aged has created a worldwide network of organizations working to improve older people's lives. Age Concern has been an advocacy group and has offered community support programs across the United Kingdom. Check out their website, as they have great resources and information about aging issues.

3. The World Health Organization Age-Friendly Environments Programme
   http://www.who.int/ageing/age_friendly_cities/en/index.html

The Age-Friendly Environments Programme is an international effort by the WHO to address the environmental and social factors that contribute to active and healthy ageing in societies. Check out the cities that are a part of this effort and the steps cities should take to become age-friendly.

4. The MetLife Foundation
   http://www.n4a.org/pdf/MOAFinalReport.pdf

The MetLife Foundation has funded an initiative, led by the National Association of Area Agencies on Aging, in partnership with the International City/County Management Association, National Association of Counties, National League of Cities, and Partners for Livable Communities, to help cities and counties better meet the needs of their aging populations. The group has published their report "The Maturing of America: Getting Communities on Track for an Aging Population."

5. City of Stockholm
   http://www.stockholm.se/FamiljOmsorg/

Check out the wide variety of community support for older adults on Stockholm's website. Be sure to use a webpage translator such as Google's page translation!

Mrs. R., age 81
London, borough of Kensington, England

I was born in Dorsett on the south coast of England, right near the sea. My father was a civil servant; my mother didn't work because she stayed home and cared for us. I came to London when I was 22 years old. I have one brother, and I did marry and have children. I have three grandchildren. My husband was an aeronautical engineer for British Airways for all his life. He was in the RAF during the war, and when that finished, he joined BA.

My typical day is I read. I don't often see the family, once a month maybe. I don't say I am very active. I've got nothing wrong with me in particular; I just have high blood pressure. That's all I take. Not bad for my age. The national health pays for my care. So when I see the doctor, the care is free, and it is not difficult to get in to see the doctor. Health care coverage hasn't changed, and it is quite good. I hardly ever see my doctor. When he asks me how I am doing, I tell him I am still breathing. He says, "Good. Keep it up!"

I get a pension from two of my employers. I get a pension from my work and also state pension. I started working when I was 14 and retired when I was 67. I find that I can manage on my pension.

Now I get help with transportation. It is what we call a Taxicard. Now if I phone for a taxi, . . . it's a common cab, . . . to come pick me up to take me shopping, say, they will ask if I need the driver to come up and help me. It costs me one pound fifty. Now if I had to pay ordinary taxi without this card, it would cost me 5 to 6 pounds. It's very convenient; I get 10 trips a month. It works very well for me. I am not housebound, because I have the taxi when I need it. The shops are far away, but we have all of these services to take us when we need it.

I don't need any help shopping, preparing meals, cleaning house, or with my personal needs. If I needed help, it is there. You go to your doctor, and once your doctor recommends it, you can get carers, people to shop for you, anything you need. You pay depending on your income. You get help paying for carers, and you get so much help based on your income. It varies based on everyone's circumstance.

I put my name on a waiting list for housing with the Council, in what was called family housing charity program, and is for people aged 60 and over. Because my husband had lots of health issues, we were able to get a flat here. There are people here Monday through Friday to help you if you need it. I pay rent for my flat, but it is based on your income. It is about £400 a month, and it includes heating and hot water, and you pay for the electricity. You can do your laundry here downstairs. You have a common room anyone can use and a communal kitchen with an oven, and if you have a small flat you can use it when you have company. They come in every 6 months to assess your needs, your income, state of health, and you can have a carer or a daily come in to help with cooking, washing, if you need it. Social services do a lot. It is marvelous in theory, but as you know, theory and practice can be different. Nothing is perfect. We have a garden and benches and a lovely view of the river.

There is an organization called 60+, a charitable organization, and they run little trips around London, have meetings going on, they have social groups and do odd jobs for you and don't charge you. They do a lot for older adults. They have a bus for people in wheelchairs. I like to send them a little donation every month. We also get a freedom pass and can use the bus and train around London for free. There is a Dial-a-Ride service that takes you shopping for £1. Here in London, if you are over age 75, you don't pay for the

TV license; it is free. We are lucky being in London, because other people outside of London don't get the services we do.

I don't feel invisible as an old person. I think it is up to you to be heard and seen, . . . cause a fuss now and again, yes, remind people you are still alive and breathing. I think it is up to the person. Some people just shut themselves up in their flat and don't do anything or go anywhere, and they let themselves go. That doesn't do anybody any good. . . . You don't know when they are ill or when they need help. I have great friends here; I have known one neighbor for 16 years, and after my husband died, he and his wife helped me out a lot. I have lots of friends here that I could ring up if I needed help.

What do I think about growing old? There is nothing I can do about it, so I just don't bother about it, . . . grin and bear it. What do I look forward to? Peace and quiet! Old age, . . . looking forward to growing older!

Katerina, Age 85, Greece

ZéBombeiro, Age, 80, Brazil

Family Caregiving Policies

> *The family in Italy still plays a dominant role in the life of old people . . . [and] thereby becomes the most important element to the quality of life for old people . . . and largely ensures assistance to non-self-sufficient old people in Italy.*
>
> —Hon. Roberto Maroni, Italian Minister of Labour and Social Policies

> *I am aware of support services as far as it affected me with [taking care of] my mother [who lived with us for 20 years]. The last period of my mother's life—she was very, very old—the last 2 years in particular. I can remember one day I was absolutely desperate, and I telephoned the local social services at the town hall, and I said, "Look, I don't need any financial help and I don't need any physical [nursing] help, but I am desperately in need of mechanical help." So they sent along a nurse to assess her . . . and within 12 hours, I had a frame for the shower (because I had to go into the shower to help shower her). They sent along a "ripple bed," and I had a frame for the bed because I was having problems lifting her, and with this she could hold on to the handle and I could as well, and I could lift her then. They were absolutely marvelous. As she was incontinent, they sent padded sheets for the bed and for her. Within 12 hours, I had everything, every single thing . . . things that I never knew about. . . . They told me what I needed. And then after that, it was quite funny, because my mother had a double bed and the nurse said, "I want you on this bed for 20 minutes every day," and I looked at her and I said, "Me?" and she said "Yes, because you need to rest as well, and this will be very helpful and soothing." After that, they came once a week to check on me (I hadn't asked for that), and also when I needed more of the disposable things, they were here within hours. They were fantastic. I didn't have to pay for anything, not anything.*
>
> —Mrs. M., age 74, London

A s individuals age, a significant number will experience physical limitations, compromises in cognitive functioning, and like Mrs. M.'s mother, need caregiving assistance. So when physical or mental impairments start to impede an older adult's ability for self-care, the question for families and communities is "Who will help ensure that his or her personal and social care needs will be met?" In this chapter, we describe how personal health and social care responsibility is shared among older adults, their families, and various levels of government. We begin by providing an overview of the demographics of caregiving and introduce a social policy framework that we use to examine family and community-based caregiving support in four different countries.

Global Demographics of Caregiving

Across the globe, families are de-facto deemed to be the social unit that bears the primary responsibility of caring for their elderly family members when they are no longer self-sufficient. However, demographic and social changes that have occurred over the past several decades throughout the world have strained the family's abilities to continue to provide direct and regular personal care to their elderly family members. As we discussed in Chapter 1, the increase in life expectancy and the decrease in fertility rates has resulted in an increase in the number of generations living in a family network. Thus, older adults have fewer children available to provide caregiving assistance, when at the same time, adult children are likely still caring for their own children, or in some cases their grandchildren. One broad indicator of this phenomenon of fewer young-old adults caring for older adults is the Parent Support Ratio (PSR). The PSR is the number of people aged 80 and over per 100 persons aged 50 to 64 years. As you can see in Figure 9.1, there were few persons over the age of 80 relative to the number of persons between the ages of 50 and 64 in 1950—with ratios of less than 10 in the United States, Canada, Western Europe, and Eastern Asia. Although every region shown in Figure 9.1 is expected to have marked increases in the PSR from 1950 to 2030, the increases in the ratio are expected to occur more rapidly and be greater in the United States, Canada, and Western Europe. For example, in the United States, the ratio in 1950 was 8, in 2000 it was 22, and it is expected to experience an increase to 33 by 2030. Western Europe is expected to see the ratio increase from 23 to 37 by 2030, and Eastern Asia is expected to increase from 10 to 23.

It is also instructive to examine the PSR for females, as they often become the primary elder care provider within the family. Using the PSR for examining the number of females aged 50 to 64 per 100 elders aged 80 or older, the support ratios show a different picture. Figure 9.2 shows the PSR for females in selected countries for the years 1950, 2000, and 2030. In all the countries listed in Figure 9.2, there were 18 or fewer older adults over age 80 for 100 young-old females aged 50 to 64 in 1950. In the United States, the ratio in 1950 was 16, whereas in the European countries listed, the ratio ranged from 11 in Germany to 18 in Canada, Sweden, and France. The ratios increased dramatically from 1950 to 2000, and they are expected to markedly increase by 2030. Japan's PSR is expected to be the highest among all regions, as there is projected to be 100 elders aged 80 and over for every 100 young-old females. The European countries listed are also expected to see dramatic rises in the PSR from 2000 to 2030, with the ratio in the United Kingdom and Italy at 73, in France at 78, and Sweden at 90. The United States and Canada are expected to have PSR ratios in the mid-60s.

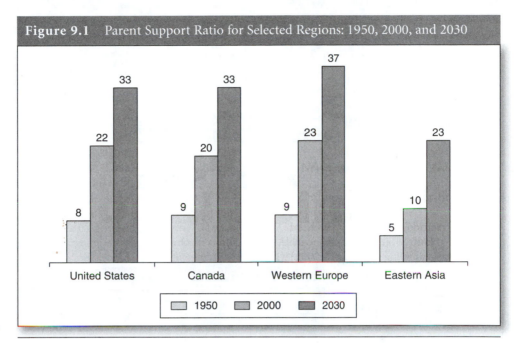

Figure 9.1 Parent Support Ratio for Selected Regions: 1950, 2000, and 2030

Notes: Western Europe includes Denmark, France, Germany, Greece, Italy, Sweden, and the United Kingdom; Eastern Asia includes China, India, Japan, and Thailand; South America includes Argentina, Brazil, and Chile.
Source: Data compiled from Kinsella and Velkoff (2001).

In addition to the demographic changes in life expectancy and fertility rates within families, women—including daughters, who are usually the primary carers after wives—have been entering the workforce to support their own family's economic needs, thus reducing their availability to provide care. The percentage of women working in the labor force in many European countries and the United States is quite high. For example, in 2007, the employment rate for women aged 15 to 64 ranged from a high of 73.4% in Denmark to 65.8% in the United Kingdom to a low of 46.3% in Italy (Eurostat, 2007). In the United States, a high percentage of single women have been employed since the 1950s (54% in 1950 to 69% in 2002), and the percentage of married women's employment has doubled, increasing from 28.5% in 1955 to 61% in 2002 (U.S. Bureau of the Census, 2003).

Thus, the demographic pressures of an aging population, combined with shrinking fertility rates and increasing numbers of employed women, are pressing governments across the globe into considering policies that address the availability of community-based care support for older adults and their families.

Family Caregiving Social Policy Framework

Providing care to an older family member is a highly personal activity, usually conducted privately within the confines of the family home. Elderly spouses or partners or adult children go about the business of arranging their lives and daily activities so that their relative receives needed assistance; some family caregivers may even quit their jobs or scale back to part-time employment to more fully engage in caregiving activities.

Figure 9.2   Parent Support Ratios for Females of Selected Countries: 1950, 2000, for 2030

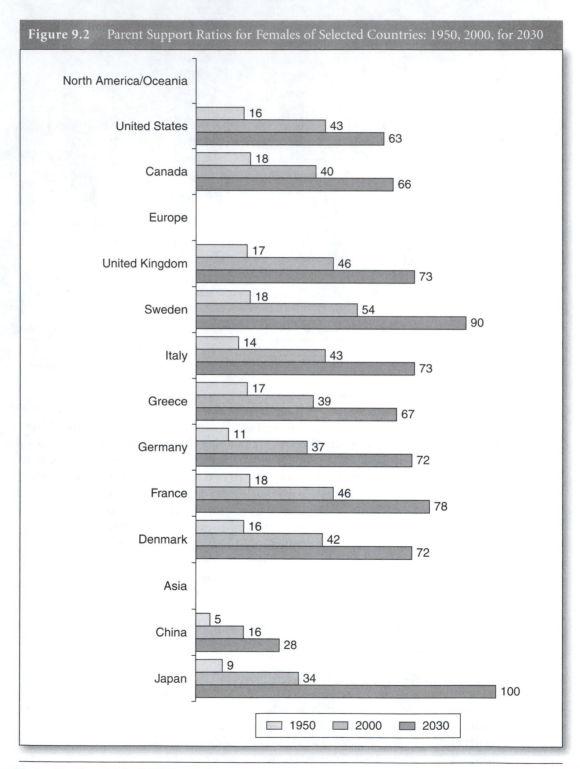

Source: Kinsella and Velkoff (2001).

Family caregivers[1] shop for food and prepare meals, provide transportation to and from appointments, do laundry, clean house, administer medications, and provide personal care and social companionship. Difficulties occur, however, when the care required is beyond the physical, social, or economic capabilities of the elder's social network and external support is needed. Thus, the social policy questions for countries, regions, and communities are "What role should government play in helping elders and their carers pay for, arrange for, and receive care so that the elder can remain living independently in the community?" and "What is the nature of the interface between government, family, voluntary/nonprofit and private sector in meeting elder care needs?" As we will see later in this chapter, countries approach this policy issue in different ways through the social policies and programs/services they enact and the eligibility criteria associated with elders and caregivers gaining access to these programs and services.

We have chosen four countries that represent four distinct types of policy approaches on a continuum of government support and assistance for community-based care for older adults. On one end of the continuum is limited government support, and by default, family members are deemed to be responsible for providing and paying for their elderly family members' social, physical, and economic needs. Here, a country's social policy approach is to rely almost exclusively on families for caregiving needs with little direction or involvement from the government. On the other end of the continuum, the government plays a more central role by enacting and funding legislation that provides a more extensive array of support and services designed to address the community-based care needs of elderly adults and their caregivers. For these countries, their social policy approach is to offer families various types of government support to address caregiving needs.

The four countries we have selected—the United States, Italy, England, and Sweden—lie at different points on the continuum, and their social policy approaches to elder care reflect those differences. The United States and Italy are characterized by limited government involvement and support; England has a moderate mix of governmental and support services; and finally, Sweden has a more extensive array of government programs to support the delivery of community-based elder care.

In order to illustrate the specifics of how these countries differ in their elder care support, we apply a framework used by Lyon and Glucksmann (2008). This framework examines the extent to which four sectors—government, family, private sector, and volunteer/nonprofit organizations—are involved in assisting with elder care support. In Figures 9.3 through 9.6, each sector's involvement will be illustrated by using a solid line that indicates direct involvement, a dashed line that indicates a subsidiary function via policy or transfer of funds, and a dotted line that represents minimal involvement. We begin our discussion with a review of United States policy.

United States

As shown in Figure 9.3, elder care in the United States is characterized by the direct involvement of the family, minimal direct involvement from the federal government, and a heavy reliance on the private and voluntary/nonprofit sectors, which receive

---

1. We use the words *caregiver* and *carer* interchangeably as these terms are used in the United States and Europe, respectively.

Figure 9.3 Elder Care in the United States

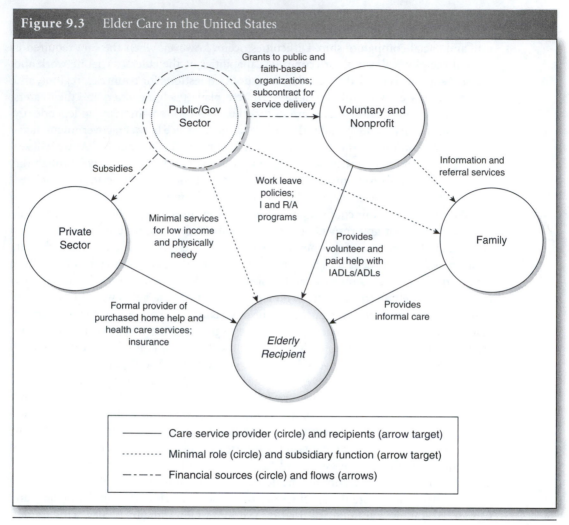

Source: Adapted from Lyon and Glucksmann (2008).

subsidies or grants from the government to provide community-based services or offer services for direct purchase. In the United States, the federal government's role has been in passing legislation authorizing leave from work policies and tax credit policies for caregivers, enacting the Medicare and Medicaid health care programs that assist with the purchase of home health care, and providing grants to the private and voluntary/nonprofit organizations, who in turn make various types of homemaker, respite, and information and referral support services available to elders.

Leave From Work and Tax Credit Policies

In the United States, there are two tax laws that offer tax breaks to a select group of caregivers—the Dependent Care Tax Credit and the Dependent Care Assistance Programs. Under the Dependent Care Tax Credit, the qualifying spouse or dependent of the taxpayer must be physically or mentally unable to provide self-care. Not being able to provide self-care is defined as not being able to dress, clean, or feed oneself because of physical or mental problems, and the dependent person must have constant attention to prevent them from injuring themselves or others. In addition, the dependent person must live with the taxpayer for more than half the tax year (Colello, 2007; Internal Revenue Service, 2008). Next, the taxpayer/caregiver and his or her spouse must be employed full- or part-time or be seeking work. The only exception applies when one spouse is physically or mentally incapable of self-care. Third, the payments for care cannot be made to the spouse of the taxpayer/caregiver or someone who is a dependent of the taxpayer/caregiver. In 2008, up to $3,000 of dependent care expenses could be made for one qualifying dependent or up to $6,000 for two or more qualifying dependents (Internal Revenue Service, 2008). The tax credit amount is 35% for taxpayers whose adjusted gross income (AGI) doesn't exceed $15,000 and is gradually reduced to 20% for taxpayers with an AGI of more than $43,000 (Colello, 2007). For example, a married couple earning $50,000 with $3,000 in qualifying expenses would be eligible for a credit of $600 (20% of $3,000). In addition, a taxpayer/caregiver's tax liability, which is offset by his or her standard deduction and/or other exemptions does not benefit from the credit. As a result, a married couple could not declare the full credit based on the $3,000 until their AGI reaches $29,001 (Colello, 2007).

Employees who work for an employer that offers a Dependent Care Assistance Plan can allocate up to $5,000 of their own pretax earnings to a dependent-care account. These funds can be used to pay for qualified dependent care expenses, which are the same as the Dependent Care Tax Credit. Tax payers/caregivers can use both tax programs as long as they are used for different expenses (Colello, 2007). There are some limitations to both of these tax policies. Not all caregiving expenses are allowed, care must be provided by someone other than an employee's dependent, funds in the Dependent Care Assistance Program are of little use if there are limited or no services available to purchase, and any unused funds in the program are forfeited at the end of the year (Neal & Wagner, n.d.).

The Family Medical Leave Act (1993) allows eligible employees to take up to 12 weeks of unpaid job-protected leave in a 12-month period for certain family medical reasons. To be eligible, employees must meet employment criteria and the family members in need of care must be defined as having a serious health condition. Employment criteria state that the employee be employed in the public agency or in a private-sector company with more than 50 employees working in 20 or more work weeks and where at least 50 employees are employed by the employer within 75 miles. In addition, the employee must have worked for the employer for a total of 12 months and for 1,250 hours over the previous 12 months (U.S. Department of Labor, 2009b). A serious health condition involves treatment connected with inpatient care (e.g., hospitalization), is a chronic condition, involves rehabilitation treatments that require periodic visits to a health care provider, or is a permanent long-term condition that does not have an effective treatment (e.g., Alzheimer's disease). An employer must maintain health coverage, and the employee, upon return to the workforce, must be given his or her job or one equivalent in pay, benefits, and other terms.

Home Health and Home Care

The majority of community-based care provided by the federal government is in the payment of in-home health care to a limited segment of the elderly population via two national health care programs—Medicare and Medicaid (both discussed in more detail in Chapter 6). These two programs are the sole means of federal government support for home health care, as access to health care in the United States is not universal and is restricted to employees whose employers offer health coverage, elderly adults with a work history, and very low-income adults.[2]

The Medicare program covers the cost of home health care if the older adult has met the following criteria. The first is to have established eligibility for Medicare by having worked a minimum number of years (10) in qualified paid employment or by purchasing Medicare out of pocket. Once Medicare eligibility is established, a second set of criteria must be met as the elder is required to (1) be considered "homebound"; (2) have a doctor's orders and a plan of care established; (3) establish that the need for skilled nursing care, physical therapy, speech language pathology, or occupational therapy is reasonable and necessary; and (4) have a need that is part-time or intermittent (less than 8 hours per day and 28 hours or less weekly). Medical social services, home health aide services, or other care services, durable medical equipment (e.g., wheelchairs, hospital beds, oxygen, and walkers), and medical supplies for use at home may also be covered under Medicare if the basic eligibility criteria discussed above are met. The services must be provided by a Medicare-certified home health agency. Coverage periods are short-term—60 days—and clients are reviewed again for eligibility. Cost for home health care includes a monthly premium for care covered under Medicare Part B that is based on yearly income and that ranges from $96.40 to $308.30, as well as a deductible of $135 per year for covered services (Centers for Medicare and Medicaid, 2010a). Medicare beneficiaries pay nothing for approved home health care services and 20% of the cost of approved durable medical equipment. Home care services for nonskilled personal care to assist with activities of daily living are covered under Medicare only if care is linked with the need for skilled nursing care; otherwise, Medicare does not cover nonskilled home help services (e.g., light housekeeping, meal preparation).

Medicaid is the federal health and long-term care program for certain low-income persons that is jointly funded by the federal government and states and is administered by the states. Medicaid allows low-income elders access to doctors, hospital care, and prescription medication as well as nursing home care. In an effort to reduce the federal government cost burden of Medicaid paying for nursing home care, the federal government passed the Home and Community-Based Services Waivers Section 1915(c) legislation that allows states to deliver long-term care services to low-income elders in the community (Centers for Medicare and Medicaid Services, 2005).

Although the federal government sets minimum income eligibility guidelines for Medicaid, states can exercise a number of different income eligibility options, and as a result, there are 56 different configurations of Medicaid programs (one in each state, four

---

2. Low-income children have access to health care services through Children's Health Insurance Program. As this goes to press, President Obama has signed into law the Patient Protection and Affordable Care Act (2010), which will serve to make health care access more universal and extend coverage of health care services.

U.S. territories, and Puerto Rico; Bruen, Wiener, & Thomas, 2003). Regardless of which state an elder lives in, to receive home care services under Medicaid, they must meet income and asset levels and functional eligibility similar to that established for low-income elders needing nursing home care. As mentioned above, states have several options to expand eligibility criteria, and the majority of states set financial eligibility at 300% of the income guideline for the Supplemental Security Income program, although approximately one-quarter of the states use the more restrictive poverty level rate used for Supplemental Security Income eligibility (Kaiser Commission on Medicaid and the Uninsured, 2007). In 2008, the income eligibility criteria for home- and community-based services was $637 a month for a single individual or $1,911 if using the 300% of the poverty level criteria (U.S. Department of Health and Human Services, 2008a).

In addition to meeting income guidelines, eligible participants must also meet functional criteria and must have difficulty performing at least three activities of daily living (e.g., bathing, dressing, transferring, toileting, and eating), although again, states may require greater levels of impairment. Many states also place a limit on the amount of service provided and have a limited number of slots available to control the overall cost of the home- and community-based care program, which results in many states having people on waiting lists (Bruen et al., 2003).

Medicaid will not pay for home help unless it is associated with eligibility for services under the Home- and Community-Based Services Waiver Program. As the intent of the Medicaid waiver program is to keep low-income elders living in the community, other services in addition to skilled care such as personal care, case management, adult day care, home care, and other services can be offered to eligible participants. In the past few years, states have been experimenting with providing a budget to elderly Medicaid recipients so they can purchase services from providers of their choosing. For example, 15 states currently have caregiver payment programs in which clients are permitted to employ, schedule, train, and supervise their own personal assistance providers and can include family members, friends, neighbors, or others if they meet the specified provider qualifications (Cash and Counseling, 2010). In general, spouses and parents of minor children cannot be paid providers of waiver services (Polivka, 2001; Wiener et al., 2004). These programs, however, reach only a small number of eligible individuals across the country.

Other Government-Funded Programs

The Corporation for National and Community Service Senior Companion Program is a federal program that trains low-income elderly volunteers to visit and assist frail elderly clients in their homes by offering companionship and friendship, providing assistance with simple chores, making phone calls for elders, providing transportation, and giving caregivers some time off (Corporation for National and Community Service [CNCS], 2009; RTI International, 2003). Federal funds are usually provided to local or county governments who are responsible for program delivery and often contract with local nonprofits to deliver such services. Volunteers receive a small stipend (e.g., in 2010, the stipend was $2.65 per hour) and provide up to 40 hours per week of service. Although the program has documented benefits to elders and caregivers, programs are not readily available in every state. There are 237 projects nationwide, enlisting 17,000 volunteers (CNCS, 2004; RTI International, 2003); however, 27 states report having three or fewer programs statewide, and 10 of these states have only one program.

As shown by the dotted line from the government to the elder and family, the federal government also plays a role in funding information referral and assistance services so elders and their caregivers can locate and access private- and public-sector services. The National Eldercare Locator Service is an information and referral assistance service that is accessed via a toll-free number or the website (www.eldercare .gov). Inquirers provide information about where they live and what services they are looking for and are given information about the state and local agencies that provide programs and services. The federal government also made funding available to state and county governments beginning in 2003 to develop Aging and Disability Resource Centers (ADRC, 2008). The intent of the ADRCs is to enhance the information and referral assistance infrastructure and thereby streamline access to multiple public benefits programs and offer information about long-term care services via a single point within county governments. For example, some ADRCs provide Medicaid applications online, others have published Internet service resource directories and online consumer decision tools, and five programs have developed exchange protocols so consumers can provide application information one time that can be used by multiple agencies (ADRC, 2008). As of 2008, there were 147 ADRCs in the United States.

Voluntary, Nonprofit, and Private-Sector Organizations

As shown in Figure 9.3, the federal government also awards grants and contracts to agencies within the nonprofit and private sector to assist in the delivery of community-based services, primarily through legislation under the Older Americans Act (OAA), enacted by Congress in 1965 (as discussed in Chapter 2). Community-based programs and services funded under the OAA are coordinated through the local AAAs. As a general rule, the AAAs do not directly deliver services authorized under the Act, but rather, the funding to support community-based care is transferred to private-sector or nonprofit agencies that agree to deliver the services that are either mandated by the OAA (e.g., meals programs) or determined to be a local need (e.g., outreach to minority elders). Services provided under the Act have universal access, as all older adults aged 60 and over are eligible; however, the emphasis is on helping older persons with the greatest economic and social needs (Wacker & Roberto, 2008). Cost sharing or charging participants for services is allowed in some circumstances, but self-declared low-income elders are to be exempt, and no one can be denied services because of inability to pay or donate.

The specific community-based care programs and services funded under Title III of the OAA that support caregiving include homemaker assistance, client assessment and case management, respite and adult day care, and home-delivered meals. Homemaker assistance is available through care management services (known by a variety of different names, such as case management, care coordination) and usually administered locally through the AAA. Under the care management program, clients are assessed to determine their physical, psychological, functional, and social needs. A trained caseworker who conducts the assessment then develops a care plan that links the older adult with the most appropriate services available in the community from the private or nonprofit sector, which may include homemaker help, home-delivered meals, and respite or adult day care services. These services are then either paid for by the AAA and/or participants are asked to provide a donation or are charged a cost-sharing fee based on their income. Low-income individuals with the greatest physical, emotional, and social needs receive the highest priority for services available through the program.

OAA Title III funding also provides partial support for respite programs delivered in the caregiver's home or in a community-based setting through adult day programs. Generally, AAA funds are given as grants to a private-sector business or nonprofit adult day care program to subsidize its operating budget and thus provide services to a targeted number of elders. In some instances, low-income elders who qualify for the home- and community-based services described above can receive vouchers to purchase respite care from a private-sector or nonprofit agency, or a payment is provided by the program directly to the agency providing the service.

Until recently, there was no articulated national policy or position in support of family caregivers, as the policies discussed above has been targeted to older adults; caregivers have not been intentionally identified as a client or consumer of services (Feinberg & Newman, 2004). The National Family Caregiver Support Program (NFCSP), enacted by Congress in 2000 under the OAA, was the first piece of legislation that provided funding for caregiver support programs. The NFCSP supports local programs that offer information and referrals to caregivers; assists caregivers in accessing supportive services; provides counseling, support groups, and caregiver training; and provides respite care and supplemental services on a limited basis to complement the care provided by caregivers. Eligibility is limited to family caregivers of older adults (age 60 and older) and grandparents and relative caregivers of children not more than 18 years. Priority is given to those persons in greatest social and economic need (with particular attention to low-income, minority individuals) and to older individuals providing care and support to persons with mental retardation and related developmental disabilities (Administration on Aging, 2010c).

As shown in Figure 9.3, private and nonprofit agencies play a direct role in the delivery of home health and other community services to the vast majority of families who do not qualify for services under Medicare or Medicaid or do not have access to OAA programs. Families, if they can afford to, purchase needed services out of pocket. In the United States, the private and nonprofit sectors are well-developed, and there are typically a wide range of community-based services available in most urban areas and, to a lesser extent, in rural communities. For example, elders who need assistance with activities of daily living can pay for homemaker service offered through a private home health business to assist with daily needs. There are 9,284 Medicare-certified home health agencies across the country (Centers for Medicare and Medicaid Services, 2008), and the average cost of a home health aid is $29 per hour (U.S. Department of Health and Human Services, 2008b). Another private-sector service that has developed to support caregiving needs is geriatric care managers. Geriatric care managers provide case management services for a fee, which includes assessment of a client's needs, arranging for services, and monitoring care on an ongoing basis. The average cost of services is $175 for an initial consultation, $168 to develop a care plan, and $74 per hour to monitor and manage service delivery (Stone, Reinhard, Machemer, & Rudin, 2002). Likewise, there are more than 3,400 privately operated adult day programs across the country, and the average cost for adult day care is $61 per day (MetLife Mature Market Institute, 2007; National Adult Day Services Association, 2009).

In the nonprofit and volunteer sector, programs such as Meals on Wheels provide home-delivered meals to elders over the age of 60 or others who are homebound. Participants pay a suggested donation for home-delivered meals ($4–$7), or their donation is reduced based on a sliding scale relative to their income. Nonprofit agencies such as local United Way agencies identify areas of community need and, primarily through local fundraising and grants, support programs that address those areas of need. For example, a United Way may provide financial support to a local adult day care center or respite services.

There are also nonprofits that exist across the country that are organized around a particular illness or social issue and act as political advocates as well as providers of information and support. For example, the Alzheimer's Association provides information, local support groups, and online resources (see www.alz.org) and lobbies government for research and other services that would assist persons with Alzheimer's. The AARP, founded in 1958, is an advocate for and resource for older adults and has more than 39 million members over the age of 50. AARP activities include informing members and the public on social, health, and economic issues; advocating about legislative, consumer, and legal issues; promoting community service; and offering a wide range of special products and services to members (AARP, 2009).

BOX 9.1   Policy to People Link: Advocacy Organizations Influencing Policy: The National Alliance for Caregiving

Established in 1996, the National Alliance for Caregiving is a nonprofit coalition of national organizations that focuses on issues of family caregiving. Alliance members include grassroots organizations, professional associations, service organizations, disease-specific organizations, a government agency, and corporations.

The Alliance initiated a 2-day conference titled "Toward a National Caregiving Agenda: Empowering Family Caregivers in America." During the 2-day meeting, participants discussed changes needed in public policies to make family caregiving in the United States a more bearable task. Their primary goal for coming together, however, was to craft and begin executing a plan for organizing family caregivers into a political voice—to create a vigorous caregiver movement.

You can review the plan at http://caregiving.org/data/summit.pdf.

In summary, the United States can be characterized as having limited government support of community-based elder care. The programs that are available, such as Medicare and Medicaid, are restricted to those who first meet eligibility criteria and physical impairment guidelines. An important piece of legislation, the OAA, does provide funding for a select type of community-based services for older adults over age 60 and their caregivers, but the small amount of funding for these programs limits the Act's scope and impact. Thus, families who are primarily responsible for providing caregiving services must navigate between qualifying for government programs and/ or paying for services in order to access community-based care for their elderly family members. Aside from an unpaid work leave policy and the OAA program—the National Family Caregiver Support Program that offers information/assistance and referral and some supportive services—caregivers do not receive any compensation for their caregiving role. We now turn our discussion to Italy.

Italy

As shown in Figure 9.4, the community-based caregiving policy framework in Italy is characterized by the primary role of the family and private sector, minimal role of government, and limited involvement of the voluntary/nonprofit sectors. Italian families are implicitly and explicitly designated as the primary carer of older family members, and this expectation is deeply rooted in Italian culture to such an extent that it is

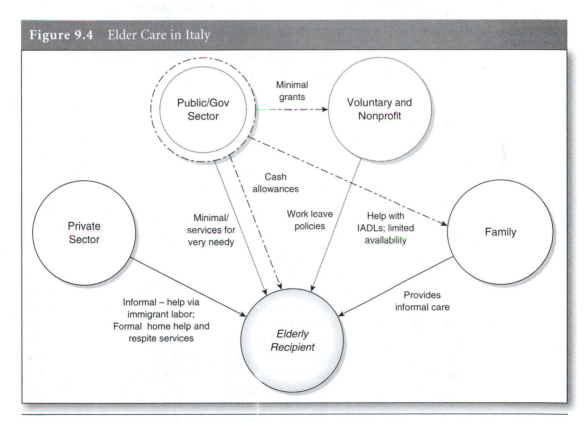

Figure 9.4   Elder Care in Italy

Source: Adapted from Lyon and Glucksmann (2008).

almost socially unacceptable for families to admit, by seeking outside assistance, that they are unable to provide elder care (Polverini et al., 2004). Moreover, Italian law requires families (to the third generation) to provide financial support to elders who are unable to support themselves, although this law has not been aggressively enforced.

The national government's role in community-based care for elders has been limited and is further complicated by the interface among the various levels of Italian government structure. This structure consists of 20 regions (*regioni*) that are divided into 100 provinces, and within the provinces are municipalities (*comuni*).

Home Health and Home Care

The national government's involvement in caregiving policy has been one of declaring the need for community-based elder care in national plans that encourage regions and municipalities to develop care assessments, home care services, and other community support services, because in Italy the regions and municipalities are responsible for providing community-based and health care services. In 1998, the Italian National Health Plan (1998–2000) articulated for the first time the need to adopt policies that supported families who had older adults in need of home care. Three years later, the Health Plan (2003–2005) reiterated the need for supporting families in their role of carer (Polverini et al., 2004). In 2000, law n 328, a National Plan of Interventions and Social Services, identified the need for supporting dependent people in their homes and directed regions to develop and provide home-based care; however, only two regions had responded 4 years later (Polverini et al., 2004).

As indicated by the dashed line from the government to the elder in Figure 9.4, the national government gives two types of cash payments that can be used for purchasing care services. A disability allowance (*indennità di inabilità*) is available to low-income and disabled adults determined to have lost at least 66% of functioning, and the allowance is payable until and if the person is qualified to receive a retirement pension (SSA, 2008a). A care allowance (*indennità di accompagnamento*) is offered to those who, regardless of age or income, are deemed to have total disability and who are not self-sufficient (Gori, 2000). On an informal basis, some regions and communities chose to make available on a limited basis an additional care allowance or voucher to low-income and/or highly dependent elders that can be used to purchase care services from the private sector.

Italians are guaranteed access, at no or low cost, to primary health care that is delivered through general practitioners via the Italian National Health System (*Sistema Sanitoria Nazionale*), which is under the control of regional governments and administered by local health authorities (*Azienda di Sanità Locale*). There are two forms of free or low-cost home health care available in Italy—the Programmed Home Care Assistance (ADP; *Assistenza Domicilare Programmata*) and Integrated Home Care (ADI; *Assistenza Domicilare Integrata*). Under the ADP program, general practitioners make home visits at designed intervals to those who have physical disabilities or health limitations (e.g., heart or respiratory disease) that make it difficult to travel (Polverini et al., 2004). Once a request for ADP services is approved by the doctor in charge of the health district, the general practitioner arranges for home visits as needed, usually weekly or monthly, with the purpose of reviewing the current living conditions and the verification of the effectiveness of any prescribed care or rehabilitation program (Lamura, Melchiorre, Quattrini, Mengani, & Albertini, 2001).

The ADI program authorizes various health professionals (e.g., doctors, nurses, and physical therapists) to make scheduled home visits to those with serious health conditions (e.g., terminal illnesses, severe pathologies, temporary disability) if approved by the general practitioner. Those receiving services through ADI are also provided with the necessary medical equipment and home helper services needed. In some local communities, home health services may be limited to a few days a week because of a lack of resources and personnel (Polverini et al., 2004). Although the medical home care services are provided free under the national health care system, home helper services must be paid for by the elder or family.

For elders who do not have serious or terminal illness and do not qualify for the integrated ADI program but who need assistance with activities of daily living, home care services are accessible in most regions or municipalities through the *Servizio di Assistenza Domiciliare* program. Request for assistance is made to the local commune office, and an assessment is conducted to determine the level of care needed and the income of the elder and, in some regions, his or her family's income as well (Gori, 2000). Because the responsibility for home help services rests at the regional and local levels, the amount of funding allocated to such services—and, therefore, the extent to which home helper services are available and the cost of such services—varies markedly across Italy (Lamura et al., 2001).

Leave From Work and Tax Credits

In Figure 9.4, the dotted line from government to the family represents legislation that provides some workplace benefits to carers. Italian caregivers do receive some benefits for providing caregiving assistance, but eligibility for and scope of these benefits are limited. For example, under Law n 335 enacted in 1995, working caregivers can be granted pension credits for leave from paid work if they are caring for someone aged 6 and older and if they are cohabitating with the care recipient. The pension credit is limited to 25 days per year with a maximum lifetime limit of 2 years (Quattrini, Melchiorre, Balducci, Spazzafumo, & Lamura, 2006).

With regard to leave from work, any worker has the right to paid leave for 3 working days per year in case of the death or documented severe disability of a spouse or other family member and unpaid leave for up to 2 years (consecutive or split time) for a documented care need under Law n 53, enacted in 2000. The employee retains his or her job without pay and must not be employed during the unpaid leave. If the working carer is aiding a severely disabled family member, the carer is entitled to 3 days of paid leave per month throughout his or her working career. Finally, Law n 342 (2000) allows the deduction from taxable income of up to €1,550 ($2,073) per year for the cost of hiring private carers (Polverini et al., 2004). Beyond the policies for working caregivers, the Italian social policy does not address the needs of the carers themselves.

Thus, while there have been a handful of national laws attempting to provide some level of support to family carers, legislation for community-based support for caring remains decentralized and fragmented across Italy (Melchiorre, Quattrini, Megani, & Lamura, 2000; Polverini et al., 2004). Specific legislation for family carers has never existed because the cost and responsibility of caring is seen as a compulsory family duty (Polverini et al., 2004).

Voluntary, Nonprofit, and Private-Sector Organizations

As shown by the solid line from the private sector to the elder in Figure 9.4, the private sector plays a direct role in providing elder care services. The private elder care sector in Italy is, however, characterized primarily by the availability of migrant workers who are hired to provide assistance with home care needs and secondarily by a limited number of businesses from which elders or their family can purchase community-based care. Recent estimates suggest that there are approximately 700,000 migrant workers who have been hired by elders and/or families, often without formal employee contracts (Polverini et al., 2004). Thus, personal care and respite care (hourly or weekend) services can be obtained in most regions by hiring immigrants or, to a lesser degree, through private businesses. According to Bettio, Mazzotta, and Solinas (2007), private, professional services tend to be accessed by the richer segment of the population, while those with low incomes rely on means-tested services described above and the middle class often resorts to migrant workers within the private sector to assist with elder care. The average cost of home care purchased within the private sector ranges from €8 ($11) to €20 ($27) per hour (Bettio et al., 2007). For example, out-of-home respite care through day care services for older adults with Alzheimer's disease is provided by the *Associazione Italiana Malattia di Alzheimer* in the city of Biella in Northern Italy for €20 per day (Alzheimer Territoriale Provincia di Biella, 2009).

Volunteer organizations that provide some assistance with short respite care and transportation to medical appointments (as shown by the dotted line in Figure 9.4) also exist in varying degrees of availability. Organizations such as *Associazione Volontari Assistenza Ammalati e Anziani* (Volunteer Association for Assistance of the Sick and Elderly) in the commune of Calusco d'Adda in Northern Italy and volunteer organizations such as *Gruppo Volontariato Vincenziano,* which is associated with the Catholic Church, in Rome, provide care and visitation services through volunteers. There are also some national organizations that advocate for and provide information to caregivers, such as the *Federazione Alzheimer Italia* (www.alzheimer.it) and the *Associazione Italiana Malattia di Alzheimer* in Rome (www.aimaroma.it).

BOX 9.2 Policy to People Link: In-Home Care, Biella, Italy

The availability and administration of home help services is the responsibility of regional and local governments in Italy. The city of Biella, which is located in the northern region of Piedmont, Italy, provides in-home care services for older adults. Older adults in need of home care services contact the local Geriatric Assessment Unit. A caseworker prepares an individual care plan that starts with a home visit to assess needs. The care plan can include such services as personal care, meal preparation, management of daily activities, and an emergency alarm. Half of the cost for these services is paid by the local government and half by the older adult. In addition, there are some nongovernmental agencies in the Piedmont region that also provide services for a fee.

If I was by myself, unable to move [to another location], with no family or any help and in need of food, there is the Comunita Montana . . . [that] comes around to your house with warm meals every day. You pay a little amount toward it, depending on your income. . . . The maximum you pay is €7 per day; they come round once a day for 5 days a week. . . . If you need someone to help you with cleaning the house, there are people who come and charge €7 per hour, which is much less than the normal rate. Basically, unless you are really poor, you need to pay for all of these services. If you are really poor and have nothing, the local town hall will investigate your case, check your bank account, and then help you out.

—Mrs. D., age 84, Biella, Italy

In summary, the Italian national government plays a secondary role in the support of community based care for older adults. Only those elderly adults whose medical needs are established through the home health program are then linked to home help care, and only those with severe physical disabilities receive a social care allowance that may be used to purchase services via a limited pool of private-sector availability. Because the responsibility to provide community-based home helper services rests with the regional and local levels of government, care services have not been widespread, may or may not be means tested, and are unevenly distributed between Northern and Southern Italy, with the north having more services (Polverini et al., 2004). The programs and services that municipalities offer are also influenced by local political cultures and organizational capacities, and these local governments are left to determine what services will be provided to whom (Polverini et al., 2004). Thus, because policies and services directed by both state and regional government are not well-developed, the result is a fragmented and decentralized landscape of social care services across Italy—an environment that serves a limited number of elderly adults.

England

Elder care in England is a mix of primary involvement by the government, nonprofit, and family sectors (see Figure 9.5). While families are deemed to be the primary carers of older adults, the national government has played an important role in providing support for both the elder and the carer (Lothian, McKee, Philp, & Nolan, 2001). Support is based on key legislation via the National Health Services, Community Care Act of 1990, Carers Recognition and Services Act of 1995, the National Strategy for Carers (Department of Health, 1999), the Health and Social Care Act (2001), and the Carers Act of 2004, which will be described below.

Figure 9.5 Elder Care in England

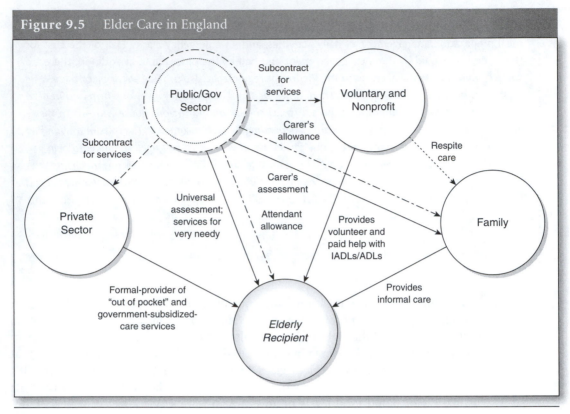

Source: Adapted from Lyon and Glucksmann (2008).

Home Health and Home Care

As health care is universally accessible in England, nursing care, rehabilitative care, and chiropodist services delivered at home are covered under the National Health Services and are provided free and are wholly reimbursable. Once the care recipient has been assessed for his or her needs, community nurses who are registered nurses make home visits to provide nursing care (e.g., changing dressings, giving injections) and help people get needed home nursing aids and, with a small deposit, any home equipment needed. They may also teach families and carers basic caregiving skills (Direct.gov.uk, 2009b).

With regard to home care or homemaker services, local departments of social services are responsible for assessment and management of these services, which are funded from a mix of general taxation and charges (Brodhurst & Glendinning, 2001). Home care services include laundry service, special transport services, an at-home hairdresser, meals, homemaker services, personal care, home maintenance and adaptations, and counseling services (Nolan, Barber, Edis, Brown, & McKee, 2004). To receive home care, elders are first assessed for their level of need and then are provided a care plan based on that assessment. Once a care plan is developed, a financial assessment is conducted to determine how much the elder can contribute to his or her cost of home care services. Those with incomes at or below the basic annual level of pension credit plus 25% (£8,063 or $15,777) will not be charged for services, and any charge an elder has to pay should not bring his or her income below this level (Help the Aged, 2007). Spouse or partner income is not included in the financial determination, unless the care recipient is legally entitled to that income. Local councils may decide to include savings and assets in the determination of how much an elder must contribute to the cost of services. Home value is excluded, and there is an upper (£21,500 or $42,000) and lower limit (£13,000 or $25,437) to how much of one's savings will be included. If an elder has more savings than the upper limit, he or she may be asked to pay the full cost of services; if the individual has less, the savings will not be included in determining how much he or she can pay. If savings amount is between the upper and lower limits, £1 ($1.50) will be added to income-level determination per week for every £250 over the lower savings limit amount (Help the Aged, 2007).

As indicated in Figure 9.5, the delivery of care can be directly provided by the local council, a subsidy can be given to a private or voluntary agency that will provide the services, or the elder can be given a cash amount, called a direct payment, to arrange and purchase his or her own services through a private or voluntary agency (Help the Aged, 2007). Spouses or other relatives living with the elder are usually not eligible to be paid for providing care. Respite care, in-home care, care at a day center, or a short-stay situation in a residential care home are also available. Access to respite care is provided through the department of social services or can be purchased privately. Another cash allowance called the Attendance Allowance is a tax-free benefit for individuals aged 65 and older who have a physical or mental disability and as a result need help with personal care (Direct.gov.uk, 2009c). Depending on the level of disability, the Attendance Allowance may be paid at the higher rate of £67 ($99) or the lower rate of £44.85 ($67) per week. If an elder is already receiving assistance via the Carer's Allowance, described below, he or she may not be able to receive this additional allowance.

As shown in Figure 9.5, the government provides direct support to family caregivers through a number of legislative acts that ensure caregivers' needs are considered and also provide a Carer's Allowance (Direct.gov.uk, 2009a). In 1999, the government published its National Strategy for Carers (Department of Health, 1999), which set forth the importance and support of carers of all ages. The strategy focused on three key elements: (1) information (having access to and receiving information about services that aid in caring activities), (2) support (involving carers in planning of needed services), and (3) care (carers have a right to have their own needs addressed). Two additional policies, the Carers and Disabled Children Act (Department of Health, 2000) and the Carers (Equal Opportunities) Act of 2004, provided additional support for carers. Carers, regardless of their income, are to be informed by local councils of their right to an assessment (even if the care recipient refuses an assessment) and to have their needs related to work, training, or leisure assessed. The Carer's Act also empowered local councils to supply certain services directly to the carers (Help the Aged, 2007; Nolan et al., 2004). Under the Act, carers are entitled to an assessment of their ability to provide care, their emotional and physical health, their other responsi-bilities, their understanding of the elder's condition, and the tasks for which they would like assistance (Carers U.K., 2007). Based on the assessment, a care plan that includes services to address the needs of both the carer and care recipient is to be developed for those eligible for assistance. Carers can then receive services directly from local coun-cils that support their caregiving role, including an integrated plan of caring, training, self-help groups, counseling, vouchers to enable carers to take a break from caring, help with taxi fares, and mobile phones for carers (if needed when they are away from the person they care for; Carers U.K., 2007).

Finally in 2006, the Department of Health published "Our Health, Our Care, Our Say," which provided an update on the 1999 National Strategic white paper. Goals for community services included a more integrated approach to the delivery of health and social care, as well as devising minimum standards, more provider choice, workforce training, and regulation. To meet these goals, the Department of Health launched the "New Deal for Carers," which establishes an information service/helpline for carers, provides an additional £25 million ($37 million) for short-term, home-based breaks for carers in crisis or an emergency situation, and funds the creation of the Expert Carers' Programme. The program will be a comprehensive model for carers training that will be delivered both face-to-face and online.

In addition to having the right to an assessment, increasing access to services, and the development of a care plan for eligible carers, a Carer's Allowance is also available (direct.gov.uk, 2009a). If carers spend 35 hours or more per week caring for a relative or friend and are caring for someone who is eligible for certain disability benefits, they are eligible for the Carer's Allowance. The Carer's Allowance weekly rate was £50.55 ($99) in 2008. Although the Carer's Allowance is not means tested, carers cannot receive both a Carer's Allowance and other state benefit if that benefit is at or greater than £50.55 ($99) or more a week. For example, if the carer receives £90 ($134) per week from the State Retirement Pension, then the carer is not eligible for the Carer's Allowance. If, however, the Carer's State Retirement Pension is £32 ($48) per week, they would receive £18 ($27) in a Carer's Allowance. For carers who are not yet retired, for every week the Carer's Allowance is paid, the carer is credited with a National Insurance contribution, which protects eligibility to the State Retirement Pension.

With regard to working caregivers, the Employment Relations Act of 1999 gave employees the right to time off from work to attend to unexpected care needs. The length of time away from work and whether the time off is paid is negotiated with the employer (Nolan et al., 2004).

The government supports the delivery of home care services through contracts with nongovernmental organizations. For example, the Princess Royal Trust for Carers (2010) was created in 1991 and is the largest provider of carer support services in the United Kingdom and has a network of 141 independently managed Carer's Centers (www.carers.org). It receives funding from the government to support carers. The organization provides advice and information to carers and professionals via its website, helpline, booklets, and factsheets and operates CarersLine (Carers U.K., 2010).

BOX 9.3   Policy to People Link: England's Caring Act and the Royal Borough of Kensington and Chelsea

In England, the delivery of home care services rests with the local departments of social services, who are responsible for assessment and management of these services. Carer program services include home visits by public nurses. In the Royal Borough of Kensington and Chelsea, the council offers a range of services, from help with personal care (such as washing and dressing) to home adaptations and safety alarms. If an older adult finds it difficult to manage at home, the Council's Adult Social Care Department will provide a free in-home assessment. If there is a need, a social worker will draw up a care plan that may include help with housework, shopping, bathing, food preparation, or other daily tasks.

Check out the other services the Royal Borough of Kensington and Chelsea provides at www.rbkc.gov.uk/healthandsocialcare/servicesforolderpeople.aspx.

In summary, community-based care for older adults in England is characterized by a moderate amount of government involvement through programs that directly support both the elder and caregiver. Elders have universal access to needed home health care services and equipment via the National Health Services health care program, under which such services are provided free of charge. Elders are also entitled to a needs assessment to determine the level of community-based care needed. Once the need for care has been established, the amount of services and the elder's ability to contribute to the cost of the care are determined. Once deemed eligible, older adults may choose to receive care directly from the local agency or from another community-based care provider. England is also unique in the direct support it provides to carers. Carers are also entitled to an assessment of their needs and, if they qualify, can receive respite services and other supportive assistance. Carers can also receive a direct payment for providing caregiving services that meet the thresholds of eligibility.

Sweden

As shown in Figure 9.6, elder care in Sweden is characterized by direct support from the Swedish government and family, secondary involvement of the private sector, and little to no involvement by the volunteer/nonprofit sector. In contrast to the United States and Italy, the Swedish government accepts an active role in supporting elders and carers through legislation that creates and finances services and through the direct delivery of community-based services in some instances. Care of older adults is seen as a public responsibility, and services are universally available to all citizens. The Swedish parliament defined national objectives that are used as a framework for social policies, which state that older persons should (1) be able to live an active life and have influence over their everyday lives, (2) be able to grow old in security and retain their

Figure 9.6   Elder Care in Sweden

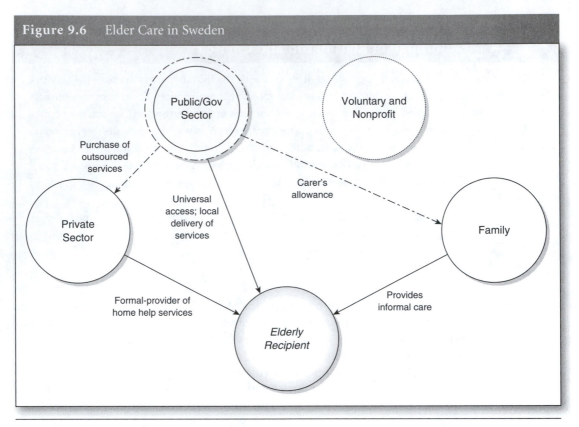

Source: Adapted from Lyon and Glucksmann (2008).

independence, (3) be treated with respect, and (4) have access to good health care and social services (Socialstyrelsen, 2008).

Three levels of government are involved in caring for older adults. The national government sets policy direction for the country via legislation, the county councils (*län*) serve at the regional level and are responsible for health care services, and the municipalities (*kommuner*) are responsible for delivering social and housing services and, in some cases, health care services. At the national level, there are three key pieces of legislation that provide the framework for community-based services. The Social Services Act of 1982 established the statutory right to receive social care services when needed, the Health and Medical Services Act of 1982 set high standards of health care and universal access for all citizens, and the 1992 Community Care Reform legislation (*Ädelreformen*) appointed the municipalities as the sole authority for care and home health care for older adults. The Social Services Act (*Socialtjäanstelagen*) established the statutory right of individuals at all ages to receive social services if the need cannot be met in any other way (Hässler, 2001). Thus, access to care services is universal and is not means tested as it is in the United States. As shown by the black line from the government to the elder in Figure 9.6, the municipality is directly involved in assessing and arranging for home health and home help services. The cost of outpatient care is decided by each county council. For example, there is a fee of SEK150 ($21) charged to consult a physician or other health care specialist. There is a cap on how much a patient pays out of pocket, and after a patient has paid a total of SEK900 ($124), all medical consultations in the 12 months following the date of the first consultation are free of charge (Socialstyrelsen, 2008).

All older adults can apply for home help services, but in most municipalities, receiving services is contingent on an assessment conducted by a municipal care manager (Socialstyrelsen, 2008). Each municipality decides if an assessment is required, which type of services to include, and the fee associated with such care. If an assessment is required, it includes meeting with the older adult—usually in his or her home—to review the request, discussing the care needs with family, and consulting with other professionals. Home help is the primary service provided, which in Sweden includes help with activities of daily living such as bathing, toileting, and dressing, as well as instrumental activities of daily living such as transportation, foot care, meals, security alarms, housing adaptations, assistive devices, and adult day care (Johansson, 2004). Care also includes overnight and weekend assistance. These services are arranged by a care manager and delivered by the public health services unit or, as shown by the line from the government to the private sector, provided by a private business. A charge for the services provided is based on the elder's and his or her spouse's or registered partner's income and cost-of-living expenses. For example, in Stockholm, the maximum cost for home help service and daytime activities three to five times per week is SEK947 ($128) per month (Stockholm Government, 2010a).

As shown in Figure 9.6, families provide direct and informal care to their elderly relatives, but the government also supports family caregivers through services that help carers directly and by providing compensation to carers. In 1998, the Social Services Act was revised to include a paragraph that directed municipalities to support the family in its role of caring for elderly, dependent, or sick family members (Johansson, 2004). A year later, the National Action Plan on Policy for the Elderly directed SEK300,000,000 ($38.5 million) to municipalities to fund services that are designed to support carers, such as a few hours of daily in-home respite care per week, respite for short-term time periods (e.g., a week), counseling and support groups, and training courses. All carers are entitled to 4 hours of respite during the week at no charge. Carers may also be eligible for either an Attendance Allowance or a Carer's Allowance (Johansson, 2004). The Attendance Allowance (or Home Care Allowance) is given to the elder, who in turn pays the family member who is providing care work beyond what is considered a normal amount. The amount of the untaxed payment is based on the level of dependency and amount of hourly caregiving provided, but compensation cannot exceed 17 hours per week. Although the amount of the allowance varies by municipality, the maximum pay is about SEK5,000 ($689) per month. Under the Carer's Allowance, caregivers receive a payment that is equal to that of a formal home help service provider employed by the municipality. This payment is taxable (Keefe, 2004), and carers receive pension credits as well.

Finally, working carers are entitled to paid and unpaid time off work when caring for an older adult. The Care Leave Act of 1989 entitles a person caring for a seriously and/or terminally ill close relative to be absent with pay from work for up to 60 days (Johansson, 2004). The carer and the person cared for must both be registered at the social insurance office (i.e., the carer must be under 65 years of age), and the care must take place in Sweden. Payments to the carer are payable at 80% of the income, and these benefits are taxed. Flexible work arrangements such as part-time or flex-time adjustments for carers are negotiated with a carer's employer (Johansson, 2004).

Although the nonprofit/voluntary sector is not directly involved in community care services, there are organizations that offer support to carers and elders. The Swedish Red Cross uses volunteers to make social visits to lonely and isolated people, mostly the elderly, at home and offers support groups to carers (Swedish Red Cross, 2009). The Dementia Association (*Demensförbundet*) and the Alzheimer's Association of Sweden (*Alzheimerföreningen i Sverige*) also provide information about dementia and support groups for carers and are advocates for those with dementia (Alzheimer's Association of Sweden, 2009; Dementia Association, 2009).

Elder care in Sweden is viewed as a public responsibility, and its social policies legislate universal access to home health and home care services that support both the elder and the caregiver. Once a need for home care has been determined, there is a comprehensive array of home services provided, including overnight care and home modifications. Needed care can be delivered by local municipalities or through a private-sector agency that receives a subsidy from the municipality. Caregivers also receive direct support via respite programs and care allowances, as well as paid leave policies that allow for payment at 80% of income for qualified caregivers.

Summary

The United States, Italy, England, and Sweden are good examples of the different ways in which countries address the growing need for elder care and support of family carers. We have summarized these differences in Tables 9.1, 9.2, and 9.3 (pages 231–237). The primary difference between the countries we described is how available services are accessed. In Italy and the United States, the pathway to accessing services begins with meeting income and physical need criteria. If these criteria are not met, then elders must turn to nongovernment sectors to purchase services out of pocket. In the United States, the exception to this is programs funded through the OAA, but funding for these programs is severely limited and is not available in all communities. In Italy, in particular, families have become heavily reliant on paying immigrant workers to provide in-home care.

In contrast, the access to services in England and Sweden is universal, as these governments have articulated that care of the elderly is a public concern. Thus, the

Table 9.1 Community-Based Services for Elder Care by Country

Service	Availability		Access		Eligibility/Cost	
In-home laundry	Gov program	IT EN SE US	Universal access	EN SE	Available private pay	IT US
	Voluntary/ nonprofit		Income and/or severity	US	Need assessed; govt provides free or wholly reimbursed	IT EN
	Private sector	IT US			Need assessed; cost share govt & elder	EN SE US
Hairdresser at home	Gov program	EN SE	Universal access	EN SE	Available private pay	IT
	Voluntary/ nonprofit		Income and/or severity		Need assessed; govt provides free or wholly reimbursed	EN
	Private sector	IT			Need assessed; cost share govt & elder	EN SE
Meals at home	Gov program	IT US EN SE	Universal access	EN SE	Available private pay	IT US EN
	Voluntary/ nonprofit	IT US	Income and/or severity	IT US EN	Need assessed; govt provides free or wholly reimbursed	IT
	Private sector	IT			Cost share govt & elder	IT US EN SE
Tele-alarms	Gov program	IT EN SE	Universal access	EN SE	Available private pay	US
	Voluntary/ nonprofit		Income and/or severity		Need assessed; govt provides free or wholly reimbursed	SE
	Private sector	US			Need assessed; cost share govt & elder	IT

(Continued)

Table 9.1 (Continued)   Community-Based Services for Elder Care by Country

Service	Availability		Access		Eligibility/Cost	
Care aids (assistive devices)	Gov program	IT US EN SE	Universal access	EN SE IT	Available private pay	US
	Voluntary/ nonprofit	US	Income and/or severity	US	Needs assessed; govt provides free or wholly reimbursed	IT EN
	Private sector	US			Needs assessed; cost share govt & elder	IT US EN SE
Home modifications	Gov program	IT EN SE	Universal access	SE	Available private pay	IT US
	Voluntary/ nonprofit	US	Income and/or severity	IT EN	Needs assessed; govt provides free or wholly reimbursed	IT EN SE
	Private sector	IT US			Needs assessed; cost share govt & elder	IT EN
Senior companion/ company	Gov program	IT SE	Universal access	SE	Available private pay	IT US EN
	Voluntary/ nonprofit	US EN	Income and/or severity		Needs assessed; govt provides free or wholly reimbursed	IT SE
	Private sector	IT			Needs assessed; cost share govt & elder	SE
Day care in-home or community center	Gov program	US EN SE	Universal access	EN SE	Available private pay	IT US
	Voluntary/ nonprofit		Income and/or severity	US	Need assessed; govt provides free or wholly reimbursed	EN
	Private sector	IT US			Need assessed; cost share govt & elder	US EN SE

Table 9.1 (Continued)   Community-Based Services for Elder Care by Country

Service	Availability		Access		Eligibility/Cost	
Night care in home	Gov program	EN SE	Universal access	SE	Available private pay	IT US EN
	Voluntary/nonprofit		Income and/or severity	EN	Need assessed; govt provides free or wholly reimbursed	EN
	Private sector	IT US EN			Need assessed; cost share govt & elder	EN SE
Private cohabitant assistant	Gov program	IT SE	Universal access	SE	Available private pay	IT US EN
	Voluntary/nonprofit		Income and/or severity	IT	Need assessed; govt provides free or wholly reimbursed	
	Private sector	IT US EN			Need assessed; cost share govt & elder	IT SE
In-home care for ADLs	Gov program	US EN SE	Universal access	EN SE	Available private pay	IT US
	Voluntary/nonprofit		Income and/or severity	US	Need assessed; govt provides free or wholly reimbursed	EN
	Private sector	IT US			Need assessed; cost share govt & elder	US EN SE

(Continued)

Table 9.1 (Continued)   Community-Based Services for Elder Care by Country

Service	Availability		Access		Eligibility/Cost	
Homemaker services	Gov program	US EN SE	Universal access	EN SE	Available private pay	IT US
	Voluntary/ nonprofit	US	Income and/or severity	US	Govt provides free or wholly reimbursed	EN
	Private sector	IT US			Cost share govt & elder	US EN SE
Case manager or social worker	Gov program	IT US EN SE	Universal access	EN SE	Available private pay	US
	Voluntary/ nonprofit		Income and/or severity	IT US	Need assessed; govt provides free or wholly reimbursed	IT EN SE
	Private sector	US			Need assessed; cost share govt & elder	US

Note: US = United States, IT = Italy, EN = England, SE = Sweden

need for services is the initial determining factor for receiving services, the payment for these services is then based on the elder's income, and the cost is shared by the elder and subsidized by the government.

The community-based services listed in Table 9.1 are described in terms of their availability and whether the service is available via government programs, the voluntary and/or nonprofit sector, and the private sector. It is possible that the service is available in more than one sector. If the service is indeed available via a government program, the next column identifies whether such a service is universally accessible or whether access is based on income and/or physical eligibility criteria. The final column indicates whether there is a cost associated with the service. Again, it is possible to have more than one cost structure for a particular service. For example, access to home laundry service through a government program is universal in England and Sweden, but government programs that provide in-home laundry are accessed in the United States after meeting income and physical health eligibility criteria. These services are also available for purchase from the private sector in both Italy and the United States. Depending on how services are accessed, the elder may have to pay out of pocket or contribute some amount as a cost share.

Table 9.2 Services for Caregivers by Country

	Availability			Access		
Services for Caregivers	No	Restricted Access	Universal Access	Government	Voluntary/ Nonprofit	Private Pay by Family
Caregiver needs assessment (formal assessment of caregiving situation)			SE EN			US
Counseling and advice (I&R)		IT US*	SE EN	IT US EN	US	US EN
Support groups		US* IT EN	SE	IT EN	IT US	
In-home respite or "granny-sitting"		US* SE EN	IT	US EN	US SE	IT EN US
Respite care		US* IT	SE EN	EN		IT EN US
Caregiver allowance/ payment	US		IT EN SE	IT EN SE		
Practical training in caregiving skills, protecting caregiver's own physical and mental health		IT EN	SE		US	

* In the United States, support for caregivers is restricted to programs funded under the Older Americans Act.

Note: US = United States, IT = Italy, EN = England, SE = Sweden

Tables 9.2 and 9.3 summarize services and financial support targeted to caregivers directly. The pattern of universal support and direct benefits provided to caregivers in England and Sweden is evident in the availability of caregiver allowances, caregiver needs, and workplace leave policies.

Each of the countries we reviewed in this chapter has and will continue to have high percentages of elders, and each will no doubt continue to adapt and adopt caregiver policies to address the need for community-based elder care. To explore how differing caregiving policies may play out in the daily lives of older adults, return to the case study presented in Chapter 1 and consider how Luciana's caregiving needs could be met if she was a resident of the countries discussed in this chapter.

Table 9.3   Benefits for Family Caregivers

Benefit	Italy	United States	England	Sweden
Caregiver Allowance (compensation directly to family member who is providing care)	Yes	No	Yes	Yes
Restrictions	Must meet income and support needs as established by municipalities		Over age 16; spend at least 35 hours per week caring; the care recipient gets Attendance Allowance or Disability Living Allowance; doesn't earn more than £95/week from work	<65
Who is paid	Family member of care recipient		Caregiver	Caregiver
Who pays?	Municipalities		Local government	Municipalities
Pension credit	No		Yes	Yes
Levels of payment/mo.	Varies by municipality 70–929 euros		£48.65 a week	Varies ~SEK14,000
Care Voucher (used to purchase services)	Yes	Yes	Yes	Yes
Restrictions	Income	Restricted to low income and those who have met disability criteria	People aged 65 or over; have long-term illness or disability	None
Who is paid	Primary caregiver	Care recipient	Care recipient	Care recipient
Who is responsible?	Municipalities	Local Area Agencies on Aging	Local government	Municipalities
Levels of payment/ mo.	Varies by municipality – (e.g., Milan 300 E)		Low and high rates; depends on extent of need	Varies ~SEK5,000

Table 9.3 (Continued)   Benefits for Family Caregivers

Benefit	Italy	United States	England	Sweden
Workplace Leave Policy for Caregivers	Yes	Yes	Yes	Yes
Restrictions	Recipient must be evaluated as severely disabled	Recipient must meet employment criteria and individual receiving care must have a serious health condition	As determined by employer	<65
Paid	Current salary	No	Negotiable	80% of income
Terms of leave	Paid leave 3 days per month; unpaid leave max. 2 years	12 weeks of unpaid job protection in a 12-month period	Flex-time, paid and unpaid time off is at the discretion of employer	Maximum 60 days
Pension credits	Must be cohabitants with care recipient; can receive pension credits 25 days per year; max. 24 mos.	No	No	Yes

For More Information

1. Carers/Caregiving Advocacy Groups

Advocacy groups play a key role in policy development on issues of concern to caregivers/carers. Here are a few of those nongovernment advocacy groups:

a. Eurocarers: European Association Working for Carers
http://www.eurocarers.org/index.htm

Eurocarers is an advocacy group for informal carers in the European Union. The website offers research reports, policy papers, best practices, and factsheets.

b. Carers U.K.
http://www.carersuk.org/Home

Carers U.K. is a membership organization of carers, led by carers for carers in England, Scotland, and Wales.

   c. Family Caregiver Alliance, United States
   http://caregiver.org/caregiver/jsp/home.jsp

Founded in 1977, Family Caregiver Alliance was the first community-based nonprofit organization in the country to address the needs of families and friends providing long-term care at home.

   d. National Alliance for Caregiving, United States
   http://www.caregiving.org/

Established in 1996, the National Alliance for Caregiving is a nonprofit coalition of national organizations focusing on issues of family caregiving.

2. Euro Famcare Caregiving Reports
   http://www.uke.de/extern/eurofamcare/

Euro Famcare provides a European review of the circumstances of family carers of older people in relation to the existence, familiarity, availability, use, and acceptability of supporting services. The joint research project of eight universities and governments provides background reports on caregiving in 23 European countries.

3. National Center on Caregiving
   http://caregiver.org/caregiver/jsp/content_node.jsp?nodeid=343

Established in 2001 as a program of Family Caregiver Alliance, the National Center on Caregiving (NCC) works to advance the development of high-quality, cost-effective policies and programs for caregivers in every state in the country. Uniting research, public policy, and services, the NCC serves as a central source of information on caregiving and long-term care issues for policymakers, service providers, media, funders, and family caregivers throughout the country.

Mr. F., age 72
Rio de Janeiro, Brazil

I was born here, in Rio de Janeiro, in Praça da Bandeira, in the north part of the city, in 1934, but I now live in Ipanema. All my family was from Rio, my parents, my two brothers and my sister, I am the youngest one. My parents died relatively young, well, in compare to today life expectation. My mother died at 65 and my dad at 60.

My father was a builder; he was a hard worker. I never saw him enjoying himself, only working. My brothers are dead, but my sister is still alive. She is 80 years old.

I am married; I have two sons and five grandchildren. Our family is very close, but unfortunately, my older son lives in São Paulo, so I only see him once a month. The other, I see him all the time. My wife used to work as an English teacher. She is now retired. She is 71 years old. I had different jobs throughout all my life, mostly working as an accountant for a public organization. I worked as a geography teacher, but I am actually graduated in social science.

My daily life? I wake up at 7. I come to the beach; my favourite spot is here sitting on this bench, the most beautiful beach of Rio. There are days that I come here by bicycle and cycle around the beach, days that I walk here and run all the way to Leblon. Sometimes I come by roller skate and stroll up and down the Copacabana board walk. I love doing sports; I like to be active. Physical activity is so important, keeps me young, healthy. What else have I got to do? I am retired; I have so much spare time. Sport is therapeutic as much for my body as for my brain. Physical activity is fundamental at any age, especially at mine; for young people as well, people that are into sport are not into drugs, and they are into a healthy lifestyle.

I meet my friends here at the beach, every day. I stay here until midday, then I go home, I have lunch, I watch a bit of TV, sleep a couple of hours, and in the afternoon I take care of my bills, go to the bank, the post, see if there are any things to be fixed in the house.

I don't go out at night; I am usually too tired to go out.

I feel great. I am 1.80 meter tall, I weight 80 kilos, I don't have a ounce of fat, my cholesterol is low 180, when the normal level is 200. I cannot complain. I am in great form.

I am retired and so I receive a pension. The pension, here in Brazil, depends from the job that you were doing when you were young, so of course, people working for the minimum salary once retired can hardly survive. My pension is a good one, because I was a civil servant and I was on a good salary, so between mine and my wife's one we don't have to worry about money. In Brazil, you can start to retire after 30 years of solid work. My wife worked a little bit more, and she retired after 32 years. I have a private health plan (JAP) that I've been paying since I start working. Was only a small percent of my wage, which now allows me to use medical facilities for free, like hospitals, dentist, physiotherapist. For some special consultations, I only pay 30%, the plan pays the rest. JAP is one of Brazil best health plans.

I do not need any help at home, because it is only me and my wife living in a small apartment; there is no need for external help. We do everything alone. But if we did, forget about the state. Brazil cannot provide for this. You cannot depend from the state. Everyone has to be able to look after himself or create the base to be able to pay someone else to do it in case something happens. If you have a private health plan or a life insurance, you don't need the state. Not Brazil or even the U.S. can stop poverty.

The poverty is in the hand of the person in need; he has to create the base to stop it. There is no point in relying on the state. You have to invest in thinking for the future. If you gain and waste at the same time, you will get nowhere.

How am I experiencing aging? Getting old is a natural process. You cannot do the same things that you were doing when you were young. For example, I cannot run the marathon anymore, but I can still run on the beach. Therefore, the limitations reflect the age.

The future of an old person is today. You have to try to live today in the best way possible in order to still have a future. If you don't maintain a healthy lifestyle, your future was yesterday.

The advantage of this age is the free time. I am travelling a lot. I take my car and drive in places that I never saw before. We have more than 8,000 km of coast line in Brazil, and I am planning to see it all. This week, for example, I was in S. Bernardo do Campo, that is 450 kms away from Rio, to see my grandchild. Two months ago, I was in the Serra Gaucha, in Rio Grande do Sul (region in the South of Brazil). You have to take advantage of life.

I am at the end of my cycle, which is what I don't like about aging. The person is born, lives, and then dies. I am in the third stage of my life; this sometimes makes me sad. It would be great if I still had all my life in front of me.

Brazilian society is starting now to respect the elders, something that was unusual until a few years ago. Now old people travel on the bus for free, pay half price in the cinema, or go to the stadium, especially to Maracana, for free. The respect is relative to who you meet; some people are extremely educated, some others are not.

Aging well, if you analyze it, depends from different factors. First and most important the health factor; you have to look after yourself and starting from when you are young to eat well, do lots of exercise, get enough sleep. Then there is the financial factor; you have to work and economize part of your salary in order to have a comfortable retirement, so you can travel when you are old, help your kids, enjoy your life until the last drop.

Part III

The Future of Aging Social Policy

Mathilde, age 85, France

Alda, age 73; Domitilla, age 77; Maria, age 74; Giannina, age 84; Marisa,
age 76; Vilma, age 77; Marisa, age 76; Stefanina, age 84, Italy

10

Aging Social Policy Challenges

❖

> *We have realized that the time has come for us to move forward from debating the numbers surrounding global aging—to developing policies to deal with the impact on the future security and dignity of our citizens, particularly in their later years. . . . We have been compelled to answer difficult questions such as "What sort of social contract does our government hold with our citizens?"*
>
> —Erik Olsen, president, AARP board member (2007)

> *How do I feel about growing older? This is a million Swiss Francs question. Aging is not that nice, before [I was] 70, I was okay and then I started to think that I had only few years left to live. I guess what really scares me is thinking about illnesses. It is normal that years go by and that you get old, but you hear it all the time about people who don't understand anything anymore or live like vegetables, and you become a burden to your relatives. Obviously, you cannot think about it all the time and you must take all of the good things that happen to you day after day. We are fortunate because without our children, our life would be very sad and flat. What do I expect from the future? Health, for us, my family and other people, too.*
>
> —Mrs. G., age 82, Bellizona, Switzerland

We began this book by presenting demographic data showing that population aging is occurring around the globe. With the exception of Africa, the percentage of those aged 65 and over and aged 80 and over is expected to nearly double in a span of 30 years in all regions; almost a quarter of the European and Canadian populations and one-fifth of the U.S. population are expected to be aged 65 and over in 2030. And while the percentage increase in older adults is likely to be smaller in most European countries and the United States, countries such as China, India, Brazil, and Thailand are expected to experience an increase in their aging populations of more than 150% from 2000 to 2030.

What has been of interest to us is how countries and their governments and citizens conceptualize the social and economic implications of population aging and how they respond through the creation of aging social policies. Throughout this book, we have illustrated the different ways in which a sampling of countries, along with the United States, have responded to aging social policy in the areas of retirement income, employment, housing, health care, mental health, community-based services, and family caregiving. These differences in policy characteristics and responses are reflective of different cultural values and ideologies about the roles and responsibilities of governments, the private sector, the nonprofit sector, families, and individuals in protecting citizens from the risks inherent in growing old—those that are both socially constructed and physically inevitable.

In this chapter, we briefly discuss three important contextual issues that are related to debates surrounding the future of old-age social policy—the population aging data, the interpretation of population aging data as a harbinger of an impending social and economic crisis, and the decision about the criteria that should be used to grant access to aging social programs. We conclude this chapter with a brief discussion about some key policy challenges in each of the topics we explored in this book.

Is There a Population Aging Crisis?

Fifty years ago, a prominent sociologist, Robert Merton, commented, "In the future . . . if life expectancy climbs to 83 . . . the result of this aging of the population [will be] to increase medical and welfare costs, to lower the efficiency of the labor force, to reduce technical and economic innovation, and to make life more orderly perhaps but also more somber and boring" (Merton & Nisbet, 1966, p. 407). Although Merton was predicting specific possible outcomes of population aging (the prediction about life being more somber and boring is interesting!), there is no alarm bell sounding a coming social and economic crisis. Fast-forward to the present. The aging of the population is frequently framed as a catastrophic social problem—a "gray tsunami"—that will bring down the functioning of governments, overwhelm the federal budget, diminish the capacity of countries to be economically viable, and fuel intergenerational warfare (Broder, 1996; Peterson, 1999; Thurow, 1996; World Bank, 1994).

The labeling of population aging as a social and economic crisis is problematic in two ways. First, population aging data projections provided by various entities are based on assumptions about fertility, mortality, and migration patterns, and such predictions are influenced by complex macro and micro social and economic factors—and, as a result, are often not precise (Gee, 2002). For example, projecting fertility rates, which is an important variable in population aging, is particularly challenging. Since 1945, the number of live births peaked to 4.3 million in 1957 and eventually declined to 3.1 million in 1973; it was not predicted, however, that 2007 would mark the highest number of births ever registered for the United States at 4.31 million (Friedland & Summer, 2005; Hamilton, Martin, & Ventura, 2009). Demographers also use low, middle, and high assumptions about the variables used in their statistical modeling, which can create dramatically different results. For example, the number of persons age 85 and over projected in 2050 varies from 16 million to 24 million, depending on which assumption you use—resulting in a difference of nearly 50% (Friedland & Summer, 2005). Which population estimate is used will also have significant policy implications. The U.S. Census Bureau projects the percentage of persons over the age of 65 in 2030 to be

69.3 million, while the Urban Institute projects the total to be 64.3 million. These figures may not seem too far from each other, but depending on which figure we use, this discrepancy translates into a difference of $76 *billion* in Social Security benefits (Friedland & Summer, 2005). Thus, it is difficult if not unwise to enact social policy changes using predictions made about population demographics 15, 20, or 30 years away. We have to understand that these data are projections that give us important information; however, these data projections should not be the only variable used to guide our social policy planning (Friedland & Summer, 2005).

Second, the interpretation of these data as proof of a coming social "crisis" has been criticized as a means to reconstruct and redefine social problems to fit certain ideological positions (Gee, 2002; Hudson, 2005). The alleged entitlement crisis concerning Social Security and Medicare in the late 1980s was centered more on the question of government responsibility and the level of private sector involvement than on expenditures and deficits (Quadagno, 1989; White, 2002). If you think about it for a moment, the story about the baby boom generation's impact on society is not new. This generation has had an enormous economic impact on the educational system (from classroom space to budgets), the workforce, housing, and health care as it moved from birth to childhood to midlife during the 1940s, 1960s, and on through the 1980s. Early on, the booming number of children was labeled as an economic boom ("Population: Babies Mean Business," 1948) not as a population crisis caused by the birth of too many children.

So what are we to make of the population-aging data? The crisis scenarios contain some elements of truth, to be sure, but are thought to be substantially exaggerated (Castles, 2002; Mullan, 2002). As population aging is not a new social phenomenon, it is believed that governments, even with modest economic growth, will have the capacity to meet the requirements of an aging population (Mullan, 2002; see Box 10.1 for a

BOX 10.1 The Graying of the Federal Budget

Much of the debate surrounding the scope of aging social policies is about the graying of the federal budget—meaning that programs for older adults such as Social Security and Medicare consume a disproportionate share of the federal budget. Friedland and Summer (2005), in their seminal work called *Demography Is Not Destiny, Revisited*, provided an interesting example of how the question about how much is too much to spend on aging social policies can be framed.

Public policy debates tend to be about what we value, yet most debates eventually narrow to the question of what we can afford. Except at the extremes, it is not easy to answer this question. We can't afford to spend all our national income on government enterprises. To do so may entail a diminished standard of living; but how much spending is too much? On the other hand, if none of our national income is spent on government programs, we may endanger future standards of living. But how much is necessary? Given a national income of more than $10 trillion, the range between not spending enough and spending too much is enormous.

At present, about $3.0 trillion of national income is collected through taxes and slightly more than $3.2 trillion is spent annually through government activities, resulting in an annual deficit of

(Continued)

(Continued)

about $200 billion. Clearly, as suggested by the cut in income tax rates in 2001 and 2002, many argue that we are spending too much. Others, however, might disagree because the cut in taxes was not met with an equal cut in expenditures. In fact, expenditures have increased, resulting in an increase in deficit spending.

On September 24, 2003, Secretary Rumsfeld appeared before the Senate Committee on Appropriations to testify on the president's emergency supplemental budget request for $87 billion for post-military operations in Afghanistan and Iraq. In his prepared remarks, Secretary Rumsfeld posed a rhetorical question: "Is $87 billion a great deal of money? Yes. But can we afford it? Without question." His point was that this request was of such high value that the money was not an issue. This request was "the price of freedom." Funding this request would send a clear "message to terrorists that we are willing to spend what it takes."

We were able to "afford" the $87 billion because it was important. Is $87 billion a lot of money? Relative to our national income, it is not. But in government program terms, $87 billion is more than enough money to fund current levels of Head Start for the next 18 years (even adjusting for anticipated inflation). Alternatively, $87 billion is enough money to finance Medicaid's current coverage of home- and community-based long-term care for the next 5 years. (Friedland & Summer, 2005, p. 77)

discussion about the graying of the federal budget). We must begin to prepare for what the future increase in the older adult population means for our retirement systems, employment policies, lifelong learning, health and long-term care support, geriatric and gerontological training for all professionals, and our communities. But we must recognize that incremental changes to social policy over time will likely be the most effective approach as circumstances change (Friedland & Summer, 2005).

The Eligibility for Aging Social Policy

As discussed in various chapters throughout the book, eligibility for old-age social policy programs is either based on age, need, citizenship, or some combination of all three criteria. Need, or means testing, as a criterion to gain access to social programs, has been in existence for quite some time, and is used in varying degrees in many countries' social welfare programs and is used extensively in the United States. Using need as a criterion for eligibility targets only those in greatest need who are at the lowest end of the socioeconomic spectrum and thus keeps expenditures on social programs to a minimum (Hill, 2006). Need-based programs have attached to them the social stigma of "being on welfare," and as a result, large numbers of eligible individuals do not apply for benefits (Walker, 2005). Moreover, the existence and funding of these programs are continually targeted for reduction or elimination as the beneficiaries of these programs are some of the least politically powerful groups.

Using age as criterion for program eligibility is a fairly recent social policy phenomenon in the United States. The development of old-age social policy in the period between 1935 and the 1960s was linked to the belief among the general population that age was a legitimate eligibility criterion, as older adults were viewed as frail, poor, and deserving of the newly created social policies, such as Social Security and Medicare (Hudson, 2005). These programs, along with those funded under the Older Americans Act, were seen by policymakers as legitimate and necessary to address the substandard social, medical, and economic status of older adults (Lubomudrov, 1987). This compassionate view helped categorize older adults as "deserving" of age-based rather than need-based aging social policy programs. Indeed, programs such as Social Security were very successful in improving the economic well-being of older adults. For example, the poverty rate of older adults in 1960 was 35% (Clark, Burkhauser, Moon, Quinn, & Smeeding, 2004) and has since dropped to 9.5% in 2007 (U.S. Bureau of the Census, 2010).

The public's perception of older adults changed dramatically in the decade between the mid-1980s and mid-1990s. Fueled by federal budget challenges, the Reagan administration's goal of reducing government spending on social programs, the projected imbalance of Social Security's revenue and expense budget, and the overall improvement of the economic and health status of older adults, the older generation was now cast as healthy adults "on the go" who were economically well-off and a greedy generation concerned only about their own well-being (Gibbs, 1988; Salholz, 1990). Older adults were now seen as taking resources away from other deserving groups, such as children. Thus, the age-based programs that were so successful in improving the quality of life of older adults now caused them to be used as a scapegoat for federal budget woes, and they were now considered to be a "social problem" (Estes, 1979). As Binstock (1983) observed, "the shrinking of [federal] resources [was] accompanied by a shrinking of compassion" (p. 136). Ironically, the efforts by gerontologists and social scientists to reverse the negative images of aging and older adults has likely inadvertently contributed to obscuring the realities and difficulties of aging (Settersten, 2007) and sent the message that older adults are doing very well, thank you very much.

As we alluded to above, using age or any other social category as a basis for public policy creation and program eligibility facilitates the labeling of groups as either deserving or undeserving. It also makes it necessary for advocates of various social groups (e.g., older adults, children, veterans, persons with disabilities) to continually work to shape the public and political perceptions of their group's deservedness over others' in order to gain a greater slice of the resource pie. Moreover, social welfare programs that have been enacted often target only single issues such as hunger or poverty and are means tested to reach only the poorest among the population. Programs such as the Supplemental Nutrition Assistance Program (food for the poor) and Supplemental Security Income are examples.

In spite of these unintended negative consequences of age-based social policies, Hudson (2005) suggests that age-based features in programs such as Social Security and Medicare have positive outcomes and support the values of dignity, social solidarity, and social justice. Estes (1979, 2001) takes a different perspective by pointing out that age-based policies and programs, such as the Older Americans Act, in reality do nothing to address the existing social structures that cause disparities such as poverty in later life. Age-based programs such as the Older Americans Act give the perception to the public that the needs of older adults have been addressed. We now turn to another type of eligibility—those that are universal in nature and are aimed at addressing social problems that affect all citizens.

Universalistic Approach

The age versus need debate exists in part because the United States lacks a comprehensive national social welfare policy (Quadagno, 1989) and has instead, as we discussed above, adopted a social welfare strategy that enacts legislation incrementally and targets certain segments of the population. The exception of course is the one universal social insurance program—Social Security—that has almost universal participation. As this book goes to press, President Obama just signed the new Patient Protection and Medical Care Act (2010), which marks the second major universal social policy enacted in the United States.

A universalistic approach is one in which social policies are aimed at addressing social problems as they affect society at large and one that provides a social insurance of sorts against risks across all stages of the life course. It emphasizes the collective responsibility of society to manage the risks of economic or health misfortunes that some in our society experience at any given time and threaten all of us over the course of a lifetime (Shactman & Altman, 2002). It changes the political discourse from what *we* (the affluent) should do for *them* (the impoverished) to an "us-us" perspective (Marmor & Mashaw, 2002). A universal framework promotes mutual responsibility between generations and a sense of reciprocity across the life course (Estes, 2001).

The lack of a more universal approach to social welfare in the United States reflects underlying ideologies of individualism, self-reliance, and that families, not government, are primarily responsible for the well-being of their members. As Hudson (2005) so aptly states, one ideological issue at the core of all aging social policy responses is the debate over the "locus of responsibility" for the care of our aged population. The question revolves around the balance among the roles of the public sector, the private sector, and individuals and families in securing the well-being of older adults. As we have seen in the various chapters in this book, other countries have a more universal or social insurance approach to social welfare. Citizenship conveys a social contract between individuals and governments for certain social and health benefits, and the access to these programs is nearly universal. To understand the difference between a need-based and a universal approach, consider our review of community services for older adults and their caregivers in Chapter 9. In Sweden and England, older adults have universal access to an assessment of their needs. Once need is assessed, some measure of the support service is provided at no or low cost based on ability to pay. In the United States, access to such services is means tested, which is the first step in gaining access to available services; those who do not qualify must turn to the private sector and pay out of pocket for needed services. Defining eligibility within various aging social policies and whether the United States will move toward a more universal approach is an issue that will continue to evolve and inspire debate.

Policy Challenges

Each of the topics we covered in this book comes with policy challenges and issues that will need to be considered in the coming years. Of particular interest in policy debates are retirement income policies. As we discussed in Chapter 3, countries vary markedly in their approach to providing retirement income, and as a result, the range of preretirement wage replacement rates varies as well. Retirement income policies in many countries have indeed been successful at alleviating financial vulnerabilities, as the percentage of older adults below 50% of median income is below 12% in most major industrial countries, with the exception of the United States, Australia, and Norway (Friedland & Summer, 2005). The main policy question revolves around how to stabilize funding so retirement program fund balances can weather the economic ups and downs and also prepare for increasing numbers of older adults who will be accessing their benefits.

Policymakers will continue to consider altering elements of retirement policies in many ways, such as raising the retirement age, cutting back on benefit amounts, and restructuring current funding structures and investment strategies to ensure fiscal stability. While all these potential changes are politically difficult for all countries, the debate in the United States will most likely continue to revolve around privatizing Social Security. The debate that began in earnest during the 1980s and 1990s has retreated a bit as the financial return on contributions into private retirement benefit programs, which are based primarily on the returns on investments in the stock and other markets, plummeted with the dot-com bust in the early 2000s and again with the Great Recession of 2009. Thus, the prospect of risking a significant portion of their retirement benefit in the private sector market has been seen as less palatable by much of the public, and the call for privatizing Social Security has, as of now, diminished—but it is certain to resurface.

Related to retirement income policies are the employment polices affecting older adults. Governments have begun to acknowledge that early and mandatory retirement policies drain both knowledge and experience from the workforce and create pressure for pension systems (Feinsod, Arthurs, & Charman, 2007). Policies are needed that promote a discrimination-free workplace for both recruitment and employment of older workers, lifelong learning opportunities, age-friendly work environments with work-schedule flexibility, job sharing and phased retirement plans, and the elimination of pension provisions that penalize employees for working beyond retirement age.

Along with retirement income, health care policy continues to be at the forefront of aging social policy discussions across the globe. Countries, both developed and developing, are at different stages of health care policy, although most major industrialized countries have enacted health systems that are universal and accessible to all their citizens. The United States' story of health care policy will now be rewritten with the passage of the Patient Protection and Medical Care Act (2010), which will expand access to health care in some fashion to all Americans. Regardless of the differences in health care policies across the globe, there are some common issues that should be considered in the arena of health care policy. Clearly, good health is fundamental to ensuring quality of life for individuals and families. Social policies are needed that support health promotion and disease prevention throughout all stages of life (Barratt, 2007). Our policies must reflect the notion that the benefits of good health and physical activity can be enjoyed even among the oldest-old. There must also be an intentional shift in our health systems to improve the delivery of care for chronic as well as the acute care needs of older adults, which is an important element of providing a more holistic approach to health and well-being. Health care systems, characterized by fragmented and uncoordinated care, must evolve to a more holistic approach that includes assessing and coordinating all of an individual's health needs—mental health, nutritional health, physical activity, and preventative health and acute, chronic, and long-term care needs (Kalache & Kickbusch, 1997). Of course the greatest challenge to all health care policies is to simultaneously balance cost, access, and quality and to eliminate the causes of health care inequalities experienced by certain subpopulations, including older women and minority and rural elders.

Mental health, an important component of overall health and wellness, faces numerous policy challenges, as the number of older adults with mental health needs such as dementia and depression will most certainly increase exponentially. Future aging policy must address the lack of quality and quantity of mental health services for older adults (Kermis, 1987) as well as the factors that cause the underutilization of the mental health services that do exist.

Housing needs of older adults will also be a significant policy issue in the coming years (McCarthy & Kim, 2005; Pynoos & Nishita, 2005). In the United States and elsewhere, the primary policy challenges will be to provide the necessary support for older adults to age in place, which includes funding programs for homes to be adapted for frail elders, funding for maintenance of older homes of low-income elders, and connecting elderly homeowners to necessary community-based and health care services (Wardrip, 2010). In addition, an expansion of affordable senior rental housing options for low-income older adults and for individuals requiring assisted living and long-term care options will be needed to meet the diverse housing needs of current and future elderly adults.

As we discussed in Chapter 9, families across the globe play the primary role of carer for older adults, and the demands on caregivers will continue to increase as the number of oldest-old increases over the next 20 to 30 years. Clearly, it is in the best interests of governments to view families as partners in providing assistance to their older adult family members and to address carers' economic, physical, and mental well-being (Levine, 2008). While some countries such as England and Sweden have begun to include carers in enacted social policy, other countries must follow their lead and provide caregiver assessments to determine needed support. Policies should also consider financial support to carers by way of tax credits, carer benefits, and credit toward state pensions while carers are out of paid employment to provide caregiving activities. Other policies must work to enhance workplace flexibility to better balance job and caregiver demands (Lamura et al., 2008).

Community-based carer support programs such as low-cost respite and day and night in-home help options are a part of a larger array of community-based services that exist to promote the health and social well-being of older adults. The policy challenge here is to determine the mix of universal and targeted community-based programs that serve to keep older adults active and engaged members of society. The United States has a more coordinated approach compared with other countries because of the existence of the Older Americans Act, which authorizes local Area Agencies on Aging to act as the coordinating body for the planning and implementation of community-based services. Although funding for Older Americans Act programs is inadequate relative to the number of older adults in the United States, meal programs, respite care, senior centers, transportation, information and referral/ assistance, and legal services do exist in communities large and small across the country. The World Health Organization's Age-Friendly Cities Programme signals a new approach that takes a macrolevel view of how structures and services can be accessible to and inclusive of older adults and their needs and encourages active ageing by "optimizing opportunities for health, participation, and security in order to enhance quality of life as people age" (WHO, 2007, p. 1). Age-friendly cities are characterized by transportation, housing, social participation, respect and inclusion, civic participation and employment, communication and information, community support and health services, and outdoor spaces that are inclusive of older adults.

In closing, we have tried throughout the book, through the interviews and photos, to remind our readers about the impact that social policies have on the daily lives of individual older adults. We also hope that you were able to use our case study of Luciana (introduced in Chapter 1) to understand how her daily life would be markedly different depending on where she resided. When considering the person-policy link, one must also be cognizant of the differential impact that policies may have on socially disadvantaged groups such as minority older adults, older women, and rural elders. For example, in the United States, Social Security benefits are tied to work histories and do not accommodate the social circumstances that minorities or women experience over the life course that cause interrupted work histories. Compensations for the issue of interrupted work histories are provided in other countries' retirement income policies that offer some portion of retirement income based on citizenship or provide credits to caregivers for the time they exit the workforce to care for their elderly parents or children.

While decades have passed since many of the aging social policies we discussed were put in place, there have been and will continue to be many heated debates over either dismantling or expanding these programs as different political parties with different ideologies gain and relinquish political power. Although we are challenged with the task of anticipating the needs of an aging population, we believe that, collectively, we have the ability to adjust and adapt. We must continue to seek the answer to the question "Who will care for our aged?" in a way that supports the dignity and well-being of our elders.

Aging social policy is constantly in motion. We hope after reading this book that you will stay tuned and stay engaged in what is happening in the arena of aging social policy. The ways in which our social policies are constructed characterize who we are as a nation, and define how we care for one another and, ultimately, how we care for ourselves.

Ms. L., age 60
Paris, France

My family originated in the Bordeaux area. I was born in 1945 at the end of the war in the free zone. I was married in 1966 but was later divorced. I have one son and three grandchildren, and they live very far from here in the South of France. I remarried in 1976, and my husband died in 1990.

My history is that I was born in a small apartment by a midwife, and my mother sent me to a family who took care of me for my whole life as their own daughter, sent me to school and to the university. My mother, the lady who took care of me, had a restaurant and bar in the country, a low-level bistro; my father was a very poor man and worked on a property, a farm, and took care of the whole property and started working when he was age 12. We were very poor people, but we were very happy people. I went to boarding school, to high school, and then to the university. I was going to be a teacher but decided to leave the university because I couldn't see myself in a classroom all day long. I applied and was accepted into another school for tourism, to learn to be an interpreter. But I let all that go when I got married in 1966 and let go of the idea of traveling around the world. I took the first job I could find, and I was a reservation agent, but I left and found another job where I wrote itineraries for travel companies, gave practical information for travelers for the sellers of tours to use. I have worked in various capacities in the tourism industry, in publicity, marketing, advertising, and planning, and as a manager of a travel company.

Then in 1998, when I was 52, the company I worked for made me redundant [made to retire]. Voilà, it was very hard, I tried to find work, and I never found any other work, as I was too old on the French market. I sent thousands of letters and no, nothing, I was too old, too experienced. I would have accepted a lower wage, but no one answered me; I had not even one interview.

When my second husband passed away, he left me money, so that was helpful. In France, there is a system of retirement, like an indemnity, so I was paid 60% of my retirement for 4 years, because I was made redundant before I reached age 58. Now I get money from my husband's pension until I die. My finances, overall, is considered to be too high, so I receive the minimum pension from the government. I am lucky. I have my own flat paid, but many people aren't so lucky. The very poor can get around €300 a month, which is not much. Many people lose their jobs around 50 or 55 and have a difficult time financially. Twenty years ago, it was impossible for a manager to fire people without any reason, but now it is totally different; people, older people, can be laid off for no reason.

A typical day for me? I stay busy every day. I sing in the chorale, I ride my motorbike, I am planning to go on a trip; my life is very free. I love love, if you know what I mean; it is very positive. My health is good, and my annual tests have come back good. I watch what I eat and have plenty of activity, and I have lots of friends. I bike, do gymnastics 1 hour most every day, hiking and swimming. I swim at least 1 hour in the morning. I like dancing and singing and riding my motorbike. I have been learning ceramics. I clean the house, do some laundry, check my e-mail and my accounts. My life is filled with wonderful relationships.

For health care in France? In France, we have now the green Carte Vitale, which is a kind of payment card for the electronic system that is connected to the Security Sociale, which refunds the doctor. You pay with the Carte Vitale, and then the Security Sociale and private insurance, if you have it, reimburses you. So the Security Sociale pays between 40% and 65% of your medical care, depending on what kind of care you need. I pay for a complementary private health assistance, which is €100 a month. For example, my hearing aid broke and it cost me €299.20 to fix. I got €9.42 from Security Sociale and €37 from my additional insurance coverage; so it cost me €252 to repair my hearing aid. If I don't have any money to pay, I don't hear. But for a visit to the specialist, it is different. My visit cost €30, Security Sociale reimbursed me €14, and my complementary insurance reimbursed me €15; so I lose €1 on each visit.

For the future? The only thing I worry about is health, is Alzheimer 's disease. We all die, and I am not afraid of that, but I am concerned about losing my health and losing my freedom. I want to be able to read, see friends, to travel. If you are in bad physical shape, you can't do anything. I have one bad eye and one bad ear, so I think about what would happen if I would lose my sight or my hearing. My mother had Alzheimer's, and she had so many people around her, my sister, me and my husband at the time, her husband, grandchildren—people around her to care for her. What should I do? I am alone. . . . If that would happen to me, I know my son wouldn't take care of me. I would have to pay for all of my care; nothing would be available, and I would have to pay for everything. I would not receive any help, any pay from the government. But if I had nothing, my son would be obligated by law to take care of me, . . . but I hope that I don't become financially ruined. . . . It won't likely to happen I guess as long as I have my pension.

How do I feel about growing older? I am not always looking in the mirror every day, . . . but it is not comfortable, because you can't do things the way you used to do. BUT BUT as far as *being older,* it's not that bad! I am feeling alright with my age. I hope that if you come in 10 years, you will find that I am still in the same physical shape and still seducing lovers! Growing older is two sides for me—you don't have to care about your future, you don't have to care about what you have done. . . . It is finished. It is over. . . . The pressure is gone. I think I am wiser today than I was. I feel better. I feel peace, much more peaceful now than when I was 20 or 30. When you are younger, you are challenged all the time, . . . pressured, . . . trying to be a good parent, trying to be a good wife, finding a job. But now I just have to take care of me. . . . It is comfortable to be out of the competition, the pressure. But growing older, the physical part is the difficult. Maybe because it is because I love to make love, and I think all of that is about to finish. How do I find a man? It is difficult when you get older, it is difficult to find a man at my age as everyone is in a couple. But I am in a good place mentally.

When I look forward to the future, I have everything I want, I am comfortable in life. I am curious, I travel. I am always active. What am I looking forward to? Certainly nothing depending on money from the material point of view . . . but to be comfortable emotionally, feel well, feel happy, feel that I exist as a woman; this is very important to me.

References

AARP. (2009). *About AARP.* Retrieved April 12, 2009, from http://www.aarp.org/about-aarp/

AARP. (2010). *About PPI.* Retrieved April 26, 2010, from http://www.aarp.org/research/ppi/about_ppi/

Administration on Aging. (2006). *Highlights from the pilot study: Second national survey of Older Americans Act Title III service recipients conducted during 2004.* Retrieved January 9, 2010, from http://www.gpra.net/nationalsurvey/files/2ndhighlights.pdf

Administration on Aging. (2008a). *Compendium of active grants fiscal year 2008 under Title IV of the Older Americans Act.* Retrieved April 3, 2010, from http://www.aoa.gov/AoARoot/Grants/Compendium/docs/compendium-2008.pdf

Administration on Aging. (2008b). *Investments in change: Enhancing the health and independence of older adults.* Retrieved April 14, 2010, from http://www.aoa.gov/AoARoot/Program_Results/docs/2008/AOA_2008AnnualReport.pdf

Administration on Aging. (2008c). *Justification of estimates for appropriations committees.* Washington, DC: Author. Retrieved from http://www.aoa.gov/AoARoot/Program_Results/docs/2009/FinalAoAFY2009CongressionalJustification01282008.pdf

Administration on Aging. (2009a). *2007 U.S. profile of OAA programs.* Retrieved January 12, 2010, from http://www.aoa.gov/AoARoot/Program_Results/SPR/2007/Profiles/us.pdf

Administration on Aging. (2009b). *Nutrition evaluations report: Program funding, costs, and efficiency.* Retrieved December 29, 2009, from http://www.aoa.gov/AoARoot/Program_results/Nutrition_Report/er_vol1ch5b.aspx

Administration on Aging. (2009c). *Nutrition services (OAA Title IIIC).* Retrieved April 18, 2010, from http://www.aoa.gov/AoARoot/AoA_Programs/HCLTC/Nutrition_Services/index.aspx

Administration on Aging. (2009d). *Older Americans Act.* Retrieved April 18, 2010, from http://www.aoa.gov/AOARoot/AoA_Programs/OAA/oaa.aspx#t4

Administration on Aging. (2009e). *A profile of older Americans: 2009.* Retrieved February 1, 2010, from http://www.aoa.gov/AoAroot/Aging_Statistics/Profile/2009/docs/2009profile_508.pdf

Administration on Aging. (2009f). *Table 4b. Clusters 3: Service units provided for selected services under Title III of OAA.* Retrieved December 30, 2009, from http://www.aoa.gov/AoARoot/Program_Results/SPR/2007/Tables/table4b.pdf

Administration on Aging. (2009g). *Table 6a. Title III service expenditures for selected services.* Retrieved December 30, 2009, from http://www.aoa.gov/AoARoot/Program_Results/SPR/2007/Tables/table6a.pdf

Administration on Aging. (2009h). *Table 10: Focal points and senior centers.* Retrieved December 30, 2009, from http://www.aoa.gov/AoARoot/Program_Results/SPR/2008/Index.aspx

Administration on Aging. (2010a). *Civic engagement initiative.* Retrieved March 14, 2010 from http://www.aoa.gov/aoaroot/aoa_programs/special_projects/civic_engagement/index.aspx

Administration on Aging. (2010b). *Historical evolution of programs for older Americans.* Retrieved August 13, 2010, from http://www.aoa.gov/aoaroot/aoa_programs/oaa/resources/history.aspx

Administration on Aging. (2010c). *National family caregiver support program (OAA Title IIIE).* Retrieved April 18, 2010, from http://www.aoa.gov/AoARoot/AoA_Programs/HCLTC/Caregiver/index.aspx

Administration on Aging. (2010d). *National Legal Resource Center.* Retrieved January 17, 2010, from http://www.aoa.gov/AoARoot/AoA_Programs/Elder_Rights/Legal/national_legal.aspx

Administration on Aging. (2010e). *Nutrition services (OAA Title IIIC).* Retrieved April 18, 2010, from http://www.aoa.gov/AoARoot/AoA_Programs/HCLTC/Nutrition_Services/index.aspx

Administration on Aging (2010f). *Older Americans Act.* Retrieved April 18, 2010, from http://www.aoa.gov/AOARoot/AoA_Programs/OAA/oaa.aspx#t4

Age Concern. (2007). *Improving services and support for older people with mental health problems: The second report from the U.K. inquiry into mental health and well-being in later life.* London: Age Concern Policy Unit. Retrieved from http://its-services.org.uk/silo/files/inquiry-full-report.pdf

Age Concern. (2009). *Public transport and concessions.* London. Retrieved from http://www.ageconcernliverpool.org.uk/uploads/documents/Fact%20Sheets%202010/may/FS26%20PublicTransportConcessions%20Nov%202009%20-%20AM062.pdf

Age Concern. (2010a). *Fit as a fiddle.* Retrieved March 1, 2010, from http://www.ageconcernle-ics.com/fiddle/

Age Concern. (2010b). *Resource centres: Activities for older people in Camden.* Retrieved March 16, 2010, from http://www.ageconcerncamden.org.uk/documents/resource_centres%20leaflet.pdf

Ageing Research Online. (2006). Ageing research online news. *Ageing Research Online News, 3.* Retrieved from http://www.aro.gov.au

Aging and Disability Resource Center. (2008). *Aging and Disability Resource Center successes 2008.* Retrieved April 23, 2009, from http://www.ct.gov/longtermcare/lib/longtermcare/adrcsuccesses08.pdf

Allen, S., Chapman, Y., O'Connor, M., & Francis, K. (2008). The evolution of palliative care and the relevance to residential aged care: Understanding the past to inform the future. *Collegian, 15,* 165–171.

Allen, S. G., Clark, R. L., & McDermed, A. A. (1993). *Post-retirement increases in pensions in the 1980s: Did plan finances matter?* Cambridge, MA: National Bureau of Economic Research.

Alliance for Health and the Future. (2005). *Promoting age equality in the delivery of health care. Issue Brief, 2*(3). New York: International Longevity Center. Retrieved from http://www.ilcusa.org/media/pdfs/Promoting%20Age%20Equality.pdf

Altenstetter, C., & Busse, R. (2005). Health care reform in Germany: Patchwork change within established governance structures. *Journal of Health Politics, Policy, and Law, 30,* 121–142.

Alzheimer Territoriale Provincia di Biella. (2009). *The day centre.* Retrieved April 16, 2009, from http://www.aimabiella.it/

Alzheimer's Association of Sweden. (2009). *Alzheimer's Association of Sweden.* Retrieved October 1, 2009, from http://www.alzheimerforeningen.se/

Alzheimer's Disease International. (2008). *The prevalence of dementia worldwide.* Retrieved from http://www.alz.co.uk/adi/pdf/prevalence.pdf

American Society on Aging. (2010). *ASA's Civic Engagement Program.* Retrieved March 14, 2010, from http://www.asaging.org/asav2/civiceng/index.cfm

Americans With Disabilities Act of 1990, P. L. No. 101-336, § 2, 104 Stat. 328 (1991). Retrieved from http://www.ada.gov/archive/adastat91.htm

Australian Bureau of Statistics. (2007). *National survey of mental health and wellbeing: Summary of results* (Report No. 4326.0). Retrieved from http://www.ausstats.abs.gov.au/Ausstats/subscriber.nsf/0/6AE6DA447F985FC2CA2574EA00122BD6/$File/43260_2007.pdf

Australian Government. (2008). *National advisory council on mental health.* Retrieved from http://www.health.gov.au/internet/mentalhealth/publishing.nsf/Content/National+Advisory+Council+on+Mental+Health

Australian Government National Health and Medical Council. (2006). *Guidelines for a palliative approach in residential aged care.* Retrieved from http://www.nhmrc.gov.au/_files_nhmrc/file/publications/synopses/pc29.pdf

Australian Health Ministers. (2000). *Mental health: Statement of rights and responsibilities.* Canberra: Australian Government Publishing Service.

Australian Health Ministers' Conference. (2006). *National framework for action on dementia 2006–2010.* Retrieved from http://www.health.gov.au/internet/main/publishing.nsf/Content/D64BD892C6FDD167CA2572180007E717/$File/nfad.pdf

Australian Institute of Health and Welfare. (2006). *Residential aged care in Australia 2004–05: A statistical overview* (Aged Care Statistics Series No. 22; AIHW Cat. No. AGE 45). Canberra: Author.

Barratt, J. (2007, February). *Major development and trends in creating enabling environments for older persons* (Briefing Paper prepared for AARP and United Nations Programme on Ageing/DESA Briefing Series on Major Developments and Trends in Global Aging United Nations, New York). Retrieved from http://www.agingsociety.org/agingsociety/links/enabenvt.pdf

Bartels, S. J., Coakley, E. H., Zubritsky, C., Ware, J. H., Miles, K. M., Areán, P. A., et al. (2004). Improving access to geriatric mental health services: A randomized trial comparing treatment engagement with integrated versus enhanced referral care for depression, anxiety, and at-risk alcohol use. *American Journal of Psychiatry, 161,* 1455–1462.

Bath & North East Somerset Council. (2009). *Community meals.* Retrieved from http://www.bathnes.gov.uk/SiteCollectionDocuments/Health%20and%20Social%20Care/Community%20Meals.pdf

BBC News. (2010, February 15). *Nicolas Sarkozy to introduce French pension reforms.* Retrieved from http://news.bbc.co.uk/2/hi/8515947.stm

Berg, J., Ernst, C., & Auer, P. (2006). *Meeting the employment challenge: Argentina, Brazil, and Mexico in the global economy.* Boulder, CO: Lynne Rienner.

Berleen, G. (2004). *A healthier elderly population in Sweden.* National Institute of Public Health. Retrieved from http://www.fhi.se/PageFiles/3172/healthierelderly0403%281%29.pdf

Bettio, F., Mazzotta, F., & Solinas, G. (2007). *Costs and prospects for home-based long-term care in Northern Italy: The Galca survey.* Università degli Studi di Salerno, Centro di Economia del Lavoro e di Politica Economica. Retrieved from http://www.unisa.it//download/75_359_2058059707_103_dp.pdf

Binstock, R. H. (1983). The aged as scapegoat: The Donald P. Kent memorial lecture. *Gerontologist, 23*(2), 136–142.

Binstock, R. H. (2005). The contemporary politics of old age policies. In R. B. Hudson (Ed.), *The new politics of old age policy.* Baltimore, MD: Johns Hopkins University Press.

Birkland, T. A. (2001). *An introduction to the policy process: Theories, concepts, and models of public policymaking.* Armonk, NY: M. E. Sharpe.

Blackman, T., Brodhurst, S., & Convery, J. (2001). *Social care and social exclusion: A comparative study of older people's care in Europe.* London: Palgrave Macmillan.

Bloch, P. (2006). Diversity and labor law in France. *Vermont Law Review, 30,* 717–747.

Boeri, T., & Brugiavini, A. (2008). *Pension reforms and women retirement plans.* Retrieved from http://ftp.iza.org/dp3821.pdf

Bradshaw, J. R. (1972). The concept of social need. *New Society, 496,* 640–643.

Bright, K. (2005). *Section 202 supportive housing for the elderly.* AARP Public Policy Institute. Retrieved from http://assets.aarp.org/rgcenter/il/fs65r_housing.pdf

Broder, D. (1996, August 11). The party's over: By 2000, the GOP or the Democrats could fade in favor of a third party. *Washington Post*, p. C1.

Brodhurst, S., & Glendinning, C. (2001). The United Kingdom. In T. Blackman, S. Brodhurst, & J. Convery (Eds.), *Social care and social exclusion: A comparative study of older people's care in Europe* (pp. 68–82). New York: Palgrave.

Bruen, B. K., Wiener, J. M., & Thomas, S. (2003). *Medicaid eligibility policy for aged, blind, and disabled beneficiaries.* Washington, DC: AARP Public Policy Institute. Retrieved from http://assets.aarp.org/rgcenter/health/2003_14_abd.pdf

Bruin, S. R. De, Oosting, S. J., Kuin, Y., Hoefnagels, E. C. M., Blauw, Y. H., Groot, L. C. P. G. M. De, et al. (2009). Green care farms promote activity among elderly people with dementia. *Journal of Housing for the Elderly, 23,* 368–389.

Bundesministerium für Gesundheit. (2009). *Health care system and health care reform in Germany.* Retrieved from http://www.bmg.bund.de/cln_178/nn_1493790/EN/Gesundheit/gesundheit__node.html?__nnn=true

Bureau of Labor Statistics and International Labor Office. (2009). *Labor force participation rates by age, 2007.* Retrieved from http://www.bls.gov/spotlight/2008/older_workers/

Burgermeister, J. (2003). Germany reaches controversial deal of healthcare reform. *British Journal of Medicine, 327,* 250.

Burwell, B., Sredl, K., & Eiken, S. (2007). *Medicaid long-term care expenditures in FY 2006.* Retrieved from http://www.hcbs.org/files/120/5958/memo.pdf

Campbell, A. L. (2003). *How policies make citizens: Senior political activism and the American welfare state.* Princeton, NJ: Princeton University Press.

Canadian Alliance on Mental Illness and Mental Health. (2006). *Framework for action on mental illness and mental health.* Retrieved from http://www.cmha.ca/data/1/rec_docs/601_CAMIMH%20English%20Lowres.pdf

Canadian Coalition for Seniors' Mental Health. (2008). *History.* Retrieved from http://www.ccsmh.ca/en/about/history.cfm

Canadian Hospice Palliative Care Association. (2009). *About us.* Retrieved from http://www.chpca.net/about_us/history.html; http://www.hc-sc.gc.ca/hcs-sss/palliat/support-soutien/chronolog-eng.php

Canadian Mental Health Association. (2009a). *Canadian Mental Health Commission.* Retrieved from http://www.cmha.ca/bins/content_page.asp?cid=5-916-919-928

Canadian Mental Health Association. (2009b). *Strategic plan: Executive summary 2007–2010.* Retrieved from http://www.ontario.cmha.ca/

Canadian Mental Health Commission. (2006). *Out of the shadows at last: Transforming mental health, mental illness, and addiction services in Canada.* Retrieved from http://www.parl.gc.ca/39/1/parlbus/commbus/senate/Com-e/SOCI-E/rep-e/rep02may06-e.htm

Capretta, J. C. (2007a). *Global aging and the sustainability of public pension systems: An assessment of reform efforts in twelve developed countries: A report of the Aging Vulnerability Index Project.* Washington, DC: Center for Strategic and International Studies, Library of Congress.

Capretta, J. C. (2007b). *Long-term care insurance partnerships: New choices for consumers: Potential savings for federal and state government.* AHIP Center for Policy and Research. Retrieved from http://www.civicenterprises.net/pdfs/policysample-ahip.pdf

Care Services Improvement Partnership. (2005). *Everybody's business.* Retrieved from http://kc.csip.org.uk/upload/everybodysbusiness.pdf

Care Services Improvement Partnership, West Midlands. (2006). *The mental health and well-being of Black and minority ethnic elders: A foundational report on the research literature and a mapping of national resources.* Retrieved from http://its-services.org.uk/silo/files/bme-elders-final-report.pdf

Carers (Equal Opportunities) Act, Chapter 15 (2004).

Carers (Recognition and Services) Act, Chapter 12 (1995).

Carers U.K. (2007). *Looking after someone: A guide to carers' rights and benefits 2007/8.* Retrieved October 13, 2009, from http://www.carersuk.org/Newsandcampaigns/CarersRightsDay/Adviceguidesforcarers

Carers U.K. (2010). *Carers U.K.: The voice of carers.* Retrieved from http://www.carersuk.org/Home

Cash and Counseling. (2007). *Program overview.* Retrieved from http://www.cashand counseling.org/about/index_html

Cash and Counseling. (2010). *Participating states.* Retrieved August 31, 2010, from http://www.cashandcounseling.org/about/participating_states

Castles, F. G. (2002). The future of the welfare state: Crisis myths and crisis realities. *International Journal of Health Services, 32*(2), 255.

Cato Institute. (2010). *About Cato.* Retrieved April 27, 2010, from http://www.cato.org/about.php

Center for Addiction and Mental Health. (2005). *Responding to older adults with substance use, mental health, and gambling challenges.* Retrieved from http://www.camh.net/Publications/Resources_for_Professionals/Older_Adults/responding_older_adults.pdf

Center for Medicare Advocacy, Inc. (2009). *Medicare coverage of mental health services* (pp. 1–5). Retrieved from http://medicareadvocacy.org

Centers for Medicare and Medicaid Services. (2005). *Medicaid at-a-glance 2005.* Baltimore, MD: U.S. Department of Health and Human Services. Retrieved from http://www.cms.gov/MedicaidGenInfo/downloads/MedicaidAtAGlance2005.pdf

Centers for Medicare and Medicaid Services. (2008). *Number of Medicare-certified home health agencies and hospices, by state, 2007.* Retrieved April 30, 2009, from http://www.nahc.org/Facts/2007hhas.pdf

Centers for Medicare and Medicaid Services. (2010a). *Medicare and you 2010.* Baltimore, MD: U.S. Department of Health and Human Services. Retrieved from http://www.medicare.gov/publications/pubs/pdf/10050.pdf

Centers for Medicare and Medicaid Services. (2010b). *Money Follows the Person grants.* Retrieved from http://www.cms.hhs.gov/DeficitReductionAct/20_MFP.asp

Chappell, N. (1997). Health care reform: Implications for seniors. *Journal of Aging Studies, 11,* 171–175.

Charman, C., Feinsod, R., & Arthurs, R. (2007). *Profit from experience: Perspectives of employers, workers, and policymakers in the G7 countries on the new demographic realities.* Washington, DC: AARP.

China Daily. (2006). *Chinese still reluctant to place loved ones in hospice.* Retrieved from http://english.peopledaily.com.cn/200604/06/eng20060406_256395.html

Chu, L., & Chi, I. (2008). Nursing homes in China. *Journal of the American Medical Directors Association, 9,* 237–243.

City of Stockholm. (n.d.). *The city of Stockholm's care plan for the elderly, 2007–2011.* Stockholm: Author. Retrieved from http://www.stockholm.se/Global/Stads%C3%B6vergripande%20%C3%A4mnen/St%C3%B6d%20&%20Omsorg/%C3%84ldreomsorg/%C3%84ldreplan_eng.pdf3.pdf

Clark, R. L., Burkhauser, R., Moon, M., Quinn, J., & Smeeding, T. (2004). *The economics of an aging society.* Oxford, UK: Blackwell.

Clawson, R. (2003). *The media portrayal of Social Security and Medicare and its impact on public opinion.* Paper presented at the annual meeting of the American Political Science Association, Philadelphia Marriott Hotel. Retrieved May 26, 2009, from http://www.allacademic.com//meta/p_mla_apa_research_citation/0/6/3/7/7/pages63770/p63770-1.php

Colello, K. J. (2007). *Family caregiving to the older population: Background, federal programs, and issues for Congress.* Washington, DC: Congressional Research Service, Library of Congress.

Retrieved from http://digitalcommons.ilr.cornell.edu/cgi/viewcontent.cgi?article=1327&context=key_workplace

Comas-Herrera, A., Wittenberg, R., Osta-Font, J., Gori, C., Di Maio, A., Patxot, C., et al. (2006). Future long-term care expenditure in Germany, Spain, Italy, and the United Kingdom. *Ageing & Society, 26,* 285–302.

Commonwealth Fund. (2008). *International health policy survey of sicker adults.* Retrieved August 22, 2010, from http://www.commonwealthfund.org/Fellowships/Australian-American-Health-Policy-Fellowships/The-Health-Care-System-and-Health-Policy-in-Australia.aspx

Commonwealth Fund. (2009). *The health care system and health policy in Australia.* New York: Author. Retrieved from http://www.commonwealthfund.org/fellowships/fellowships_show.htm?doc_id=372961

Commonwealth Institute. (2010). *About us.* Retrieved April 27, 2010, from http://www.common wealinstitute.org/about-us

Commonwealth of Australia. (2009). *The national palliative care strategy.* Retrieved from http://www.health.gov.au/internet/main/publishing.nsf/Content/palliativecare-strategy.htm

Contini, B., & Leombruni, R. (2006). From work to retirement: A tale of bumpy routes. *Review of Political Economy, 18,* 359–378.

Cook, M. (2006). Policy changes and the labor force participation of older workers: Evidence from six countries. *Canadian Journal on Aging, 25,* 387–400.

Copeland, C. (2010). *Labor force participation rates: The population age 55 and older, 2008.* Retrieved from http://www.law.cornell.edu/supct/html/98-536.ZS.html

Cornell University Law School Legal Information Institute. (1999). *Olmstead v. L. C. (98-536)527 U.S. 581.* Retrieved from http://www.law.cornell.edu/supct/html/98-536.ZS.html

Corporation for National and Community Service. (2004, December). *State profiles and performance report, program year 2002–2003.* Washington, DC: Office of Research and Policy Development. Retrieved from http://www.nationalservice.gov/pdf/CNCS_Performance_Report_04.pdf

Corporation for National and Community Service. (2009). *Annual financial report.* Washington, DC: Author. Retrieved from http://www.nationalservice.gov/pdf/afr_2009_fullreport.pdf

Costa-Font, J., & Patxot, C. (2005). The design of the long-term care system in Spain: Policy and financial constraints. *Social Policy and Society, 4,* 11–20.

Costa-Font, J., & Rovira-Forns, J. (2008). Who is willing to pay for long-term care insurance in Catalonia? *Health Policy, 86,* 72–84.

Council of the European Union. (2003). *Joint report by the commission and the council on supporting national strategies for the future of health care and care for the elderly.* Brussels: Author. Retrieved from http://ec.europa.eu/employment_social/soc-prot/healthcare/elderly_en.pdf

Cowan, E. (1978). Background and history: The crisis in public finance and social security. In M. J. Boskin & G. F. Break (Eds.), *The crisis in social security: Problems and prospects.* San Francisco: Institute for Contemporary Studies.

Crowley, J. S. (2006). *Medicaid long-term services: Reforms in the Deficit Reduction Act* (#7486). Washington, DC: Kaiser Family Foundation.

Da Piedade Morais, M., & de Oliveira Cruz, B. (2010). Housing demand, tenure choice, and housing policy in Brazil. In S. V. Lall, M. Freire, B. Yuen, R. Rajack, & J. Helluin (Eds.), *Urban land markets: Improving land management for successful urbanization* (pp. 253–282). Netherlands: Springer.

Dal Santo, T. S. (2009). *Senior center literature review: Reflecting and responding to community needs.* Sacramento: California Commission on Aging. http://www.ccoa.ca.gov/res/docs/senior-cntr/Literature_Review.pdf

De Vos, S., & Andrade, F. (2005). Race and independent living among elderly Brazilians since 1980. *Journal of Comparative Family Studies, 36*, 567–581.

Dementia Association. (2009). *About the Dementia Association.* Retrieved from http://www.demensforbundet.se/

Department for Communities and Local Government. (2010). *Welcome to FirstStop!* Retrieved March 19, 2010, from http://www.firststopcareadvice.org.uk/

Department for Transport. (2009). *Guidance on local transport plans.* London: Department for Transport, Great Minster House. Retrieved from http://www.dft.gov.uk/adobepdf/165237/ltp-guidance.pdf

Department for Work and Pensions. (2005). *Opportunity age.* Retrieved March 15, 2010 from http://webarchive.nationalarchives.gov.uk/20100406213018/http://dwp.gov.uk/policy/ageing-society/strategy-and-publications/opportunity-age-first-report/

Department for Work and Pensions. (2009). *Building a society for all ages.* Norwich: Stationery Office. Retrieved from http://www.hmg.gov.uk/media/33830/fullreport.pdf

Department of Health. (1999). *Caring about carers: A national strategy for carers.* HM Government, Secretary of State for Health by Command of Her Majesty. Retrieved from http://www.dh.gov.uk/prod_consum_dh/groups/dh_digitalassets/@dh/@en/documents/digitalasset/dh_4049323.pdf

Department of Health. (2000). *Carers and Disabled Children Act.* Retrieved from http://www.dh.gov.uk/en/Publicationsandstatistics/Publications/PublicationsPolicyAndGuidance/DH_4118023

Department of Health. (2001). *National service framework for older people* (Royal College of General Practitioners Summary Paper 2001/02). Retrieved from http://www.rcgp.org.uk/pdf/ISS_SUMM01_02.pdf

Department of Health. (2006). *Our health, our care, our say: A new direction for community services.* HM Government, Secretary of State for Health by Command of Her Majesty. Retrieved from http://www.dh.gov.uk/prod_consum_dh/groups/dh_digitalassets/@dh/@en/documents/digitalasset/dh_4127459.pdf

Department of Health. (2007). *Mental health: New ways of working for everyone* (Gateway No. 7938). Retrieved from http://www.dh.gov.uk/dr_consum_dh/groups/dh_digitalassets/@dh/@en/documents/digitalasset/dh_074495.pdf

Department of Health. (2009). *Mental Health Act 1983.* Retrieved from http://www.dh.gov.uk/en/Healthcare/Mentalhealth/DH_4001816

Department of Health. (2010). *Intergenerational demonstrator programme: Generations together.* Retrieved February 15, 2010, from www.dh.gov.uk/en/SocialCare/Deliveringadultsocialcare/Olderpeople/DH_097784

Direct.gov.uk. (2009a). *Carer's allowance.* Retrieved October 11, 2009, from http://www.direct.gov.uk/en/CaringForSomeone/MoneyMatters/CarersAllowance/index.htm

Direct.gov.uk. (2009b). *Community nurses and health visitors.* Retrieved November 1, 2009, from http://www.direct.gov.uk/en/DisabledPeople/HealthAndSupport/WhosWhoInHealthServices/DG_4003759

Direct.gov.uk. (2009c). *Financial support.* Retrieved October 11, 2009, from http://www.direct.gov.uk/en/DisabledPeople/FinancialSupport/index.htm

Duckett, S. (2004). *Health care in Australia.* Retrieved from http://www.medhunters.com/articles/healthcareInAustralia.html

Dye, T. R. (1976). *Policy analysis: What governments do, why they do it, and what difference it makes.* Tuscaloosa: University of Alabama Press.

Elderly Mental Health Care Working Group. (2002). *Guidelines for mental health care planning for best practices for health authorities.* British Columbia Ministry of Health Services.

Retrieved from http://www.health.gov.bc.ca/library/publications/year/2002/MHA_elderly_mentalhealth_guidelines.pdf

Employee Benefit Research Institute. (2008). *EBRI databook on employee benefits.* Washington, DC: Author. Retrieved from http://www.ebri.org/publications/books/index.cfm?fa=databook

Employee Benefit Research Institute. (2009). *Fundamentals of employee benefit programs.* Washington, DC: Employee Benefit Research Institute Education and Research Fund.

Employment Relations Act of 1999, Chapter 26.

Estes, C. L. (1979). *The aging enterprise: A critical examination of social policies and services for the aged.* San Francisco: Jossey-Bass.

Estes, C. L. (1993). The aging enterprise revisited. *Gerontologist, 33*(3), 292–298.

Estes, C. L. (2001). Crisis, the welfare state, and aging: Ideology and agency in the Social Security privatization debate. In C. L. Estes & Associates (Eds.), *Social policy and aging: A critical perspective* (pp. 95–118). Thousand Oaks, CA: Sage.

European Commission. (2007). *Employment in Europe 2007.* Belgium: Author.

European Policy Information Research for Mental Disorders Consortium. (2008). *European Policy Information Research for Mental Disorders: Final report.* Retrieved from http://www.epremed.org/

Eurostat. (2010). *Average exit age from the labour force by gender.* European Commission. Retrieved from http://epp.eurostat.ec.europa.eu/portal/page/portal/structural_indicators/indicators/employment

Experience Works. (2009). *What we do.* Retrieved from http://www.experienceworks.org/site/PageServer?pagename=WhatWeDo_Main#leadership

Exter, A., Hermans, H., Dosljak, M., & Busse, R. (2004). *Health care systems in transition: Netherlands.* Copenhagen: WHO Regional Office for Europe on behalf of the European Observatory on Health Systems and Policies. Retrieved from http://www.euro.who.int/document/e84949.pdf

Family Medical Leave Act of 1993, 5 U.S.C. § 6381 *et seq.,* 29 U.S.C. §§ 2601 *et seq.,* 2631 *et seq.* (1993).

Federal Ministry of Health. (2009). *Long-term care insurance.* Retrieved from http://www.bmg.bund.de/cln_178/SharedDocs/Downloads/DE/Standardartikel/P/Glossar-Pflegeversicherung/Long-term-care-insurance,templateId=raw,property=publicationFile.pdf/Long-term-care-insurance.pdf

Feeding America. (2010). *About us.* Retrieved on March 13, 2010, from http://feedingamerica.org/about-us.aspx

Feinberg, L. S., & Newman, S. L. (2004). A study of 10 states since passage of the National Family Caregiver Support Program: Policies, perceptions, and program development. *Gerontologist, 44*(6), 760–769.

Feinsod, R., Arthurs, R., & Charman, C. (2007). *Perspectives of employers, workers, and policy-makers in the G7 countries on the new demographic realities.* Washington, DC: AARP, Global Aging.

Fischer, D. L. (1978). *Growing old in America.* New York: Oxford University Press.

Fjelltun, A-M. S., Henriksen, N., Norberg, A., Gilje, F., & Normann, H. K. (2009). Nurses' and carers' appraisals of workload in care of frail elderly awaiting nursing home placement. *Scandinavian Journal of Caring Science, 23,* 57–66.

Focarelli, D., & Zanghieri, P. (2005). Labour force participation of older workers in Italy: Trends, causes, and policy issues. *Geneva Papers, 30,* 711–723.

Folkbildningsrådet. (n.d.). *Folkbildning in Sweden.* Retrieved February 20, 2010, from http://www.folkbildning.se//Documents/Q%20översättningar/översättning_webb_final_071210_en_gr.pdf

Försäkringskassan. (2008a). *General information about maintenance support [underhållsstöd] [Allmänt om underhållsstöd].* Retrieved October 1, 2009, from http://www.forsakringskassan

.se/irj/go/km/docs/fk_publishing/Dokument/Publikationer/Faktablad/Andra_sprak/Engelska/underhallsstod_eng.pdf

Försäkringskassan. (2008b). *Guarantee pension [Garantipension].* Retrieved October 1, 2009, from http://www.pensionsmyndigheten.se/Garantipension.html

Försäkringskassan. (2008c). *Income pension [Inkomstpension].* Retrieved October 1, 2009 from http://www.pensionsmyndigheten.se/Inkomstpension.html

Försäkringskassan. (2008d). *Premium pension.* Retrieved October 1, 2009, from http://www.pensionsmyndigheten.se/PremiumPension_en.html

Francke, A. L. (2003). *Palliative care for terminally ill patients in the Netherlands* (International Publication Series Health, Welfare, and Sport: No. 16). The Hague: Dutch Government.

Friedland, R. B., & Summer, L. (1999). *Demography is not destiny.* New York: Commonwealth Fund. Retrieved from http://www.agingsociety.org/agingsociety/pdf/destiny1.pdf

Friedland, R. B., & Summer, L. (2005). *Demography is not destiny, revisited.* New York: Commonwealth Fund.

Garcez-Leme, L. E., Leme, M. D., & Espino, D. V. (2005). Geriatrics in Brazil: A big country with big opportunities. *Journal of the American Geriatrics Society, 53,* 2018–2022.

Gavrilov, L. A., & Heuveline, P. (2003). Aging of population. In P. Demeny & G. McNicoll (Eds.), *The encyclopedia of population* (pp. 32–37). New York: Macmillan.

Gee, E. M. (2002). Misconceptions and misapprehensions about population ageing. *International Journal of Epidemiology, 31*(4), 750–753.

Giambiagi, F., & de Mello, L. (2006). *Social security reform in Brazil: Achievements and remaining challenges* (Working Paper No. 534). Paris, France: OECD.

Giarchi, G. G. (1996). *Caring for older Europeans: Comparative studies in 29 countries.* Aldershot, UK: Ashgate.

Gibbs, N. R. (1988, February 22). Grays on the go. *Time, 131,* pp. 66–75.

Gill, D. G., & Ingman, S. R. (1994). *Eldercare, distributive justice, and the welfare state: Retrenchment or expansion.* Albany: State University of New York Press.

Goh, C. (2008). *Palliative care development in Asia.* Retrieved from http://www.eapcnet.org/download/forAuspices/Antea2008/Wednesday12-Goh.pdf

Gomez Jimenez, M. A., & Koebel, C. T. (2007). A comparison of Spanish and American housing policy frameworks addressing housing for the elderly. *Journal of Housing for the Elderly, 20*(4), 23–37.

Gordon, R., Eagar, K., Currow, D., & Green, J. (2009). Current funding and financing issues in the Australian hospice and palliative care sector. *Journal of Pain and Symptom Management, 38,* 68–74.

Gori, C. (2000). Solidarity in Italy's policies toward the frail elderly: A value at stake. *International Journal of Social Welfare, 9,* 261–269.

GovBenefits.gov. (2010). *About us.* Retrieved January 13, 2010, from http://www.benefits.gov/about-us

Government of New Brunswick. (2009). *Low-income senior's benefit.* Retrieved August 1, 2009, from http://saintjohn.cioc.ca/record/HDC0705?Number=1

Haley, B. A., & Gray, R. W. (2008). *Section 202 supportive housing for the elderly: Program status and performance measurement.* Washington, DC: U.S. Department of Housing and Urban Development, Office of Policy Development and Research.

Hamilton, B. E., Martin, J. A., & Ventura, S. J. (2009, March 18). Births: Preliminary data for 2007. *National Vital Statistics Reports: From the Centers for Disease Control and Prevention, National Center for Health Statistics, National Vital Statistics System, 57*(12), 1–23.

Hassett, A., Fortune, T., & Smith, B. (2007). Mental health care for our ageing Australian population. *Australasian Psychiatry, 15,* 480–483.

Hässler, R. (2001). Sweden. In I. Philip (Ed.), *Family care of older people in Europe* (pp. 237–254). Amsterdam: IOS Press.

Health and Medical Services Act. (1982:763). Ministry of Health and Social Affairs, Sweden.

Health and Social Care Act, Chapter 15 (2001).

Health Canada. (2009). *Federal support to palliative and end-of-life care.* Retrieved from http://www.hc-sc.gc.ca/hcs-sss/palliat/support-soutien/index-eng.php

Heijink, R., Koopmanschap, M. A., & Polder, J. J. (2006). *International comparisons of cost of illness.* Rotterdam, Netherlands: RIVM, Centre for Public Health Forecasting. Retrieved from http://www.rivm.nl/bibliotheek/rapporten/270751016.html

Help the Aged. (2007, April). *Care at home.* London: Author. Retrieved August 5, 2007, from http://helptheaged.org.uk/care_at_home_is.pdf

Herd, P., & Kingson, E. R. (2005). Reframing Social Security: Cures worse than the disease. In R. B. Hudson (Ed.), *The new politics of old age policy.* Baltimore, MD: Johns Hopkins University Press.

Hessel, R. (2009). *European papers in the new welfare: The need for age-neutral training in the "Silver Society."* Retrieved from http://eng.newwelfare.org/2009/01/08/the-need-for-age-neutral-training-in-the-%E2%80%98silver-society%E2%80%99/

Hew, C. (2006). *Healthcare in China: Towards greatest access, efficiency, and quality.* IBM Healthcare. Retrieved from https://www-935.ibm.com/services/us/imc/pdf/g510-6268-healthcare-china.pdf

Highgate Newtown Community Centre. (2010). *Activities for senior citizens.* Retrieved March 17, 2010, from http://www.highgatenewtown.org/activities_seniors.htm

Higo, M., & Yamada, A. (2009). *Japan public policy.* Boston: Sloan Center on Aging & Work. Retrieved from http://www.bc.edu/research/agingandwork/meta-elements/pdf/publications/GPB02_Japan.pdf

Hill, M. J. (2006). *Social policy in the modern world: A comparative text.* Malden, MA: Blackwell.

Hospice Association of America. (2009). *Hospice facts and statistics.* Retrieved from http://www.nahc.org/facts/HospiceStats09.pdf

Hudson, R. B. (2005). Contemporary challenges to age-based public policy. In R. B. Hudson (Ed.), *The new politics of old-age policy.* Baltimore, MD: Johns Hopkins University Press.

Ingraham, P. W. (1987). Toward more systematic consideration of policy design. *Policy Studies Journal, 15*(4), 611–628.

Inter-American Commission on Human Rights. (1997). *Report on the situation of human rights in Brazil: Chapter IX.* Retrieved from http://www.cidh.oas.org/countryrep/brazil-eng/Chaper%209%20.htm

Internal Revenue Service. (2008). *Child and dependent care expenses* (Publication 503). Washington, DC: U.S. Department of the Treasury. Retrieved from http://www.irs.gov/pub/irs-pdf/p503.pdf

International Labor Organization. (2008). *LABORSTA Internet: Total economically active population.* Retrieved from http://laborsta.ilo.org/

Invest in Sweden Agency. (2007, February). *Occupational pension and insurance.* Retrieved from http://investsweden.se/Sverige/

Italian Republic. (2003). *Implementation of Directive 2000/78/EC on equal treatment in employment and work conditions.* Retrieved from http://europa.eu/legislation_summaries/employment_and_social_policy/employment_rights_and_work_organisation/c10823_en.htm

Ius Laboris. (2009). *Age discrimination internationally: Brazil.* Retrieved from www.agediscrimination.info/international/Pages/Brazil.aspx#top

Izuhara, M. (2002). Care and inheritance: Japanese and English perspectives of the "generational contract." *Ageing & Society, 22,* 61–77.

Jakubowski, E., & Busse, R. (1998). *Health care systems in the EU: A comparative study* (Report No. SACO 101 EN). Luxembourg: European Parliament.

Jenike, B. R. (2003). Parent care and shifting family obligations in urban Japan. In J. W. Traphagan & J. Knight (Eds.), *Demographic changes and the family in Japan's aging society* (pp. 177–202). New York: State University of New York Press.

Jerit, J., & Barabas, J. (2006). Bankrupt rhetoric: How misleading information affects knowledge about Social Security. *Public Opinion Quarterly, 70*(3), 278–303.

Johansson, L. (2004, August). *Services for supporting family carers of elderly people in Europe: Characteristics, coverage, and usage.* EUROFAMCARE, National Background Report for Sweden. Retrieved from http://www.uke.de/extern/eurofamcare/documents/nabares/nabare_sweden_rc1_a5.pdf

Jones, A. L., Dwyer, L. L., Bercovitz, A. R., & Strahan, G. W. (2009). *The national nursing home survey: 2004 overview data from the National Health Care Surveys* (DHHS Publication No. [PHS] 2009–1738). Hyattsville, MD: U.S. Department of Health and Human Services, Centers for Disease Control and Prevention National Center for Health Statistics.

Kaiser Commission on Medicaid and the Uninsured. (2006). *Private long-term care insurance: A viable option for low and middle-income seniors* (#7459). Washington, DC: Kaiser Family Foundation.

Kaiser Commission on Medicaid and the Uninsured. (2007, December). *Medicaid home and community-based service programs: Data update.* Washington, DC: Henry J. Kaiser Family Foundation. Retrieved from http://www.kff.org/medicaid/upload/7720.pdf

Kaiser Commission on Medicaid and the Uninsured. (2009). *Medicaid home and community-based service programs: Data update* (#7720-03). Washington, DC: Kaiser Family Foundation.

Kaiser Family Foundation. (2009). *Medicare fact sheet: Medicare advantage* (#2052-12). Menlo Park, CA: Author.

Kaiser Family Foundation. (2010). *Medicare: A primer* (#7615-03). Menlo Park, CA: Author.

Kalache, A., & Kickbusch, I. (1997). A global strategy for healthy ageing. *World Health, 50*(4), 4–5.

Karagiannaki, E. (2005). *Changes in the living arrangements of elderly people in Greece: 1974–1999* (Les Sticerd Research Paper No. CASE 104). Retrieved from http://papers.ssrn.com/sol3/papers.cfm?abstract_id=1159335

Karlin, B., & Duffy, M. (2004). Geriatric mental health policy: Impact on service delivery and directions for effecting change. *Professional Psychology: Research and Practice, 35,* 509–519.

Keefe, J. M. (2004). *Policy profile for compensating family caregivers: Sweden.* Retrieved January 15, 2008, from http://www.msvu.ca/mdcaging/PDFs/Profile_Sweden_final.pdf

Kermis, M. D. (1987). Equity and policy issues in mental health care of the elderly: Dilemmas, deinstitutionalization, and DRGs. *Journal of Applied Gerontology, 6,* 268–283.

Kerr, D. (1993). Terminal care in China. *American Journal of Hospice and Palliative Care 1993, 10,* 18–26.

Kinsella, K., & He, W. (2009). *An aging world, 2008: International population reports.* Washington, DC: U.S. Department of Health and Human Services.

Kinsella, K. G., & Velkoff, V. A. (2001). *An aging world: 2001.* Washington, DC: U.S. Dept. of Commerce, Economics and Statistics Administration, U.S. Census Bureau.

Klees, B. S., Wolfe, C. J., & Curtis, C. A. (2009). Medicaid program description and legislative history. *U.S. Social Security Administration: Office of Retirement and Disability Policy.* Retrieved from http://www.ssa.gov/policy/docs/statcomps/supplement/2009/medicaid.html

Koff, T. H., & Park, R. W. (1999). *Aging public policy: Bonding the generations.* Amityville, NY: Baywood.

Kosberg, J. I. (1994). *International handbook on services for the elderly.* Westport, CT: Greenwood Press.

Kotlikoff, L., & Hagist, C. (2005). *Who's going broke? Comparing health care in ten OECD countries.* National Bureau of Economic Research. Retrieved from http://ideas.repec.org/p/nbr/nberwo/11833.html

Krugman, P. (2004, December 7). Inventing a crisis. *New York Times.* Retrieved from http://www.nytimes.com/2004/12/07/opinion/07krugman.html?scp=539&sq=&st=nyt

LABORSTA Internet. (2010). *Total and economically active population.* ILO Department of Statistics, International Labour Organization. Retrieved from http://laborsta.ilo.org/

Lamura, G., Melchiorre, M. G., Quattrini, S., Mengani, M., & Albertini, A. (2001). In I. Philip (Ed.), *Family care of older people in Europe* (pp. 97–134). Amsterdam: IOS Press.

Lamura, G., Mnich, E., Nolan, M., Wojszel, B., Krevers, B., Mestheneos, L., et al. (2008). Family carers' experiences using support services in Europe: Empirical evidence from the EUROFAMCARE study. *Gerontologist, 48*(6), 752–771.

Lawrence, D., & Liu, J. (2009). *China's $124 billion health care plan aims to boost consumption.* Retrieved from http://www.bloomberg.com/apps/news?sid=aXFagkr3Dr6s&pid=newsarchive

Lawson, J. (2009). The transformation of social housing provision in Switzerland mediated by federalism, direct democracy, and the urban/rural divide. *European Journal of Housing Policy, 9,* 45–67.

Lawton, M. P. (1980). Housing elderly: Residential quality and residential satisfaction. *Research on Aging, 2,* 309–328.

Lawton, M. P., & Nahemow, L. (1973). Ecology and the aging process. In C. Eisdorfer & M. P. Lawton (Eds.), *Psychology of adult development and aging* (pp. 619–674).Washington, DC: American Psychological Association.

Leadership Council of Aging Organizations. (2010). *Our mission.* Retrieved April 26, 2010, from http://www.lcao.org/our_mission.htm

Leanse, J., Tiven, M., & Robb, T. B. (1977). *Senior center operation: A guide to organization and management.* Washington, DC: National Institute of Senior Centers, National Council on the Aging.

Lee, M. (2007). *Improving services and support for older people with mental health problems.* Retrieved from http://www.mhilli.org/documents/Inquiryfinalreport-FULLREPORT.pdf

Lee, R. D. (2007). Demographic change, welfare, and intergenerational transfers: A global overview. In J. Veron, S. Pennec, & J. Legare (Eds.), *Ages, generations, and the social contract* (pp. 17–43). New York: Springer.

Legal Aid Authority. (2007). *Legal aid in Sweden.* Sundsvall, Sweden: Author. Retrieved from http://www.rattshjalp.se/Publikationer/Informationsmaterial/Legal_aid_in_Sweden.pdf

Legal Services Commission. (2007a). *Annual report and accounts 2008/09.* London: Author. Retrieved from http://www.official-documents.gov.uk/document/hc0809/hc07/0731/0731.pdf

Legal Services Commission. (2007b). *Paying for your legal aid.* London. Retrieved from http://www.opsi.gov.uk/acts/acts2007/ukpga_20070029_en_1

Legal Services Corporation. (2010). *What is the Legal Services Corporation?* Retrieved January 12, 2010, from http://www.lsc.gov/about/lsc.php

Legal Services Corporation Act, 42 U.S.C. § 2996 *et seq.* (1974).

Levine, C. (2008). Family caregiving. In M. Crowley (Ed.), *From birth to death and bench to clinic: The Hastings Center Bioethics briefing book for journalists, policymakers, and campaigns.* Garrison, NY: Hastings Center. Retrieved from http://www.thehastingscenter.org/uploadedFiles/Publications/Briefing_Book/family%20caregiving%20chapter.pdf

Lloyd-Sherlock, P. (2000). Population ageing in developed and developing regions: Implications for health policy. *Social Science and Medicine, 51,* 887–895.

Lokiec, P. (2008). Chapter 4: Discrimination law in France. In R. Blanpain, H. Nakakubo, & A. Takashi (Eds.), *New developments in employment discrimination law* (pp. 77–92). Frederick, MD: Aspen.

Lothian, K., McKee, K., Philp, I., & Nolan, M. (2001). United Kingdom. In I. Philp (Ed.), *Family care of older people in Europe* (pp. 255–280). United Kingdom: IOS Press.

Lowi, T. J. (1964). American business, public policy, case studies, and political theory. *World Politics, 16*(4), 677–693.

Lubomudrov, S. (1987). Congressional perceptions of the elderly: The use of stereotypes in the legislative process. *Gerontologist, 27*(1), 77–81.

Lundy, J., & Finder, B. D. (2009). *Cost sharing for health care: France, Germany, and Switzerland* (#7852). Menlo Park, CA: Kaiser Family Foundation.

Lyon, D., & Glucksmann, M. (2008). Comparative configurations of care work across Europe. *Sociology, 42*(1), 101–118.

MacAdam, M. (2008). *Frameworks of integrated care for the elderly: A systematic review.* Canadian Policy Research Networks. Retrieved from http://www.cprn.org/documents/49813_EN.pdf

MacCourt, P. (2004). *Senior mental health policy lens.* Retrieved from http://www.seniorsmental health.ca/PolicyLensENG_17_06.pdf

Marmor, T. R., & Mashaw, J. L. (2002). The case for universal social insurance. In S. H. Altman & D. Shactman (Eds.), *Policies for an aging society.* Baltimore, MD: Johns Hopkins University Press.

Marques, R. M., & Batich, M. (2003). The labor market and social security in Brazil. *International Journal of Political Economy, 30*(4), 49–67.

Maser, K., & Bégin, J. (2003). *Canada's retirement income programs: A statistical overview (1990–2000).* Ottawa: Statistics Canada, Income Statistics Division, Pensions and Wealth Program. Retrieved from http://dsp-psd.pwgsc.gc.ca/Collection-R/Statcan/74-507-XIE/0010074-507-XIE.pdf

Mauch, D., Kautz, C., & Smith, S. A. (2008). *Reimbursement of mental health services in primary care settings* (HHS Pub. No. SMA-08-4324). Rockville, MD: Center for Mental Health Services, Substance Abuse and Mental Health Services Administration.

McCarthy, L., & Kim, S. (2005). *The aging baby boomers: Current and future metropolitan distributions and housing policy implications.* Washington, DC: U.S. Department of Housing and Urban Development, Office of Policy Development and Research. Retrieved from https://pantherfile.uwm.edu/kim/www/papers/HUD_report%5Bfinal%5D.pdf

McGarry, K., & Schoeni, R. F. (2000). Social security, economic growth, and the rise in elderly widow's independence in the twentieth century. *Demography, 37,* 221–236.

Meeks, C. B., Nickols, S. Y., & Sweaney, A. L. (1999). Demographic comparisons of aging in five selected countries. *Journal of Family and Economic Issues, 20,* 223–250.

Melchiorre, M. G., Quattrini, S., Megani, M., & Lamura, G. (2000). L'assistenza dei famigliari agli anziani disabili. *Prospettive Sociali e Sanitarie, XXX*(10), 1–4.

Merton, R. K., & Nisbet, R. A. (Eds.). (1966). *Contemporary social problems* (2nd ed.). New York: Harcourt, Brace, & World.

MetLife Mature Market Institute. (2007). *The MetLife market survey of adult day services and home care costs.* Connecticut: Author and LifePlans, Inc. Retrieved from http://www.agapelongtermcare.com/resources/metlife_survey_adult_daycare_0709.pdf

MetLife Mature Market Institute. (2009). *The 2009 MetLife market survey of nursing home, assisted living, adult day services, and home care costs.* New York: Author.

Milbank Memorial Fund. (2006). *Public housing and supportive services for the frail elderly: A guide for housing authorities and their collaborators.* Retrieved from http://www.milbank.org/reports/0609publichousing/0609publichousing.html

Ministerie van Sociale Zaken en Werkgelegenheid. (2008). *The old age pension system in the Netherlands.* Den Hage, Netherlands: Author. Retrieved from http://docs.minszw.nl/pdf/135/2009/135_2009_1_23649.pdf

Ministry of Health, Labor, and Welfare. (2007). *White paper on aging society.* Tokyo: Office of Government Public Relations. Retrieved from http://www8.cao.go.jp/kourei/english/annual report/2007/2007.pdf

Ministry of Health and Social Affairs. (2007). *Care of the elderly in Sweden.* Stockholm, Sweden: Author

Ministry of Health and Social Affairs. (2008). *A stable pension system.* Regeringskansliet, Government Offices of Sweden. Retrieved from http://www.regeringen.se/content/1/c6/12/02/06/d0e2c9f7.pdf

Ministry of Health and Social Affairs. (2009). *Selection of issues and meetings in the field of health and social affairs during the Swedish Presidency of the EU 2009.* Retrieved from http://ec.europa.eu/eahc/documents/news/technical_meetings/Swedish_Priorities.pdf

Ministry of Health and Social Affairs/Riksförsäkringsverket. (2003). *The Swedish national pension system.* Retrieved from http://www.sweden.gov.se/content/1/c6/02/42/21/aa589a7c .pdf

Ministry of Integration and Gender Equality. (2008). *Policy on nongovernmental organisations and popular movements.* Retrieved from http://www.sweden.gov.se/integrationministry

Ministry of Labor. (2004). *Nondiscrimination Act 21/2004.* Retrieved from http://www.finlex.fi/ fi/laki/kaannokset/2004/en20040021.pdf

Ministry of Social Affairs and Employment. (2009). S*ocial assistance.* Retrieved November 1, 2009, from http://english.szw.nl/index.cfm?menu_item_id=14639&hoofdmenu_item_id= 14632&rubriek_item=392436&rubriek_id=391971&set_id=3615&doctype_id=6&link_ id=128095

Minshull, P. (2007). *Age equality: What does it mean for older people's mental health services?* Retrieved from http://www.psige.org/psige-pdfs/Age%20Equality%20Guidance%20 CSIP%20April2007.pdf

Moon, M., & Mulvey, J. (1996). *Entitlements and the elderly: Protecting promises, recognizing reality.* Washington, DC: Urban Institute Press.

Mullan, P. (2002). *The imaginary time bomb: Why an ageing population is not a social problem.* London: Tauris.

Naegele, G., & Walker, A. (2007). *A guide to good practice in age management.* Dublin: European Foundation for the Improvement of Living and Working Conditions.

Napili, A. (2008). *Older Americans Act: FY2008 funding and FY2009 budget request* (CRS Report for Congress). Washington, DC. Retrieved from http://aging.senate.gov/crs/aging16.pdf

National Adult Day Services Association. (2009). *About adult day services.* Retrieved April 26, 2009, from http://www.nadsa.org/knowledgebase/col.php?pid=29&tpid=15

National Association of Area Agencies on Aging. (2009). *Fast facts about the Eldercare Locator.* Retrieved December 2, 2009, from http://www.n4a.org/programs/eldercare-locator/?fa= fast-facts

National Association of Area Agencies on Aging. (2010a). *Advocacy in action center.* Retrieved April 30, 2010, from https://www.n4a.org/advocacy/aging-policy-briefing/index.cfm

National Association of Area Agencies on Aging. (2010b). *FY 2011 labor-HHS-Education and other appropriations as of April 1, 2010.* Retrieved April 30, 2010, from http://www.n4a.org/ files/advocacy/campaigns/fy2011-april-appropriations-chart.pdf

National Committee to Preserve Social Security and Medicare. (2008). *The Medicare Improvements for Patients and Providers Act (MIPPA): Summary of key provisions.* Retrieved from http://www.ncpssm.org/news/archive/mippa_summary/

National Council on Aging. (2010a). *About the National Council on Aging.* Retrieved April 27, 2010, from http://www.ncoa.org/about-ncoa/

National Council on Aging. (2010b). *National Center for Benefits Outreach and Enrollment: About us.* Retrieved January 10, 2010, from http://www.centerforbenefits.org/mission.html

National Council on Aging. (2010c). *NCOA issue brief: Older Americans Act appropriations.* Retrieved April 10, 2010, from http://www.ncoa.org/assets/files/pdf/IB10-OAA-Approps.pdf

National Federation of Shopmobility. (2010). *Welcome to the NFSUK website.* Retrieved February 15, 2010, from http://www.shopmobilityuk.org

National Health Service. (2010). *Carers Direct.* Retrieved March 30, 2010, from http://www.nhs .uk/carersdirect/Pages/CarersDirectHome.aspx

National Hospice and Palliative Care Organization. (2009). *Facts and figures on hospice care in America.* Retrieved from http://www.nhpco.org/files/public/Statistics_Research/NHPCO_ facts_and_figures.pdf

National Institute of Senior Centers. (2005). *Facts about senior centers.* Washington, DC: Author. Retrieved December 30, 2009, from http://www.ncoa.org/press-room/fact-sheets/senior-center-fact-sheet.html

National Union of Public and General Employees. (2008). *2009 CPP benefits increase; OAS and GIS benefits remain unchanged.* Retrieved August 1, 2009, from http://www.nupge.ca

National Union of Public and General Employees. (2009). *2008 benefit rates increases for OAS, GIS, and CPP.* Retrieved from http://www.nupge.ca/print/268

Navarete, F. F., & Palanca, I. (2005). Mental health care in Madrid. *European Psychiatry, 20,* S279–S284.

Neal, M. B., & Wagner, D. L. (n.d.). *Working caregivers: Issues, challenges, and opportunities for the aging network.* National Family Caregiver Support Program Issue Brief. Retrieved April 13, 2008, from http://www.caregiverslibrary.org/Portals/0/Working%20Caregivers %20-%20Issues%20for%20the%20Aging%20Network%20Fin-Neal-Wagner.pdf

New York Times Company. (1985). *The longest-running game in town.* Produced by a.s.a.p. A project of Families USA, Washington, DC.

Nolan, M., Barber, L., Edis, A., Brown, J., & McKee, K. (2004, August). *Services for supporting family carers of elderly people in Europe: Characteristics, coverage, and usage.* EUROFAMCARE, National Background Report for the United Kingdom. Retrieved from http://www.uke.de/ extern/eurofamcare/documents/nabares/nabare_uk_rc1_a5.pdf

Norwegian Ministry of Health and Care Services. (2008). *Dementia plan 2015: Subplan of care plan 2015* (Publication No. I-1129E). Oslo: Norwegian Government Administration Services.

Norwegian Ministry of Local Government and Regional Development. (2004). *On housing policy: Summary in English* (Report No. 23). Oslo: Housing and Building Department.

Nyce, S. A., & Schieber, S. J. (2005). *The economic implications of aging societies: The costs of living happily ever after.* Cambridge, UK: Cambridge University Press.

Nyyssola, K., & Hamalainen, K. (2001). *Lifelong learning in Finland: The extent to which vocational education and training policy is nurturing lifelong learning in finland.* Luxembourg: Office for Official Publications of the European Communities.

Office of the Privacy Commissioner of Canada. (2006). *Legal information related to the Personal Information Protection and Electronic Documents Act (PIPEDA).* http://www.priv.gc.ca/ leg_c/leg_c_p_e.cfm#contenttop

Older Americans Act of 1965, Pub. L. No. 89-73, 42 U.S.C. § 3001 *et seq.*

Olivera, J., Benabarre, S., Lorente, T., Rodríguez, M., Pelegrín, C., Calvo, J., et al. (2008). Prevalence of psychiatric symptoms and mental disorders detected in primary care in an elderly Spanish population. *International Journal of Geriatric Psychiatry, 23,* 915–921.

Organisation for Economic Co-operation and Development. (2004a). *Executive Summary: Ageing and Employment Policies: Finland.* Paris: Author.

Organisation for Economic Co-operation and Development. (2004b). *Executive Summary: Ageing and Employment Policies: Japan.* Paris: Author.

Organisation for Economic Co-operation and Development. (2004c, September). *Private health insurance in OECD countries. OECD Observer,* 1–8. Paris: Author.

Organisation for Economic Co-operation and Development. (2005a). *Executive Summary: Ageing and Employment Policies: France.* Paris: Author.

Organisation for Economic Co-operation and Development. (2005b). *Long-term care for older people: The OECD Health Project* (#53867). Paris: Author.

Organisation for Economic Co-operation and Development. (2005c). *OECD pensions at a glance: Public policies across OECD countries.* Paris: Author.

Organisation for Economic Co-operation and Development. (2006). *Ageing and employment policies: Live longer, work longer.* Paris: Author.

Organisation for Economic Co-operation and Development. (2007). *Pensions at a glance 2007: Retirement-income systems in OECD countries.* Paris: Author.

Organisation for Economic Co-operation and Development. (2009a). *Health data 2009.* Paris: Author.

Organisation for Economic Co-operation and Development. (2009b). *Pensions at a glance 2009: Retirement-income systems in OECD countries.* Paris: Author.

Organisation for Economic Co-operation and Development. (2009c). *Society at a glance 2009: OECD social indicators.* Paris: Author.

O'Shaughnessy, C. (2004). *Older Americans Act: History of appropriations, FY1966–FY2004.* Washington, DC: Congressional Research Service, Library of Congress.

O'Shaughnessy, C. (2008). *The aging services network: Accomplishments and challenges in serving a growing elderly population.* Washington, DC: George Washington University.

Palme, M., & Svensson, I. (1997). *Social security, occupational pensions, and retirement in Sweden* (Working Paper Series No. 184). Cambridge, MA: National Bureau of Economic Research. Retrieved from http://swopec.hhs.se/hastef/papers/hastef0184.pdf

Palmer, E. E. (2000). *The Swedish pension reform model: Framework and issues.* Washington, DC: World Bank.

Pareja Eastaway, M., & San Martin Varo, I. (2002). The tenure imbalance in Spain: The need for social housing policy. *Urban Studies, 39,* 283–295.

Paulli, A., & Tagliabue, M. (2002). Active strategies for older workers in Italy. In M. Jepsen, D. Foden, & M. Hutsebaut (Eds.), *Active strategies for older workers* (pp. 275–298). Brussels: European Trade Union Institute.

Pestieau, P. (2003). Ageing, retirement, and pension reforms. *World Economy, 26,* 1447–1457.

Peterson, P. G. (1999). Gray dawn: The global aging crisis. *Foreign Affairs, 78*(1), 42–55.

Philp, L., & Appleby, L. (2005). *Securing better mental health for older adults.* Retrieved from http://www.dh.gov.uk/dr_consum_dh/groups/dh_digitalassets/@dh/@en/documents/digitalasset/dh_4114992.pdf

Polivka, L. (2001). *Paying family members to provide care: Policy considerations for states.* San Francisco: Family Caregiver Alliance. Retrieved from http://www.caregiver.org/caregiver/jsp/content/pdfs/op_2001_10_policybrief_7.pdf

Polverini, F., Principi, A., Balducci, C., Melchiorre, M. G., Quattrini, S., Gianelli, M. V., et al. (2004, August). *EUROFAMCARE: National background report for Italy.* Retrieved from http://www.uke.de/extern/eurofamcare/documents/nabares/nabare_italy_rc1_a5.pdf

Population and Housing Census. (2001). *Spain at the beginning of the 21st century.* Retrieved from http://www.ine.es/en/prodyser/pubweb/folletocenso01/folletocenso01_en.htm

Population: Babies mean business. (1948, August 9). *Newsweek.*

Portney, K. E. (1986). *Approaching public policy analysis: An introduction to policy and program research.* Englewood Cliffs, NJ: Prentice-Hall.

President's New Freedom Commission on Mental Health. (2003). *A report on the public comments submitted to the President's New Freedom Commission on Mental Health.* Retrieved from http://www.mentalhealthcommission.gov/reports/comments_011003.pdf

Princess Royal Trust for Carers. (2010). *Help for carers.* Retrieved from http://www.carers.org/

Psychiatric Services Online. (2008). Report highlights reimbursement barriers to provision of mental health services in primary care. *Psychiatric Services, 59,* 1072–1073. Retrieved from http://www.psychiatryonline.org

Purcell, P. J. (2008). *Pension sponsorship and participation: Summary of recent trends.* Washington, DC: Congressional Research Service, Library of Congress. Retrieved from http://assets.opencrs.com/rpts/RL30122_20080908.pdf

Pynoos, J., & Nishita, C. M. (2005). The changing face of senior housing. In R. B. Hudson (Ed.), *The new politics of old-age policy.* Baltimore, MD: Johns Hopkins University Press.

Quadagno, J. (1989). Theories of the welfare state. *Annual Review of Sociology, 13,* 109–128.

Quattrini, S., Melchiorre, M. G., Balducci, C., Spazzafumo, L., & Lamura, G. (2006). *Services for supporting family carers of elderly people in Europe: Characteristics, coverage, and usage.*

National Survey Report for Italy, EUROFAMCARE. Retrieved from http://www.uke.de/extern/eurofamcare/documents/deliverables/nasure_it.pdf

Queen's Crescent Community Association. (2010). *About QCCA.* Retrieved March 10, 2010, from http://qcca.org.uk/

Ramadge, J. (Ed.). (2000). *Australian nursing practice and palliative care: Its origins, evolution, and future.* Deakin, Australia: Royal College of Nursing.

Reinhardt, U. E. (2003). Does the aging of the population really drive the demand for health care? *Health Affairs, 22*(6), 27–39.

Reuters. (2010, March 27). *French pension reform top priority, PM Fillon says.* Retrieved from http://www.todayszaman.com/tz-web/detaylar.do?load=detay&link=205699

Rodríguez Cabrero, G. (2002). *Long-term care: Context, debates, policies, and prospects.* Unidad de Politicas Comparadas. Retrieved from http://www.iesam.csic.es/doctrab2/dt-0214e.pdf

Rojo Perez, F., Fernandez-Mayoralas, G., Pozo Rivera, F. E., & Rojo Abuin, J. H. (2001). Ageing in place: Predictors of the residential satisfaction of elderly. *Social Indicators Research, 54,* 173–208.

Romanow, R. J. (2002). *Building on values: The future of health care in Canada: Final Report.* Commission on the Future of Health Care in Canada. Retrieved from http://dsp-psd.pwgsc.gc.ca/Collection/CP32-85-2002E.pdf

RTI International. (2003, March). *Final report of the senior companion quality of care evaluation.* Washington, DC: Corporation for National and Community Service. Retrieved from http://www.seniorcorps.gov/pdf/final_scp_report.pdf

Ruggles, S. (2007). The decline of intergenerational coresidence in the United States, 1850–2000. *American Sociological Review, 72,* 964–989.

Rymkevitch, O., & Villosio, C. (2007). *Age discrimination in Italy.* Retrieved from http://www.laboratoriorevelli.it/_pdf/wp67.pdf

Salholz, E. (1990, October 29). Blaming the voters: Hapless budgeteers single out "greedy geezers." *Newsweek,* p. 36.

Salvador-Carulla, L., Haro, J. M., & Ayuso-Mateos, J. L. (2006). A framework for evidence-based mental health care and policy. *Acta Psychiatrica Scandinavica, 114,* 5–11.

Sass, S. A. (1997). *The promise of private pensions: The first hundred years.* Cambridge, MA: Harvard University Press.

Sass, S. A. (2003). *Reforming the U.S. retirement income system: The growing role of work.* Chestnut Hill, MA: Center for Retirement Research at Boston College.

Schneider, N., Buser, K., & Amelung, V. E. (2006). Improving palliative care in Germany: Summative evaluation from experts' reports in Lower Saxony and Branderburg. *Journal of Public Health, 14,* 148–154.

Schneider, N., Lueckmann, S. L., Behmann, M., & Bisson, S. (2009). Problems and challenges for palliative care: What are the views of different stakeholders on the meso and macro level of the health system? *Health Policy, 93,* 11–20.

Schoen, C., Osborn, R., How, S. K. H., Doty, M. H., & Peugh, J. (2009). In chronic condition: Experiences of patients with complex health care needs, in eight countries, 2008. *Health Affairs, 28*(1), 1–16.

Schulz, J. H. (2005). *The economics of aging.* Westport, CT: Auburn House.

SeniorNet Sweden. (2010). *SeniorNet Sweden.* Retrieved February 21, 2010, from http://www.seniornet.se/

Seniors Psychosocial Interest Group. (2004). *Seniors' mental health psychosocial research agenda for Canada.* Retrieved from http://www.seniorsmentalhealth.ca/

Service Canada. (2009a). *Canadian Pension Plan (CPP): Payment rates.* Retrieved August 1, 2009, from http://www.servicecanada.gc.ca/eng/isp/pub/factsheets/rates.shtml

Service Canada. (2009b). *Canada Pension Plan retirement pension.* Retrieved August 1, 2009, from http://www.servicecanada.gc.ca/eng/isp/pub/factsheets/rates.shtml

Service Canada. (2009c). *Guaranteed income supplement.* Retrieved on July 30, 2009, from http://www.servicecanada.gc.ca/eng/sc/oas/gis/guaranteeddincomesupplement.shtml

Service Canada. (2009d). *Income assistance for seniors.* Retrieved August 1, 2009, from http://www.servicecanada.gc.ca/eng/audiences/seniors/benefits.shtml

Service Canada. (2009e). *Old Age Security (OAS) payment rates.* Retrieved August 1, 2009, from http://www.servicecanada.gc.ca/eng/isp/oas/oasrates.shtml

Service Canada. (2010a). *Allowance for the survivor.* Retrieved on February 1, 2010, from http://www.servicecanada.gc.ca/eng/isp/pub/oas/allowsurv.shtml

Service Canada. (2010b). *Services for seniors.* Retrieved February 1, 2010, from http://www.servicecanada.gc.ca/eng/audiences/seniors/index.shtml

Settergren, O. (2001). *Automatic balance system Swedish pension system.* Riksförsäkringsverket (Swedish National Social Insurance Board). Retrieved from http://www.forsakringskassan.se/irj/go/km/docs/fk_publishing/Dokument/Rapporter/Working_papers/wp0102_the_automatic_balance_mechanism_of_the_swedish_pension_system.pdf

Settersten, R. A., Jr. (2007). Ten reasons why shake-ups in the life course should change approaches to old-age policies. *Aging and Public Policy Report, 17*(3), 1, 21–27.

Shactman, D., & Altman, S. H. (2002). Overview: Issues and options for an aging population. In S. H. Altman & D. Shactman (Eds.), *Policies for an aging society.* Baltimore, MD: Johns Hopkins University Press.

Shugarman, L. R., Campbell, D. E., Bird, C. E., Gabel, J., Louis, T. A., & Lynn, J. (2004). Differences in Medicare expenditures during the last 3 years of life. *Journal of General Internal Medicine, 19,* 27–35.

Silfverhielm, H., & Kamis-Gould, E. (2000). The Swedish mental health system: Past, present, and future. *International Journal of Law and Psychiatry, 23,* 293–307.

Sivis, R., McCrae, C. S., & Demir, A. (2005). Availability of mental health services for older adults: A cross-cultural comparison of the United States and Turkey. *Age and Mental Health, 9,* 223–234.

Small, N. R. (1988). Evolution of nursing homes. In N. R. Small & M. B. Walsh (Eds.), *Teaching nursing homes: The nursing perspective* (pp. 31–46). Owings Mills, MD: National Health Publishing.

Smith, K. B., & Larimer, C. W. (2009). *The public policy theory primer.* Boulder, CO: Westview Press.

Social Security Administration. (2008a). *Social security programs throughout the world (SSPTW) Europe: Italy.* Washington, DC: Author. Retrieved from http://www.ssa.gov/policy/docs/progdesc/ssptw/2008-2009/europe/italy.pdf

Social Security Administration. (2008b). *Social security programs throughout the world (SSPTW): Europe: Sweden.* Washington, DC: Author. Retrieved from http://www.ssa.gov/policy/docs/progdesc/ssptw/2008-2009/europe/sweden.pdf

Social Security Administration. (2009). *Social Security, understanding the benefits* (SSA publication No. 05-10024). Baltimore, MD: Author.

Social Security Administration. (2010a). *Fact sheet, Social Security: 2010 Social Security changes.* Retrieved March 13, 2010, from http://www.ssa.gov/pressoffice/factsheets/colafacts2010.pdf

Social Security Administration. (2010b). *What is the maximum Social Security retirement benefit?* Retrieved March 13, 2010, from http://ssa-custhelp.ssa.gov/app/answers/detail/a_id/5/~/the-maximum-social-security-retirement-benefit

Social Services Act. (1982). *SFS 1980:620,* Stockholm.

Socialstyrelsen. (2008). *Developments in the care for the elderly in Sweden 2007.* Article # nr 2008-126-37. Retrieved from http://www.socialstyrelsen.se

Srinivasan, R. (2007). *India's overlooked "grey market" workforce.* Retrieved from http://www.hindustantimes.com/StoryPage/Print/236210.aspx

Stähl, A. (1999). *Public transport or special service or mix?* Lund University, Department of Technology and Society. Proceedings from the KFB research conference on Urban Transport Systems, Lund, Sweden.

Stamso, M. A. (2009). Housing and the welfare state in Norway. *Scandinavian Political Studies, 32,* 194–220.

Statistics Netherlands. (2008). *Old people receiving more and more care.* Retrieved from http://www.cbs.nl/en-GB/menu/themas/gezondheid-welzijn/publicaties/artikelen/archief/2008/2008-2368-wm.htm

Steinbrook, R. (2006a). Imposing personal responsibility for health. *New England Journal of Medicine, 355,* 753–756.

Steinbrook, R. (2006b). Private health care in Canada. *New England Journal of Medicine, 354,* 1661–1664.

Stockholm Government. (2010a). *Fees.* Retrieved February 21, 2010, from http://www.stockholm.se/FamiljOmsorg/Aldreomsorg/Avgifter-for-aldreomsorg/

Stockholm Government. (2010b). *Mature direct (Äldre direkt).* Retrieved February 22, 2010, from http://www.stockholm.se/FamiljOmsorg/Aldreomsorg/Ring-Aldre-direkt/

Stone, R., Reinhard, S. C., Machemer, J., & Rudin, D. (2002). *Geriatric care managers: A profile of an emerging profession* (Data Digest No. 82). Washington, DC: Public Policy Institute, AARP. Retrieved from http://www.careersinaging.com/careersinaging/geriatric_care_managers.pdf

Sun, R. (2004). Worry about medical care, family support, and depression of the elders in urban China. *Research on Aging, 26,* 559–585.

Surgeon General U.S. Public Health Service. (1999). *Chapter 5: Older adults and mental health.* Retrieved from http://www.surgeongeneral.gov/library/mentalhealth/chapter5/sec1.html

Swedish Association of Local Authorities and Regions. (2007). *Care of the elderly in Sweden today, 2006.* Retrieved from http://english.skl.se/web/Publications_and_reports.aspx

Swedish Institute. (2007a). *Elderly care in Sweden.* Retrieved from http://www.sweden.se/eng/Home/Society/Elderly-care/Facts/Elderly-care/

Swedish Red Cross. (2009). *Developing social security.* Retrieved October 1, 2009, from http://www.redcross.se/rksf/sfdesign.nsf/main?openagent&Layout=engelsk&docid=AF6B3E5CB1163664C12571950048520D&menu0=0&menu1=7

Swedish Social Insurance Agency. (2008). *The Orange Report: Annual report of the Swedish pension system 2008.* Retrieved from http://www.forsakringskassan.se/irj/go/km/docs/fk_publishing/Dokument/Publikationer/arsredovisningar/orange_rapport_2008_engelsk.pdf

Takagi, E., Silverstein, M., & Crimmins, E. (2007). Intergenerational coresidence of older adults in Japan: Conditions for cultural plasticity. *Journal of Gerontology: Social Sciences, 62,* 330–339.

Tanner, M. (2008a). *The grass is not always greener: A look at national health care systems around the world* (Policy analysis). Washington, DC: CATO Institute.

Tanner, M. (2008b, April 25). Health care around the world: Canada. *Healthcare Economist.* Retrieved from http://healthcare-economist.com/2008/04/25/health-care-around-the-world-canada/

Taskforce on the Aging of the American Workforce. (2008). *Report of the Taskforce on the Aging of the American Workforce.* Retrieved from http://www.aging.senate.gov/letters/agingworkforcetaskforcereport.pdf

Thurow, L. C. (1996, May 19). The birth of a revolutionary class. *New York Times Magazine,* pp. 46–47.

Torjman, S. (2002). *The Canada Pension Plan disability benefit.* Ottawa: Caledon Institute of Social Policy, Office of the Commissioner of Review Tribunals Canada Pension Plan/Old Age Security. Retrieved from http://www.ocrt-bctr.gc.ca/dapdep/r012002/r012002-eng.pdf

Trollor, J. N., Anderson, T. M., Sachdev, P. S., Brodaty, H., & Andrews, G. (2007). Prevalence of mental disorders in the elderly: The Australian National Mental Health and Well-Being Survey. *American Journal of Geriatric Psychiatry, 15,* 455–466.

Turner, J. A., Toft, C., & Witte, H. A. (2008). *Lifelong learning for an aging population: Lessons from Scandinavia.* Washington, DC: AARP.

U.K. Acts of Parliament. (1990). *The National Health Service and Community Care Act* (1990 c19, as amended). Retrieved from http://www.legislation.gov.uk/ukpga/1990/19/contents

U.K. Acts of Parliament. (2000). Transport Act (2000 c38, as amended). Retrieved from http://www.opsi.gov.uk/acts/acts2000/pdf/ukpga_20000038_en.pdf

U.K. Acts of Parliament. (2007a). *Concessionary Bus Travel Act 2007, c13, as amended.* Retrieved from http://www.opsi.gov.uk/acts/acts2007/pdf/ukpga_20070013_en.pdf

U.K. Acts of Parliament. (2007b). *Legal Services Act 2007, c29, as amended.* Retrieved from http://www.opsi.gov.uk/acts/acts2007/ukpga_20070029_en_1

United Nations. (1983). *Vienna international plan of action on aging.* New York: Author. Retrieved from http://www.monitoringris.org/documents/norm_glob/vipaa.pdf

United Nations. (1991). *Principles for older persons* (General Assembly res. 46/91, Annex, U.N. Doc. A/RES/46/91). Retrieved from http://www1.umn.edu/humanrts/instree/unprinciples-olderpersons.html

United Nations. (1992). *Proclamation on ageing: Resolution* (General Assembly 47th session: 1992–1993). New York: Author.

United Nations. (1995). *World summit for social development.* New York: Author. Retrieved from http://wwwupdate.un.org/esa/socdev/wssd/index.html

United Nations. (1998). *International plan of action on ageing and United Nations principles for older persons.* New York: Author. Retrieved from http://www.un.org/esa/socdev/ageing/un_principles.html#Principles

United Nations. (2002). *Report of the second World Assembly on Ageing.* New York: Author. Retrieved from http://www.un.org/ageing/secondworld02.html

United Nations. (2005). *Living arrangements of older persons around the world.* Department of Economic and Social Affairs/Population Division. Retrieved June 3, 2009, from http://www.un.org/esa/population/publications/livingarrangement/report.htm

United Nations. (2007). *World population ageing 2007, series: Population studies.* New York: UN Department of Economic and Social Affairs, Population Division.

United Nations. (2008). *World population prospects: The 2006 revision.* Population Division of the Department of Economic and Social Affairs of the United Nations Secretariat. Retrieved from http://esa.un.org/unpp/

United Nations. (2009a). *Conference on the world financial and economic crisis and its impact on development.* Retrieved August 1, 2009, from http://www.un.org/esa/desa/financialcrisis/document/s-g_fin_crisis_final_advance.pdf

United Nations. (2009b). *Directory of ageing resources on the Internet.* New York: Author. Retrieved from http://www.un.org/esa/socdev/ageing/documents/Web_Links/directory June09.pdf

United Nations. (2009c). *United Nations Programme on Ageing.* Retrieved April 7, 2009, from http://www.un.org/ageing/index.html

United Nations. (2009d). *World population ageing 2009.* Retrieved April 17, 2010, from http://www.un.org/esa/population/publications/WPA2009/WPA2009_WorkingPaper.pdf

United Nations Department of Economic and Social Affairs. (2007). *World economic and social survey 2007: Development in an ageing world.* Retrieved March 22, 2010, from http://www.un.org/esa/policy/wess/wess2007files/wess2007.pdf

United Nations Economic and Social Council (1991, January 1). First session: Implementation of the International Plan of Action on Ageing and related activities. New York: United Nations.

United Nations General Assembly (45th session: 1990–1991), Third Committee. (1990). *Report of the Third Committee. Resolutions adopted on the report of the Third Committee. International Day for the Elderly.* http://www.un.org/documents/ga/res/45/a45r106.htm New York: UN

United We Ride. (2007, November). *Family of transportation services.* Retrieved from http://www.unitedweride.gov/FTS.pdf

U.S. Bureau of the Census. (2003). *Marital status of women in the civilian labor force: 1900 to 2002.* Statistical Abstracts of the United States. Retrieved from http://www.census.gov/statab/hist/HS-30.pdf

U.S. Bureau of the Census. (2010). *Historical tables: Table 15. Age distribution of the poor.* Retrieved May 24, 2010, from http://www.census.gov/hhes/www/poverty/data/historical/people.html

U.S. Department of Agriculture. (2009a). *Commodity Supplemental Food Program.* Retrieved December 29, 2009, from http://www.fns.usda.gov/fdd/programs/csfp/pfs-csfp.pdf

U.S. Department of Agriculture. (2009b). *The Emergency Food Assistance Program.* Retrieved December 29, 2009, from http://www.fns.usda.gov/fdd/programs/tefap/pfs-tefap.pdf

U.S. Department of Agriculture. (2009c). *A short history of SNAP.* Retrieved December 29, 2009, from http://www.fns.usda.gov/snap/rules/Legislation/about.htm

U.S. Department of Agriculture. (2010). *Supplemental Nutrition Assistance Program: Eligibility.* Retrieved December 29, 2009, from http://www.fns.usda.gov/snap/applicant_recipients/eligibility.htm#special

U.S. Department of Education. (2009). *Independent living services for older individuals who are blind.* Retrieved from http://www2.ed.gov/programs/rsailob/index.html

U.S. Department of Energy. (2010). *Weatherization assistance program.* Retrieved February 2, 2010, from http://apps1.eere.energy.gov/weatherization/

U.S. Department of Health and Human Services. (2006). *Executive summary: Low-income home energy assistance report to congress for FY 2006.* Retrieved from http://www.acf.hhs.gov/programs/ocs/liheap/report/06report.pdf

U.S. Department of Health and Human Services. (2008a). *Income and resource guidelines.* Retrieved from https://www.cms.gov/MedicaidEligibility/07_IncomeandResourceGuidelines.asp#TopOfPage

U.S. Department of Health and Human Services. (2008b). *Paying for LTC: Overview.* National Clearinghouse for Long-Term Care Information. Retrieved October 20, 2008, from http://www.longtermcare.gov/LTC/Main_Site/Paying_LTC/Costs_Of_Care/Costs_Of_Care.aspx

U.S. Department of Health and Human Services. (2009). *LIHEAP brochure.* Retrieved from http://www.acf.hhs.gov/programs/ocs/liheap/brochure/brochure.html

U.S. Department of Health and Human Services. (n.d.). *HCBS waivers Section 1915 (c).* Retrieved from http://www.cms.gov/MedicaidStWaivProgDemoPGI/05_HCBSWaivers-Section1915(c).asp

U.S. Department of Labor. (2004). *Employment and training administration, 20 CFR Part 641, Senior Community Service Employment Program, final rule.* Washington, DC: Author. Retrieved from http://www.doleta.gov/Seniors/other_docs/etaOAreg.pdf

U.S. Department of Labor. (2008). *Fact sheet: The Mental Health Parity Act.* Retrieved from http://www.dol.gov/ebsa/newsroom/fsmhparity.html

U.S. Department of Labor. (2009a). *About SCSEP.* Retrieved from http://www.doleta.gov/SENIORS/html_docs/AboutSCSEP.cfm

U.S. Department of Labor. (2009b). *Leave benefits: Family and medical leave.* Retrieved October 26, 2009, from http://www.dol.gov/dol/topic/benefits-leave/fmla.htm#

U.S. Department of Labor. (2009c). *Trade Act program: TAA for workers.* Retrieved March 10, 2010, from http://www.doleta.gov/tradeact/

U.S. Department of Labor. (2010). *Current population survey: Civilian labor force participation rate.* Retrieved from http://www.bls.gov/data/home.htm

U.S. Department of Transportation. (2010). *FTA programs fact sheets.* Retrieved from http://fta .dot.gov/printer_friendly/index_6538.html

U.S. Government Accountability Office. (2004). *Transportation-disadvantaged seniors: Efforts to enhance senior mobility could benefit from additional guidance and information: Report to the chairman, Special Committee on Aging, U.S. Senate.* Washington, DC: Author.

U.S. Government Accountability Office. (2005). *Elderly housing: Federal housing programs that offer assistance for the elderly.* Retrieved May 26, 2010, from http://www.gao.gov./new.items/ d05174.pdf

Valença, M. M., & Bonates, M. F. (2010). The trajectory of social housing policy in Brazil: From the National Housing Bank to the Ministry of the Cities. *Habitat International, 34,* 165–173.

Van Wezemael, J. E., & Gilroy, R. (2007). The significance of demographic change in the Swiss approach to private rented housing: A potential for ageing in place? *Housing Studies, 22,* 597–614.

VanWey, L. K., & Cebulko, K. B. (2007). Intergenerational coresidence among small farmers in Brazilian Amazonia. *Journal of Marriage and Family, 69,* 1257–1270.

Van Zeeland, C. M. C., & Barendrecht, J. M. (2003). *Legal aid systems compared: A comparative research into three legal aid systems.* Tilburg, Netherlands: Centre for Liability Law, Tilburg University. Retrieved from http://www.tilburguniversity.nl/faculties/law/research/tisco/ publications/reports/legal-aid-systems.pdf

Vårdguiden Stockholm. (2010). *Paratransit (Färdtjänst).* Retrieved February 20, 2010, from http://www.vardguiden.se/Sa-funkar-det/Stod/Fardtjanst/

Vidlund, M. (2009). *Pension contribution level in Sweden.* Helsinki, Finland: Finnish Centre for Pensions. Retrieved from http://www.etk.fi/Binary.aspx?Section=42909&Item=63897

Wacker, R. R., & Roberto, K. A. (2008). *Community resources for older adults: Programs and services in an era of change.* Los Angeles: Sage.

Waldman, S. (1985). A legislative history of nursing home care. In R. J. Vogel & H. C. Palmer (Eds.), *Long-term care: Perspectives from research and demonstrations* (pp. 507–535). Rockville, MD: Aspen.

Walker, R. (2005). *Social Security and welfare: Concepts and comparisons.* Maidenhead, UK: Open University Press.

Wang, T. (2009). *China takes a stab at universal health care.* Retrieved from http://forbes .com/2009/01/22/china-health-care-markets-econ-cx_twdd-0122markets04.html

Wardrip, K. (2010). *Strategies to meet the housing needs of older adults.* AARP Public Policy Institute. Retrieved from http://assets.aarp.org/rgcenter/ppi/liv-com/i38-strategies.pdf

Watkins, D. A., & Watkins, J. M. (1984). *Social policy and the rural setting: Vol. 4. Springer series on social work.* New York: Springer.

White, J. (2002). The entitlement crisis that never existed. In S. H. Altman & D. Shactman (Eds.), *Policies for an aging society.* Baltimore, MD: Johns Hopkins University Press.

White House Conference on Aging. (2005). *The booming dynamics of aging: From awareness to action. December 11–14, 2005: Report to the president and the Congress.* http://www.whcoa .gov/Final_Report_June_14nowater.pdf

White House Conference on Aging. (2010). *History.* Retrieved April 21, 2010, from http://www .whcoa.gov/about/history.asp

Whiteford, H., & Buckingham, B. (2005). The process of transforming mental health services in Australia. *International Journal of Mental Health, 34,* 55–71.

Wiencek, T. (1991). How the Older Workers' Benefit Protection Act affects employers. *Practice Lawyer, 37,* 69–76.

Wiener, J. M., Brown, D., Gage, B., Khatutsky, G., Moore, A., & Osber, D. (2004). *Home- and community-based services: A synthesis of the literature* (Report No. 07147.019.003). Waltham, MA: RTI International.

Wikipedia. (2010). *United States House Permanent Select Committee on Aging.* St. Petersburg, FL: Wikimedia Foundation. Retrieved April 21, 2010, from http://en.wikipedia.org/wiki/United_States_House_Permanent_Select_Committee_on_Aging

Williamson, J. B., & Higo, M. (2009).Why Japanese workers remain in the labor force so long: Lessons for the United States? *Journal of Cross Cultural Gerontology, 24,* 321–337.

Woolley, J. T., & Peters, G. (n.d.). *The American Presidency Project* [online]. Santa Barbara, CA. Retrieved from http://www.presidency.ucsb.edu/ws/?pid=27079

World Bank. (1994). *Averting the old-age crisis: Policies to protect the old and promote growth* (World Bank policy research report). Oxford, U.K.: Oxford University Press.

World Bank. (n.d.). *Notional accounts: Notional defined contribution plans as a pension reform strategy.* Retrieved from http://siteresources.worldbank.org/INTPENSIONS/Resources/395443–1121194657824/PRPNoteNotionalAccts.pdf

World Health Organization. (2003). Mental health in WHO's European Region. Retrieved from http://www.euro.who.int/__data/assets/pdf_file/0007/87694/RC53_edoc07.pdf

World Health Organization. (2005a). *Mental health atlas 2005: Global results.* Retrieved from http://www.who.int/mental_health/evidence/atlas/global_results.pdf

World Health Organization. (2005b). *Mental health atlas 2005: Profile of countries A–B.* Retrieved from http://www.who.int/mental_health/evidence/atlas/profiles_countries_a_b.pdf

World Health Organization. (2005c). *Mental health atlas 2005: Profile of countries S.* Retrieved from http://www.who.int/mental_health/evidence/atlas/profiles_countries_s1.pdf

World Health Organization. (2005d). *Mental health atlas 2005: Profile of countries T–Z.* Retrieved from www.who.int/mental_health/evidence/atlas/profiles_countries_t_z.pdf

World Health Organization. (2007). *Global age-friendly cities: A guide.* Geneva, Switzerland: Author. Retrieved from http://www.who.int/ageing/publications/Global_age_friendly_cities_Guide_English.pdf

World Health Organization. (2009). *Mental health: A state of well-being.* Retrieved from www.who.int/features/factfiles/mental_health/en/

Wright, B. (2004). *Assisted living in the United States.* Washington, DC: AARP Public Policy Institute. Retrieved from http://assets.aarp.org/rgcenter/post-import/fs62r_assisted.pdf

WRVS. (2010). *Facts.* Retrieved February 14, 2010, from http://wrvs.org.uk/standard.aspx?page_id=41

Wu, B., Mao, Z., & Xu, Q. (2008). Institutional care for elders in rural China. *Journal of Aging & Social Policy, 20,* 218–239.

Wu, B., Mao, Z., & Zhong, R. (2009). Long-term care arrangements in rural China: Review of recent developments. *Journal of the American Medical Directors Association, 10,* 472–477.

Yamada, Y. (2009). *Aging in Japan: Current conditions and challenges: Summary of white paper on an aging society 2009.* Retrieved from http://www.jarc.net/int/?p=271

Zahradnik, N. (2007, winter). Minding our elders: Mental health in long-term care. *Network Magazine: Canadian Mental Health Association.* Retrieved from http://www.ontario.cmha.ca/network_story.asp?cID=7439

Zaidi, A. (2008). *Features and challenges of population aging: The European perspective.* Vienna, Austria: European Centre for Social Welfare Policy and Research.

Zavoretti, R. (2006). Family-based care for China's ageing population: A social research perspective. *Asia Europe Journal, 4,* 211–228.

Zhang, T., & Chen, Y. (2006). Meeting the needs of elderly people in China. *British Medical Journal, 333,* 363–364.

Zunzunegui, M. V., Beland, F., & Otero, A. (2001). Support from children, living arrangements, self-rated health, and depressive symptoms of older people in Spain. *International Journal of Epidemiology, 30,* 1090–1099.

Zweifel, P., Felder, S., & Werblow, A. (2004). Population ageing and health care expenditure: New evidence on the "Red Herring." *Insurance, 29,* 652–666.

Index

About the Authors

Robbyn R. Wacker, PhD, is assistant vice president for Research, dean of the Graduate School and International Admissions, and professor of Gerontology at the University of Northern Colorado in Greeley. Her research interests include international aging social policy and psychosocial predictors of community service use among older adults. Prior to obtaining her doctorate, she provided legal assistance to older adults through the Title III Legal Services program. Along with her administrative duties, Dr. Wacker continues to be an active researcher in the field of gerontology. She has published more than 60 referred presentations, scholarly articles, books (including *Community Resources for Older Adults: Resources and Services in an Era of Change*, 3rd ed., with Roberto, 2008), and conference proceedings. Dr. Wacker has earned numerous university and professional awards, including UNC's Academic Leadership Excellence Award, Outstanding Achievement Award in Sponsored Programs, and Mortar Board Excellence Award for Teaching, and was selected by the Harvard Graduate School of Education to attend its summer Management Development Program for leaders in higher education.

Karen A. Roberto, PhD, is professor and director of the Center for Gerontology and the Institute for Society, Culture, and Environment at Virginia Polytechnic Institute and State University in Blacksburg, Virginia. Her research examines the intersection of health and social support in later life. Her primary interests include older women's adaptation to chronic health conditions, family relationships and caregiving, and elder abuse and mistreatment. She is the author of more than 100 scholarly articles and 30 book chapters and the editor or author of 9 books, including *Community Resources for Older Adults: Resources and Services in an Era of Change*, 3rd ed. (with Wacker, 2008) and *Pathways of Human Development: Explorations of Change* (with Mancini, 2009). Dr. Roberto is a fellow of the Association for Gerontology in Higher Education, the Gerontological Society of America, the National Council on Family Relations, and the World Demographic Association and served as the 2009 chair of the Behavioral and Social Sciences section of the Gerontological Society of America. She is the recipient of numerous university and professional awards, including the Gordon Streib Academic Gerontologist Award from the Southern Gerontological Society and the Virginia Tech Alumni Award for Research Excellence.

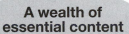